Finding Source Code on the Web for Remix and Reuse

Susan Elliott Sim • Rosalva E. Gallardo-Valencia
Editors

Finding Source Code on the Web for Remix and Reuse

 Springer

Editors

Susan Elliott Sim
Many Roads Studios
Toronto, ON, Canada

Rosalva E. Gallardo-Valencia
Intel Corporation
Santa Clara, CA, USA

ISBN 978-1-4899-9446-2   ISBN 978-1-4614-6596-6 (eBook)
DOI 10.1007/978-1-4614-6596-6
Springer New York Heidelberg Dordrecht London

Printed on acid-free paper

Springer is part of Springer Science+Business Media (www.springer.com)

For my students and my children, who have taught me much
   -SES
   For my parents, Vitaliano Gallardo Cuadra and Yolanda Valencia Lara, whom I admire and love so much
   -RGV

Preface

In June, 2010, a small number of us met in Mannheim, Germany to continue discuss an emerging area of research. This meeting was an informal continuation of the conversations we had at the inaugural Workshop on SUITE (Search-driven development: Users, Infrastructure, Tools and Evaluation) held at ICSE 2009 in Vancouver, Canada. At that meeting, we latched on to the term "code retrieval in the web," because it encompassed both the technological and behavioral aspects of the phenomenon we were studying collectively. From a technological standpoint, we and other researchers were using algorithms and concepts from information retrieval, program analysis, and software reuse to facilitate code search. From a behavioral standpoint, software developers were searching for code but this was qualitatively different from what had been observed previously in an IDE (integrated development environment), in a web browser for documents, or in a library with expert guidance.

We agreed that we needed to have a single edited volume to lay the foundation for code retrieval on the web as a research area, and so the idea for this book was sown. Thank you to Oliver Hummel, Werner Janjic, and Oleksandr Panchenko for the inspiration and motivation. We now pass the baton to you for the next volume.

We will be donating the royalties from this book to two charities, The Fistula Foundation and Sembrando (Sowing in Peru). Because this is an edited volume, we felt that this was the most equitable distribution of the proceeds. The Fistula Foundation (http://www.fistulafoundation.org/) is a non-profit organization that funds hospitals that repair obstetric fistulas in 11 countries around the world, including Ethiopia, Afghanistan, and Bangladesh. Their work has been the subject of a documentary, "A Walk to Beautiful" and has been promoted by Pulitzer Prize-winning journalist, Nicholas Kristof. Sembrando (http://www.sembrando.org.pe/) is an initiative of Instituto Trabajo y Familia that seeks to improve the social and economic conditions of extremely poor families living in the High Andes. Its patron is Pilar Nores, economist and former first lady of Peru.

It took 2 years and much labour to bring this book to fruition. We could not have done it without others joining and aiding our project. We are especially grateful to the authors who contributed chapters.

At Springer Verlag, Jennifer Maurer and Courtney Clark provided editorial advice and assistance during the prepartion of this book.

We would like to thank our reviewers who graciously gave their time: Eduardo Almeida, Claudia Ayala, Sushil Bajracharya, Joel Brandt, Rahul De', Xavier Franch, Mark Grechanik, Raphael Hoffman, Werner Janjic, Oliver Hummel, Ken Krugler, Kumiyo Nakakoji, Joel Ossher, Denys Poshyvanyk, C. Albert Thompson, Medha Umarji, and Halli Villegas.

Toronto, Canada   Susan Elliott Sim
Santa Clara, USA   Rosalva E. Gallardo-Valencia

Contents

Part II From Data Structures to Infrastructure

Contributors

Megha Agarwala
Columbia University, New York, NY, USA, e-mail: ma3037@columbia.edu

Eduardo Santana de Almeida
Federal University of Bahia and RiSE Salvador, Salvador, Bahia, Brazil
e-mail: esa@dcc.ufba.com.br

Colin Atkinson
Software Engineering Group, University of Mannheim, Mannheim, Germany
e-mail: atkinson@informatik.uni-mannheim.de

Claudia Ayala
Technical University of Catalunya, Barcelona, Spain, e-mail: cayala@essi.upc.edu

Sushil Krishna Bajracharya
Black Duck Software, Burlington, MA, USA, e-mail: sbajra@acm.org

Ohad Barzilay
Blavatnik School of Computer Science, Tel-Aviv University, Tel-Aviv, Israel
e-mail: ohadbr@tau.ac.il

Reidar Conradi
Norwegian University of Science and Technology, Trondheim, Norway
e-mail: conradi@idi.ntnu.no

Daniela Cruzes
Norwegian University of Science and Technology, Trondheim, Norway
e-mail: dcruzes@idi.ntnu.no

Rahul De'
Indian Institute of Management Bangalore, Bangalore, India
e-mail: rahul@iimb.ernet.in

Xavier Franch
Technical University of Catalunya, Barcelona, Spain, e-mail: franch@essi.upc.edu

Rosalva E. Gallardo-Valencia
Intel Corporation, Santa Clara, CA, USA, e-mail: rgallardovalencia@acm.org

Oliver Hummel
University of Mannheim, Mannheim, Germany
e-mail: hummel@informatik.uni-mannheim.de

Werner Janjic
University of Mannheim, Mannheim, Germany
e-mail: werner@informatik.uni-mannheim.de

Micah Joel
Sunnyvale, CA, USA, e-mail: micah@micahjoel.info

Ken Krugler
Scale Unlimited, Nevada City, CA, USA, e-mail: kkrugler@scaleunlimited.com

Jingyue Li
DNV Research & Innovation, Høvik, Norway, e-mail: jingyue.li@dnv.com

Kumiyo Nakakoji
Software Research Associates Inc., Tokyo, Japan, e-mail: kumiyo@acm.org

Yoshiyuki Nishinaka
Software Research Associates Inc., Tokyo, Japan, e-mail: nisinaka@motr.jp

Joel Ossher
University of California, Irvine, Irvine, CA, USA, e-mail: jossher@uci.edu

Ravi A. Rao
Indian Institute of Management Bangalore, Bangalore, India
e-mail: ravi.rao10@iimb.ernet.in

Marcus Schumacher
University of Mannheim, Mannheim, Germany,
e-mail: schumacher@informatik.uni-mannheim.de

Susan Elliott Sim
Many Roads Studios, Toronto, ON, Canada, e-mail: ses@drsusansim.org

Erik Stenberg
University of California, Irvine, Irvine, CA, USA, e-mail: ebstenberg@gmail.com

Phitchayaphong Tantikul
University of California, Irvine, Irvine, CA, USA, e-mail: ptantiku@gmail.com

C. Albert Thompson
University of British Columbia, Vancouver, Canada, e-mail: leetcat@cs.ubc.ca

Christoph Treude
University of Victoria, Victoria, BC, Canada, e-mail: ctreude@uvic.ca

Medha Umarji
Symantec Corporation, Mountain View, CA, USA
e-mail: medha_umarji@symantec.com

Yasuhiro Yamamoto
Tokyo Institute of Technology, Yokohama, Japan, e-mail: yxy@acm.org

Alexey Zagalsky
Tel-Aviv University, Tel-Aviv, Israel, e-mail: alexeyza@tau.ac.il

Chapter 1
Introduction: Remixing Snippets and Reusing Components

Susan Elliott Sim and Rosalva E. Gallardo-Valencia

Abstract In this introductory chapter, we map out "code retrieval on the web" as a research area and the organizational of this book. Code retrieval on the web is concerned with the algorithms, systems, and tools to allow programmers to search for source code on the web and the empirical studies of these inventions and practices. It is a label that we apply to a set of related research from a software engineering, information retrieval, human-computer interaction, management, as well as commercial products. The division of code retrieval on the web into snippet remixing and component reuse is driven both by empirical data, and analysis of existing search engines and tools.

1.1 Introduction

Code retrieval on the web is concerned with the algorithms, systems, and tools to allow programmers to search for source code on the web and the empirical studies of these inventions and practices. The name builds on two concepts in computing: code search and information retrieval. Code search traditionally happens within an editor or integrated development environment. Information retrieval is the set of technologies to retrieve documents from large online collections and information behaviour is the study of how people use these tools. Adding the qualifier "on the web" particularlizes the study to a modern context, with open source repositories, Web 2.0, crowdsourcing, and code-specific search engines. It's a label that we apply to a set of related research from a variety of disciplines, as well as commercial products.

S.E. Sim (✉)
Many Roads Studios, Toronto, ON, Canada
e-mail: ses@drsusansim.org

R.E. Gallardo-Valencia
Intel Corporation, Santa Clara, CA, USA
e-mail: rgallardovalencia@acm.org

S.E. Sim and R.E. Gallardo-Valencia (eds.), *Finding Source Code on the Web
for Remix and Reuse*, DOI 10.1007/978-1-4614-6596-6_1,
© Springer Science+Business Media New York 2013

Our earliest work on code retrieval on the web was an extension of our previous work on code search within an IDE. In preparation to conduct an empirical study, we conducted a literature search. We found relevant papers on this topic in many disciplines. Although, we used software engineering and program comprehension as a starting point, we were quickly led to software reuse, human-computer interaction (HCI), information retrieval, and even further afield to areas such as consumer behavior.

One observation that we made repeatedly, both during the literature search and in our subsequent research, is that there were two kinds of code search on the web. One kind would be recognized by the software reuse community and involved the reuse of source code in components with little or no modification. However, these components or projects were not necessarily reused as intended by their original designers. The other kind would be more familiar to those in HCI, where source code is used as raw material in a creative process. The title and organization of this book reflects this division.

In this chapter, we give an introduction to code retrieval on the web. In Sect. 1.2, we give some context to the emergence of this area. Next, we explain the organization of this book and give an overview of the chapters.

1.2 Emergence of Code Search on the Web

Code search has long been a critical part of software development. A study of software engineering work practices found that searching was the most common activity for software engineers [35]. They were typically locating a bug or a problem, finding ways to fix it and then evaluating the impact on other segments. Program comprehension, code reuse, and bug fixing were cited as the chief motivations for source code searching in that study. A related study on source code searching found that the search goals cited frequently by developers were code reuse, defect repair, program understanding, feature addition, and impact analysis [28]. They found that programmers were most frequently looking for function definitions, variable definitions, all uses of a function and all uses of a variable.

The recognition that search is powerful and useful has led to advances in code search tools. Software developers have needed tools to search through source code since the appearance of interactive programming environments. It started with simple keyword search and when regular expressions were added, it became possible to specify patterns and context [37]. An important improvement was made when search techniques started using program structure, such as identifiers of variables and functions, directly in expressing search patterns [1, 27].

Another approach to syntactic search involves processing the program and storing facts in a database file of entity-relations [6, 23]. Alternatively, the code can be parsed and transformed into other representations, such as data flow graphs or control flow graphs, and searches can be performed on those structures [26]. While some of these ideas have not been widely adopted, searches using regular expressions and program structure are standard in modern IDEs.

Code search in IDEs is the common origin for both component reuse and snippet remixing. These new practices have emerged in response to new technologies, such as open source, and Web 2.0. Open source is the ethic of making source code available with the executable for a software program. Centralized repositories, such as Source Forge[1] and Github,[2] were created for the purpose of sharing these programs. Web 2.0 technologies has allowed anyone with a web browser to contribute content to web sites. This material has included personal blogs, tutorials, online discussion forums, and snippet repositories, such as Snipplr,[3] and Smipple.[4]

Nowadays, they search the web to find information in order to solve the problems they encounter while working on software development tasks. A recent study [4] found that developers spend 19 % of their programming time on the web. The mechanisms for specifying searches and making source code searchable are equally applicable to code search on the web. However, there are two important differences: scale and the information sought. Conventional code search is concerned with searching for specific information within the context of a single project. A project could be very large and even have multiple programming languages, but it would still be a single project with a constrained set of compilation units. With code retrieval on the web, the challenge is to examine the contents of many different projects, i.e. thousands of projects and billions of lines of code. Also, in this context, the software developer is less concerned with finding whether a variable or function is defined, and more interested in finding functionality, a typical concern in code reuse. It is also common to use the web as a giant desk reference. Gone are the days of programmers keeping thick reference manuals on their desks.

We can see evidence of these two kinds of search both in how software developers think about code retrieval and how tool designers approach the problem.

1.3 Programmers Think Differently About Component Reuse and Snippet Remixing

The differences in how programmers approach component reuse and snippet remixing can be characterized by two dimensions: the quantity of source code being reused and the degree to which the source code will be adapted to the new setting.

Drawing on years of research into social and cognitive aspects of code search and expertise search within organizations [40, 41, 42], Kumiyo Nakakoji, Yasuhiro Yamamoto, and Yoshiyuki Nishinaka (Chap. 2) identified two dimensions efficacy and attitude for code retrieval on the web. Efficacy can occur when a literal line of code or "texture" is copied into the program under construction. Or efficacy can occur when "functionality" is copied in whole cloth. For attitude, the programmer

---

[1] http://sourceforge.net/.

[2] https://github.com/.

[3] http://snipplr.com/.

[4] http://www.smipple.net/.

either uses the code as an "element" in her own code or as a "substrate" upon which to build software. These dimensions form a 2×2 matrix. Component reuse aligns with texture/element. In turn, snippet remixing aligns with functionality/substrate. Nakakoji et al. continue on in "Unweaving Code Search toward Remixing-Centered Programming Support" to describe how various scenarios of code retrieval on the web play out within these dimensions and what kinds of tool support is needed.

In analyzing data from an exploratory survey, Medha Umarji and Susan Elliott Sim (Chap. 3) also arrive at two similar dimensions, "target size" and "motivation." Points along the target size spectrum were characterized as block, subsystem, and system. The endpoints of the motivation spectrum were as-is reuse and reference example. Both of these dimensions also align with Nakakoji's characterization. Component reuse aligns here with subsystem or system and as-is reuse. Whereas, snippet remixing involves blocks, but not purely as reference examples. In the remainder of "Archetypal Internet-Scale Source Code Searching," Umarji and Sim consider other aspects of the search process, such as the tools used and information sources, in a qualitative fashion.

Susan Elliott Sim, Megha Agarwal, and Medha Umarji (Chap. 4) conducted a quantitative, controlled laboratory experiment as a follow-on study. They provided subjects with a scenario, derived from data from the survey, and asked them to search for code using five search engines. They found statistically significant differences between searches for reference examples and as-is reuse. Searching for reference examples required more effort, as measured by average the number of terms per query, average number of queries, clickthrough rate, and time spent. Searches for blocks were similar. Further details of this study can be found in "A Controlled Experiment on the Process Used by Developers During Internet-Scale Code Search."

These differences between snippet remix and component reuse were apparent not only the analyses generated by researchers, but also in how programmers themselves thought about code retrieval targets. We took the results of the exploratory survey, distilled them down into 27 examples, and asked programmers to place them into categories using a card sorting task.

Table 1.1 shows the list of search targets provided. We asked participants to classify these examples into at least two and no more than eight categories based on similarities or differences. After participants were done with card sorting task, we asked them about the criteria that they used for classification and to provide a name for each category.

We ran a total of 12 sessions with 24 participants (22 graduate and 2 undergraduate computer science students). They were between the ages of 20 and 49, and they had between 1 and 15 years of experience developing software. Each pair of software developers were given 27 index cards and asked to classify these examples into at least two and no more than eight categories based on similarities or differences.

We took the examples and the categories generated by every group and performed a Formal Concept Analysis (FCA) on them. FCA is a data analysis technique that takes a matrix of objects and properties of objects and derives an ontology, called a concept lattice [30]. This technique has been used in a number of areas, including

1. Tomcat bug report on improper shutdown of AJP connector	15. Class to connect to Oracle using JDBC
2. A JavaScript tutorial	16. Class to represent a bank transaction
3. Apache Struts 2.2.1	17. Patch for ANT to allow multiple elements in a single property
4. Openbravo ERP	18. Form post on different behaviors in a Thread
5. Implementation of diff	19. OpenMRS
6. Implementation of binary search	20. MySQL bug report on strings short than defined length
7. Implementation of circular linked list	21. Java.util package
8. Implementation of stack	22. Patch for WebdavServelet
9. Javadocs for Log4J	23. Spring Framework
10. Javadocs for Java 2 Platform 5.0	24. Apache Commons Collections API
11. Code to convert Array to Map in Java	25. JUnit package
12. Method to validate email address	26. Forum post on how Hibernate binds values to prepared statements
13. Article on Java Management Extensions JMX	27, MySQL server
14. The Standard Widget Toolkit	

Table 1.1: Source code search targets used in card sorting task

artificial intelligence, software clustering, and genetics [9, 19, 21]. We used Concept Explorer to produce a concept lattice Fig. 1.1. For expository purposes, we use a simplified version here.

The white boxes are the search targets from Table 1.1. The grey boxes are the categories created by the participants. When targets or categories always appeared together, they were collapsed into a single box. The organization and layout of the lattice are generated automatically and it reflects the relationships between the concepts. More specific concepts appear closer to the bottom of the lattice, and more general ones appear to the top. Circles are placed where different objects are joined to create more general concepts. Larger circles indicate greater confidence in the concept. Some circles are barely visible and not labeled, as these have been created by the analysis process and were not part of the input data. Circles where the bottom half is colored black indicate an exact match with categories created by the participants. Circles where the top half is shaded indicate an exact match with search targets in the study. Edges in the lattice depict a relationship between concepts, with line thickness showing the strength.

In this concept lattice, examples and snippets are in the far left half. Documentation in the form of tutorials and forums are in the middle. To the right of these, are bugs and patches. On the far right are components such as systems, products, and frameworks. The arrangement from left to right was selected by Concept Explorer to create the simplest layout possible, by minimizing edge crossings. It is noteworthy that the snippets group on the left is placed on the opposite side of the page from the components group on the right. Two search targets, a class to represent a bank transaction and a class to connect to a database appear in the middle with links to both snippets and components. This makes sense, because they are both small pieces of code and a means to access these larger systems.

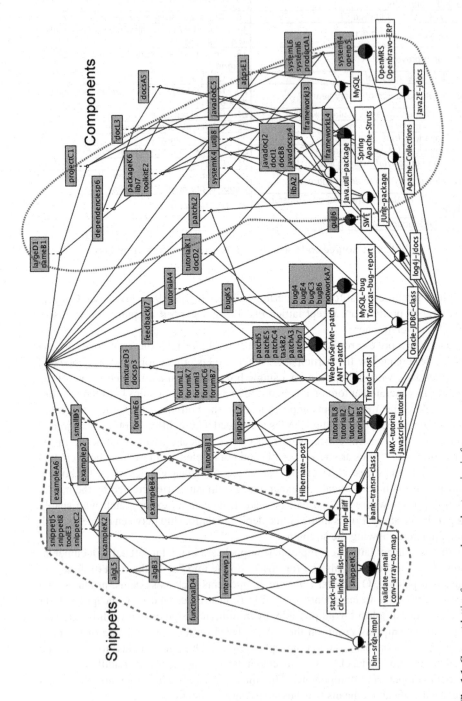

Fig. 1.1 Concept lattice for examples and categories in focus groups

There are eight clear, consistent concepts where the categories and search targets match: "snippet," "tutorials," "patches," "bug reports," "SWT," "frameworks," and "open source systems." Only one falls int the snippet group, while indicates that this concept is more unitary. In contrast, three of these fall in the component group. Open source systems and frameworks are not identical to each other, but both have integrity as components.

This lattice is surprisingly consistent, given the diversity of stimuli and number of pairs in the focus groups. This regularity supports the our assertion that software developers think differently about snippets to remix than components to reuse.

1.4 Tools for Retrieving Code on the Web

Looking at the wide range of tools for code retrieval on the web, we arrive at three categories: those designed for snippet searches, those designed for component searches, or those designed for both kinds of searches. The tools in the first two categories used either snippets or components as the starting point in their design. Tools that can be used for both were either (i) intended to be used with components and support for snippets were a side-effect, or (ii) a general purpose tool, not specifically designed for use with source code, e.g. Google. Table 1.2 shows the classification of these tools.

We used this taxonomy to guide the selection of articles for Parts II–IV of this book. Part II, "From Data Structures to Infrastructure," is on the design of search engines, with a focus on the back end. Chapter 5 "Artifact Representation Techniques for Large-Scale Software Search Engines" by Oliver Hummel, Colin Atkinson, and Marcus Schumacher give a historical overview of the data structures used in code retrieval engines. A history of the evolution of the Krugler search engine given by Ken Krugler in Chap. 6. Together these two chapters describe how our understanding of how to build code search engines from an academic and an industrial perspective, respectively. The similarities between the two are more significant than the differences.

The authors of the next two chapters advanced code search technology in novel ways. Eduardo Santana de Almeida has worked on a series of code search engines that introduced novel mechanisms for characterizing components, including Folksonomy, and facets. Conventionally, labels and keywords in component repositories were defined a priori and additions to the repository must conform to these terms. A Folksonomy is based on tags that are added ad hoc. Facets are discovered using data

---

[1] http://demo.spars.info/j/.

[2] http://www.koders.com.

[3] http://www.google.com/codesearch/.

[4] http://www.krugle.com/.

[7] http://www.google.com/.

	Snippets	Components	Both
API and example code search	Prospector [24] Strathcona [14] MAPO [39] Mica [36] XSnippet [32] PARSEWeb [38] STeP_IN_Java [41] SNIFF [5] Blueprint [3] SAS [2]	JSearch [34] XFinder [8]	Assieme [13]
Web-based code search engine		Agora [33] SPARS-J[5] [18] JBender [12]	Koders[6] Google code search[7] Krugle[8] Merobase [17] Sourcerer [22] S6 [31] Exemplar [11]
Test-driven code search		Code Conjurer [17] CodeGenie [20]	Extreme harvesting [16]
Code snippet web search engine	Sniplr Smipple		
Project hosting site		SourceForge	Github
Reuse opportunity recommender	CodeBroker [40] Rascal [25]		
Source code integration	Jigsaw [7]	Gilligan [15]	
General purpose web search engine			Google[9]
Others	Codetrail [10]		JIRISS [29]

Table 1.2: Tool classification by type of searches

mining techniques. Lessons learned from implementing these innovations are described in Chap. 7. In Chap. 8, Sushil Krishna Bajracharya considers code retrieval engines not solely as a stand-alone tool or service, but as infrastructure or platform for building applications for mining or reusing open source components.

1.4.1 Component Retrieval

Developers perform searches for components when they want to reuse complete frameworks or systems. Developers expect to find complete components or systems that they could reuse, but the expectation changes according to what they find available on the Web. The types of tools that mainly support developers seeking open source projects are web-based code search engines [11, 12, 17, 18, 22, 31, 33], source code integration tools [15], test-driven code search [16, 17, 20], and project-hosting sites. Only a few of these tools take into consideration the current development context of the developer to suggest components or to help in the evaluation of results.

When developers evaluate open source components and projects, they look not only at the functionality, but also at other aspects such as compatibility of the license, the support and level of activity of the open source community in case of problems and questions, the quality of the software, and the reputation of the developers. After selecting a suitable component or project, developers will adapt their current code, and possibly the found code, to integrate them. There are few tools that help developers with this integration.

In Part III, "Reuse: Components and Projects," are four papers on component reuse; two of these are empirical studies and the second two are on technologies for improving component retrieval on the web. In Chap. 9, Claudia Ayala, Xavier Franch, Reidar Conradi, Jingyue Li, and Daniela Cruzes report a study where they interviewed 19 practitioners on the criteria that they used for selecting open source components for use in their own projects. Rahul De' and Ravi A. Rao conducted a similar study, where they interviewed senior IT managers on how high level goals of an organization influenced the decision to use open source components. These goals are also known as strategic imperatives, and includes examples such as maintaining hypercompetitiveness or entering a new sector. This study can be found in Chap. 10.

Joel Ossher and Cristina Lopes brought together established technologies from two fields to arrive at a novel improvements to component retrieval, and these are described in Chap. 11. They combine algorithms and frameworks from information retrieval for searching and returning documents from a large corpus, with algorithms from program analysis for extracting characteristics from source code. Similarly, Oliver Hummel and Werner Janjic combine infrastructure for information retrieval, and a software development technique called "test first." to arrive at their tool. Queries for suitable components are created by specifying test cases, and the their tool, "Extreme Harvester," which is described in Chap. 12, returns only those components that pass the tests.

1.4.2 Snippet Retrieval

Developers perform searches for snippets to learn how to use an API, to acquire a new concept, or to remind them of syntax. Developers expect to find some lines of code that they could copy and paste with or without the need to adapt the code to integrate it to their current development task. The types of tools that mainly help developers find snippets are API and example code search tools [2, 3, 5, 13, 14, 24, 32, 36, 38, 39, 41], code snippet Web search engines, reuse opportunity recommenders [25, 40], and source code integration tools [7]. Many of these tools, especially the ones in the first and third group in the list, make use of the current context of the user to suggest potentially related code snippets. A few tools in the project-hosting sites, test-driven code search, and general-purpose search engine group also help developers look for code snippets. Many tools in the listed groups support both snippet and component searches, but only the reuse opportunity recommender group and code snippet search engines support exclusively snippet searches. When developers evaluate the result set given by the tools, they mainly pay attention to the functionality of the code snippet. Not many tools offer support for integrating code snippets, mainly, because they assume developers will copy and paste them.

Part IV, "Remix: Snippets and Answers," contains three papers. Chapter 13 by Rosalva E. Gallardo-Valencia and Susan Elliott Sim is on "Software Problems that Motivate Web Searches." They observed software developers as they worked and paid particular attention to the searches that they performed. They found that searches for snippets were examples of opportunistic problem solving. Software developers engaged in these types of searches when they needed information to solve a problem that they encountered in their daily work. Gallardo-Valencia and Sim also found a stark division between searches for snippets and searches for components. The latter took more time and the selection process took more factors into consideration.

These results informed the design and implementation of a search engine for Java snippets described in Chap. 14. Using information retrieval infrastructure, similar to those described elsewhere in this volume, Phitchayaphong Tantikul, C. Albert Thompson, Rosalva E. Gallardo-Valencia, and Susan Elliott Sim, used tutorial web pages rather than open source projects as source material. The examples in the tutorials were the "documents" in the repository and the surrounding text was used as metadata.

An increasingly important resource for software developers is Stack Overflow, a web site where one can post programming-related questions and expect answers from other users. While many questions and answers contain code snippets, not all of them do. Nevertheless, software developers often search the site for information. In Chap. 15, Ohad Barzilay, Christoph Treude, and Alexey Zagalsky report on a study that they conducted on Stack Overflow and a tool that they developed to help software developers to remix the found snippets or examples into their own software.

1.5 Concluding

We conclude this book with Part V, "Looking Ahead," which contains two provocative articles that look at broader issues. Chapter 16 by Susan Elliott Sim and Erik B. Stenberg is on "Intellectual Property Law in Source Code Reuse and Remix."

They conduct a series of thought experiments in which they apply current U.S. intellectual property law to a scenario where source code is being reused. The emphasis of their analysis on the maintaining access to a large body of source code for future software developers. The last chapter of this book is the winner of a science fiction short story contest, "Singular Source," on the future of programming. This work by Micah Joel, entitled, "Richie Boss: Private Investigator Manager," is a film noir-themed mystery where the protagonist makes a startling foray into an archive of computer programs. We wanted to include a work of fiction as a final chapter, both to inspire future researchers and to probe the boundaries of code retrieval on the web.

This book represents a first collection of works on this topic, with historical retrospectives, syntheses of multiple studies, and current research. In this introduction, we argued that 'code retrieval on the web' bifurcates into two kinds of information seeking behavior: component reuse and snippet remix. Searches for components are methodical and involve careful consideration of multiple criteria. The found components are subsequently reused with minimal modification. Searches for snippets are opportunistic and are typically conducted to obtain information. The found snippets are used in a variety of ways, including copy and paste, and read and understand.

The two types of search are often conflated because they share a common origin, specifically code search in IDEs, and they have a single apparent action, typing queries into a search engine. Closer consideration of how software developers think about code retrieval on the web reveals two distinct patterns: searches for components and searches for snippets reveals. Each kind of search is distinct enough to warrant individual treatment in research and design of tools. We hope that this book promotes and encourages research in these and other directions.

References

[1] Alexander Aiken and Brian R. Murphy. Implementing regular tree expressions. In *Proceedings of the 1991 Conference on Functional Programming Languages and Computer Architecture*, pages 427–447. Springer-Verlag, 1991.

[2] Sushil Bajracharya, Joel Ossher, and Cristina Lopes. Searching API usage examples in code repositories with sourcerer api search. In *Proceedings of 2010 ICSE Workshop on Search-driven Development: Users, Infrastructure, Tools and Evaluation*, pages 5–8, Cape Town, South Africa, 2010. ACM.

[3] Joel Brandt, Mira Dontcheva, Marcos Weskamp, and Scott R. Klemmer. Example-centric programming: Integrating web search into the development environment. In *Proceedings of the 28th International Conference on Human Factors in Computing Systems*, pages 513–522, Atlanta, Georgia, USA, 2010. ACM.

[4] Joel Brandt, Philip J. Guo, Joel Lewenstein, Mira Dontcheva, and Scott R. Klemmer. Two studies of opportunistic programming: interleaving web foraging, learning, and writing code. In *Proceedings of the 27th international conference on Human factors in computing systems*, pages 1589–1598, Boston, MA, USA, 2009. ACM.

[5] Shaunak Chatterjee, Sudeep Juvekar, and Koushik Sen. SNIFF: A search engine for Java using free-form queries. In *Proceedings of the 12th International Conference on Fundamental Approaches to Software Engineering*, Lecture Notes in Computer Science, pages 385–400, Berlin/Heidelberg, 2009. Springer.

[6] Y.-F. Chen, M.Y. Nishimoto, and C.V. Ramamoorthy. The C information abstraction system. *IEEE Transactions on Software Engineering*, 16(3):325–334, 1990.

[7] Rylan Cottrell, Robert J. Walker, and Jorg Denzinger. Jigsaw: a tool for the small-scale reuse of source code. In *Companion of the 30th International Conference on Software Engineering*, pages 933–934, Leipzig, Germany, 2008. ACM.

[8] Barthélémy Dagenais and Harold Ossher. Automatically locating framework extension examples. In *Proceedings of the 16th ACM SIGSOFT International Symposium on Foundations of Software Engineering*, pages 203–213, Atlanta, Georgia, 2008. ACM.

[9] Bernhard Ganter, Gerd Stumme, and Rudolf Wille. *Formal Concept Analysis: foundations and applications*, volume 3626 of *Lecture Notes in Artificial Intelligence*. Springer Verlag, 2005.

[10] Max Goldman and Robert C. Miller. Codetrail: Connecting source code and web resources. *Journal of Visual Languages and Computing. Special Issue on Best Papers from VL/HCC 2008*, 20(4):223–235, 2009.

[11] Mark Grechanik, Chen Fu, Qing Xie, Collin McMillan, Denys Poshyvanyk, and Chad Cumby. A search engine for finding highly relevant applications. In *Proceedings of the 32nd ACM/IEEE International Conference on Software Engineering*, pages 475–484, Cape Town, South Africa, 2010. ACM.

[12] F. Gysin. Improved social trustability of code search results. In *Proceedings of the International Conference on Software Engineering*, Cape Town, South Africa, 2010.

[13] Raphael Hoffmann, James Fogarty, and Daniel S. Weld. Assieme: finding and leveraging implicit references in a web search interface for programmers. In *Proceedings of the 20th Annual ACM Symposium on User Interface Software and Technology*, Newport, Rhode Island, USA, 2007. ACM.

[14] Reid Holmes, R. J. Walker, and G. C. Murphy. Approximate structural context matching: An approach to recommend relevant examples. *IEEE Transactions on Software Engineering*, 32(12):952–970, 2006.

[15] Reid Holmes and Robert J. Walker. Supporting the Investigation and Planning of Pragmatic Reuse Tasks. In *Proceedings of the 29th International Conference on Software Engineering*, pages 447–457, Los Alamitos, CA, 2007. IEEE Computer Society Press.

[16] O. Hummel and C. Atkinson. Extreme harvesting: test driven discovery and reuse of software components. In *Proceedings of the 2004 IEEE International Conference on Information Reuse and Integration*, pages 66–72, Las Vegas, Nevada, USA, 2004. IEEE.

[17] Oliver Hummel, Werner Janjic, and Colin Atkinson. Code conjurer: Pulling reusable software out of thin air. *IEEE Software*, 25(5):45–52, 2008.

[18] K. Inoue, R. Yokomori, T. Yamamoto, M. Matsushita, and S. Kusumoto. Ranking significance of software components based on use relations. *IEEE Transactions on Software Engineering*, 31(3):213–225, 2005.

[19] Mehdi Kaytoue-Uberall, Sébastien Duplessis, and Amedeo Napoli. Using formal concept analysis for the extraction of groups of co-expressed genes. *Modelling, Computation and Optimization in Information Systems and Management Sciences*, pages 439–449, 2008.

[20] Otavio Augusto Lazzarini Lemos, Sushil Bajracharya, Joel Ossher, Paulo Cesar Masiero, and Cristina Lopes. Applying test-driven code search to the reuse of auxiliary functionality. In *Proceedings of the 2009 ACM symposium on Applied Computing*, pages 476–482, Honolulu, Hawaii, 2009. ACM.

[21] Christian Lindig and Gregor Snelting. Assessing modular structure of legacy code based on mathematical concept analysis. In *Proceedings of the 19th international conference on Software engineering*, pages 349–359. ACM, 1997.

[22] Erik Linstead, Sushil Bajracharya, Trung Ngo, Paul Rigor, Cristina Lopes, and Pierre Baldi. Sourcerer: mining and searching internet-scale software repositories. *Data Mining and Knowledge Discovery*, 18(2):300–336, 2009.

[23] M.A. Linton. Implementing relational views of programs. *ACM SIGPLAN Notices*, 19(5):132–140, 1984.

[24] David Mandelin, Lin Xu, Rastislav Bodik, and Doug Kimelman. Jungloid mining: helping to navigate the api jungle. *ACM SIGPLAN Notices*, 40(6):48–61, 2005.

[25] Frank McCarey, Mel Ó Cinnéide, and Nicholas Kushmerick. Knowledge reuse for software reuse. *Web Intelligence and Agent Systems*, 6(1):59–81, 2008.

[26] Gail C. Murphy and David Notkin. Lightweight lexical source model extraction. *ACM Transactions on Software Engineering and Methodology*, 5:262–292, July 1996.

[27] Santanu Paul and Atul Prakash. A framework for source code search using program patterns. *IEEE Transactions on Software Engineering*, 20(6):463–475, 1994.

[28] Susan Elliott Sim, Charles L. A. Clarke, and Richard C. Holt. Archetypal source code searches: A survey of software developers and maintainers. In *Proceedings of the Sixth International Workshop on Program Comprehension*, pages 180, Los Alamitos, CA, 1998. IEEE Computer Society.

[29] Denys Poshyvanyk, Andrian Marcus, and Yubo Dong. JIRiSS - an eclipse plug-in for source code exploration. In *Proceedings of the 14th IEEE International Conference on Program Comprehension*, pages 252–255, Athens, Greece, 2006. IEEE Computer Society.

[30] Ute Priss. Formal concept analysis in information science. *Annual review of information science and technology*, 40(1):521–543, 2006.

[31] Steven P. Reiss. Semantics-based code search. In *Proceedings of the 2009 IEEE 31st International Conference on Software Engineering*, pages 243–253, Vancouver, Canada, 2009. IEEE Computer Society.

[32] Naiyana Sahavechaphan and Kajal T. Claypool. XSnippet: mining for sample code. In *Proceedings of the 21st Annual ACM SIGPLAN Conference on Object-Oriented Programming, Systems, Languages, and Applications*, pages 413–430, New York, NY, 2006. ACM Press.

[33] R. C. Seacord, S. A. Hissam, and K. C. Wallnau. Agora: A search engine for software components. *IEEE Internet Computing*, 2(6):62–70, 1998.

[34] Renuka Sindhgatta. Using an information retrieval system to retrieve source code samples. In *Proceedings of the 28th international conference on Software engineering*, pages 905–908, Shanghai, China, 2006. ACM.

[35] Janice Singer, Timothy Lethbridge, Norman Vinson, and Nicolas Anquetil. An examination of software engineering work practices. In *Proceedings of the 1997 Conference of the Centre for Advanced Studies on Collaborative Research*, page 21. IBM Press, 1997.

[36] Jeffrey Stylos and Brad A. Myers. Mica: A web-search tool for finding api components and examples. In *IEEE Symposium on Visual Languages and Human-Centric Computing, 2006. VL/HCC 2006*, pages 195–202, Brighton, United Kingdom, 2006. IEEE.

[37] Ken Thompson. Programming techniques: Regular expression search algorithm. *Communications of the ACM*, 11(6):419–422, 1968.

[38] Suresh Thummalapenta and Tao Xie. Parseweb: a programmer assistant for reusing open source code on the web. In *Proceedings of the Twenty-second IEEE/ACM International Conference on Automated Software Engineering*, pages 204–213, New York, NY, 2007. ACM Press.

[39] Tao Xie and Jian Pei. MAPO: Mining API usages from open source repositories. In *Proceedings of the 2006 International Workshop on Mining Software Repositories*, pages 54–57, Shanghai, China, 2006. ACM.

[40] Yunwen Ye and Gerhard Fischer. Supporting reuse by delivering task-relevant and personalized information. In *Proceedings of the 24th Interntional Conference on Software Engineering*, pages 513–523, New York, NY, 2002. ACM Press.

[41] Yunwen Ye, Yasuhiro Yamamoto, and Kumiyo Nakakoji. A socio-technical framework for supporting programmers. In *ESEC/SIGSOFT FSE*, pages 351–360, New York, NY, USA, 2007. ACM.

[42] Yunwen Ye, Yasuhiro Yamamoto, Kumiyo Nakakoji, Yoshiyuki Nishinaka, and Mitsuhiro Asada. Searching the library and asking the peers: Learning to use Java APIs on demand. In *Proceedings of the 5th International Symposium on Principles and Practice of Programming in Java*, pages 41–50, Lisboa, Portugal, 2007. ACM

Part I
Programmers and Practices

This section consists of three diverse papers on software developers and how they search. The theory and empirical data serve to inform subsequent algorithm and software tool design that appear in later chapters.

Nakakoji, Yamamoto, and Nishinaka's paper in Chap. 2 is on "Unweaving Code Search toward Remixing-Centered Programming Support." Armed with many years of experience developing tools to help developers search for expertise in an organization, Nakakoji et al. present a framework for cognitive, social, and practical aspects of reusing source code.

In Chap. 3, Umarji and Sim present the results from their landmark survey of source code searching on the web. It was an exploratory study and represents a first effort in categorizing the kinds of code search behavior that programmers engage in when searching for code on the web. "Archteypal Internet-Scale Source Code Searching" is an important study, because it forms the foundation of much of their subsequent work.

"A Controlled Experiment on the Process Used by Developers During Internet-Scale Code Search" by Sim, Agarwala, and Umarji in Chap. 4 is a very different kind of study from the one in the previous chapter. This controlled laboratory experiment seeks to test specific hypotheses using statistics.

Chapter 2
Unweaving Code Search Toward Remixing-Centered Programming Support

Kumiyo Nakakoji, Yasuhiro Yamamoto, and Yoshiyuki Nishinaka

Abstract Recognizing that programming is basically remixing, this chapter looks into the cognitive, social, and practical aspects of searching for and using existing code in a programming task. A code search mechanism undoubtedly plays an essential supporting role in a developer's search for code in his or her own programming task. Supporting code search activities, however, demands more than code search mechanisms. At the same time, code search mechanisms also help a developer in a wider spectrum of programming activities. We present the anatomy of the cognitive activity in which a developer searches for existing code, and we propose *efficacy* and *attitude* as two dimensions depicting code search activity. We discuss areas of necessary technical and socio-technical support for code search activities in addition to code search mechanisms. We conclude the chapter by calling for a developer-centered remixing-oriented development environment.

2.1 Unweaving Code Search

Everything is a remix.[1] A large part of software is built by using existing code from open source software (OSS) via the Web. Programming is now viewed as basically remixing.

As Henning [19] noted, development style has changed from the 1970s and 1980s, when developers pretty much wrote everything from scratch. A number of

K. Nakakoji (✉) • Y. Nishinaka
Software Research Associates Inc., 2-32-8 Minami-Ikebukuro, Toshima,
Tokyo, 171–8513, Japan
e-mail: kumiyo@acm.org; nisinaka@motr.jp

Y. Yamamoto
Tokyo Institute of Technology, 4259 Nagatsuta, Midori, Yokohama, 226–8503, Japan
e-mail: yxy@acm.org

[1] http://www.everythingisaremix.info/.

S.E. Sim and R.E. Gallardo-Valencia (eds.), *Finding Source Code on the Web for Remix and Reuse*, DOI 10.1007/978-1-4614-6596-6_2,
© Springer Science+Business Media New York 2013

studies have found that developers constantly engage in searching for code, for documents, and for discussion forums. Developers almost always start their programming by searching the Web [22]. They begin to compose their own code only after making sure that there are no Application Program Interfaces (APIs) or libraries that are usable for their current tasks. Developers also use Web search results for a variety of problem-solving activities [5], and for different reasons [15], software developers use a bricolage of resources [5].

Text search mechanisms have been serving developers as essential tools. The UNIX *grep* command has been one of the most frequently used tools by developers for decades, and *emacs* has offered incremental search and another variety of text search mechanisms from the very beginning. All popular Integrated Development Environments (IDEs) are equipped with powerful text search engines.

This chapter looks into the cognitive, social, and practical aspects of searching for and using existing code in a programming task. The approach we have taken is distinguishing the issues and challenges in code search activities from those in code search mechanisms (Fig. 2.1).

The underlying motivation for this approach is our concern that casually claiming research on code search for software development might blur the essential aspects of a research question addressing a code search activity versus a code search mechanism. A code search mechanism undoubtedly plays an important role in supporting a developer searching for code in his or her own programming task. Supporting code search activities, however, demands more than code search mechanisms. At the same time, code search mechanisms also help a developer in a wider spectrum of programming activities, not just searching for code.

The next section presents the anatomy of the cognitive activity in which a developer uses existing code (i.e., code reuse). We propose efficacy and attitude as two dimensions for depicting a code search activity, and describe the scenarios of three typical types of code reuse by using these dimensions. The following two sections discuss areas of necessary technical support for code search activities other than code search mechanisms. Section 2.3 discusses how some aspects of code search

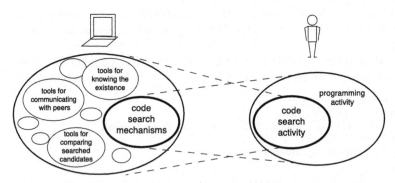

Fig. 2.1 Search technology is useful not only for a developer's search activities but for other development activities. A developer's search activities involve not only technology but also other computational support

activities call for such technical support. Section 2.4 outlines issues and challenges in using peers as information resources in code search, and addresses cognitive as well as social issues in communicating with the "right" person to obtain the sought information in a timely manner. Finally, Section 2.5 lists how the existing search mechanisms would further help a developer in interacting with source code.

2.2 Anatomy of Code Reuse

This section focuses on a developer's code search activity (see the small right oval in Fig. 2.1). From the cognitive perspective for the activities involved in code search, we present two dimensions for depicting code reuse[2] that underlie a wide variety of code search activities.

The first dimension is for what purpose a developer uses existing code for a current programming task. The second dimension is the way in which the developer uses existing code.

2.2.1 The Efficacy Dimension of Code Reuse

The first dimension, which we call the *efficacy* of code reuse, characterizes the purpose of, the motivation for, or the developer's foreseeable gain in using existing code.

There are two types of efficacy in code reuse. The first one is *efficacy through code texture*, and the other is *efficacy through code functionality* (Fig. 2.2).

Efficacy through code texture is established when a developer brings the texture (i.e., literal character strings) of an existing code segment into the program that he or she is currently editing.

Efficacy through functionality is recognized by a developer when the developer is provided with the functionality of an existing code segment that he or she needs in a program.

Fig. 2.2 The efficacy dimension: through code texture (*left*) and through code functionality (*right*)

code texture   code functionality

---

[2] Note that by "code reuse," we mean a developer's action of simply using existing code in the developer's task, and do not necessarily mean a part of more established areas of research on software reuse in software engineering.

Different cognitive activities are involved, depending on the type of efficacy a developer seeks in reusing code. When a developer seeks efficacy through texture in reusing code, the developer must read the source code of potentially reusable parts of the code. In contrast, when a developer seeks efficacy through functionality in reusing code, the developer does not necessarily have to read its source code. Instead, the developer is likely to pay more attention to its documentation and reputation by peers and other developers.

2.2.2 The Attitude Dimension of Code Reuse

The second dimension, which we call the *attitude* toward code reuse, characterizes the style, or the way in which the developer uses existing code in terms of the developer's own code that he or she is currently editing.

The attitude here is along a spectrum with two ends (Fig. 2.3). The one end portrays the attitude of a developer when the developer uses an existing code segment *as an element* in his or her own program. The other end portrays the attitude of a developer when the developer uses existing code *as a substrate*, on top of which the developer builds his or her own program.

Needless to say, this attitude is not the property of a developer, but that of a context consisting of who is reusing which code in what task.

When a developer takes the as-an-element attitude in reusing code, he or she is likely to search for potentially usable code candidates, try using one of them, and perhaps replace it with another if the chosen one does not fit well to the task. In contrast, when exhibiting the as-an-substrate attitude in reusing code, the choice of which code to reuse would have a significant impact on the developer's subsequent coding task. The developer is likely to spend a significant amount of time investigating a few potentially useful candidates by carefully comparing them to decide which one to use. Once the choice is made, he or she is unlikely to replace the chosen one.

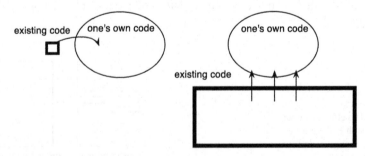

Fig. 2.3 The attitude dimension: along the spectrum between as-an-element (*left*) and as-a-substrate (*right*)

2.2.3 *Illustrating Three Typical Code Reuse Scenarios*

This subsection illustrates scenarios of three typical types of code reuse in terms of the dimensions of efficacy and attitude.

2.2.3.1 Searching for Previously Experienced Code

A developer often searches for a segment of code that he or she has either written before or read before to literally copy and paste it into the current code being editing (Fig. 2.4).

This is a typical example of a developer seeking efficacy through code texture with an as-an-element attitude.

A developer may remember previously writing a code, or reading the code (written by peer developers or by some OSS developers) that seems to be close to what he or she needs in the current program. Once the code segment is identified and pasted, the developer reads it, may modify it if necessary, or may completely discard it if it does not seem to work.

2.2.3.2 Using a Framework

A framework is a collection of program modules that provide a set of necessary functionality in a specific domain or service. Deciding which framework to use has a significant effect on a developer's programming task because it is likely to determine the architecture of the system to implement and how the program is written (Fig. 2.5).

This is a typical example of a developer seeking efficacy through code functionality with an as-a-substrate attitude.

Often a software architect of a software development project is the one who searches for potentially useful frameworks and decides which framework to use

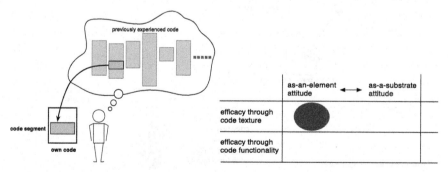

Fig. 2.4 Using a segment of previously experienced code. The challenge here is to find the segment of interest in vaguely remembered code locations

after comparing and studying several alternatives for the project. Once decided, it is not likely that the developer would casually replace the framework; replacing a framework possibly involves a large amount of maintenance cost.

2.2.3.3 Using a Code Example for a Web-Service API

A developer often uses a piece of example code for an API to use an external service (Fig. 2.6). This typical practice illustrates the type of code reuse in which a developer seeks both efficacy through texture (i.e., an example code) and efficacy through functionality (i.e., an external service), with an as-an-element attitude.

A developer who is interested in using a particular service functionality searches for documents and discussion forums about APIs for using that service. Typically, providers of such services promote their services to other developers and tend to provide detailed information resources for using their API, to make it easier to search for such information through Google and other Web search engines.

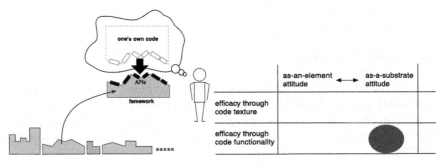

Fig. 2.5 Using a framework. A developer needs to develop some understanding about a framework before deciding to use it

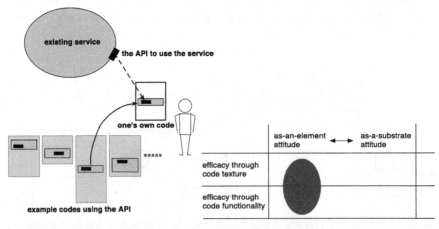

Fig. 2.6 Using a code example for a Web-service API. A challenge is to choose among multiple candidates the "right" example to copy that fits to the current programming needs

A rich source of examples of API usage is available on the Web [6], enabling developers to gain the efficacy of code reuse through code texture. The search result for API code examples is likely to consist of several candidates. Typically, a developer copies and pastes one of them in the current program, test-runs the program, and checks whether it successfully produces the desired effect. If it fails the developer's expectation, the developer replaces the pasted part with another result from the search, and then checks whether that one works. The developer may not fully understand the pasted statement, for instance, which parameter does what, but if it works, he or she may just leave it as is in the program.

2.3 Areas of Technical Support for Code Search Activities

From the perspective of a developer's cognitive activity on code search, code search mechanisms are necessary but not sufficient. Other areas of technical support should be taken into account to smoothly and effectively help a developer engaging in code reuse and remix (see the larger left oval in Fig. 2.1).

This section lists some aspects of a code search activity that would demand such technical support. We discuss existing tools and then outline future research agendas together with relevant existing research in addition to software engineering.

2.3.1 Knowing the Nonexistence of Potentially Usable Existing Code

Developers often want to make sure that there is no reusable code before they start writing their own code. Developers usually have a rather good understanding of what they want to achieve in their own programming tasks. In this sense, the code search is fact-finding rather than exploratory [25].

It remains as a challenging task to know the nonexistence of potentially usable code for the current task. When one does not find usable code among a list of queried results, it is often difficult to distinguish whether such code does not exist or whether it exists but has not been located due to inadequate queries. A developer is likely to specify a query for a desired functionality in his or her own context, but what could be suitable for the task may not be associated with such a vocabulary set [24].

2.3.2 Helping to Formulating Queries

Tools have been studied to address the challenge of adequately formulating queries. CodeBroker used a latent-semantic indexing mechanism to associate terms used in program comments and method signatures with methods stored in code repositories

[33]. Blueprint automatically generates queries with code context for a developer and presents a code-centric view of Google search results in an IDE [6]. Mica makes it easier for a developer to explore Google search results by providing appropriate relevance cues for the information that he or she wants to know [30]. The approach by Bajracharya et al. helps developers obtain example code that uses similar set of APIs by using code usage similarity measurements, reformulating a query by showing a tag-cloud of popular words for the current query, and narrowing down results according to popularity [2]. API Explorer recommends related APIs to a developer by using API Exploration Graph, which models the structural relationships between API elements [10].

We may also resort to crowd sourcing for query formulation if we could use search query logs of tens of thousands of developers searching the Web. Such query logs are typically not publicly available but can be mined through search suggestion services [3]. Fourney et al. [13] mine the Google search query log to generate a Query-Feature (QF) graph, which encodes associations between user goals articulated in queries and the specific features of a solution element relevant to achieving those goals. Using Google Suggestion and other publicly available search query suggestion services, their technique performs a standard depth-first or breadth-first tree traversal "by expanding partial queries one character at a time," starting with the keyword a user specifies. The approach has currently been applied in the CUTS (characterizing usability through search) framework, helping users to access usability information of an application system and to identify similar application systems on the Web [14]. This technique seems to be straightforwardly extendable to help developers identify potentially usable APIs, libraries, and frameworks when they are not sure about how to specify queries.

2.3.3 Locating a Previously Experienced Code Segment Through Personal Information Management

When a developer has a particular code segment in mind to reuse, the developer may remember only its existence but not its location, or may even remember it wrongly (e.g., the code segment was written at some point of time but not saved in a file).

If a developer is unable to find the source code where he or she remembered it, the developer has to search for it. The developer may use a character string that he or she has in mind as a query, or use temporal relationships, such as "that's the code I was working on when the new manager came to our project," as a retrieval cue to located potentially related files. Once presented with a searched result, the developer immediately knows whether it is what he or she has been seeking.

This type of search poses a challenge similar to the one found in the studies on personal information management [4]. Proposed tools and empirical studies in the field are applicable to help developers in this situation. For instance, using a tool such as Stuff I've Seen, which provides a unified index for email messages, Web pages, and other types of personal documents through their temporal relationships

[11], a developer would be able to search the code that he or she has previously written by using his or her own experience as a contextual cue. Another example is the HCB (History-Centric Browsing)-tempo, which helps a user revisit previously visited Web pages by indexing a large volume of Web page history using the search query-based slicing (SQS) technique [29].

2.3.4 Using Related Documents to Judge Code Reuse Potential

A number of developers have mentioned that cognitive cost is quite high when reading source code written by someone else. A developer tends to resort to related documents and information or forums to judge whether to use a specific API, service, library, or framework, rather than reading their source code, by addressing questions such as:

- Is this API well-documented?
- How often does this library go through major updates?
- When was this answer provided in the Q&A forum?
- Which projects use this framework?
- How does this library rank in Google search? How about for the last 6 months?
- Which API results in more search results?
- How lively is this forum?

Discussions in forums often complement the documents created by the library/API designers by providing what the library/API owners have not tested; documents often fail to accurately explain in which contexts the library is not operational, only because it has not been tested.

2.3.5 Judging the Credibility of Existing Code

The number of search results on each of the few potentially usable libraries helps a developer compare which ones are more popular. Limiting the search to a certain period of time (e.g., for the period of the last 6 months) helps the developer to better understand the trends of their uses.

The ranking of search results helps developers infer how popular or commonly used an API is. Popularity is often a good indication of the adequate maintenance of the API/library, unless it provides a particular service or functionality.

Timestamps attached to each question and answer in discussion forums provide a valuable resource to judge whether the library is well maintained. If the information in the forum is relatively obsolete, developers may assume that an alternative library should be available that had replaced the current library, and they should start over searching.

2.3.6 Limiting Search Space by Using Social Information

Currently available Web search engines are good for understanding the popularity and reputation of a library and API at large, but are not helpful for a developer investigating whether it is used by those the developer trusts and respects. A socio-technical approach that combines social network systems with Web search mechanisms would significantly benefit a code-searching developer in this context.

Another socio-technical approach would be to share search histories among the members of a project, a group, an organization, or a community. The information necessary to understand a framework may have already been studied by the architect of the project when deciding to use the framework from among other alternatives. Such information that the architect had used could be valuable resources for project members when they study the framework later in the development process.

2.3.7 "Tasting" Existing Code

To examine the memory consumption or the execution speed of library APIs, developers need to try out the library in their own project context. Using tools such as Maven[3] may ease the task of building processes of a target library, but it remains cumbersome to "taste" a library API, especially if it is written in an unfamiliar programming language. Experimentability and penetrability are featured as factors affecting the usability of APIs [28], and tool support to improve such aspects is warranted.

2.3.8 Understanding the Implication of the Use of Existing Code Before Reusing It

To decide whether to use a particular framework, developers need to have some understanding about a set of potentially complicated APIs the framework provides. APIs are the visible interfaces between developers and the abstractions provided by the framework [19]. Human-related factors, such as the design of APIs [19], the usability of APIs [7], the learnability of APIs [28], and the necessary conceptual knowledge about APIs [24], are becoming key considerations in deciding which framework to use. Tools such as APATITE (Associative Perusal of APIs That Identifies Targets Easily) [12], which helps a developer browse APIs through incremental, column-based presentation of API graphs filtered by popularity of usage, have been developed to help in understanding the framework being used. However, few tools are available to help the developer understand a framework prior to starting to use it.

---

[3] http://maven.apache.org/.

2.3.9 Comparing the Effects of Using Texture of Existing Code Segments

Existing program editors do not naturally support the trial-and-error process of finding a usable example code from multiple candidates. When pasted in an editor, the copied segment is merged into the existing program and becomes indistinguishable unless the developer deliberately inserts some visual cues (e.g., blank lines or comments) to designate which part is currently being tested with a pasted code segment.

Some graphic editors use a tracing paper metaphor and employ *layers* to produce variations of the current drawing area. Terry et al. explored a way to simultaneously develop alternative solutions to the current problem situation [31]. Similar techniques would help developers in the process of choosing a usable example code from multiple candidates.

2.3.10 Motivation to Search Existing Code

Although perhaps less common than in the past, a problem still remains when a developer is not motivated to search for potentially useful code. One of the early systems, CodeBroker [32], monitors a programming editor (*emacs*), infers the programmer's interest by parsing comments and message signatures, and pushes potentially relevant information to the developer in a subtle manner (i.e., in a small sub-pane located in the bottom of the *emacs* editor). The argument for such an editor is that information delivered in this way should minimize interruption, and that the system should incrementally present more in-depth information only when the developer requests it [33].

2.4 Socio-technical Support for Code Search Activities

Peer developers serve as precious information resources in identifying the existence of potentially usable code through face-to-face communication [23] and in discussion forums [20]. STeP_IN_Java (Socio-Technical Platform for In-situ Networking for Java programming) [34] is an example of an approach that identifies experts who might know the existence of potentially useful information for a developer. Help-MeOut suggests possibly relevant solutions made by peer developers to a novice programmer who is facing a compiler error message or a runtime exception [18].

A developer's ability to search, rank, and triage code, documents, and peer developers that are seamlessly integrated in an IDE may be ideal. However, code and documents are things, whereas peer developers are humans [34]. A challenge involves how to balance a developer's needs for communication for help in searching code with another developers' needs for a concentrated flow experience [26].

2.4.1 Searching for Developers for Help Is Not Equal to Finding the Name of a Person to Ask

Addressing the challenge of having school teachers as knowledge resources, Illich stated that whereas a thing is available at the bidding of a user, a person becomes a knowledge resource only when he or she consents to do so, restricting time, place, and methods as he or she chooses [21].

Using humans as information resources is costly, especially if the sought humans are not dedicated to helping and providing information because they have their own time-pressing tasks.

When finding a peer developer for a question, it is necessary to search for those who not only can answer the question, but also are willing to answer the question. The search for a peer developer for an answer needs to include considerations on how to select participants for communication, what timing to use to start communication, how to invite people to participate in the communication, which communication channel to use, and how to use the resulting communicative session (i.e., communication archives) [26].

2.4.2 Searching for Developers Adds a Social Cost to the Cost of Information Search

Finding a person and asking him or her a question involves a social cost. Those who seek information demonstrate different asking behaviors, depending on whether they are in public, in private, communicating with a stranger, or communicating with a friend, due to the different levels of perceived psychological safety in admitting their lack of knowledge [8]. At the same time, whether developers can successfully get their questions answered depends on how they ask it, including their rhetorical strategies, linguistic complexity, and wording choice [8]. A classic study has found that engineers tend to rely on knowledge resources that are easier to access rather than maximizing gains [16], a fact that does not seem to have changed much for the last 40 years.

The perceived social burden on a potential answerer may affect how easy it is for a developer to ask a question. A field study of Answer Garden reports that because the information-seeker's identity is not revealed in Answer Garden, the information-seeker feels less pressure in asking questions and bothering experts [1]. It might also become easier for an information-seeking developer to ask a question when he or she knows that the recipients have the option and freedom to ignore the request.

2.4.3 The Social Cost of Communication Can Be Reduced by Using a Social-Aware Communication Mechanism

The benefit of a question-answer communication would primarily go to the one who asks, and the cost is primarily paid by those who are asked. Such cost includes stopping his or her own ongoing development task, collecting relevant information if necessary, composing an answer for the information-seeking developer, and then going back to the original task [36]. This type of communication is different from coordination communication, which has a symmetric or reciprocal relation in terms of cost and benefit between those who initiate communication and those who are asked to communicate [27].

A developer being asked may feel different levels of social pressure, depending on who is requesting information and through which communication channel the request is coming. For instance, it is harder to ignore a request if asked face-to-face. Developers may respond to a question not because they want to answer it but because they do not want to ignore it. Even though helping is costly, taking no action or saying "no" may also incur a social cost.

The STeP_IN framework [34] provides a social-aware communication mechanism called DynC (Dynamic Community); a temporal mailing list is created every time an information-seeking developer posts a question, with the recipients decided dynamically. Whereas the sender's identity is shown to the recipients, the recipients' identities are not revealed unless they reply to the request. If some of the recipients do not answer, for whatever reasons, nobody will know it; therefore, refusing to help becomes socially acceptable. If one of the recipients answers the question, his or her identity is revealed to all the members of the DynC mailing list. This asymmetrical information disclosure is meant to reinforce positive social behaviors without forcing developers into untimely communication.

2.4.4 Asking a Question to a Thing Relieves the Social Pressure of Communication

Social skills have been recognized as indispensable for developers, who often have to obtain necessary information from other developers using the APIs of interest both within an organization and outside of organizations over the Internet. This, however, should not necessarily be so.

STeP_IN_Java [35] allows a developer to post a question to a function API of Java libraries, relieving the developer of social pressure in posting a question to a large mailing list or identifying a peer programmer who is likely to help. The system identifies expert peer developers to the specific API by keeping track of who used the API in previous project histories, filters out the experts who have formerly had little social correspondences with the developer, formulates a temporary mailing list with the remaining experts for the question, and forwards the question to the mailing list. If someone on the mailing list posts the answer, the system brings the answer back to the asking developer.

2.4.5 Searching for Developers for Help Should Balance the Benefit of Individuals with the Cost of Group Productivity

Broadcasting a question may give a developer a better chance to find the right answer more quickly. However, if developers are frequently interrupted to offer help, their productivity is significantly reduced, resulting in lower group productivity.

Attention has been rapidly becoming the scarcest resource in our society [17]. We have estimated how much attention (in terms of time) is collectively spent in the Lucene mailing list and found that roughly more than 1,000 h were collectively spent every month over the 2,282 developers [36]. In an organizational setting, this collective cost might even outweigh the benefits of developers obtaining answers from other developers. One way to reduce this cost is by limiting the recipients of the question to only those who are both able and very likely to be willing to answer the question [34].

2.4.6 Archiving Communication Turns the Need for Developer Search into That of Information Search

Compared to other professional communities, software developers' communities have historically taken advantage of digital media for communication, and their archives have served as rich information resources for other developers, transforming pieces of information originally available only by direct human contact into sources stored in artifacts.

Recent trends in social networking systems, such as Twitter, Facebook, and LinkedIn, open up new possibilities to collect information on a daily basis from individual developers. Such collections of information would become rich knowledge resources for developers, and make it possible to access knowledge that resides in a developer's mind without requiring social skills.

2.5 Interacting with Code Through Code Search Mechanisms

This section briefly describes situations in which code search mechanisms help a developer interact with code (see the larger left oval in Fig. 2.1)

- Compose through selection
  A developer start typing the initial part of the name of an API and through IDEs that are now equipped with auto-completion mechanisms, the system incrementally searches for possible names starting with the typed string and matching the current program context. Together with a rich and fast-enough auto-completion mechanism, a developer may incrementally compose a program through a cycle of typing a few letters and selecting one of the auto-completed candidates.

- Generate clickable links
  A developer uses search mechanisms to generate clickable links to directly jump
  to the exact location of interest for quicker access, rather than typing a URL
  or navigating through browsers. In this way, a developer types the major part
  of the name of the library portal site and Google returns a link to the site that
  the developer then simply clicks for instant connection, even if the developer
  remembers the exact URL. In addition, a developer can insert tags in the code in
  Eclipse so that he or she can later search for a particular tag to which the IDE lists
  all the program components as clickable links to their corresponding locations.
- Translate technical messages
  A developer uses Google search as a technical translator to make sense of cryptic
  errors and debugging messages by searching them on the Web [5].
- Be reminded of unsure names
  A developer frequently conducts a Google search to use as a reminder of the
  correct name of an API or library for what the developer has in mind. Google
  Suggest and Google search results usually come up with a list of the variation of
  the name, from which a developer is likely to easily recognize the correct one.
- Debug through structural patterns
  A developer can interactively search for a specified structure in a half-billion
  lines of a Java program repository within one second by using CodeDepot [37],
  a browser-based code search tool. The developer searches for a pattern in which
  a specific set of APIs are called, and by looking at the searched results, he or she
  may notice that the specific order of the API calls is necessary.
- Observe coding standard/styles/convention
  A developer can find code segments within his or her project that do not observe
  a given coding standard or convention by using a structure search mechanism.
- Deal with code clones
  A developer can pay attention to the code clones of the program segment in which
  he or she has found a bug through CodeDepot [37] to avoid the possibility of the
  same bug in its cloned code.
- Be proactive to code clones
  A developer can be warned when he or she is about to edit a code segment that
  is likely to have clones through CloneTracker [9], a code structure search mechanism integrated within an IDE.

2.6 Concluding Remarks

By focusing on the remixing aspect of the coding experience, this chapter has described code search activities from a cognitive perspective. Our view is not that code
is a remix but that coding is remixing. Searching for code is an essential activity in
code remixing, which calls not only for search mechanisms but also for other technical and socio-technical support.

The remixing style of programming has changed through the last decade, and now developers often use existing code without knowing its details. Developers resort to documents and code examples, as well as the reputations of other developers, to judge whether to use the code for their current task. Developers take different strategies to decide when to reuse, how to reuse, and what code to reuse, depending on the efficacy they envision and the attitude they take.

Software development has come to form an ecosystem in which each developer remixes existing code to produce new systems. A developer-centered, remixing-oriented development environment must take this dynamism of programming into account. The depiction of code search activities as well as the list of technical and socio-technical needs discussed in this chapter should help in designing and building such environments.

References

[1] Ackerman, M.S.: Augmenting organizational memory: A field study of Answer Garden. ACM Trans Info Sys, 16(3), 203–224 (1998)

[2] Bajracharya, S.K., Ossher, J., Lopes, C.V.: Leveraging usage similarity for effective retrieval of examples in code repositories. Proc. FSE '10, ACM, New York, 157–166 (2010)

[3] Bar-Yossef, Z., Gurevich, M.: Mining search engine query logs via suggestion sampling, Proc. VLDB'08, Auckland, New Zealand, 54–65 (2008)

[4] Boardman, R., Sasse, M.A.: Stuff goes into the computer and doesn't come out: A cross-tool study of personal information management, Proc. CHI '04, ACM, New York, 583–590 (2004)

[5] Brandt, J., Guo, P.J., Lewenstein, J., Dontcheva, M., Klemmer, S.R.: Two studies of opportunistic programming: interleaving web foraging, learning, and writing code, Proc. CHI '09, ACM, New York, 1589–1598 (2009)

[6] Brandt, J., Dontcheva, M., Weskamp, M., Klemmer, S.R.: Example-centric programming: integrating web search into the development environment, Proc. CHI '10, ACM, New York, 513–522 (2010)

[7] Clarke, S.: Measuring API usability. Dr Dobb's Journal Special Windows/NET Supplement, http://drdobbs.com/cpp/184405654 (2004)

[8] Cross R., Borgatti, S.P.: The ties that share: Relational characteristics that facilitate information seeking. In: Huysman M., Wulf V., Social Capital and Information Technology, pp. 137–161. The MIT Press, Cambridge, MA (2004)

[9] Duala-Ekoko, E., Robillard, M.P.: Clone region descriptors: Representing and tracking duplication in source code. ACM Trans. Softw. Eng. Methodol. 20, 1, Article 3, 3:1–3:31 (July 2010)

[10] Duala-Ekoko, E., Robillard, M.P.: Using structure-based recommendations to facilitate discoverability in APIs, Proc. 25th European Conf. on Object-Oriented Programming, 79–104 (July 2011)

[11] Dumais, S., Cutrell, E., Cadiz, J.J., Jancke, G., Sarin, R., Robbins, D.C.: Stuff I've seen: A system for personal information retrieval and re-use, Proc. ACM SIGIR Conference on Research and Development in Information Retrieval, Toronto, Canada, 72–79 (2003)

[12] Eisenberg, D.S., Stylos, J., Myers, B.A.: Apatite: a new interface for exploring APIs. Proc. CHI '10, ACM, New York, 1331–1334 (2010)

[13] Fourney, A., Mann, R., Terry, M.: Query-feature graphs: Bridging user vocabulary and system functionality, Proc. UIST '11, ACM, New York, 207–216 (2011)

[14] Fourney, A., Mann, R., Terry, M.: Characterizing the usability of interactive applications through query log analysis, Proc. CHI '11, ACM, New York, 1817–1826 (2011)

[15] Gallardo-Valencia, R.E., Sim, S.E.: What kinds of development problems can be solved by searching the web?: A field study, Proc. SUITE '11, ACM, New York, 41–44 (2011)

[16] Gerstberger P.G., Allen T.J.: Criteria used by research and development engineers in the selection of an information source. J. Appl. Psych. 52(4), 272–279 (1968)

[17] Goldhaber M.H.: The attention economy. First Monday 2(4), (1997).

[18] Hartmann, B., MacDougall, D., Brandt, J., Klemmer, S.R.: What would other programmers do: Suggesting solutions to error messages, Proc. CHI '10, ACM, New York, 1019–1028 (2010)

[19] Henning, M.: API design matters, ACM Queue 5(4), 24–36 (May 2007)

[20] Hou, D., Li, L: Obstacles in using frameworks and APIs: An exploratory study of programmers' newsgroup discussions, Proc. Program Comprehension (ICPC) 2011, IEEE, 91–100 (June 2011)

[21] Illich, I.: Deschooling sSociety, Harper and Row, New York (1971)

[22] Ko, A.J., Myers, B.A., Coblenz, M.J., Aung, H.H.: An exploratory study of how developers seek, relate, and collect relevant information during software maintenance tasks. IEEE Transactions on Software Engineering, 33(12),971–987 (December 2006)

[23] Ko, A.J., DeLine, R., Venolia, G.: Information needs in collocated software development teams. Proc. ICSE 2007, 344–353 (May 2007)

[24] Ko, A. J., Riche, Y.: The role of conceptual knowledge in API usability. IEEE Symposium on Visual Languages and Human-Centric Computing (VL/HCC), Pittsburgh, PA, 173–176 (2011)

[25] Marchionini, G.: Exploratory search: From finding to understanding. Commun. ACM 49(4), 41–46 (April 2006)

[26] Nakakoji, K., Ye, Y., Yamamoto, Y.: Supporting expertise communication in developer-centered collaborative software development environments. In: Finkelstein, A., Grundy, J., van den Hoek, A., Mistrik, I., Whitehead, J. (eds.), Collaborative Software Engineering, chap. 11, pp. 152–169. Springer-Verlag, (May 2010)

[27] Nakakoji, K., Ye, Y., Yamamoto, Y.: Comparison of coordination communication and expertise communication in software development: Motives, characteristics, and needs, In: Nakakoji, K., Murakami, Y., McCready, E. (eds.) New Frontiers in Artificial Intelligence, pp. 147–155. Springer-Verlag, LNAI6284 (August 2010)

[28] Robillard, M.P., DeLine, R.: A field study of API learning obstacles. Empirical Software Engineering, 16(6), 703–732 (2011)

[29] Shirai, Y., Yamamoto, Y., Nakakoji, K.: A history-centric approach for enhancing Web browsing experiences, Extended Abstracts of CHI2006, 1319–1324 (April 2006)

[30] Stylos, J., Myers, B.A.: Mica: A Web-search tool for finding API components and examples. Proc. VLHCC '06, IEEE Computer Society, Washington, DC, 195–202 (2006)

[31] Terry, M., Mynatt, E.D., Nakakoji, K., Yamamoto, Y.: Variation in element and action: Supporting simultaneous development of alternative solutions, Proc. CHI2004, ACM, New York, 711–718 (2004)

[32] Ye, Y., Fischer G.: Supporting reuse by delivering task-relevant and personalized information. Proc. ICSE '02, ACM, New York, 513–523 (2002)

[33] Ye, Y., Fischer G.: Reuse-conducive development environments. Int. J. Automat. Softw. Eng. 12(2), 199–235 (2005)

[34] Ye, Y., Yamamoto, Y., Nakakoji, K.: A socio-technical framework for supporting programmers, Proc. ESEC/FSE 2007, ACM Press, Dubrovnik, Croatia, 351–360 (September 2007)

[35] Ye, Y., Yamamoto, Y., Nakakoji, K., Nishinaka, Y., Asada, M.: Searching the library and asking the peers: Learning to use Java APIs on demand, Proc. PPPJ2007, ACM Press, Lisbon, Portugal, 41–50 (September 2007)

[36] Ye, Y., Nakakoji, K., Yamamoto, Y.: Understanding and improving collective attention economy for expertise sharing, Proc. CAiSE 2008, Montpellier, France, 167–181, Lecture Notes in Computer Science, Vol. 5074, Springer, Berlin, Heidelberg (June 2008)

[37] Ye, Y., Nakakoji, K.: CodeDepot: A one-stop code search environment based on the character and structural search methods, J. Digital Practices, Information Processing Society of Japan, 2(2), 117–124 (in Japanese) (April 2011)

Chapter 3
Archetypal Internet-Scale Source Code Searching

Medha Umarji and Susan Elliott Sim

Abstract To gain a better understanding of what, how, and why programmers search for code on the Internet, we conducted a web-based survey to understand the source code searching behavior of programmers, specifically, their search motivations, search targets, tools used, and code selection criteria. Data was collected from 69 respondents, including 58 specific examples of searches. We applied open coding to these anecdotes and found two major archetypes and one minor archetype, as well as, a range of sizes for search targets. The first archetype was searching for source code that could be excised and dropped into a project. The second archetype was searching for examples of source code to provide information, for example, using the World Wide Web as an enormous desk reference. The targets of these searches could vary in size from a few lines of code to an entire system. The minor archetype was searching for reports and repairs of defects. Factors affecting the final selection of a candidate piece of code included: peer recommendations; availability of help from other programmers; and the level of activity on a project.

3.1 Introduction

With the increasing popularity of open source, a rapidly growing quantity of source code is available on the Internet. Software developers are now using this rich resource in their work. Evidence of this practice can be found in the number of project hosting sites, code repositories, and source code search engines that have appeared. Among these are Koders.com with over 226 million lines of code (MLOC), Krugle.com with over 2 billion lines of code, csourcesearch.net with over

M. Umarji (✉)
Symantec Corporation, Mountain View, CA, USA
e-mail: medha_umarji@symantec.com

S.E. Sim
Many Roads Studios, Toronto, ON, Canada
e-mail: ses@drsusansim.org

S.E. Sim and R.E. Gallardo-Valencia (eds.), *Finding Source Code on the Web for Remix and Reuse*, DOI 10.1007/978-1-4614-6596-6_3,
© Springer Science+Business Media New York 2013

283 MLOC, and Google Code Search with over 1 billion lines of code. These source code search engines treat Internet-scale code searching in much the same manner as code search within a single project in an integrated development environment. But, there are other kinds of searches that can take place on the Internet and we need to know more.

This study was conducted to characterize Internet-scale source code searching: What do developers look for? How do they find what they are looking for? What tools do they use? When do they decide to search? To this end, we conducted a questionnaire-based survey of software developers contacted using availability sampling over the Internet. The design of this study is based on previous surveys by Eisenstadt [3], and Sim, Clarke, and Holt [12]. Using an online questionnaire, we collected data from over 70 programmers who were solicited using Google Groups and mailing lists.

Their responses and anecdotes were analyzed systematically to find common themes, or archetypes. An archetype is a concept from literary theory. It serves to unify recurring images across literary works with a similar structure. In the context of source code searching, an archetype is a theory to unify and integrate typical or recurring searches. As with literature, a set of them will be necessary to characterize the range of searching anecdotes.

We found that there are two major search archetypes and one minor one. The first archetype was searching for a piece of code that can be reused. For example, a text search engine, or a graphical user interface (GUI) widget. The second archetype was searching for reference information, that is, for examples of code to learn from. In this archetype, developers are using the World Wide Web as a very large desk reference. The minor archetype was searching for reports and repairs of bugs, i.e. patches. The two major archetypes had search targets that varied in size, while the minor one did not. The search targets could be small-grained, such as a block of code, medium-grained, such as a package, or large-grained, such as an entire system. The results reported in chapter are an extension of the work reported in an earlier paper [21].

3.2 Related Work

The work in this paper has evolved from past research and current trends in software development. The two trends that motivate this research are the increasing availability of source code on the Internet, and the emergence of tools for accessing the source code. The source code available on the web comes from open source projects, web sites that support communities of practice, and language-specific archives. Collectively, these sites contain billions of lines of code in countless languages. As is the case with web pages, it can be difficult to locate a particular resource. General-purpose search engines, such as Google and Yahoo!, can be used, but they do not take advantage of structural information in the code. To fill this need, code-specific search engines have been created. These software tools leverage the technology and know-how from source code searching tools within programming environments. However, code search on the Internet at times is more similar to code reuse than the find function in an IDE. In this section, we will review the trends and results that motivate and inform our research.

3.2.1 Source Code on the Internet

The open source movement has dramatically increased the quantity of source code available on the Internet. While the open source concept has been around for decades, it is only in the last 10 years or so that it has become commonplace. For-profit corporations are now contributing source code and person-hours to open source projects [5]. The most obvious benefit of the open source movement is that it makes available a "rich base of reusable software" [15].

Communities of practice have evolved from this sharing of programs and knowledge amongst people having common goals and interests, within the open source world. A community of practice is formed by a group of people united by a joint enterprise, who develop mutually beneficial social relationships in the process of working towards things that matter to them [6]. Artifacts, advice/tips and other relevant knowledge are contributed by members to provide a shared repertoire of resources for the community.

In the open source world, project hosting sites, technology-specific mailing lists and social networking sites are examples of such communities of practice. Sourceforge.net and freshmeat.net host thousands of projects and have an infrastructure that supports the sharing of programs and knowledge. The infrastructure for these projects is provided by developers, and so is the source code – all through extensive collaboration over individual projects.

Technology specific mailing lists such as PHP.net and CPAN.org are a compilation of code snippets, bug reports, patches, discussions and how-to guides related to a specific technology or programming language. These sites are frequented by developers who are interested in learning a particular language or technology, or building on top of it. The lists contain not only source code, but also contributions of helpful tips on what works, what doesn't, and what is the best way to solve a certain problem. Since it is the culture in open source to share software developed by using open source technology, these archives of source code are increasing exponentially.

Blogs, social bookmarking and other social networking sites have the capability to tag websites containing source code relevant to a particular topic and are excellent sources of reference on latest technologies and trends.

3.2.2 Code Search Engines

General purpose search engines such as Google and Yahoo! are used for code search most often. Users are familiar with these tools and due to their effectiveness in retrieving documents on the web they are easily the most popular. However, they are effective in broad searches for functionality, when good search terms are available. These search engines are not able to exploit the context and relationships between source code snippets, as they treat source code like a bag of words.

Code-specific search engines index public source code, cache it in a repository and enable users to search based on a variety of attributes such as class/function names, code licenses, programming languages and platforms. While the search is limited to the repository, the amount of code available is huge, many millions of lines of code or classes.

Three of the major code-specific search engines are Krugle, Koders, and Google Code Search. Like Google Code Search, Koders has options for searching by language and license. It also allows users to explicitly search for class, function, and interface definitions using regular expressions. Krugle returns links not only to source code, but also to tech pages, books and projects. It has a visualization for browsing code repositories and also supports tab-based searching. The searches can be applied to different segments: source code, comments, and definitions (class or method). Google Code Search includes support for regular expressions, search within file names and packages, and case-sensitive search.

To leverage the advantages afforded by open source code, we need search capabilities that are closely integrated with the way that software is developed in open source. The code search engines do not support the social interaction processes that are the lifeline of any project. For example, they do not search for keywords within mailing lists or forums related to a particular topic, users have to use a general-purpose search engine for that purpose. Neither do they support the formation and sustenance of communities of practice that are so essential for learning and sharing in any domain [6].

3.2.3 Source Code Searching

A study of software engineering work practices by Singer et al. [14] found that searching was the most common activity for software engineers. Program comprehension, reuse and bug fixing were cited as the chief motivations for source code searching in that study. A related study on source code searching by Sim et al. [12] found that the search goals cited frequently by developers were code reuse, defect repair, program understanding, feature addition and impact analysis.

Source code searching for program comprehension involves matching of words or code snippets within an IDE or source code module to a search term, typically using the Unix-based grep facility, the find command in Unix and also the File Find command under Microsoft Windows [12]. It was also found that programmers used only strings or regular expressions to form their search terms, even though they were searching for semantically significant pieces of code. Grep is by far the most popular search facility due to ease of specification of search terms, a command-line interface, and a direct match with the search model of the programmer [13]. Programmers trust grep because it is successful most of the times, and the cost of failure is insignificant.

Program comprehension tools can be categorized as (i) extraction tools such as parsers (Rigi) [8], (ii) analysis tools for clustering, feature identification and slicing (Bauhaus tool [2]), and (iii) as presentation tools such as code editors, browsers and visualizations [16, 20].

Lethbridge et al. [13] in their study on grep discuss that searching within source code is used for locating the bug/problem, finding ways to fix it and then evaluating the impact on other segments. Sim et al. [12] found that programmers were most frequently looking for function definitions, variable definitions, all uses of a function and all uses of a variable.

However, none of these existing tools have capabilities to search for software components based on functionality and purpose – which is the basic idea behind Internet-scale source code searching.

3.2.4 Software Reuse

It is evident from the discussion so far that source code searching on the Internet has more commonalities with the phenomenon of software reuse, than with traditional source code searching for program understanding and bug fixing.

Reuse is a common motivation for Internet-scale source code searching [15]. Programmers do not want to "re-invent the wheel," especially when the open source world allows reuse to occur at all levels of granularity, starting from a few lines of code, to an entire library; from a tool to an entire system.

Reuse in proprietary settings involved indexing and storing software components in a way that would make retrieval and usage easy (for example, the structured classification technique, by Prieto-Diaz [10]). Complex queries had to be formed to retrieve such components and the process of translating requirements into search terms posed a cognitive burden for software engineers. Fischer et al. [4] also discuss the gap between the system model of the software and the user's situation model, which makes it difficult for the user to express a requirement in a language that the system can understand. They also discuss the technique of retrieval by reformulation – a continuous refinement process that forms cues for retrieval of components that are not well-defined initially.

The problem of discourse persists through the open source era as the primary method of searching continues to be keywords and regular expressions. Support provided for locating and comprehending software objects does not scale up to the actual potential for reuse even in open source projects.

Reuse of open source code occurs with an understanding that effort will be expended in contextualizing, comprehending and modifying a piece of software – while traditionally, the reuse concept assumed little or no modification of components. Another interesting difference is that in open source the options available for a given search query are tremendous as opposed to a company-wide repository of source code, which may or may not have relevant reusable code.

3.3 Method

Online surveys have become increasingly common over the last decade, as Internet usage has grown by leaps and bounds. Surveys have become an established empirical method, especially for human behavior on the Internet [19].

These studies have been conducted to improve understanding of why users look for information, their search requirements, their search strategies, backgrounds and experiences, and their comparative assessment of available search mechanisms [9, 11, 18, 22]. Sim, Clarke, and Holt [12] conducted an online survey in late 1997 of source code searching among programmers that served as the model for this research. Underpinning these research designs are traditional survey methods that have been used in the social sciences for many years [1]. The design of this study is presented in this section.

3.3.1 Research Questions

In this study, we wanted to gain an understanding of how software developers currently search for source code on the Internet. The search features on project hosting sites and the emergence of source code-specific search engines hint at the kinds of search taking place, but empirical data is needed. Therefore the research questions for this study were as follows.

- What tools do programmers use to search for source code on the Internet?
- What do they look for when they are searching source code?
- How do they use the source code that is found?

Data on what tools are used provide information about the skills and tendencies of programmers when searching the web. The search targets and usage patterns for the code suggest new features. Answers to the last two questions were obtained from the open ended questions, when analyzed resulted in search archetypes.

3.3.2 Data Collection

We designed an online survey with 11 closed-ended questions and 2 open-ended questions. This chapter is focused on the results from one of the open-ended questions, which asked:

> Please describe one or two scenarios when you were looking for source code on the Internet. (Please address details such as: What were you trying to find? How did you formulate your queries? What information sources did you use to find the source code? Which implementation language were you working with? What criteria did you use to decide on the best match?)

Our goal was to cover a wide range of people that search for source code often, to get a representative sample. The population was any programmer who had searched for source code on the Internet. However, it was not possible to obtain a systematically random sample, and availability sampling also known as convenience sampling was the chosen sampling technique.

Convenience sampling may pose a threat to external validity of the results. However, this was an exploratory study and the goal was to collect data on a variety of behavior, and not its prevalence, so availability sampling was considered adequate for this task. We solicited participants from a number of mailing lists and newsgroups. We attempted to solicit participants through open source news web sites, but were declined. This strategy gave us access to a large number of developers and users of open source software, as well as developers who worked on proprietary and commercial software.

The survey was open for 6 months in 2006–2007 to collect responses. Invitations to participate in the survey were posted to the Javaworld mailing list, and the following mailing lists beginners-cgi@perl.org, comp.software-engg, comp.lang.c, and comp.lang.java. We chose these web sites, because had they had users with a variety of interests, the discussions were high technical in nature, and there was little overlap between the groups.

3.3.3 Data Analysis

The data was analyzed using a combination of quantitative and qualitative techniques. The multiple-choice questions were coded using nominal and ordinal scale variables. For the open ended questions, the responses were text descriptions that were analyzed qualitatively. We analyzed them for recurring patterns using open coding [7] and a grounded theory approach [17]. Without making prior assumptions about what we would find, we developed codes for categories iteratively and inductively. The two authors analyzed the data separately, and we found a high level of agreement in our categories. Subsequently, we combined our codes and refined the categories for clarity of presentation.

3.3.4 Threats to Validity

The main shortcoming of this study is generalizability, i.e. the sample of respondents is not sufficiently representative of the population. This is a basic problem with empirical research in software engineering is there is not a reliable model of population characteristics so that the representativeness of a sample can be assessed.

This study is no exception. Furthermore, we only solicited participants from mailing lists and newsgroups. Therefore, we are not trying to quantify the prevalence of certain types of behavior, nor are we using inferential statistics. Instead, we are looking for a variety of search behaviors and patterns (or archetypes), which is appropriate for an exploratory study.

3.4 Results

A total of 69 people responded to the survey and provided descriptions of 58 situations where they searched for source code on the Internet. The quality of the responses varied greatly. Some respondents only filled in the multiple-choice questions. Others provided very terse descriptions of search situations. Yet others provided extremely detailed descriptions of more than one situation.

A majority of the developers that responded to our survey were programmers in Java (77 %), C++ (83 %) and Perl (60 %). A few had contributed to an open source project, though most were users of open source Applications. Within the criteria guiding final selection of source code, 77 % users based their decisions on available functionality, 43 % considered the licensing terms and 30 % considered the amount of user support available. Amongst the information sources consulted while searching for source code, documentation ranked highest, followed by mailing lists and other people. Most of the respondents (59 %) had experience working on small teams with 1–5 people.

3.4.1 Situations

We analyzed 58 scenarios of source code searching. They ranged in length from one to ten lines. Figure 3.1 below is an example of a good response that we received.

The anecdotes were categorized among a number of dimensions. Clear patterns emerged regarding two aspects of their searches: (i) what programmers were searching for; and (ii) how they searched for it.

Sometimes; I did a source code searching when I don't know how to use a class or a library. For an example; I didn't know how to create a window using SWT class. I did a Google search with the description of what I want to do. I decided on the best match based on whether I understand the example code.

Fig. 3.1 Example search description

3.4.2 Object of the Search

In terms of what programmers were searching for, anecdotes were categorized along two orthogonal dimensions: the motivation for the search and the size of the search target (Table 3.1). Some responses had multiple search targets and motivations, and in such cases, each was coded separately. The most specific code that was appropriate for the search was selected, based on the information given by the participant. In Fig. 3.1, the motivation was coded as "reference example" and the size of search target was coded as "subsystem".

Code for reuse	As-is reuse	Reference example	Row total
Block	8	4	12
Subsystem	21	11	32
System	5	2	7
Column total	37	22	51

Table 3.1: Purpose by target size

3.4.2.1 Motivations for Searching

Detailed analysis of scenarios showed that respondents were either searching for reusable code (37) or reference examples (22). Reusable code is source code that they could just drop into their program, such as an implementation of trie tree data structure, quick sort algorithm, and two-way hash table. A reference example is a piece of code that showed how to do something, for instance, how to use a particular GUI widget, what is the syntax of a particular command in Java. Searches of this type essentially use the web as a large desk reference. These two motivations emerged very clearly in the anecdotes, and almost all the scenarios could be neatly classified into either of these two motivations.

A key difference between the two motivations is the amount of modification that searcher intended to perform. Programmers seeking reusable code planned to find pieces that could be dropped into a project and used right away. For example,

Needed to convert uploaded images of all types into jpeg and then [generate] thumbnails. Due to timescales; it could not be done in house...

Those seeking reference examples intended to re-implement or significantly modify the code found. One respondent wrote,

I typically search for examples of how to do things; rather than code to use directly. The products that I work on are closed-source, one can't [use] most open source directly.

On occasion, the search that was seeking reusable code would fail and become a search for reference information. A programmer needed a mutable string class in Java, but the results from search engines either had only a minimal implementation or an inappropriate open source license. He wrote, "... in the end I just rolled my own," and only used the other implementations for ideas.

3.4.2.2 Size of Search Targets

Across both types of searches, the size of the search target varied in a similar fashion. The sizes of the search targets were classified as a block (12), a subsystem (32), or a system (7). A block was a few lines of code, up to an entire function in size.

Common block-sized targets were wrappers and parsers (3), and code excerpts (8). A number of the searches for code excerpts were for PHP and JavaScript. Programs in these languages tended to be small and plentiful, which meant it was easier to make use of a few lines of code. There were searches for a small section of code that solved a specific problem, such as "encode/decode a URL" and "RSS feed parser."

A subsystem was a piece of functionality that was not a stand-alone application, and the programmer searching intended to use it as a component. Categories of subsystem targets are implementations of well-known algorithms and data structures (14), GUI widgets (9), and uses of language features (6). Some examples from the data include "a Java implementation of statistical techniques like t-test" and "wrapper code for the native pcap library."

A system was an application that could be used on its own. Searchers often intended to use these as a component in their own software. Respondents were "looking for some big piece of code that would more or less do what I want..." or something that would show them "how to do it."

3.4.3 Process of Search

With respect to the process of search, anecdotes were categorized on the starting point for the search, the tools used, and the criteria used to make the final selection. In Fig. 3.1, the starting point was a recommendation from a friend, the tool used was search.cpan.org, and no selection criterion was mentioned.

3.4.3.1 Starting Point for Search

A common starting point for Internet-scale code searches was recommendations from friends to use a particular piece of software. Other potential starting points were reviews, articles, blogs, and social tagging sites. When no such starting point was available, programmers went straight to search tools.

3.4.3.2 Search Tools Used

By far, the most popular tool for finding source code on the web was general-purpose search engines, such as Google and Yahoo! The search feature on specific web sites and archives was also popular. Interestingly, the source code-specific search engines were used only occasionally.

3.4.3.3 Selection Criteria

A number of common themes also emerged among the criteria that programmers used to make a final selection among different options. Often the choices were limited, so there were few degrees of freedom in the final selection. Criteria that were mentioned by the respondents were level of activity on the project, availability of working experience, availability of documentation, and ease of installation. Surprisingly, code quality and the user license for the source code were low priorities in the selection criteria.

The results are presented as archetypal searches in Sect. 3.5 and as observations about the search process in Sect. 3.6.

3.5 Archetypal Searches

By examining the motivations for search and the size of search targets, we found common or more frequent relationships. These patterns, or archetypes, are presented in this section, as well as, some unusual, but interesting searches.

3.5.1 Common Searches

The most common type of search was a subsystem that could be reused. Archetypes 1, 3, and 4 fell into this category. The next most common search, archetype 2, was for a system that could be modified or extended to satisfy the needs of the project. Archetypes 5–8 are searches for examples of how to do something, such as using a component or implementing a solution. The final archetype is searching for reports and patches for bugs.

1. *Reusable data structures and algorithms to be incorporated into an implementation.*
   Eight of the reported searches were for algorithms and data structures, such as "two-way hash tables," "B+ trees," "Trie trees," and "binary search algorithm." were included at this level of granularity. We suspect that this was the most prevalent because there was a close match between the vocabulary for describing the

object in code and the vocabulary for describing the search. Furthermore, abstract data structures are a well-understood basic building block in computer science.

2. *A reusable system to be used as a starting point for an implementation.*
   While creating a new system, developers often look for systems that they can use as a starting point. There were seven such searches by developers who were looking for "stand-alone tools" or a "backbone for an upcoming project" or just a "big piece of code that does more or less what I want." Examples of search targets included an application server, an ERP package or a database system. We conjecture that this type of search is common because a system does not need to be de-contextualized before it is used in a new project. Also, systems are easy to find because they typically have web sites or project pages that contain text descriptions of the software. Finally, customizing an existing application saves a lot of time in comparison to implementing from scratch.

3. *A reusable GUI widget to be used in an implementation.*
   Developers often looked for widgets for graphical user interfaces and there were seven searches of this kind in our data. Users searched by keywords of the functionality that they desired, for example "inserting a browser in a Java Swing frame." Searches for functionality are somewhat independent of the source code implementation underneath, but are mainly concerned with feature addition. Other examples include a "Java interface for subversion" and a source code that creates a "SeeSoft-like visualization." We believe that searches for GUI widgets are popular, because these components are easy to reuse. A software developer need only ensure that the widget is compatible with the GUI framework being used on the project. As well, GUI widgets can be displayed visually, therefore, making it easier for a developer to quickly assess the appropriateness of the search result.

4. *A reusable library to be incorporated into an implementation.*
   There were six searches for a reusable library, sometimes called a package or API. Programmers were generally looking for a subsystem that could be dropped in and used immediately. Some examples of the searches were for "speech processing toolkits," "library for date manipulation in Perl" and "Java implementations of statistical techniques."

5. *Example of how to implement a data structure or algorithm.*
   In six instances, developers looked for source code snippets to verify their solution or to aid reimplementation, e.g. "to verify the implementation of a well-known algorithm." There were six searches were for a piece of code to use as a reference in order to develop the same functionality. An implementation was more informative than a description or pseudocode, because the implementation had been tested and could execute. Respondents believed that a reference example would show them the right way to do something, and a running program had a lot of credibility.

6. *Example of how to use a library.*
   Developers looked for examples of how to use a library, for instance, "Sometimes, I did a source code searching when I don't know how to use a class or a library." There were six anecdotes reporting this kind of search. Libraries and

APIs can be complex to use, with arcane incantations for calling methods or instantiating classes. A reference example is easier to use than documentation, because it gives the programmer a starting point that can be tweaked to suit the situation.

7. *Example of how to use features of a programming language.*
   In four anecdotes, respondents reported that reference examples of language syntax and idioms were helpful when working with an unfamiliar programming language. Users who haven't programmed in a language before, or have forgotten parts of it, or are using the language in a new way (e.g. new hardware), searched for source code to serve as a language reference. One respondent wrote, "...mostly I look for code for syntax, I don't always like to refer to books for syntax if it is readily available on my desktop."

8. *A block of code to be used as an example.*
   Developers look at a block of code to learn how to do something. There were four situations that described this type of search. Programmers were not looking for reusable components, but their goal was to learn through examples, such as "examples of javascript implementation of menus" and "examples of thread implementation in python."

9. *Confirmation and resolution of bugs*
   There were five searches that were looking for solutions to a bug. Sometimes the can be in the form of of a report or post to a form that confirmed the presence of an actual bug. At other times, there was a patch that repaired the bug. Three of the searches led developers to find relevant information in mailing lists and forums. Developers prefer to search for a patch or quick-fix by forming natural language queries with the keywords from an error message or keywords based on the functionality deviation caused by a bug. The need for code in such situations is very specific in terms of implementation language, platform, version information, size of patch and licensing requirements. In the process of debugging, if the problem seems to occur while compiling a library or at run-time, users examine the source code of a library to determine the exact problem.

3.5.2 Uncommon Searches

There were a few uncommon searches that are worthy of attention. These were looking for a system to be used as a reference example, seeking a reference example for using a GUI framework or widget, and searching for examples of language syntax usage.

While developing or modifying a system, programmers look at existing similar systems for ideas. Searches for systems that can be understood and the logic/principles can be borrowed to construct new systems. Two searches were for systems with similar functionality as the current or to-be system. This technique was mainly used in a proprietary environment or when it was easier to construct a new system rather than adopt an existing one.

There were also two searches for examples of how to use GUI widgets. These included searches for code samples on how to use a particular component from Swing and Microsoft Foundation Classes.

Finally, there was one anecdote from a programming language designer who searched to find examples "in the wild" of syntax from the language. This information was used to evaluate requests for changes and suggestions for features.

3.6 Discussion

In this section, we explore how social interaction processes supported by the right search tools can help programmers to arrive at the right code snippet, component or exemplar.

As discussed previously, a typical search begins with a cue such as advice from a colleague or use of the immensely popular general purpose search engines.

Search mechanism	Count
Google, Yahoo, MSN search etc.	60
Domain knowledge	37
Sourceforge.net, freshmeat.net	34
References from peers	30
Mailing lists	16
Code-specific search engines	11

Table 3.2: Tools/information sources used in search

Our survey showed that 60 of the 69 respondents used general purpose search engines (refer to Table 3.2). More than half the respondents relied on their domain knowledge to find the right source code. Project hosting sites came next, with 34 of the respondents using them for source code search.

Elements from the social network were used frequently especially peer references (30) and mailing lists (16). In our descriptive data we observed that social tagging sites (del.icio.us) and compilation sites created by a group of programmers featured often.

Once users have access to the source code that matches their requirements, the problem of narrowing down the list of retrieved items arises.

3.6.1 Documentation

An initial assessment is done using web pages and documentation, as one user put it, "... (the core developer) had a good documentation of his code with lots of comments too (by which I could also modify his code), hence I decided to use that code."

A piece of software with the required functionality may be eliminated if it can't be easily determined whether it has the required features and documentation. The basic functionality has to be in place, and supported by requisite documentation.

3.6.2 Peer Recommendations

Peer recommendations were the most trusted and valued – especially if the person has used the software before. For instance, one respondent stated that "... friends recommended Graph.pm; searched for that on search.cpan.org, and found it was just what I needed." In the absence or inaccessibility of peer advice programmers then look for availability of help from people within their online social network, or within the project context.

3.6.3 Help from One's Social Network

Help from a local expert, an electronic forum, a mailing list archive, or active users who are doing similar tasks and are willing to answer questions is a major consideration while choosing open source software. One respondent said he looked for "... issues which are then found by people, solved and posted on mailing lists of discussion forums." A glance at the forums tells the users how friendly a project is and how likely they are to obtain help when needed.

Availability of help is also determined from the project activity. Respondents preferred large open source projects that were very active. For example, "The criteria that I used were: (1) if the tool was in java (2) if the tool was web based (3) the activity of the project." Activity can be quantified as the number of contributors, frequency of builds and updates, traffic on newsgroups, and number of users. Larger projects have more resources, are more responsive, and are more likely to rank highly on these criteria.

Overall, social characteristics of the project, such as the level of activity, presence of discussion forums, and recommendations by peers seem to have precedence over characteristics of the source code, such as code quality (i.e. whether the code is peer reviewed and tested), and reliability (Table 3.3).

Criteria	Count
Available functionality	54
Terms of license	30
Price	26
User support available	21
Level of project activity	18

Table 3.3: Criteria for selecting a code component

3.6.4 Feature Suggestions

Developers not only look for code, they also look for a social system through which they can contribute their knowledge and expertise as well as learn from their counterparts. As reported in Table 3.2, the domain knowledge and social networking are key ingredients of the search process in addition to search engines.

We also observed that programmers use social tagging websites for technical information and applications. The current source code repositories should be appended with a recommender system wherein programmers could obtain not just code components, but also real subjective opinions of people who have used those components.

3.7 Conclusions

The goal of this research study was to gain an understanding of Internet-scale source code searching in order to inform the design and evaluation of tools for web-based source code retrieval. We observed that programmers mainly search for either reusable components or reference examples. The granularity of search targets varies from a block of code to an entire system. Some directions for future research in this area are: Which search engines are better than others with respect to code search? Does search engine performance depend on types of tasks?

References

[1] D.A. deVaus. *Surveys in Social Research.* UCL Press, London, fourth edition. edition, 1996.

[2] T. Eisenbarth, R. Koschke, and D. Simon. Aiding program comprehension by static and dynamic feature analysis. In *Proceedings of the IEEE International Conference on Software Maintenance.*, pages 602–611, 2001. TY - CONF.

[3] Mark Eisenstadt. My hairiest bug war stories. *Communications of the ACM*, 40(4):30–37, 1997.

[4] Gerhard Fischer, Scott Henninger, and David Redmiles. Cognitive tools for locating and comprehending software objects for reuse. In *Proceedings of the 13th international conference on Software engineering*, pages 318–328, Austin, Texas, United States, 1991. IEEE Computer Society Press.

[5] R. Goldman and R.P. Gabriel. *Innovation Happens Elsewhere: Open Source as Business Strategy*. Morgan Kaufmann Publishers, San Francisco, CA, 2005.

[6] Jean Lave and Etienne Wenger. *Situated Learning: legitimate peripheral participation*. Cambridge University Press, England, 1991.

[7] M. B. Miles and A. M. Huberman. *Qualitative data analysis*. Sage Publications, Thousand Oaks, CA, 1994.

[8] H. A. Muller and K. Klashinsky. Rigi-a system for programming-in-the-large. In *Proceedings of the 10th international conference on Software engineering*, pages 80–86, Singapore, 1988. IEEE Computer Society Press.

[9] E. B. Parker and W. J. Paisley. Information retrieval as a receiver-controlled communication system. *Education for Information Science*, pages 23–31, 1965.

[10] Ruben Prieto-Diaz. Implementing faceted classification for software reuse. *Communications of the ACM*, 34(5):88–97, 1991.

[11] Soo Young Rieh. Judgment of information quality and cognitive authority in the web. *Journal of the American Society for Information Science & Technology*, 53(2):145–161, 2002.

[12] S. E. Sim, C. L. A. Clarke, and R. C. Holt. Archetypal source code searches: A survey of software developers and maintainers. In *Proceedings of the 6th International Workshop on Program Comprehension*, page 180, Los Alamitos, CA, 1998. IEEE Computer Society.

[13] Janice Singer and Timothy Lethbridge. What's so great about 'grep'? implications for program comprehension tools. Technical report, National Research Council, Canada, 1997.

[14] Janice Singer, Timothy Lethbridge, Norman Vinson, and Nicolas Anquetil. An examination of software engineering work practices. In *Proceedings of the 1997 conference of the Centre for Advanced Studies on Collaborative research*, page 21, Toronto, Ontario, Canada, 1997. IBM Press.

[15] Diomidis Spinellis and Clemens Szyperski. Guest editors' introduction: How is open source affecting software development? *IEEE Software*, 21(1):28–33, 2004.

[16] Margaret-Anne D. Storey. Theories, tools and research methods in program comprehension: past, present and future. *Software Quality Journal*, 14(3): 187–208, 2006.

[17] Anselm Strauss and Juliet Corbin. *Basics of Qualitative Research: Grounded Theory Procedures and Technique*. Sage Publications, Thousand Oaks, 1990.

[18] Louise T. Su. A comprehensive and systematic model of user evaluation of web search engines: I. theory and background. *Journal of the American Society for Information Science & Technology*, 54(13):1175–1192, 2003.

[19] V. M. Sue and L. A. Ritter. *Conducting Online Surveys*. Sage Publications, Thousand Oaks, CA, 2007.

[20] Scott R. Tilley, Dennis B. Smith, and Santanu Paul. Towards a framework for program understanding. In *Proceedings of the 4th International Workshop on Program Comprehension (WPC '96)*, page 19. IEEE Computer Society, 1996.

[21] Medha Umarji, Susan Elliott Sim, and Cristina V. Lopes. Archetypal internet-scale source code searching. In Barbara Russo, editor, *OSS*, page 7, New York, NY, 2008. Springer.

[22] H. Wang, M. Xie, and T. N. Goh. Service quality of internet search engines. *Journal of Information Science*, 25(6):499–507, 1999.

Chapter 4
A Controlled Experiment on the Process Used by Developers During Internet-Scale Code Search

Susan Elliott Sim, Megha Agarwala, and Medha Umarji

Abstract It has become common practice for developers to search the Web for source code. In this paper, we report on our analysis of a laboratory experiment with 24 subjects. They were given a programming scenario and asked to find source code using five different search engines. The scenarios varied in terms of size of search target (block or subsystem) and usage intention (as-is reuse or reference example). Every subject used five search engines (Google, Koders, Krugle, and Google Code Search, and SourceForge). We looked at how these factors influenced three phases of the search process: query formulation, query revision, and judging relevance. One consistent trend was searching for reference examples required more effort, as measured by average number of terms per query, average number of queries, clickthrough rate, and time spent. This additional effort paid off in a higher rate of precision for the first ten results.

4.1 Introduction

Searching for information on the Web has become a daily occurrence. This practice has also extended into the world of software development. Programmers often search for source code examples to remind themselves of syntax and for components to reuse on projects. The search process used by software developers during

S.E. Sim (✉)
Many Roads Studios, Toronto, ON, Canada
e-mail: ses@drsusansim.org

M. Agarwala
Columbia University, New York, NY, USA
e-mail: ma3037@columbia.edu

M. Umarji
Symantec Corporation, Mountain View, CA, USA
e-mail: medha_umarji@symantec.com

S.E. Sim and R.E. Gallardo-Valencia (eds.), *Finding Source Code on the Web for Remix and Reuse*, DOI 10.1007/978-1-4614-6596-6__4,
© Springer Science+Business Media New York 2013

software development can have significant impact on whether a project is completed on time, with the allocated budget and with the desired functionality. Some Internet-scale code search engines, such as Koders, Google Code Search, SourceForge and Krugle, have emerged to fill this niche. But little work has been conducted to understand developers' search process when using these tools.

We conducted an experiment to better understand how people search for code on the Web. Twenty-four subjects participated in the study. They were given a scenario and asked to search for source code to satisfy the task described. When the subjects settled on a query that produced satisfactory results, they were asked to judge the relevance of the first ten results (P@10). The scenarios varied along two dimensions: intention of search (as-is reuse or reference example) and size of the search target (block or subsystem) [17]. We used these two dimensions as between-subjects independent variables in our experiment. There are also different kinds of search engines that can be used to locate code on the Web and we used this factor as a within-subjects independent variable with five levels (Google, Koders, Krugle, Google Code Search, and SourceForge). The dependent variables were the length of the query, the number of queries in a session, the clickthrough rate on results, precision of the first ten results (P@10), and the duration of the session. Each of these variables provided insight into different stages of the search process. The findings reported in this chapter are complementary to a paper previous published using the same data [14] that focused on the P@10 dependent variable and insights into the search engines.

On average, the developers used each search engine for 6 min. During that time, they entered an average of 2.4 queries with 4 terms each. They navigated to 62 % of the search results overall, but a higher proportion (81 %) of relevant results, compared to irrelevant ones (47 %).

We obtained a variety of statistically significant results, including some interaction effects. Participants used more terms in their queries when carrying out search on Google or when searching for reference examples. They made more query revisions when searching for blocks of code and for reference examples. When they specialize their query by adding more terms, their next likely step is to generalize their query by removing terms. They had a lower clickthrough rate on SourceForge or when searching for code to reuse. Furthermore, they spent more time searching for reference examples or blocks of code or when using Google. We found that searches for reference examples gave a higher P@10, or a higher proportion of relevant results. Google gave the most relevant results. Koders and Krugle gave more relevant results on searches for subsystems and Google gave more relevant results for blocks.

One consistent trend across all the dependent variables is more effort was expended on searches for reference examples than for components to reuse as-is. Reference example searches involved more terms per query on average, more queries per session, a higher clickthrough rate, and more time. The additional effort was rewarded by more relevant results among the first ten matches.

In comparison to Web search, developers performing code search issued more queries, longer queries and made greater use of advanced features than users of Web search. We synthesized these statistical results into a model of user behavior during code search on the Web. We compare this model with user behavior in other kinds of search and we discuss implications for design.

4.2 Background

4.2.1 Internet-Scale Code Search

By some estimates, there are billions of lines of code available on the Internet. With this embarrassment of riches, comes a problem: locating the code that one wants. In response, many web sites, repositories, and tools have been created. Research into tools to support Internet-scale code search has clustered around two use cases: searching for examples and searching for components.

Developers frequently reuse open source components. Prototypes, such as Sourcerer [12], Merobase [9], and Exemplar [5], use a variety of approaches to return classes, files, or projects. Sourcerer uses the CodeRank metric to present the most frequently called/used components earlier. Merobase allows searches on binaries as well as source code. Exemplar matches search to concepts in the APIs used by an application to return relevant candidates.

Developers often want a snippet of code to see an example solution to a problem or how to use an API (Application Program Interface). Tools such as Strathcona [7], Assieme [6], XSnippet [13] and many others return a "snippet" of code that can be adapted or cut-and-pasted into a project. Strathcona provides examples of how to use an API, while Assieme helps a developer find an appropriate API. XSnippet provides examples of how to instantiate a certain type of object.

4.2.2 Studying User Behavior

There are a number of approaches to studying user behavior, including log analysis, field observations, and experiments.

Transaction logs from Web search engines have been analyzed to learn about query structure and query revision strategies of users [10]. Logs are a good source of data, because they are intrusive and can be used to obtain data from a large number of users.

Observational field studies can also be used to study user behavior [16]. In these studies, a researcher observes users, with or without search mediators, as they conduct searches in naturalistic settings. Although labor intensive, observational studies provide richer data than logs and insight into how people satisfy their own information needs, rather than ones that have been assigned by the experimenter.

Controlled experiments can also be used to study user behavior in Web searching to examine a wide variety of phenomena, such as differences between novices and experts [8] and where searchers look on a results page [4]. This approach allows researchers to look for general trends and tendencies in user behavior, by having multiple subjects perform the same task.

In a previous study, we found that searches for code on the Web tend to vary along two continuous dimensions [17]. The first dimension is the intention behind the search. The endpoints on the continuum are reference example and as-is reuse. Points along the continuum are distinguished by the amount of additional code that needs to be written. Reference examples are reminders of syntax or how-to do something. Once found, the developers usually write the code needed from scratch. During searches motivated by as-is reuse, the developer is looking for components to use without modification. The second dimension is the size of the source code desired. We draw attention to three points along the continuum: block (few lines of code); subsystem (class, package, or library); and system (a program that can be used on its own).

Bajracharya and Lopes [2] analyzed the log of a code search engine to identify common search topics. Brandt et al. [3] looked at how developers search for examples of how to use an API, using both logs and a laboratory experiment. They concluded that the Web is used for learning and reminding. To our knowledge, there are no observational field studies of code search on the Web. This paper reports on a laboratory experiment where we studied how developers searched for source code.

4.3 Method

In this section, we describe the design of the laboratory experiment. Many of the design decisions, such as the independent variables, search scenarios, and search engines, were motivated by a previous study [17].

4.3.1 Independent Variables

There were three independent variables in this study and our analysis: size of search target, intention of search and the search engine. Size of search target and intention of search were between-subjects factors.

Size of search target refers to the amount of source code searched by the developers on the Web. This variable had two levels: block or a subsystem. Block refers to few lines of code, for e.g. a function. Subsystem is a piece of functionality that is not a stand-alone application and is used as a component.

Intention of search refers to the motivation for searching source code on the Web. This variable had two levels: reuse as-is or reference example. Reusable code is source code that can be simply dropped in a program without any modification. A reference example is a piece of code that gives a direction to do something, for e.g. how to use a particular GUI widget.

Search engine was a within-subjects independent variable with five levels: Koders, Google Code Search, SourceForge, Google and Krugle.

4.3.2 Dependent Variables

In our analysis, we used five dependent variables: number of terms in a query, number of queries in a session, clickthrough percentage, P@10 and time spent on a search engine. These dependent variables helped us to study the search process of developers.

A query term is defined as any string of characters separated by some delimiter such as a space, a colon, or a period, depending on the syntax of the search specification. We counted Boolean operators or search filters in a query as one term. For example, the query "apache access log parser, lang:python" has five terms.

We counted as a query any search specification that was entered and results were returned (including a null set).

Clickthrough percentage is the proportion of returned matches that a user clicked on to view in detail.

P@10 is the relevance of the first ten matches as judged by the subject.

A session is considered to start when a user begins using a search engine and to end when the relevance judgment is provided. The duration of a session is the amount of time spent in seconds.

4.3.3 Scenarios

Multiple scenarios were constructed for every treatment. Two scenarios were generated for searches for blocks and three were constructed for searches for subsystems. A complete list of scenarios has been described elsewhere [14]. An example is presented below:

You are working in the Python programming language, and need to have multi-threading functionality in your program. You have never used threads before, and would like to know how to create threads, to switch between threads, and so on. Look for examples by which you can learn. Any thread implementations of Python programs are relevant. Remember you will not be using the code directly, you would like to learn how to use it.

4.3.4 Procedure

The experiment consisted of three stages: training, experiment task, and debriefing.

In the training stage, the participants were given a warm up task to make them familiar with the experimental setup and the think aloud procedure. To train the participants on think aloud, we asked them to identify how many windows were in their parents' house. Generally, to answer this question they had to mentally walk through the house and count the windows. To train the participants on the experiment procedure, we asked them to conduct a web search for a binary search tree. Each participant was trained individually.

During the experiment, participants were randomly assigned a search scenario, which was a combination of intention of search and size of search target. They had to conduct the search using five search engines. They could choose the engines in any order. They were free to change their query as many times they wished. Once they found a page with satisfactory results, they had to rate the relevance of the first ten matches (P@10). Finally, in the debriefing stage, the participants completed a questionnaire on their preferences and background in code search.

4.3.5 Subjects

Twenty-four subjects participated in this study. They were recruited on the criteria that they should have some prior programming experience in either a professional or an academic setting. The average age of subjects was 27.3 and on average they had 4.3 years of programming experience. All of them had searched for source code on the Web previously, worked with multiple programming languages and had worked with a team. Fifty percent of the subjects searched for source code "frequently", 33 % searched for it "occasionally," and only 16 % of the subjects searched for source code "rarely." Sixty-seven percent of the subjects declared their primary job responsibility as "Programming." Twenty-three subjects had experience with Java, 22 subjects had experience with HTML, 21 subjects had experience with C and 20 subjects had experience with C++. Seventy-one percent of the subjects had worked on small sized teams and 29 % of the subjects had worked on medium sized teams.

4.3.6 Hypotheses

We planned to examine the effect of intention, size of search target, and search engine on the search process. We identified the following hypotheses to be tested in our study.

4.3.6.1 Main Effects

Since there were three independent variables, there were three main effects in our analysis.

H_1^I: The search process is affected by the intention of search, i.e. user behavior is different when searching for reference examples than when searching for code to reuse as-is.

H_1^S: The search process is affected by the size of the search target, i.e. user behavior is different when searching for blocks of code than when searching for subsystems.

H_1^E: The search process is affected by the search engine used, i.e. user behavior is different when searching with Google, Koders, Google Code Search, Krugle and SourceForge.

4.3.6.2 Interaction Effects

With the three independent variables, we had four possible interactions. We expected two of them to be significant, so we describe them here.

The first one is the interaction effect between intention of search and search engine. We expected that user behavior with a particular search intention would be affected by the search engine used. Some search engines would be better for reference examples than others, e.g. Google versus SourceForge.

H_1^{IE}: The search behavior when searching with a particular search intent (i.e. reuse or reference example) is dependent on the search engine used.

The second interaction effect was between the size of search target and the search engine. We predicted that user behavior when searching for a particular target size would be affected by the search engine used. Some search engines would be better at locating components than others.

H_1^{SE}: The search behavior when searching for a particular size of code (blocks or subsystems) is dependent on the search engine used.

4.4 Results

We transcribed the audio, video, and screen recordings of the experiment. Using the recordings and the transcripts, we coded for our independent variables. The significant effects are summarized in Table 4.1.

4.4.1 Query Length

Overall, the average number of terms per query was found to be 4. The distribution of the number of terms in a query is given in Fig. 4.1.

We conducted an analysis of variance (ANOVA) on the number of terms in the query and found four statistically significant effects. The query length was affected by the intention of the search $(F(1,265) = 9.29, p < 0.01)$. Searches for reference examples involved 4.3 terms on average, while searches for components had only 3.8 terms on average. Query length was also affected by the search engine $(F(4,265) = 4.06, p < 0.01)$. Searches using Google tended to have the most terms (4.7) (Table 4.2).

		Dependent Variables			
	Number of Terms	Number of Queries	P@10	Clickthrough Rate	Time Spent
Size	-	Block > system $p < 0.04$	-	-	Block > subsystem $p<0.01$
Intention	Reference > reuse $p<0.001$	Reference > reuse $p<0.01$	Reuse > reuse $p<0.05$	Reference > reuse $p<0.001$	Reference > reuse $p<0.03$
Engine	Google highest $p<0.001$	-	Google highest, SF lowest $p<0.01$	Google highest, SF lowest $p<0.001$	Google highest $p<0.02$
Size x Intention	Block x reference higher $p<0.001$	-	-	-	-
Intention x Engine	-	-	-	Google x reference highest $p<0.04$	-
Size x Engine	Block x Krugle lowest $p<0.03$	-	Google x block highest $p<0.001$	-	-
Size x Intention x Engine	-	-	-	-	-

(Independent Variables)

Table 4.1: Summary of statistically significant results

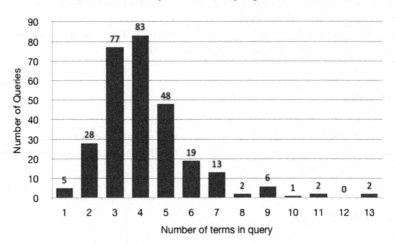

Fig. 4.1 Distribution of query length

Google	Koders	Krugle	GCS	SourceForge
4.7	4.1	3.7	4.2	3.8

Table 4.2: Average terms per query by search engine

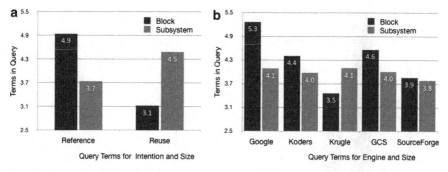

Fig. 4.2 Interaction effects on average terms per query. (**a**) Query terms for intention and size and (**b**) query terms for engine and size

An interaction effect was found between size of the search target and intention of the search ($F(1,265) = 45.63, p < 0.01$) as shown in Fig. 4.2a. More terms were used when searching for block-sized reference examples than for subsystems to be reused as-is. Another interaction was found between size of the search target and search engine ($F(4,265) = 2.83, p < 0.05$). More terms were entered in Google for block-sized code, but fewest when using Krugle to search for subsystems.

4.4.2 Query Revision

We found that on average, 2.38 queries were entered per subject per search engine. The distribution of session length is depicted in Fig. 4.3. Over all the queries, 42.2 % used a filter and 8.7 % used a Boolean operator.

The ANOVA found two statistically significant effects. The number of queries made in a session was affected by the intention of the search ($F(1,100) = 6.55, p < 0.05$). More queries were entered when searching for reference examples (2.8) than when searching for code to reuse as-is (1.8). The number of queries was also affected by the size of the search target ($F(1,100) = 4.57, p < 0.05$). More queries were entered when searching for blocks (2.7) than for subsystems (1.9).

After looking at the number of queries in a session, we examined how the queries changed within a session. We coded the modifications between query n and n + 1. We used a coding scheme based on the one used by Brandt et al. [3] with adaptations to fit with our study. The coding scheme had six different kinds of query refinements.

A **generalization (G)** refinement had a new search string with one of the following properties: it was a substring of the original, it contained a proper subset of the tokens in the original, it split a single token into multiple tokens and left the rest unchanged, or it led to removal of a filter.

A **specialization (S)** refinement had a new search string with one of the following properties: it was a superstring of the original, it added tokens to the original, it

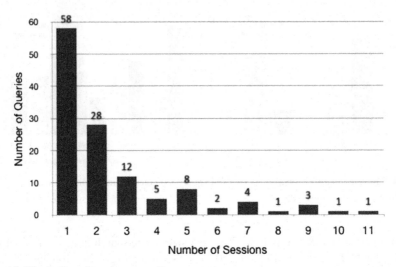

Fig. 4.3 Distribution of queries per session

combined various tokens from the original into one and left the rest unchanged, or it led to the adding of a filter.

A **reformulation (R)** refinement had a new search string that contained some tokens in common with the original but was neither a generalization nor a specialization. It consisted of moving a token into a filter and vice versa or changing a filter within a search engine.

A **new query (N)** had no tokens in common with the original.

Spelling (SP) refinement was any query where spelling errors were corrected, defined as a Levenshtein Distance (LD) [11] between 1 and 3. Changes with larger LDs were placed in one of the other categories.

A **No Change (NC)** refinement was any query that had all tokens in common with the original.

There were a total of 286 queries issued by the subjects in our study, which led to 144 refinements. The number of each type of query refinement is as given in Table 4.3. We analyzed the sequences of query revisions occurring at query n and its immediate next query, numbered $n + 1$. We used a χ-squared test of two-way contingency tables to identify which sequences of refinements were significant. The test would indicate if certain combinations of query revisions were more or less likely to occur from other combinations.

Generalization	Specialization	Reformulation	New	Spelling	No change
13	61	57	4	7	2

Table 4.3: Number of query refinements by type

When we looked at all of the queries, without regard to the independent variables, we found two statistically significant query sequences at $p < 0.05$: specialization $\rightarrow$ generalization, and new $\rightarrow$ null.

We found that when developers specialized their query, their next likely step was to generalize their query. We refer to this transition as SG, i.e. a specialization followed by a generalization. We also found that developers often used a single query to carry out search without reformulating the query. We refer to this transition as N-null transition, i.e. a new query followed by no reformulation. In other words, it was a session that consisted of a single query.

Further, we analyzed the sequence of query revisions by size of search target, intention of search, and the search engine. The significant results are presented in the Tables 4.4–4.6.

Size of search target	Significant query transitions
Block	SG, RS, NR, N-null
Subsystem	N-null

Table 4.4: Effect of target size on revision sequences

Intention of search	Significant query transitions
As-is reuse	N-null
Reference examples	SG, N-null

Table 4.5: Effect of intention on revision sequences

Search engine	Significant query transitions
Koders	SG, NR, N-null
Google code search	SG, N-null
SourceForge	SG, N-null
Google	RR, NS, N-null
Krugle	N-null

Table 4.6: Effect of search engine on revision sequences

4.4.3 Evaluating the Matches

We used two dependent variables to characterize how searchers evaluated the matches: the proportion of the first ten matches that were judged as relevant (P@10) and the proportion of these matches that were further investigated (clickthrough rate).

The overall average P@10 was 0.35. We found three statistically significant effects using ANOVA: intention, engine, and size × engine. The first was a between-subjects effect, because each subject only worked with one search scenario. The latter two were within-subjects effects, because each subject used all five search engines (Table 4.7).

There was a main effect from the intention of the search (F(1, 32) = 4.99, $p < 0.05$) (Fig. 4.4). Searches for reference examples yielded a higher proportion of relevant results than searches for code to reuse as-is (0.43 versus 0.32). There was a main effect of search engine: Google gave more relevant results ($F(4, 128) = 4.11, p < 0.01$). As well, there was an interaction effect between size of search target and the search engine used ($F(4, 128) = 4.08, p < 0.01$). Koders and Krugle performed better with subsystems, while Google was better when searching for block-sized code (Fig. 4.5).

	df	Sum of squares	Mean sum of squares	F value	$p <$
Between subjects					
Size	1	0.00	0.00	0.02	0.89
Intention	1	0.53	0.53	4.99	0.03*
Size × intention	1	0.01	0.01	0.14	0.72
Residuals	32	3.42	0.11		
Within subjects					
Engine	4	0.98	0.25	4.11	0.00*
Size × engine	4	0.97	0.24	4.08	0.00*
Motivation × engine	4	0.11	0.03	0.44	0.78
Size × intention × engine	4	0.26	0.07	1.09	0.36
Residuals	128	7.64	0.06		

*The difference is statistically significant at the p < 0.05 level

Table 4.7: ANOVA results on P@10

The overall clickthrough rate was 62 %. The developers visited a larger proportion of relevant results (81 %) than irrelevant results (47 %). An ANOVA found three significant effects. There was a main effect from the intention of the search ($F(1, 100) = 18.75, p < 0.01$). There was a much higher clickthrough rate when searching for reference examples (92 %) than when searching for code to reuse as-is (48 %). The search engine used also had an effect on clickthrough rate ($F(4, 100)$

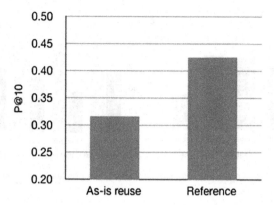

Fig. 4.4 Effect of intention on P@10

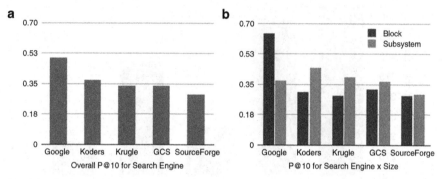

Fig. 4.5 Effect of search engines and interaction effect search engine and size

$= 6.44, p < 0.01$). The highest rate occurred when using Google, whereas the lowest rate occurred with SourceForge, as shown in Fig. 4.6a. An interaction effect was found between intention of the search and the search engine ($F(4, 100) = 2.55, p < 0.05$). On SourceForge, the clickthrough rate was higher when searching for code to reuse as-is than for reference examples; the opposite was true for all the other search engines.

4.4.4 Time Spent

The search session as a whole was characterized by time spent. We found that developers spent an average of 6 min on any search engine for searching. An ANOVA revealed three significant effects (Fig. 4.7).

There was a main effect from the intention of search ($F(1, 100) = 4.66, p < 0.05$). More time was spent looking for reference examples (417 s) than code to reuse as-is (334 s). The size of the search target also affected the duration of the

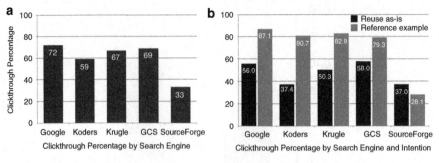

Fig. 4.6 Effect of search engine and interaction effect of intention and search engine

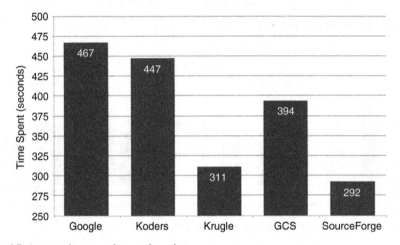

Fig. 4.7 Average time spent by search engine

search session $(F(1,100) = 6.96, p < 0.01)$. More time was spent looking for blocks of code (426 s) than subsystems (325 s). Finally, the search engine used had an effect $(F(4,100) = 3.24, p < 0.05)$. The most time was spent when using Google, and the least with SourceForge.

4.4.5 Order Effects

In the experiment, subjects were given a list of search engines and were allowed to choose the engines in any order. Consequently, we need to check whether the order in which search engines were selected affected the dependent variables.

The original list consisted of search engines in the following order: Koders, Google Code Search, SourceForge, Google, and Krugle. Thirteen out of twenty-four participants used Koders first, nine subjects started with Google and only two subjects started with Google Code search. Finally, 19 people used Krugle at the end.

We analyzed the effect of order of search engines used on the different dependent variables: number of terms in a query, number of queries, click-through percentage, and time spent on the search engine. P@10 was not influenced by the order of use of search engines. In other words, any given search engine received the same P@10 regardless of whether it was used first, last, or anywhere in between.

We found two statistically significant order effects. An ANOVA revealed that the clickthrough percentage was affected by order $(F(4,92) = 2.89, p < 0.05)$. There was a dip in clickthrough rates at the middle of the experiment session. In other words, subjects navigated to a smaller proportion of matches than at the beginning or end of the session, as shown in Table 4.8.

Source	Sum of squares	df	Mean sum of squares	F	Pr > F
Subject	5.98	23	0.26	3.07	0.00*
Engine	0.98	4	0.24	2.89	0.03*
Residual	7.80	92	0.08		

*The difference is statistically significant at the $p < 0.05$ level

Table 4.8: ANOVA for order effect on clickthrough

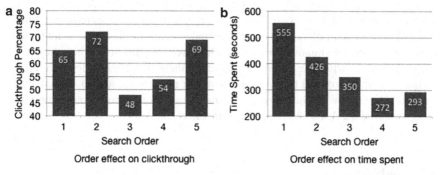

Fig. 4.8 Order effects. (a) Order effect on clickthrough and (b) order effect on time spent

There was an order effect on the time spent $(F(4,92) = 11.36, P < 0.01)$. Subjects tended to spend more time on earlier search engines and spent less time on subsequent search engines (Table 4.9).

Figure 4.8b shows the amount of time spent on the search engines decreased from the first engine to fifth engine. The small increase in time from fourth engine to fifth engine was not significant.

Source	Sum of squares	df	Mean sum of squares	F	Pr > F
Subject	2,155,478.19	23	93,716.44	3.36	0.00*
Engine	1,267,185.88	4	316,796.47	11.36	0.00*
Residual	2,564,786.52	92	27,878.11		

*The difference is statistically significant at the $p < 0.05$ level

Table 4.9: ANOVA for order effect on time spent

4.4.6 Threats to Validity

The participants in our study had no special training or background on the use of search engines. Consequently, different results are possible with subjects who are more expert in creating and refining queries. However, our results are likely typical for average users.

Another threat to the validity of the results is the fact that scenarios were assigned by the researchers and did not come from the searchers themselves. As well, they were not required to use the search results. When one self-identifies a need for source code, one likely has more background knowledge and more stringent criteria for evaluating relevance. A similar argument could be made for judging suitability for use in a project versus the relevance of a search result. In this study, we elected to look at relevance only on assigned tasks, because this is standard practice in information retrieval, which allows us to compare results from that research community.

Finally, using multiple search engines to find code for one scenario is not typical behavior. In normal situations, users switch search engines only when they have difficulty finding what they want. In our study, there was likely a learning effect on query formulation and query refinement, but none was detected by statistical analysis. The story with clickthrough rate and duration of session is more complex, as indicated by the ANOVA results for order effect.

4.5 Analysis

4.5.1 Main Effect of Size (H_1^S)

The independent variable of size had two levels in our study, block and subsystem. This variable affected the number of terms that subjects used in a query, number of query revision, and the time spent on the engine. When searching for blocks of code, subjects used more queries with more terms, made more revisions to the queries, and spent more time.

It is possible that more effort is required to locate blocks because they are smaller and tend to be embedded in a Web page. Additional terms in the query are needed because the block is highly specific and focused on one topic or concept. More queries are needed because the subject is trying to force more relevant results to the top of the list. In addition to the extra work, it takes longer to judge the relevance of a match, because the subject has to navigate to the Web page and read portions of it.

4.5.2 Main Effect of Intention (H_1^I)

The intention of the search affected all the dependent variables. This was the only independent variable that had an effect across the board. Reference examples had a positive effect on the values of all variables. Subjects expended more effort – queries with more terms, sessions with more queries, a higher clickthrough rate, and longer session duration and were rewarded with better results, i.e. a higher P@10 rate.

The additional time, queries, and terms indicate that the subjects were trying a wider variety of searches. They were tweaking their queries by adding a term (specialization), which was often followed by removing a term (generalization.) They were trying out search keywords and filters to reduce the large number of matches and to bring the most relevant ones to the top of the results set.

Relevant reference examples were easier to find, likely because the criteria for judging relevance were more flexible. Overall, subjects had a higher clickthrough rate with relevant results. So the higher proportion of relevant results when searching for reference examples led to the higher clickthrough rate.

4.5.3 Main Effect of Search Engine (H_1^E)

The search engine used affected all the dependent variables except for the number of queries. Google seemed to stand out from the others: subjects used more terms, judged greater P@10, navigated to more matches, and spent more time.

These differences were likely due to the larger quantity and variety of Web pages that were available through Google and subjects' previous experience using this search engine. Since Google indexes the entire Web, more pages were available, so subjects had to be more specific in their queries by using more terms. The larger number of pages likely contributed to the higher relevance rate. The variety of pages likely led to the higher clickthrough rate and time spent, i.e. subjects had to look more carefully at the matches.

4.5.4 Interaction Effects

We found four statistically significant interaction effects, each with a different combination of independent and dependent variables.

There was an interaction effect on the number of terms in a query under combinations of size and intention. Searches for blocks to be used as reference examples led to search specifications with more terms. When searching for block sized reference example, the developers issued the longest queries (4.9 terms) compared to searches for subsystems to reuse (3.1 terms). It is likely that this effect arose due to the greater specificity needed to search for blocks (as discussed in Sect. 4.5.1) and the additional constraints when searching for reference examples (as discussed in Sect. 4.5.2).

The different combinations of size and engine (H_1^{SE}) also had an effect on the number of terms in a query. Fewer terms were used on Krugle when searching for a block than for subsystems. The opposite was true for the other search engines. This effect was likely due to Krugle being used last by a large number of subjects (19/24).

There was an interaction effect on the clickthrough rate under combinations of search intention and the search engine (H_1^{IE}). Subjects had to look at more matches when using SourceForge to find code to reuse, but fewer when looking for reference examples. The opposite was true for every other search engine. This difference likely arose because it was quicker to judge that a project returned by SourceForge was not relevant to a task that needed a reference example.

Lastly, there was an interaction effect on P@10 from combinations of size and search engine. A higher proportion of results returned by Google were judged to be relevant when looking for blocks of code. It was easier to find blocks using Google, because Web pages tend to have more descriptive text on them, making it easier to narrow down to relevant blocks.

4.5.5 Overall Process of Search

All of these statistically significant main and interaction effects are synthesized here in the context of the overall search process. Figure 4.9 shows the different steps of a search, the dependent variables associated with each step, and the independent variables that had an effect.

Query formulation was affected by the size, intention, search engine, and two interaction effects. In other words, the number of terms in a query was highly sensitive to the independent variables. This trend suggests us that users would be responsive to support for choosing search terms and filters. This is a promising direction for improving code search on the Web.

Query revision was affected by only intention and size. It may be the case that searching for blocks and reference examples involves more experimentation. We suspect that searching for blocks to use as reference examples may be an unexplored niche for code search engines.

Evaluation of matches was affected by intention, search engine, and two interaction effects. We are dubious of the effect of intention, but this is clearly a question that requires more research. The effect of engine suggests that the presentation can affect evaluation. Presenting the appropriate details in the list of search results may reduce the clickthrough rate.

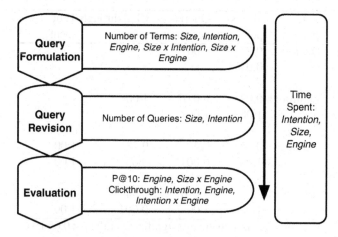

Fig. 4.9 Effect of independent variables on search process

The time spent on a search was affected by all the independent variables and no interactions. This dependent variable is a good reflection of the amount of effort required to find matches in different settings. Levels of the independent variables that led to more time spent are kinds of searches that can be made more efficient.

4.5.6 Correlations Among Dependent Variables

We calculated the pairwise Pearson product-moment correlation coefficients (r^2) to determine if there was any relationship between the dependent variables. Table 4.10 shows the r^2 statistic and their significance levels; statistically significant effects are denoted by an asterix. A correlation greater than 0.7 is considered strong, below 0.3 is weak, and between these thresholds is a moderate relationship. We used a Bonferroni adjustment for the significance calculations, because these tests were performed post hoc.

We found four statistically significant correlations. Correlation only indicates a relationship, not causality, so we must consider the underlying phenomenon to interpret the statistic. The number of terms per query is moderately related with the number of queries ($r^2 = 0.27, p < 0.04$). This positive correlation is consistent with our findings on query revision. Making more queries within a session is indicative of experimentation and of creating more complex queries. The duration of a session was related to the number of queries ($r^2 = 0.46, p < 0.001$) and to the clickthrough rate ($r^2 = 0.28, p < 0.03$). These relationships are not surprising, because making more queries and clicking on more search results takes time, thereby increasing session duration.

There is a moderate, but strongly significant relationship, between the click-through rate and P@10 ($r^2 = 0.44, p < 0.001$). It is not clear whether a higher clickthrough rate resulted in a higher P@10 rate, or vice versa, or if some other

r^2 / p-value	Terms per query	Queries per session	Clickthrough rate	Time spent
Queries	0.27 0.04*	1.00		
Clickthrough	0.02 1.00	−0.02 1.00	1.00	
Time	0.15 1.00	0.46 0.001*	0.28 0.03*	1.00 1.00
P@10	0.02 1.00	−0.10 1.00	0.44 0.001*	0.03 1.00

*The difference is statistically significant at the $p < 0.05$ level

Table 4.10: Table of correlation coefficients and p-values

factor cause both to rise together. The "mere exposure effect" tells us that we tend to prefer items that we are more familiar with [18]. The increased exposure could be greater frequency or greater total time. In this context, participants may have been more likely to consider an item relevant if they had clicked through on it previously. But we also know that participants clicked on a higher proportion of relevant matches than irrelevant ones, which suggests a causal relationship in the opposite direction. A clear explanation will require further study.

4.6 Discussion

We compare user behavior when searching for code on the Web with other kinds of search.

4.6.1 Comparison with General Search

User behavior when searching for code on the Web shared a mix of characteristics with user behavior in other kinds of search. A prior study by Jansen and Pooch [10] summarized characteristics of user behavior when using Web search engines, traditional information retrieval systems, and online public access catalogs (OPAC). An example of a traditional information retrieval system would be the INSPEC database of scholarly articles in engineering, physics, and other fields. Historically, these databases were available only in libraries and designed to be used primarily by librarians. OPAC are more commonly known as online library catalogs and the designed to be used primarily by patrons. We reproduce their table here and add our data.

Code search uses a similar number of queries in a session compared to Web searches and OPAC searches, but fewer than traditional IR systems. Users conducting Web code searches use a larger number of terms in their queries compared to Web search and OPAC search, but fewer than traditional IR search. We required the subjects in our study to examine ten matches, so it is difficult to compare the number of documents viewed per session.

Users conducting Web code searches are far more likely to use advanced features in the search engine than in the other three kinds of searches. The percentage of queries that use Boolean operators is similar to Web searches, but far more than OPAC searches and far less than traditional IR searches. We were not able to measure failure rate in our study, so no comparison is possible (Table 4.11).

Category	Code search in our study	Web system	Traditional IR systems	OPAC systems
Session length (number of queries per user per session)	2.38	1–2	7–16	2–5
Query length (number of terms per query)	4.19	2	6–9	1–2
Relevant documents viewed (number per session)	10 required	≤10	≈10	<50
Use of advanced features (proportion of queries)	42 %	9 %	9 %	8 %
Use of boolean operators (proportion of queries)	8.7 %	8 %	37 %	1 %
Failure rate (proportion improperly formatted queries)	N/A	10 %	17 %	7–19 %

Table 4.11: Comparison of user behavior during search

4.6.2 Comparison with Log Analysis

Bajracharya and Lopes [1] analyzed 1 year of log data from Koders, a commercial code-specific search engine. Overall, we found the results from our respective studies to be consistent, and in some cases virtually identical. They found that the average number of terms per query was 1.31, which was fewer than our study where subjects used an average of four terms. This difference may be due to how we counted query terms. In the Koders log, the average number of queries per session was 2.62 and in our study, the same figure was nearly the same at 2.38 queries per session. Bajracharya and Lopes found only 43 % of search sessions included a download. This figure is close to our overall P@10 of 0.35. Most sessions were short: 84 % were 3 min or less in duration and only 3.5 % had durations of greater than 10 min.

In our study, subjects spent on average 6 min, but they were required to judge the relevance of the first ten results. When conducting a search on the web, it is more common to take the first good match and stop. The distribution of all these variables followed an exponential curve, similar to the ones in our study.

4.6.3 Comparison of Searches for Reference Examples and Components to Be Used As-Is

The independent variable of Intention had a consistent effect on every dependent variable. Searches for reference examples required more effort than searches for components to be reused as-is, and yield a higher proportion of results. The breadth of this effect suggests that there is an important difference between these two kinds of searches.

The separation between reference examples and as-is reuse searches was previously identified in an online survey [17]. A similar separation can be seen in prototypes search tools. As mentioned in Sect. 4.2, some tools were designed to search for components, while others are intended to retrieve snippets. Components tend to be reused as-is, or with a minimum of modification, adapting, or wrapping. Snippets tend to be modified most extensively, or only consulted as an example, so that a developer can make use of that knowledge.

We speculate that snippets for reference and components for reuse tap into different ways of thinking about programming. Components are black boxes of technology, assumed to work, with internals that are not necessarily understood. Snippets are pieces of knowledge that needs to be understood well enough in order to be reused. They are kind of how-to knowledge that is embedded in the context of an example.

4.6.4 Implications for Design

A consistent trend in our study is developers expended more effort to search for reference examples than for code to reuse, and were rewarded with more results that were perceived to be relevant. These findings suggest that creating tools to help find components to reuse as-is will be a challenge. Developers seem to be less willing to expend effort, and there are additional constraints on the suitability of the search results, for example, architectural match and compatibility of the software license. However, we found it encouraging that subjects were willing to experiment with query terms and features in the search engines.

Subjects using Google employed a higher average number of terms per query, a higher average clickthrough rate, and more time overall. Again, this additional effort was rewarded by a more matches that were perceived relevant. The success of Google was likely due to the number and variety of pages that it indexes and participants' familiarity with the search engine. Both aspects pose additional challenges for searching for code to reuse as-is, because they are difficult to overcome. Repository size is a more tractable problem, because building a large corpus only requires effort, albeit a significant one. In contrast, user comfort and familiarity with Google is almost insurmountable. One possible solution is to make searching with keywords more robust, by improving algorithms behind a simple search box. For example, Exemplar uses information retrieval and static analysis techniques to improve matching [5]. Another approach is to avoid querying entirely and build a recommender system into the IDE for code to reuse, as was done by Code Conjurer [9].

Taken together, these observations suggest that a "scaffolded" approach to Internet-scale code search might be effective [15]. The starting point could be a familiar and comfortable text box, with the search results presented along with a variety of additional information to facilitate exploration. This approach is similar to the one used in geographical searches, e.g. when looking for restaurants in a region using Google Maps. Advanced features could be added to the results page to allow filtering by a characteristic, viewing of additional details about a match, and further searching within the results.

4.7 Conclusion

We conducted a study of user behavior during code search on the Web. In a laboratory study, subjects were given a scenario and asked to find code to satisfy the scenario using five different search engines. We measured the effect of the size of the desired source code, the intention behind the scenario, and the search engine used on the number of terms in a query, the number of queries in a session, the clickthrough rate, relevance judgments, and duration of a search session. We found statistically significant main effects and interaction effects and here we summarize their effects on the user behavior.

- Query formulation, as indicated by number of terms in the query, was most sensitive to the independent variables. This finding suggests that users would be highly receptive to tool support for creating queries.
- Query revision, as indicated by the number and type of modifications, was affected by manipulations on the scenario. This result suggests that specialized search tools may be beneficial for specific kinds of searches, such as looking for blocks of code to use as reference examples.
- Evaluation of matches returned was influenced by the search engines used. The presentation of the matches clearly had an effect on how subjects performed their evaluations.
- The duration, or time spent, on a search was also affected by all the independent variables. This trend also indicates that certain kinds of searches require more effort than others using existing tools.

Our study represents initial work on this topic. Further study is needed to better understand some of the effects that we found. For instance, we were skeptical of one result, the effect of intention on query revision. We were surprised that more queries were needed to find reference examples than code to reuse as-is. This may be an artifact of our experiment design, but we do not yet have the data to give a definitive answer. To our knowledge, there have been no observational field studies of developers as they search for source code as part of their daily work. Such a study would be a helpful complement to the experiment reported on here and would aid in validating and expanding the results.

Acknowledgements This material is based upon work supported by the NSF under Grant No. IIS-0846034. Any opinions, findings, and conclusions or recommendations expressed in this material are those of the authors and do not necessary reflect the views of the NSF.

References

[1] Sushil Bajracharya and Cristina Lopes. Mining search topics from a code search engine usage log. In *Proceedings of the 6th IEEE Working Conference on Mining Software Repositories*, pages 111–120, 2009.

[2] Sushil Bajracharya, Joel Ossher, and Cristina Lopes. Searching API usage examples in code repositories with sourcerer api search. In *Proceedings of 2010 ICSE Workshop on Search-driven Development: Users, Infrastructure, Tools and Evaluation*, pages 5–8, Cape Town, South Africa, 2010. ACM.

[3] Joel Brandt, Philip J. Guo, Joel Lewenstein, Mira Dontcheva, and Scott R. Klemmer. Two studies of opportunistic programming: interleaving web foraging, learning, and writing code. In *Proceedings of the 27th international conference on Human factors in computing systems*, pages 1589–1598, Boston, MA, USA, 2009. ACM.

[4] L. Granka, T. Joachims, and G. Gay. Eye-tracking analysis of user behavior in www search. In *Proceedings of the Conference on Research and Development in Information Retrieval (SIGIR)*, pages 478–479, 2004.

[5] Mark Grechanik, Chen Fu, Qing Xie, Collin McMillan, Denys Poshyvanyk, and Chad Cumby. A search engine for finding highly relevant applications. In *Proceedings of the 32nd ACM/IEEE International Conference on Software Engineering*, pages 475–484, Cape Town, South Africa, 2010. ACM.

[6] Raphael Hoffmann, James Fogarty, and Daniel S. Weld. Assieme: finding and leveraging implicit references in a web search interface for programmers. In *Proceedings of the 20th Annual ACM Symposium on User Interface Software and Technology*, Newport, Rhode Island, USA, 2007. ACM.

[7] Reid Holmes, Robert J. Walker, and Gail C. Murphy. Strathcona example recommendation tool. In Michel Wermelinger and Harald Gall, editors, *ESEC/SIGSOFT FSE*, pages 237–240. ACM, 2005.

[8] C. Holscher and G. Strube. Web search behavior of internet experts and newbies. *Computer Networks*, 33(1–6):337–346, 2000.

[9] Oliver Hummel, Werner Janjic, and Colin Atkinson. Code conjurer: Pulling reusable software out of thin air. *IEEE Software*, 25(5):45–52, 2008.

[10] Bernard J. Jansen and Udo Pooch. A review of web searching studies and a framework for future research. *Journal of the American Society for Information Science and Technology*, 52(3), 2001.

[11] V. Levenshtein. Binary codes capable of correcting deletions, insertions and reversals. *Sov. Phys. Dokl.*, 10(8), 1966.

[12] Erik Linstead, Sushil Bajracharya, Trung Ngo, Paul Rigor, Cristina Lopes, and Pierre Baldi. Sourcerer: mining and searching internet-scale software repositories. *Data Mining and Knowledge Discovery*, 18(2):300–336, 2009.

[13] Naiyana Sahavechaphan and Kajal T. Claypool. XSnippet: mining for sample code. In *Proceedings of the 21st Annual ACM SIGPLAN Conference on Object-Oriented Programming, Systems, Languages, and Applications*, pages 413–430, New York, NY, 2006. ACM Press.

[14] Susan Elliott Sim, Medha Umarji, Sukanya Ratanotayanon, and Cristina V. Lopes. How well do internet code search engines support open source reuse strategies? *ACM Transactions on Software Engineering and Methodology*, 21(1), December 2011.

[15] Janice Singer and Timothy Lethbridge. What's so great about 'grep'? implications for program comprehension tools. Technical report, National Research Council, Canada, 1997.

[16] Amanda Spink. Study of interactive feedback during mediated information retrieval. *Journal of the American Society for Information Science*, 48(5), 1997.

[17] M. Umarji, S. E. Sim, and C. Lopes. Archetypal internet-scale source code searching. In B. Russo, E. Damiani, S. Hissam, B. Lundell, and G. Succi, editors, *IFIP International Federation for Information Processing 275: Open Source Development, Communities and Quality*, pages 257–263. Springer, 2008.

[18] R. B. Zajonc. Attitudinal effects of mere exposure. *Journal of personality and social psychology*, 9(2), 1968.

Part II
From Data Structures to Infrastructure

The creation of ground-breaking search engines for code retrieval required ingenuity in the adaptation of existing technology and in the creation of new algorithms and data structures. This section provides glimpses into this process at the macroscopic and the microscopic levels.

In Chap. 5, "Artifact Representation Techniques for Large-Scale Software Search Engines," Hummel, Atkinson, and Schumacher give a historical overview of the data structures and representations behind the search engines. They start with the relational databases in use at the turn of the century and include contemporary experiments with XML databases and object-oriented databases.

A more personal history is given by Ken Krugler in Chap. 6, "Krugle Code Search Architecture." In this article, he traces the evolution of Krugle over 7 years, and includes lessons learned on web crawling, system architecture, and source code analysis.

The final two chapters in this Part follows more recent innovations. In Chap. 7, Almeida writes about his "Experiences and Lessons Learned with the Development of a Source Code Search Engine." As part of this process, he experimented with alternative indexing and matching techniques, including facets and Folksonomy. Finally, Bajracharya considers the code retrieval engine as a starting point for a suite of software development tools. He writes about this work in Chap. 8, "Infrastructure for Building Code Search Applications for Developers."

Chapter 5
Artifact Representation Techniques for Large-Scale Software Search Engines

Oliver Hummel, Colin Atkinson, and Marcus Schumacher

Abstract The first generation of software retrieval systems developed some 25 years ago used simple bibliographic indexing techniques adapted from library science to support the retrieval of relatively small numbers of in-house software artifacts. While these were sufficient at the time, they were completely unscaleable to the vast numbers of software artifacts available today. The second generation of software search engines, representing the state-of-the-practice today, tackles this problem by using full-text search frameworks such as Lucene to support text-based searches on large software collections. However, these typically provide no inherent support for sophisticated search use cases which exploit the structure and "meaning" of software artifacts. In this chapter we describe the core techniques used in current text-based code search engines and advanced techniques that can be used to support sophisticated forms of searches that exploit the structure of software. We then survey the challenges and opportunities encountered in the development of the next (third) generation of software search engines based on new, currently emerging data storage platforms.

5.1 Introduction

In the early years of software reuse research, the notion of "software retrieval" was essentially confined to the problem of finding potentially reusable software artifacts from a relatively small library of self-written, in-house software components [2, 3, 4, 6]. Since the number of components was so small (rarely reaching three figures), the efficiency of storage and retrieval technologies was of no great concern and bibliographic indexing techniques adapted from library science were thus

O. Hummel (✉) • C. Atkinson • M. Schumacher
Software Engineering Group, University of Mannheim, 68131 Mannheim, Germany
e-mail: hummel@informatik.uni-mannheim.de; atkinson@informatik.uni-mannheim.de; schumacher@informatik.uni-mannheim.de

S.E. Sim and R.E. Gallardo-Valencia (eds.), *Finding Source Code on the Web for Remix and Reuse*, DOI 10.1007/978-1-4614-6596-6__5,
© Springer Science+Business Media New York 2013

considered sufficient. Even in the late 1990s, when software component collections had grown to a few hundred artifacts and several new software retrieval techniques had been developed, as described by Mili et al. [7], relatively simple systems were still able to deliver usable results. However, as Mili et al. predicted, the ever increasing size of modern software repositories (particularly those generated by the open source movement) quickly created the need for more powerful software retrieval solutions with better efficiency.

At the turn of the millennium, software researchers were therefore faced with the challenge of developing a new generation of software search engines that were able to cope with the dramatically increased numbers of software components that had become available. The most mature platform for handling such large quantities of data at the time was Relational Database Management Systems (RDBMS) which had become (and still are) the dominant data storage technology for mainstream software applications and information systems. RDBMS products offer a mature technology supporting the efficient, reliable and scaleable storage of large amounts of information of any type, including text. They also provide robust and efficient mechanisms for managing concurrent updates and searches (transaction management) over such data. However, traditional RDBMS products have a couple of significant weaknesses when it comes to supporting search engine functionality. First, they are optimized for structured SQL queries based on a relational table model rather than for keyword-based searches on unstructured text. Second they do not provide a relevance ranking for the elements in result sets. Since this second feature is commonly seen as a central element of modern search engines [1] it is obviously also a fundamental requirement for software search engines.

An alternative platform that became mature enough to use for this purpose around the turn of the millennium was Full-Text Search Frameworks (FTSF). The most well known example is the open source Lucene framework initially developed by Doug Cutting, which became an Apache project in 2001 [16]. FTSFs such as Lucene were developed to accelerate exactly the weak text search functionality of traditional RDBMSs. They specialize in creating indices from the textual elements of documents (i.e. words) and are optimized for full text searches with relevance estimates and ranking for the members of result sets. Since all the data necessary to support searches is stored in the indices, no other repository of information (such as a normal database) is needed to drive a search engine. The second generation of software search engines that started to emerge around 2005 (e.g. Koders [21], Krugle [19], Sourcerer [20], Merobase [18]) was therefore predominately based on such FTSFs, most notably Lucene, although some of them were supported by RDBMs as well.

Using an FTSF alone to drive a search engine also has disadvantages, however. First, pure full-text search engines provide no inherent support for structured queries on the properties and relationships of the concepts indexed. Second, they provide only rudimentary support for concurrent read and write access, based on simple locking concepts. Thus, updating the index is an expensive, time consuming operation compared to relational databases. The first of these issues is particularly challenging and raised the key research question of whether it is possible to efficiently support structured queries in a software search engine built on top of an FTFS.

Given the growing importance of making information accessible and searchable over the Internet in the last few years, the value of integrating the capabilities of traditional RDBMSs and FTSFs into a single, off-the-shelf product has become apparent for all types of data. Most vendors of modern RDBMS products therefore are now working on integrating full-text searching capability into their products. This provides the foundation for a new, "third" generation of code search engines built on top of such hybrid (relational/indexed) databases and other advanced forms of databases.

In the remainder of this chapter we describe the techniques used in the current generation of software search engines to support sophisticated search use cases on top of an FTSF. We begin in the next section by summarizing the different indexing techniques used in the first generation of code search engines and the various categories of storage and retrieval techniques they developed. The following three sections then describe the techniques used to represent software components in the current (second) generation of software search engines. Section 5.3 describes how FTSFs can form the underlying platform for these engines. Section 5.4 then goes on to describe the basic software representation techniques used in FTSF-based software search engines, while Sect. 5.5 describes some advanced techniques that can be used to support more sophisticated search use cases, such as interface (API) based searches, on top of an FTSF index. Section 5.6 then discusses some of the issues faced by the emerging third generation of software search engines based on more sophisticated data storage platforms. The final section then concludes with a summary and some final remarks.

5.2 First Generation Software Retrieval Concepts

Most work in the area of software retrieval before the turn of the millennium was driven by the desire to support the reuse of existing software artifacts in the creation of new applications in order to avoid programming them from scratch. Since the main goal of the software reuse research community at that time was to create a library of reusable artifacts, most early publications in this area were influenced by ideas from general library science. Frakes and Pole [5], for example, defined the representation of software artifacts in a retrieval system as "a language used to describe a set of objects [...] [that] allows operations that would be more difficult or impossible on the represented object itself." As an example they describe bibliographic records of books that are easier to sort and maintain than the books themselves. Indexing in this context is the process of creating the records, i.e. translating the actual objects into the logical model used to store the information. The same basic approach is still used today in all kinds of search engines, whether it be for books, websites or software artifacts.

Again, according to Frakes and Pole, library science has developed four basic representation methods that can be used in the context of software retrieval as well, namely

1. *Controlled vocabularies* that use a set of predefined keywords to describe an artifact,
2. *Enumerated classification* schemes that separate an area into mutually exclusive, typically hierarchical classes to create a taxonomy,
3. *Free text indexing* that uses the complete text in an artifact itself, or metadata about the artifact, to create searchable records,
4. *Faceted classification schemes* [6] that combine multiple facets describing an artifact from different viewpoints usually ordered by descending generality.

Most modern (software) search engines rely on some kind of faceted classification approach and store content and metadata about artifacts in various fields of name/value pairs. These fields may contain data from controlled vocabularies, enumerated classification schemes or indexed free text and can usually be searched independently from each other. Thus, facets can be used to constrain searches in certain ways. For example, as well as allowing search terms to be concatenated with Boolean operators, Google's general web search engine contains a facet for the filetype of the indexed document so that searches can be restricted to PDF files (by adding filetype:pdf to a query), for instance. Most existing software search engines (cf. Hummel et al. [26] for a comprehensive overview) offer similar features in order to limit keyword based searches to a given programming language or to a specific portion of the code (such as class or operation names). While today's large-scale collections obviously require automated indexing based on special parsers, early prototypes often required manual indexing of artifacts.

5.2.1 Retrieval Approaches

Although the relatively simple approaches adapted from bibliographic retrieval techniques worked reasonably well on small collections of software artifacts, researchers quickly recognized that the idiosyncrasies of software often stretched the precision of searches to their limits since the structure and the "meaning" of software artifacts were not taken into account. Various enhancements were therefore developed during the 1990s as summarized in Mili et al.'s systematic survey [7] that identified the following six main classes of software retrieval approaches:

1. Information retrieval methods
2. Descriptive methods
3. Denotational semantics methods
4. Operational semantics methods
5. Structural methods
6. Topological methods

Information retrieval and *descriptive methods* basically cover the text-based and bibliographic retrieval approaches introduced before. While the former focus on keyword matching "within" the artifacts, the latter usually rely on externally obtained metadata (such as language, domain etc.) for retrieval. In general, Mili et al. characterize descriptive methods as a subset of information retrieval methods, but since this family of approaches was so widely used at the time of their survey they decided to list it as a separate category. *Denotational semantics methods* drive the retrieval process based on signatures (see e.g. [11]) resp. formal specifications [13] of the indexed assets. While signature matching is considered useful in practice, software retrieval based on formal specifications suffers from a variety of disadvantages. For instance, the specifications are difficult to create and evaluate (e.g. due to the complexity of the associated decision problems) and cause a significant creation and maintenance overhead. *Operational semantics approaches* use exemplary input values (or so-called "samples" [30]) to execute syntactically matching artifacts contained in a collection. Although they are quite expensive to execute they have recently received a lot of attention in association with test-driven reuse approaches (as described in another chapter of this book [10]). *Structural methods* do not deal with the code of the assets directly but rather with internal program patterns or designs. Since, the formulation of queries for approaches of this class is not yet well understood, it remains an academic research area for the time being. The common property of the *topological methods*, the sixth group listed by Mili et al., is that they calculate some kind of "distance" between the query and the results. Hence, today, they would be better classified as approaches supporting the ranking of search results.

5.2.2 Limitations

Although this basic classification provided a good starting point, it quickly became clear that modern software collections containing potentially millions of (open source) artifacts quickly stretch these traditional methods to their limits. Not only that, since manual indexing is impossible with collections of this size, the precision of the above approaches is simply not sufficient. Suppose, for example, that a text-based software search engine is requested to find a reusable stack data structure. Simply searching for the string *stack* within the indexed artifacts typically delivers thousands of results that merely contain this string somewhere in their source code. Thus, many of the delivered results will not actually be stacks but may merely use a stack somewhere in their implementation. The same holds true for pure signature matching techniques that can also deliver thousands of results for sufficiently generic signatures (more examples and some preliminary investigation results on this can be found in a previous publication [26]).

In order to support more practical software search use cases (as e.g. listed by Sim et al. [12] or more recently by Janjic et al. [31]), more precise and specialized query possibilities are urgently required. In particular, more sophisticated types of queries that allow the form of software artifacts to be taken into account are needed.

One of the most important examples is the ability to search for software artifacts offering a specific provided interface (i.e. API). This need is reinforced by a recent study by Hoffmann et al. [8] showing that the majority of queries related to Java in a mainstream search engine are for APIs. Other scenarios that purely text-based search engines struggle to support include searches for API usage examples [33] or for the set of artifacts impacted by envisaged changes to a piece of code in a maintenance context [29].

5.3 Full-Text Search Frameworks

The advent of Lucene [16] at the turn of the millennium made a powerful and efficient FTSF freely available as an open source product. Lucene not only offers a very fast full-text search capability with relevance ranking, which is vital for all search engines as understood today, but is supported by a suite of other helpful tools such as the crawler Nutch or the index browsing tool Luke. On contemporary hardware, the Lucene tool suite has become mature enough to be used out-of-the-box for implementing large-scale search engines as underlined by the "powered by" section [14] on the Lucene website currently listing about 150 search engines including high profile websites such as Wikipedia, for example. The typical approach used to create such an index with Lucene is sketched in Fig. 5.1. Documents containing text usually coming from the Internet (though other data sources such as local fileservers are also possible) are crawled with the help of Nutch which forwards them to an appropriate document parser based on their filetype (such as HTML, PDF etc.). Once the pure text is extracted, it can be analyzed, tokenized and mapped in a document that is stored in the actual index. Beyond the mere content, a document may contain other fields for its title, its origin (i.e. URL), its headings etc. that allow more targeted searches.

Technically, FTSFs such as Lucene usually index the terms (i.e. the tokens) found in a set of documents in a so-called term-document-matrix, i.e. they store the number

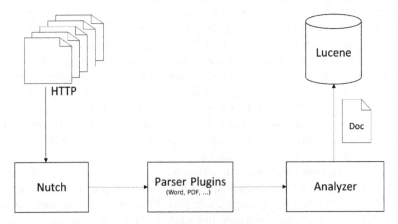

Fig. 5.1 Basic structure of a Lucene-based search engine implementation

of occurrences of each term per document. A single document is thus represented as a vector, the so-called term-document-vector, with one dimension per unique term found over all documents. Searches for a keyword can then be easily carried out by looking up the desired term (on all or just a limited set of fields) and delivering all documents where the term appears. To optimize the search process, such an index is actually stored either in a hashtable or as a B-Tree based data structure. Clearly, the usage of Boolean operators (AND, OR, NOT) is also straightforward to implement in this context.

Even a comparison of two documents is easy using mathematical tools such as the so-called cosine measure. In its simplest form only Boolean values (i.e. zeros or ones) are used to represent each term (resp. dimension in the vector) indicating whether it is present in a given document or not. More sophisticated approaches store the number of occurrences of each term per document (the so-called term frequency) or even multiply this value with the inverse number of occurrences over all documents (which is called inverse document frequency). This yields the so-called TFIDF (term frequency inverse document frequency) that reduces the impact of terms appearing too frequently. Standard information retrieval textbooks (such as [15] or [16]) provide more details on these technical aspects.

5.4 Representing Software in an FTSF

Since they are optimized for text-based searches and include relevance ranking for the members of result sets, FTSFs such as Lucene intuitively provide a better foundation for more efficient and scaleable software search engines than databases. Consequently, around the middle of the previous decade a new generation of software search engines based on Lucene begun to emerge. Some of the main examples include Krugle [16], Merobase [18] and Sourcerer [24]. Others such as Google Code Search used similar full-text search approaches based on proprietary FTSF implementations. Although they are based on a much more powerful indexing and retrieval platform these search engines still essentially indexed software in the same basic way as the first generation of search engines, treating software artifacts as natural language documents in the first place. In other words, they essentially treated source code artifacts as "just another text document" and indexed them in the traditional way as shown in Fig. 5.2 that is largely identical to Fig. 5.1. Only Merobase and Sourcerer are already providing advanced structural searches as discussed later.

Just as it is valuable to extract certain kinds of elements from textual documents in general search engines as described before, it is also helpful to extract additional information about a software artifact in order to store it in additional fields of the document (e.g. methods or unit names, superclasses etc.). This can easily be achieved by extending the basic Nutch crawler with programming language parsers which can analyze source code syntax. The remainder of this section illustrates a basic representation scheme used in an FTSF-based code search engines to index software artifacts. It actually describes the Merobase [18] Lucene document

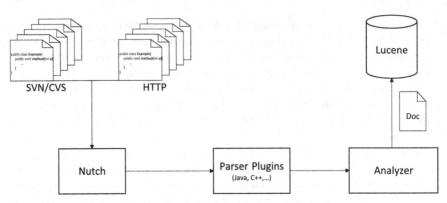

Fig. 5.2 Using Lucene to implement a software search engine

structure, but other Lucence based implementations (such as Sourcerer [20] or Krugle [19]) are very similar in this regard. In terms of the approaches described by Milli et al., this corresponds to a faceted classification scheme: each field in the Lucene document template describes a different facet of the software artifact as described in Table 5.1. There, each field is described by its name, a brief description of its content, how often it can appear per document (i.e. its multiplicity) and the actual approach used to index it.

Table 5.1: Overview of commonly used fields in software search engines

Field	Description	Multipl.	Vocabulary
content	Source code	1	Free text
url	The URL the artifact was retrieved from	1	Free text
host	The hostname contained in the URL	1	Free text
name	The artifact's name	1	Free text
lang	Programming language	1	Controlled
form	Source or binary	1	Controlled
requires	URL's of recognized dependencies	0...*	Free text
kind	If recognized, a special kind of artifact such as applet, test case, EJB etc.	0...1	Controlled
namespace	The artifact's namespace	0...1	Enumerated
extends	Direct superclass of the artifact	1	Enumerated
implements	Names of implemented interfaces	0...*	Free text
method	The contained operation names	0...*	Free text

license	(Open source) license	0...1	Controlled
lictype	Classification according to copyleft	1	Enumerated
author	Author(s) of the artifact	0...*	Free text

Since an artifact will usually require fields that have a multiplicity larger than 1 (for instance for storing the operation names of an artifact) it is useful that Lucene allows several entries per document to be stored with the same field name. During the indexing process the content of each of the above fields is tokenized. This means that before it is actually indexed it is fed to Lucene's standard analyzer that separates it into a stream of searchable tokens (i.e. typically words). Since software developers often concatenate words to create more expressive operation or variable names using approaches such as "camel case", enhancing the Lucene analyzer to reverse this process may improve search quality (see Bajracharya et al. [24], for example).

In order to avoid maintaining an extra database with additional information about the indexed artifacts that can be used for result presentation (as well as more advanced searches, as e.g. implemented in Sourcerer [20]), it makes sense to store a number of additional fields that are not directly used in the search process. Examples include the date when a document was added, various source code metrics and a unique hash value that allows simple duplicate recognition. Furthermore, since Lucene used to "destroy" all formatting information (i.e. upper and lower casing), free text fields that are of interest to the user need to be stored a second time in a non-tokenized and non-searchable way for optimized result presentation. Although this practice increases the index size considerably, the impact on search speed is negligible. Fortunately, more recent versions of Lucene are even able to handle this internally so that copying the fields is no longer necessary. With this relatively simple index structure, the full performance of Lucene's query engine (as e.g. described in [16]) including wildcards, range queries etc. is available on the tokenized fields and can be used to support keyword based retrieval of software artifacts (see [36] for the full Merobase Lucene index built on these principles).

5.5 Advanced Representation Techniques

As mentioned above, Lucene allows values to be stored in different fields and thus supports faceted retrieval approaches (as we discussed in Sect. 5.4) out of the box. This makes it possible to index the source code of software artifacts and to enhance records with metadata such as the artifact's language, project environment, documentation, etc. The ranking of search results is also included so that the best matching result is always delivered first. The drawback, however, is that Lucene's fields cannot be relationally connected as in a database, which makes it difficult to search for operation signatures, for example. Queries such as "give me all artifacts containing two methods *add* and *sub* receiving two *int* parameters and returning an *int*" are thus not directly feasible. Using Boolean operators makes it possible to concatenate fields from simple searches for individual operation interfaces (as proposed for Sourcerer [24], for instance), but this is still too limited for precise signature- and API-based searches. Consider the previous request as an example. Even if there were additional fields for parameters and return types in the same style as before, the maximum possible precision of a query of the form –

method:add AND method:sub AND param:int AND return:int

would retrieve all artifacts that have a method add, a method sub and any arbitrary method with at least one int parameter and one with int as return type. The reason for this behavior is – as indicated before – that fields cannot be related to one another in an FTSF. In other words, because no relational information is present in the index, the search engine cannot work out whether the specified operation names and the desired types belong to the same operation. Hence, no higher-level structural information related to the structure of software artifacts (e.g. class structure, methods structure, parameter structure etc.) can be utilized for searching. Clearly, such structural information would be directly available in an RDBMS system (as e.g. additionally used in Sourcerer for this purpose, cf. [35] in chapter 8 of this book), but for search engines based on an FTSF index alone it is not automatically present.

Therefore, to support more sophisticated, structure-based queries it is necessary to employ additional techniques that capture important code-related structure within the facetted storage approach that underlies FTSF-based indices such as those presented before. Many superficially appealing techniques do not work in practice on closer analysis, however. For example, why not directly store complete operation interfaces (such as e.g. *public int doSomethingUseful(int i, String s)*) extracted from a programming language parser in order to overcome the challenge just described? Unfortunately, such a relatively simple implementation is not possible since tokenization during the indexing would tear the operation signature apart into individual tokens, which would make it impossible to subsequently distinguish between the various elements again. The only apparent way to overcome this problem is by forcing the FTSF to deliver only exact matches. However, even if the parameter names were ignored through the help of wildcards, or not stored at all, the FTSF would still deliver only those results with identical parameter order so that searches would still be limited. Another approach that worked in theory was supported by Google Code Search (which was closed down in early 2012 [23], however). This not only supported simple wildcards, but full regular expressions that allowed users to specify appropriate searches. However, the resulting queries for that purpose were so complicated that they were barely usable in practice (cf. [25]).

It is, nevertheless, possible to apply some relatively simple "tricks" to significantly enhance the sophistication of the queries that can be supported on a FTSF-based search engine. In the following we explain how we enhanced the current version of the Merobase search engine in this way. The basic idea is to store operation signatures in a "flattened" form (in database terminology this might be called a "de-normalized" form) in non-tokenized fields in a way that ignores parameter orders, i.e. that yields the same entry for a method no matter in what order the parameters appear (i.e. *int, String* or *String, int*). This is possible by sorting parameter types alphabetically and by concatenating ("flattening") method names, parameter and return types into a single field as shown in the following example:

mn:doSomethingUseful_rt:int_pt:int_pt:String

In order to avoid confusing operation names with parameter types and visibility, special separators are added to the field entry for the sake of human readability. To enable searches with and without visibility modifiers, the above example can be stored twice, once as shown and once with e.g. "vs:public" added to it to indicate its visibility. It should be obvious that search requests have to be translated into this format by an appropriate query parser before searches are executed in order to increase usability. We discuss this issue in more detail in the next subsection.

Unfortunately, wildcard searches on these structures (e.g. ignoring the method name) are not possible due to internal restrictions of Lucene. However, it is possible to enable at least pure signature matching [11] for the operations by storing another, largely identical field without the method name merely containing parameter and return types. In the case of the above example, this would yield:

rt:int_pt:int_pt:String

Yet another problem can occur in this context when an identical signature is required more than once in one artifact since it is not directly possible to specify the number of required occurrences. Again, it is possible to circumvent the problem, this time by preceding each signature with a counter of the number of times it appears in the component, i.e.

1_rt:int_pt:int_pt:String
2_rt:int_pt:int_pt:String

When an incoming search request is "translated" appropriately, this makes it possible to search for classes that contain the required signature once as well as twice, or any required number of times. As shown in Table 5.2, Merobase adds five more fields to the previously described index template based on the concepts just described.

Table 5.2: Additional index fields for structural searches

Field	Example
methodHeader	*mn:doSomething_rt:int_pt:int_pt:String*
methodHeaderV	*mn:doSomething_rt:int_pt:int_pt:String_vs:public*
methodSignature	*rt:int_pt:int_pt:String*
constrHeader	*pt:int_pt:String*
constrHeaderV	*pt:int_pt:String_vs:public*

In addition to the three fields for method headers there are two special fields for class constructors. Fortunately, we do not need to store the class name here as this is unique for every stored entity and can thus be added as necessary via an AND query on the name field.

5.5.1 Query Parsing

Although it might seem simple at first sight, finding a good approach to generically formulate queries for software search engines is an interesting problem in its own right since at least three different styles of query formulation need to be supported – namely free text queries, signature-based queries and API-based queries. Once a search infrastructure as described above is in place it is in principle possible to use the field structure of the index to support searches on directly expressed queries. In simple cases this might be satisfactory (as e.g. for name-based queries in the commercial Koders search engine), however, for API-driven searches this would require a deeper knowledge and understanding of the internal index structure and hence is definitively an unintuitive approach.

In order to overcome this challenge, it makes sense to support a query formulation and parsing approach that only uses concepts that are already familiar to software developers (i.e. the users of a software search engine). To our knowledge, Merobase is currently the only software search engine that supports such an approach directly by accepting code in supported programming languages as queries (the Eclipse plugin CodeGenie has a similar capability on the client side, though [34]). Thus, all queries in Merobase are first fed to a modified Java/C# parser that is able to recognize class and method interfaces such as the following API-based search for a simple Matrix class:

```
public class Matrix {
        public Matrix add(Matrix m) { }
        public Matrix multiply(Matrix m) { }
}
```

This approach easily allows developers to search in their favorite programming language and even makes the development of recommender tools that issue searches directly from a development environment straightforward. However, since a query interface should ideally be programming language independent and customizable, Merobase also includes a small intuitive retrieval language that supports method headers (such as random(float,float):float;) and class interface descriptions as programming language independent input. It is based on the textual representation of operations in UML class diagrams. The following snippet provides an example:

```
Customer (
        getAddress():String;
```

```
        setAddress(String):void;
)
```

In contrast to ordinary programming languages, this language also supports additional search constraints (such as lang:java) – or in other words, issuing faceted searches – and even special wildcards that finally make formulating pure signature-based searches possible as well. In order to not interfere with Lucene, the dollar sign can be used to replace all names in an interface, i.e. either *Customer*, *getAddress* or *setAddress* in case of the above example, yielding *$(String):void* for the last method, for instance.

5.5.2 Retrieval Heuristics

It is intuitively clear that the more complex an API-based query becomes, the less components are likely to match it [32]. Thus, the number of retrieved results usually drops quickly with the size of the desired API. A similar observation has been made by Zaremski and Wing in the context of signature matching [11]. They therefore propose so called "relaxed searches" that also allow imperfect matches in the result set. The basic idea is to implement a signature-aware relevancy estimation approach that boosts the relevancy of search results that are likely to better conform to the users expectations. Consider the "matrix" example used previously: Lucene's standard ranking algorithm would assign the highest relevancy to those artifacts that contain the term "matrix" most often. An actual matrix implementation that perhaps contains the term just once in its class definition will therefore usually receive a rather low relevancy in contrast to artifacts using it multiple times. This can be overcome by attaching certain fields (such as class or method names) to the query with extra weight (in Lucene terminology the terms are "boosted"). In order to avoid "overlooking" the term in the actual content when it does not appear in the name the fields are concatenated with a Boolean OR as in the following simple example:

content:matrix OR name:matrix^2

Although the term "matrix" is searched for within the whole content of the index entries, special attention is given to the name of the class since this is assigned double importance. Hence a result file that is actually named Matrix will be automatically ranked higher by Lucene than one that just contains the string "matrix" somewhere. This approach can be easily extended with methods to –

content:matrix content:add content:multiply OR name:matrix^2
OR method:multiply OR method:add

Similar approaches are possible to better support camelCased search terms (e.g.

addItem could be split into *add OR item*, more on this approach can also be found in another chapter of this book [35]) or even signature and API based searches.

Since FTSFs such as Lucene not only support the boosting of search terms during query time, but also the boosting of documents (i.e. artifacts) when they are indexed, it should also be straightforward to implement the Component Rank approach developed by Inoue et al. [17] with an FTSF. A search engine based on this approach would simply assign a higher boost value to those artifacts that are more often used by other artifacts during the indexing process and the FTSF would deal with ranking the search results during searches.

As with every information retrieval system, the use of synonyms still remains a significant challenge for software retrieval, not only for text-based queries. Since programmers might use different names describing identical concepts, it is currently not possible to recognize signatures that contain different object types (such as CharSequence instead of String) even if they might be compatible. While it might be possible to add additional entries based on a kind of "programming thesaurus" for fairly standard cases such as the one just mentioned, already the "Matrix vs. MatrixImpl" example demonstrates that this would significantly increase the index size and require a thesaurus for artifact names and common programming terminology that to our knowledge does not exist so far. At the time of writing, however, a detailed investigation of the effects of each heuristic on result quality has yet to be carried out [9].

5.6 Towards Third Generation Code Search Engines

The FTSFs-based technology described in the previous three sections successfully met the challenge of scaling software search engines up to the vast numbers of open-source software artifacts available over the Internet. Most online search engines today index well over a million software artifacts. Table 5.3, for example, gives an idea of the size of the Merobase index, which is one of the largest software search engines currently available on the Web.

Table 5.3: Number of components services indexed in Merobase

Programming language	No. of files	Percentage
Java	8,011,883	79.57
Source	3,927,475	49.02
Binary	4,084,408	50.98
C#	207,092	2.06
C	1,399,455	13.90
WSDL	3,228	0.03
.NET assemblies	447,801	4.45
Total	10,069,459	100

This also illustrates that the FTSF platform is versatile enough to support source code in various common languages such as Java, C# and C as well as online web services and binary code (not containing searchable source content, of course) as well. Based on a (rather low end) contemporary Ubuntu Linux server with 4 cores (2.6 GHz each), 300 GB disk space, 8 GB RAM, and Lucene 3.4.0, searches on the above index (requiring slightly over 50 GB disk space with the index structure explained before) are usually carried out in around 1.5 s in the case of a single keyword and require up to around 3–5 s if more complex searches for APIs are issued. Hence, the base FTSF technology should be easily capable of handling even more artifacts by upgrading the underlying server or by distributing it to a number of machines as soon as the index becomes too large to handle on one. Lucene already provides basic support for distributed searches, and a more sophisticated tool for that purpose is available in the form of Solr [16].

5.6.1 Limitations of FTSF-Based Search Engines

As mentioned previously, the central weakness of the current generation of FTSF-based search engines is their limited support for structured queries that exploit the structure and semantics of software artifacts. Using the techniques described in the previous section it is possible to support certain kinds of structured searches (i.e. searches based on the structure of interfaces), but these have to be defined a-priori and are thus fixed. It is not possible for users to define new kinds of structured searches on-the-fly that were not foreseen when an index was created. Hence, an ideal platform would combine the full-text search capabilities of an FTSF such as Lucene with the arbitrary structured search capabilities of an RDBMS on a single, unified data repository. This would allow users to perform full-text searches and all imaginable, software-relevant structured searches on a single logical corpus of software artifacts. Hence, it should allow keyword, signature and API matching to be integrated as described in this chapter with other interesting applications such as API recommendations [33] and maintenance-driven search approaches [29].

It is also likely that further advances in software search technology will increase the demand from practitioners as well as researchers for such more advanced forms of queries. A recent (but probably still not exhaustive) overview of software retrieval usage scenarios was presented by Janjic et al. [26]. This identifies a dozen applications that might benefit from powerful software retrieval tools and illustrates in which phases of the software development lifecycle these are likely to be used. In the next subsection we discuss some of the emerging platforms that could serve as the basis for such "third generation" software search engines.

5.6.2 Ongoing Work

The most obvious approach for creating such a platform is to integrate a relational database and full-text search index into a single logical product. Practically, all large database vendors now offer full text search capabilities as part of their database products, such as *Oracle Text* or *MySQL Fulltext*. However, performance still seems to be an issue in this context since Linping and Lidong [27] have found in a recent comparison of simple keyword searches in Lucene and Oracle Text that Lucene is about an order of magnitude faster as long as the result set does not become too large (under roughly 1,500 results). Since it is likely that a combination with various join operations required for API-based retrieval will slow down RDBM-based retrieval even further it is clear that pure FSTF platforms using the techniques outlined above will still be superior for some time. An interesting practical alternative is to run a database alongside an FTSF index on the same corpus of artifacts (as e.g. already done in the backend of Sourcerer [35]), with software to automatically keep the latter up to date with the former. Hibernate Search [22] is a recently developed open source framework that achieves this by making text search available on a domain model stored in a database by the object-relational mapper Hibernate. This offers the user the best of both worlds in terms of querying options, but at the expense of supporting two stores of the search base, one in the RDBMs and the other in the FTSF (i.e. Lucence).

The database part of such a hybrid system can be searched using standard SQL queries, thus allowing arbitrary structured searches to take advantage of its relational structure. For example, the new schema for the upcoming version of Merobase, built using Hibernate Search, is shown in Fig. 5.3 as a UML class diagram. A similar scheme for the Sourcerer search engine is documented in another chapter of this book [35]. The main advantage of Hibernate Search is that it automatically creates, and synchronizes, a Lucene full-text search index from the content in the RDBMs. The overall memory required is obviously greater, but the Lucene index itself is much leaner than the original and the new version of Merobase therefore supports all the FTFS capabilities of the original, but allows SQL queries to be applied to the same search base. The transaction-safe updating capabilities of the RDBS also allow the content of the search base to be updated much more dynamically by multiple concurrent crawlers and data mining engines.

Using a relational database it is also possible to support precise searches for components with particular combinations of properties on-the fly, for example searching for a specific version of a component that is used as a parameter in a method. Consider the case of a developer who is faced with the task of learning to use a particular framework. With an FTFS-based system it is only possible to filter for the version of the actual search result, i.e. the file that illustrates how to use a framework. However, searches may often deliver many unsuitable results using outdated tutorials or documents describing the use of old versions of the framework containing deprecated methods, or old orchestrations of component that are no longer applicable (e.g. initialization). A software developer trying to discover how to use the latest version of a framework would find it extremely helpful to be able

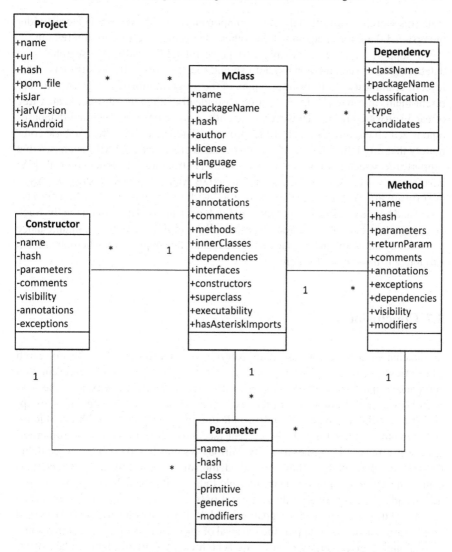

Fig. 5.3 Hibernate Search data model for the next version of the Merobase search engine

to search for examples using a specific version of a framework. The following SQL statement illustrates this with the help of an example where a developer is looking for the QueryBuilder of Hibernate Search version 4.0:

```
Hibernate :
SELECT c.name FROM MClass c
        LEFT JOIN c.methods AS ms LEFT JOIN ms.parameters AS p
        WHERE p.paramClass.project.jarVersion = '4.0'
        AND p.type = 'QueryBuilder'
```

With this search capability only those components using the required QueryBuilder in version 4.0 are returned, and all the other "deprecated" results are filtered out.

To support even more flexible and powerful ad-hoc structure searches, the database side of such a hybrid system should ideally store software artifacts at the level of granularity of the abstract syntax of the programming language used to represent them. In other words, the search base ideally stores the abstract syntax tree of each software artifact. However, efficiently storing trees in relational databases (and in search engines) is a non-trivial problem. A recent trend in the database community that might become helpful in this context are so-called XML databases that support tree structures due to the way XML is structured. Panchenko et al. [28] have recently sketched how to use the MonetDB/XQuery system to store the ASTs of software artifacts that can then be queried with the help of the XPath query language and hence would allow defining all kinds of structured queries on the fly. Such an approach is currently regarded as especially useful for supporting maintenance activities by allowing queries such as "give me all files in project x where the global variable y is used in an if statement".

5.7 Conclusion

In this chapter we have presented an overview of the evolution of software search and retrieval in the last 25 years with a special focus on the data representation approaches that have been developed to describe software artifacts with the help of full-text search frameworks in the last 5 years. While the first generation of approaches was largely based on simple indexing ideas adapted from library science and were thus rather limited, the current (second) generation has made internet-scale software search engines a reality. Various systems based upon freely available full-text search frameworks have recently demonstrated that software search engines containing millions of artifacts are feasible today. With the help of special heuristics (or additional databases) these are not only able to support simple text-based searches, but also searches for signatures and APIs of software artifacts. Advanced ranking approaches also support the retrieval of imperfectly matching search results.

Although a great variety of software search engines are available today, so far none of them supports the complete state of the art in retrieval techniques (i.e. API-based searches, usage relations, and advanced text-processing techniques from information retrieval), so we are still waiting for the first engine that stretches pure FTSF-based techniques to its limit. Furthermore, it is not yet clear to what degree the various search techniques support existing (and upcoming) usage scenarios since most approaches have not been systematically evaluated and comparisons of approaches have not been carried out so far due to the large effort involved in such an undertaking. Thus, we also expect to see increasing efforts put into the systematic investigation of the retrieval performance of various software retrieval approaches in the near future.

Since one current trend in software retrieval seems to go into the direction of better utilizing the structure of software artifacts for search, whether it be for API-based searches, API usage recommendations or maintenance-oriented applications, we expect to see a number of solutions optimized for these purposes in the future. Given these prerequisites it is no surprise that various research groups are working towards utilizing new hybrid data storage solutions that integrate the power of relational or XML-based data representation and full-text search capabilities for software search. Although it is not yet foreseeable, it is nevertheless likely that this third generation of software search engines will also facilitate new and exciting applications such as code clone detection or automation of refactorings, for example, in the not too distant future.

Acknowledgements The authors would like to thank Philipp Bostan, Matthias Gutheil, Werner Janjic and Dietmar Stoll from the Software Engineering Group at the University of Mannheim for their contributions to developing the tools described in this chapter.

References

[1] Page, L., Brin, S., Motwani, R., Winograd, T.: The Pagerank Algorithm: Bringing Order to the Web. Proceedings of the International Conference on the World Wide Web (1998)

[2] McIlroy, D.: Mass-Produced Software Components. Software Engineering: Report of a conference sponsored by the NATO Science Committee (1968).

[3] Krueger, C.W.: Software reuse. ACM Computing Surveys, vol. 24, no 2. (1992)

[4] Frakes, W.B., Nejneh, B.: An Information System for Software Reuse. Software Reuse: Emerging Technology, Computer Society Press (1987)

[5] Frakes, W.B.: An empirical study of representation methods for reusable software components. IEEE Transactions on Software Engineering, Vol. 20, no.8 (1994)

[6] Prieto-Diaz, R., Freeman, P.: Classifying Software for Reusability. IEEE Software, Vol. 4, No. 1 (1987)

[7] Mili, A., Mili, R., Mittermeir, R.: A Survey of Software Reuse Libraries. Annals of Software Engineering 5 (1998)

[8] Hoffmann, R. and Fogarty, J. and Weld, D.S.: Assieme: Finding and Leveraging implicit References in a Web Search Interface for Programmers. Proceedings of the ACM Symposium on User Interface Software and Technology (2007)

[9] Hummel, O.: Facilitating the comparison of software retrieval systems through a reference reuse collection. Proceedings of the ICSE Workshop on Search-driven Development: Users, Infrastructure, Tools and Evaluation (2010)

[10] Hummel, O., Janjic, J.: Test-Driven Reuse: Key to Improving Precision of Search Engines for Software Reuse. In Sim and Gallardo (eds.): Code Retrieval on the Web, Springer (2012)

[11] Zaremski, A.M., Wing, J.M.: Signature Matching: A Tool for Using Software Libraries. ACM Transactions on Software Engineering and Methodology, Vol. 4, No. 2 (1995)

[12] Umarji, M. and Sim, S. and Lopes, C.: Archetypal internet-scale source code searching. Open Source Development, Communities and Quality, Springer (2008)

[13] Zaremski, A.M., Wing, J.M.: Specification Matching of Software Components. ACM Transactions on Software Engineering and Methodology, Vol. 6, No. 4 (1997)

[14] Applications and web applications using lucene, http://wiki.apache.org/lucene-java/PoweredBy (2012)

[15] Baeza-Yates, R., Ribeiro-Neto, B.: Modern Information Retrieval. Addison-Wesley (1999)

[16] Hatcher, E., Gospodnetic, O., McCandless, M.: Lucene in Action (2nd edition). Manning (2010)

[17] Inoue, K., Yokomori, R., Fujiwara, H., Yamamoto, T., Matsushita, M., Kusumoto S.: Ranking Significance of Software Components Based on Use Relations. IEEE Transactions on Software Engineering, Vol. 31, No. 3 (2005)

[18] Merobase - Software Component Search Engine, http://www.merobase.com (retr. 2012)

[19] Krugle - Open Search, http://opensearch.krugle.org (retr. 2012)

[20] Sourcerer, http://sourcerer.ics.uci.edu/sourcerer (retr. 2012)

[21] Koders, http://koders.com (retr. 2012)

[22] JBoss Community: Hibernate-Search, http://hibernate.org/subprojects/search.html (retr. 2012)

[23] Google Blog: A fall Sweep, http://googleblog.blogspot.com/2011/10/fall-sweep.html (2011)

[24] Bajracharya, S., Ossher, J., Lopes, C.: Leveraging usage similarity for effective retrieval of examples in code repositories. In Proceedings of the Int. ACM SIGSOFT Symposium on Foundations of Software Engineering (2010)

[25] Hummel, O.: Semantic Component Retrieval in Software Engineering. PhD dissertation, University of Mannheim (2008)

[26] Hummel, O., Janjic, W., Atkinson, C.: Evaluating the efficiency of retrieval methods for component repositories. Proceedings of the International Conference on Software Engineering and Knowledge Engineering (2007)

[27] Linping, Q., Lidong, W.: An Evaluation of Lucene for Keywords Search in Large-scale Short Text Storage. Computer Design and Applications (2010)

[28] Panchenko, O., Müller, S., Plattner, H., Zeier, A.: Querying Source Code Using a Controlled Natural Language. Proceedings of the International Conference on Software Engineering and Applications (2011)

[29] Panchenko, O., Karstens, J., Plattner, H., Zeier, A: Precise and Scalable Querying of Syntactical Source Code Patterns Using Sample Code Snip-

pets and a Database. Proceedings of the International Conference on Program Comprehension (2011)

[30] Podgurski, A., Pierce, L.: Retrieving reusable software by sampling behavior. ACM Transactions on Software Engineering and Methodology, Vol.2, No. 3 (1993)

[31] Janjic, W., Hummel, O., Atkinson, C.: More archetypal usage scenarios for software search engines. Proceedings of the ICSE Workshop on Search-driven Development: Users, Infrastructure, Tools and Evaluation (2010)

[32] Sametinger, J.: Software engineering with reusable components. Springer (1997)

[33] Thummalapenta, S. Xie, T.: Parseweb: a programmer assistant for reusing open source code on the web. Proceedings of the International Conference on Automated Software Engineering (2007)

[34] Lemos, O., Bajracharya, S., Ossher, J.: CodeGenie: a tool for test-driven source code search. Proceedings of the International Conference on Object-Oriented Programming (2007)

[35] Bajracharya, S.: Infrastructure for Building Search Tools for Developers. In Sim and Gallardo-Valencia (eds.): Finding Source Code on the Web for Remix and Reuse, Springer, 2012.

[36] Software Engineering Group, University of Mannheim: Merobase Data Sets, http://merobase.informatik.uni-mannheim.de/sources (retr. 2012)

Chapter 6
Krugle Code Search Architecture

Ken Krugler

Abstract Krugle was one of the earliest commercial portals for searching open source software. This chapter reviews the history of Krugle from initial inception to present day. It follows the search engine from the initial public version to the enterprise offering, with a particular focus on lessons learned from design decisions on topics such as web crawling, indexing, system architecture, and deployment.

6.1 Introduction

Krugle is a search engine for searching in source code and related technical information. There is a public site at Krugle.org, which has information on the top 3,500 open source projects, including project descriptions, licenses, software configuration management activity, and most importantly the source code—more than 400 million lines and growing.

There is also an enterprise version, which runs inside of company firewalls and provides the same search functionality against internal code and technical information.

In this chapter, I'll be describing the Krugle architecture, how it evolved over time, and the lessons we learned during that process.

6.2 Background

In 2004 I got actively involved in my first open source project, the ill-fated Chandler PIM. It slowly dawned on me that there were literally billions of lines of open source

K. Krugler (✉)
Scale Unlimited, 14860 Uren St, Nevada City, CA, USA
e-mail: kkrugler@scaleunlimited.com

S.E. Sim and R.E. Gallardo-Valencia (eds.), *Finding Source Code on the Web
for Remix and Reuse*, DOI 10.1007/978-1-4614-6596-6_6,
© Springer Science+Business Media New York 2013

code available, but no good way to find error messages, examples of API usage, or even the source for an open source component being used.

At the same time, a friend at a startup mentioned to me that the most powerful tool their developers had wasn't a debugger, or an IDE, or a build system—it was Google. This then led me to start thinking about how you'd create the ultimate programmer's search tool, and (in a broader sense) what "search-driven development" would look like.

In 2005 I started development of Krugle with a small team of friends. We got our first round of venture capital funding in September, and unveiled the Krugle site at the 2006 DEMO conference in February.

In 2006 we started work on the enterprise version of the product, which had a very different architecture. This was released to beta customers in April 2007.

In 2008 we switched the public site from the original distributed architecture to a version that uses a single large Krugle Enterprise appliance.

In 2011 the public site switched to the third version of our architecture, though still running on a Krugle Enterprise appliance.

6.3 Initial Public Version

We collected three types of information—web pages, source code and project descriptions. Each had its own collection, processing and searching infrastructure.

The web page and source code processing infrastructure was based on an early version of Hadoop, running on a cluster of 14 slave servers and one master.

The project descriptions were extracted and processed on a single server, coordinating with a MySQL database running on another server.

6.3.1 Web Page Crawling

We used Nutch to crawl technical web pages, collecting and extracting information that would be of use to software developers. Examples of such "interesting" pages included open source projects, programming tutorials, mailing lists, and bug databases.

We modified Nutch to implement a "focused crawler." The diagram below explains the fundamental steps in a focused crawl—the key point is that each "fetch loop" only fetches a percentage of all known URLs, and the pages with the highest estimated score are fetched first. This allows us to focus the crawler on areas of the web that would prove most likely to contain quality pages (Fig. 6.1).

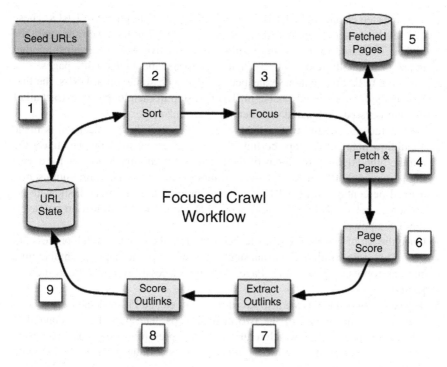

Fig. 6.1 Focused crawl in initial public version

URL State Database   This database (often called a "CrawlDB") maintains one entry for each unique URL, along with status (e.g. "have we fetched this page yet?"), the page score of fetched pages, and the link score. The actual approach used for this database varies, depending on the scale of the crawl, the availability of a scalable column-based DB or key/value store, etc.

Page Score   Every fetched page is processed by a page scorer. This calculates a numeric value for the page, where higher values correspond to pages that are of greater interest, given the focus of the crawl. A page scorer can be anything from a simple target term frequency calculation to a complex NLP (natural language processing) analyzer.

Link Score   Every URL has a score that represents the sum of page scores from all pages that contain an outbound link that matches the URL. Page scores are divided up across all outbound links, thus the increase in a URL's link score from a page with many outbound links will be minimized.

Fetched Pages Database   This is where all fetched pages are stored, using the URL as the key. Typically this isn't a real database, but rather an optimized, compressed read-only representation.

With terminology out of the way, we can discuss the steps in a focused crawl workflow.

1. The first step is to load the URL State database with an initial set of URLs. These can be a broad set of top-level domains such as the 1.7 million web sites with the highest US-based traffic, or the results from selective searches against another index, or manually selected URLs that point to specific, high quality pages.
2. Once the URL State database has been loaded with some initial URLs, the first loop in the focused crawl can begin. The first step in each loop is to extract all of the unprocessed URLs, and sort them by their link score.
3. Next comes one of the two critical steps in the workflow. A decision is made about how many of the top-scoring URLs to process in this loop. The fewer the number, the "tighter" the focus of the crawl. There are many options for deciding how many URLs to accept—for example, based on a fixed minimum score, a fixed percentage of all URLs, or a maximum count. More sophisticated approaches include picking a cutoff score that represents the transition point (elbow) in a power curve.
4. Once the set of accepted URLs has been created, the standard fetch process begins. This includes all of the usual steps required for polite and efficient fetching, such as robots.txt processing. Pages that are successfully fetched can then be parsed.
5. Typically fetched pages are also saved into the Fetched Pages database.
6. Now comes the second of the two critical steps. The parsed page content is given to the page scorer, which returns a value representing how closely the page matches the focus of the crawl. Typically this is a value from 0.0 to 1.0, with higher scores being better.
7. Once the page has been scored, each outlink found in the parse is extracted.
8. The score for the page is divided among all of the outlinks.
9. Finally, the URL State database is updated with the results of fetch attempts (succeeded, failed), all newly discovered URLs are added, and any existing URLs get their link score increased by all matching outlinks that were extracted during this loop.

At this point the focused crawl can terminate, if sufficient pages of high enough quality (score) have been found, or the next loop can begin.

In this manner the crawl proceeds in a depth-first manner, focusing on areas of the web graph where the most high scoring pages are found.

In the end we wound up with about 50 million pages, and a "crawlDB" that contained around 250 million URLs, of which about half were scored high enough such that we would eventually want to crawl them.

6.3.2 Web Page Processing

Once we had fetched a web page (or document, such as a PDF) then we'd parse it, to extract the title and text. Again, we leveraged the support that was already there in Nutch.

We also extracted information about source code repositories during the crawl, which allowed us to build a large list of CVS and SVN repositories for the source code crawler.

6.3.3 Web Page Searching

Finally, we used Nutch's search support (built on top of Lucene) to support searching these web pages. The actual indexes were stored on multiple page searchers, since (at that time) a typical 4 core box with 8 GB of ram could comfortably handled 10–20 M pages, and our index was bigger than that. Nutch provided the support to distribute a search request to multiple searchers, each with a slice ("shard") of the index, then combine the results.

6.3.4 Source Code Crawling

The source code crawler was also based on Nutch. We added "protocol handlers" for CVS and SVN, which let us leverage the distributed fetching and parsing support that was built into Nutch.

The "crawlDB" for the source code crawler contained HTTP-based URLs to SVN and CVS repositories. We manually entered many of these URLs that were found via manual searching, but we also included URLs that were discovered during the web page crawl as described previously. Finally, the project processing code (see below) also provided us with repository information.

One of the challenges we ran into was deciding whether to only get the trunk of project's code, or some number of the tags and branches as well. Initially we just went after the trunk, but eventually we settled on logic that would fetch the trunk, plus the "most interesting" tags, which we defined as being the latest point release for each major and minor version. Thus we'd go for the 1.0.4, 2.0 and 2.1.3 tags, but not 1.0.1, 1.0.2, 1.0.3, 2.1.0, etc.

We also found out quickly that we needed to be careful about monitoring and constraining the load that we put on CVS and SVN repositories. Due to a bug in the code, we accidentally wound up trying to download the complete Apache.org SVN repository—the trunk and all branches and tags from every project. This was crushing their infrastructure, and the ops team at Apache wisely blocked our crawler IP addresses, to prevent melt down. After some groveling and negotiations, plus more unit tests, we were unblocked and could resume the crawl at a more reasonable rate.

For some of the larger repositories, we looked into mirroring them, and eventually did set up an rsync of several. Unfortunately we were never able to negotiate a mirroring agreement with SourceForge, which was the biggest single repository that we needed to crawl. And the total number of unique repositories (more 100) made it impractical to negotiate that many data sharing deals, especially since many of these repositories only consisted of a few projects.

The situation in 2012 would be better suited to specific data mirroring agreements with a few repositories, given the larger number of code hosting sites that have significant number of projects (e.g. Google Code, GitHub). Note, though, that we would still need to crawl project descriptions independent of the code, as very few hosting sites or projects have adopted the use of standardized project metadata such as DOAP (description of a project) or fully specified Maven pom.xml files.

In the end, we wound up crawling over 130,000 projects found on more than 100 sites.

6.3.5 Source Code Processing

The meat of our system was the parsing infrastructure that we built, using ANTLR 3.0 grammars. We developed over 30 grammars, which we use to turn source code into something internally we refer to as a "use-def tree."

As an example of what ANTLR grammar looks like, heres a snippet from the python.g file:

```
classdef
scope EnclosingScope;
    :    'class' (NAME->class(name={$NAME.text},
                  begin={start($NAME)},
                  end={stop($NAME)}))
         { $EnclosingScope::st = $classdef.st; }
         (LPAREN testlist RPAREN)? COLON
         { $st.setAttribute("comments", comments()); }
         suite
         // catch comment in classes without func defs
         {$st.setAttribute("containedComments",
         comments());}
    ;
```

This tree, which we saved as XML, essentially tagged text in the source file as being comments, code, or whitespace. In addition the code sections would be further tagged as class definitions, function definitions, and function calls.

An example of the resulting XML for a Java file looks like:

```
<krugleparse version="0.3">
<uri>test/EndianUtils.udt</uri>
<language>Java</language>
<udt>
<c b="0" e="803"><![CDATA[/*   * Licensed
to i£¡   */]]></c>
```

```
<pkg n="org.apache.commons.io" b="813" e="833">
  <im n="java.io.EOFException" b="844" e="863"/>
  <im n="java.io.IOException" b="873" e="891"/>
  <im n="java.io.InputStream" b="901" e="919"/>
  <c b="952" e="1636"><![CDATA[/**  * Utility code
  if¡   */]]></c>
  <im n="java.io.OutputStream" b="929" e="948"/>
  <cd n="EndianUtils" b="1651" e="1661">
    <c b="1670" e="1748"><![CDATA[/* Instances
    should ...*/]]></c>
    <fd n="swapShort" b="2038" e="2046">
    </fd>
```

In order to pick the right parser, we had a preliminary analysis step that used the file name and regex patterns to determine the programming language.

We also ran additional tools over the code, including one that calculated actual lines of code, and another that extracted open source license information from source file comments and non-code text files. These results were then fed back into the project processing phase (see below) to add additional metadata to each project.

As part of a "virtuous cycle," we also found URLs in comments, and added these to the crawlDB. This in turn helped us find pages with references to additional code repositories, which we could then crawl and parse—and the cycle repeats.

Finally, we processed the parse trees to create Lucene documents. Each XML document for one source file would become one Lucene document, with many of the fields (e.g. "function call") being multi-valued, since one XML file could have many separate sections for each type of entity identified in the source.

We stored the actual source code separately, in regular files. One of our challenges became the management of large amounts of data—we were using custom-built filers (servers with lots of drives) to store many terabytes of source code, and keeping everything in sync, up to date, backed up, and available for processing was one of the major daily headaches. At this time Hadoop was not yet mature enough for us to trust it with our data—in fact we lost **all** of our crawl data once due to a bug in one of the first releases.

In the end we wound up with 2.6 billion lines of real source code in about 75 million source files.

6.3.6 Source Code Searching

Finally, we again used Nutch's search support to handle searching the source code. A search request would be distributed to multiple code searchers, each with a slice of the total index. Nutch would then handle combining the results.

We did wind up having to add a few enhancements to the search process, specifically enabling time limits on queries. The problem was that certain complex queries could take up to minutes to get results, and during this time they would cause all other queries to "stack up," leading to poor search performance for all users. Our solution was to enable early search termination at a low level (in Lucene), where after a specified amount of time the search would terminate even if it hadn't reached the end of the index. This would then return potentially different results, if the set of documents found prior to termination didn't include all of the top results that would normally be returned, but we felt this was an acceptable tradeoff.

Source code searching required a special query parser, to support custom tokenization and other tweaks that we did to improve code searching. This query parsing was handled by the master search server, before queries were sent out to the four search slaves.

6.3.7 Project Crawling

Initially we were only "crawling" projects (scraping pages) to find the repository information needed for our source code crawler. In early 2006, however, we realized that rich project metadata was critical to providing context for source code search results.

This changed the nature of our project crawling support, as it was no longer sufficient to use a page to extra repository data—instead, we needed to create a web mining system that could determine things like the project license.

The project crawl was all about discovering the URLs to project home pages. This typically involved custom Python code to do a very specific "discovery crawl" on an open source hoster site, e.g. Java.net. We also used data dumps from SourceForge.net and a few other sites that provided project listings in a format where we could then easily construct project home page URLs.

6.3.8 Project Processing

Once the discovery crawl had found a number of project home page URLs, we would web mine those pages to extract the project name, license, and other useful metadata.

Each open source hosting site had its own HTML page format, which meant writing detail extractors (again, in Python) for each hoster. As you might imagine this wasn't the most interesting thing to be working on, but it was critical for us to have structured data about projects to help augment code search results, as otherwise it was very challenging for end-users to understand and evaluate code search results. Providing project details added context that significantly improved the user experience.

The results of this web mining would be saved to a MySQL database, where our librarian could review and correct any obvious errors. With over 130,000 projects it wasn't possible to review each one, so we ranked projects by their size and level of activity.

Packaging up the results included getting statistics out of the source code project (see the source code processing section), determining the location of the source on the code filer, and building a searchable index.

6.3.9 Project Searching

By the time we added support for projects as separate entities in the system, CNet had open-sourced their enterprise search application ("Solr"). Solr provided a nice layer on top of Lucene, which simplified the work we had to do to add project-centric search support.

We created a Solr index schema that had the following fields, among others (Table 6.1):

Field Name	Description
name	The "user friendly" project name
exactname	A unique name for the project, used as a key
description	A short description of the project
license	The open source license for the project
language	The programming languages(s) used by the project
os	The target operating system(s) for the project
homepage	A URL to the project's home page
filesurl	A URL to the top location on the code filer for the project's code files
metrics	Text containing various code metrics extracted from the project's data
boost	A floating point number used to alter search results, based on the project's size, popularity, and level of activity

Table 6.1: Excerpt from solr index schema for projects

6.4 Public Site Architecture

The above describes a mixture of ad hoc back end systems, and the components used to provide search services. The actual architecture used to handle both end user (browser-based) queries and partner/enterprise API requests is a combination of a few additional systems (Fig. 6.2).

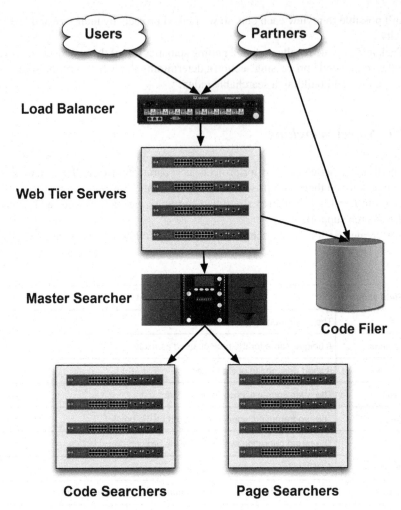

Fig. 6.2 Architecture of public Krugle site

6.4.1 Load Balancer

At the very top of the stack we had a load balancer, coupled with a firewall. All requests, either from end users (browsers) or via the Krugle API would go through a firewall and then to a load balancer, which would distribute the request to one of four servers sitting in the web tier.

6.4.2 Web Tier

The four web tier servers all ran identical versions of Perl code that acted as an intermediary between the lower-level Krugle API (implemented in Java, uses XML) and higher-level requests coming from web pages, partners, and external Krugle Enterprise boxes.

This Perl layer gave us extra flexibility, which meant we could quickly fix problems in the lower-level API and add additional functionality without having to rebuild and redeploy the search infrastructure sitting below the web tier.

In retrospect I think we should have spent more time making sure the Krugle API was correct and complete, versus back-filling and patching via Perl code in the web tier. We didn't have a good way to test the web tier layer, versus the many unit tests we implemented against the Krugle API.

6.4.3 Master Searcher

The single main searcher used a bigger hardware configuration, with more memory. The master searcher was responsible for the Krugle API, which was used by everybody (web tier, partners, and Krugle enterprise systems) to interact with the search indexes and data maintained by the public site.

The main searcher also ran the Solr search server responsible for project search requests.

6.4.4 Page Searchers

We had four servers, each with one large/slow disk to store the web page content, and a second faster disk to store to the search index. These four "slave" searchers provided distributed search across the index, and a separate front-end process running on a master search server then combined the results.

6.4.5 Code Searchers

Similar to web pages, we had four servers, though each of these had two fast disks to store to the search index. The actual code files were stored on a separate file server called the code filer.

6.4.6 Code Filer

All of the actual code files were stored on a separate "code filer", which was a big server stuffed with drives that were RAIDed together.

These files were fronted by the Lighttpd web server, which was configured to require a time-limited token for authorized access.

6.4.7 Live Versus Stand-by Versus Dev Systems

The actual infrastructure was even more complex than what has been described above. The code searchers, page searchers, master searcher and code filer all comprised a snapshot of the state of the system, for both code and data. As such, we had three copies of these—one in production, one on standby, and one being provisioned as the next "live" system.

6.4.8 Release Process

Whenever our "dev" system was sufficiently tested, we would do a "flip." This consisted of switching the VIPs (virtual IP addresses) for the master server and code filer to the new system, which would then cause the web tier to start using the new code and data. The previously live system would become the backup, which we could easily flip back to if the new live system had serious problems. And the previous backup system would become the new dev system, which we would start provisioning as the next live system.

This continuous rotation of systems worked well, but at the cost of lots of extra hardware. We also spent a lot of time pushing data around, as provisioning a new server meant copying many terabytes of data to the searchers and the filer from our back-end systems.

6.4.9 Post Mortem

The public search system worked, but required a lot of manual labor to build and deploy updates to the data, and had a lot of moving pieces. This complexity resulted in a lot of time spent keeping the system alive and happy, versus improving and extended the search functionality.

In retrospect it would have made more sense to first focus on the Krugle Enterprise system, and handle the public site via setting up multiple instances of these servers, each with a slice of the total projects. Then the delta between a stock Krugle

Enterprise system and the public site would have been a top-level "master" that handles distributing search requests and combining the results.

We would still have needed a back-end system to handle crawling web pages and handling search requests, but that's a much more isolated problem, and one with better existing support from Nutch.

6.5 Krugle Enterprise

The architecture described above worked well for handling billions of lines of code, but it wasn't suitable for a stand-alone enterprise product that could run reliably without daily care and feeding. In addition, we didn't have the commit comment data from the SCM systems that hosted the project source code, which was a highly valuable source of information for both searches and analytics.

So we created a workflow system (internally called "the Hub") that handled the crawling and processing of data, and converted the original multi-server search system into a single-server solution ("the API").

The enterprise version doesn't support crawling web pages, and it relies on users manually defining projects—specifying the repository type and location, the description of the project, etc. This information is still stored in a MySQL database.

6.5.1 SCM Comments

We added support for fetching, parsing and searching SCM comments that we retrieved from SCM systems. These comments were stored in the same Solr search server used for project search, but in a different Solr "core."

We created a Solr index schema that had the following fields, among others (Table 6.2):

6.5.2 SCMI Architecture

Early on we realized that it would be impossible to install and run all of the many different types of source code management system (SCM) clients on the enterprise server. For example, a ClearCase SCM requires a matching client, which in turn has to be custom installed.

Our solution was to define a standard protocol between the Hub and "helper" applications that could run on other servers. This SCM interface (SCMI) let us quickly build connectors to many different SCM systems, including ClearCase, Perforce, StarTeam, and git, as well as non-SCM sources of information such as Jira and Bugzilla.

Field Name	Description
uid	A unique id generated for each SCM comment.
projectUid	The unique id (project name) for the corresponding project.
projectName	The "user friendly" project name
revision	The revision number for the corresponding SCM commit.
author	User name of the person who did the SCM commit.
date	Date of the commit.
description	User-provided description of the commit.
files	List of files that were changed, added, or deleted.
activityScore	A float that describes the impact of the commit, measured by number of files changed, added, or deleted.

Table 6.2: Excerpt from Solr index schema for SCM data

6.5.3 Performance

For an enterprise search appliance, a basic issue is how to do two things well at the same time—updating a live index, and handling search requests. Both tasks can require extensive CPU, disk and memory resources, so it's easy to wind up with resource contention issues that kill your performance.

We made three decisions that helped us avoid the above. First, we pushed a significant amount of work "off the box" by putting a lot of the heavy lifting work into the hands of small clients called Source Code Management Interfaces (SCMIs). These run on external customer servers instead of on our appliance, and act as collectors for information about projects, SCM comments, source code and other development-oriented information. The information is then partially digested before being sent back to the appliance via a typical HTTP RESTful protocol.

Second, we use separate JVMs for the data processing/indexing tasks versus the searching/browsing tasks. This let us better control memory usage, at the cost of some wasted memory. The Hub data processing JVM receives data from the SCMI clients, manages the workflow for parsing/indexing/analyzing the results, and builds a new "snapshot." This snapshot is a combination of multiple Lucene indexes, plus all of the content and other analysis results. When a new snapshot is ready, a "flip" request is sent to the API JVM that handles the search side of things, and this new snapshot is gracefully swapped in.

On a typical appliance, we have two 32-bit JVMs running, each with 1.5 GB of memory. One other advantage to this approach is that we can shut down and restart each JVM separately, which makes it easier to do live upgrades and debug problems.

Finally, we tune the disks being used to avoid seek contention. There are two drives devoted to snapshots, while one is serving up the current snapshot, the other is being used to build the new snapshot. The Hub also uses two other drives for raw data and processed data, again to allow multiple tasks to run in a multi-threaded manner without running into disk thrashing.

The end result is an architecture that looks like this (Fig. 6.3):

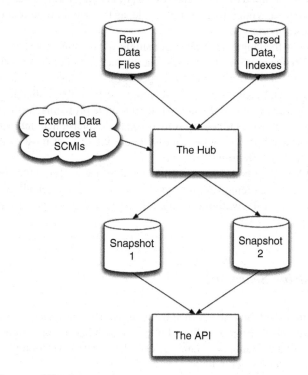

Fig. 6.3 Architecture of Krugle enterprise

6.5.4 Parsing Source Code

During early beta testing, we learned a lot about how developers search in code, with two in particular being important. First, we needed to support semi-structured searches, for example where the user wants to limit the search to only find hits in class definition names.

In order to support this, we had to be able to parse the source code. But "parsing the source code" is a rather vague description. There are lots of compilers out there that obviously parse source code, but full compilation means that you need to know about include paths (or classpaths), compiler-specific switches, the settings for the macro preprocessor in C/C++, etc. The end result is that you effectively need to be able to build the project in order to parse it, and that in turn means you wind up with a system that requires constant care and feeding to keep it running. Often that doesn't happen, so the end result is shelfware.

Early on we made a key decision, that we had to be able to process files individually, without knowledge of build settings, compiler versions, etc. We also had to handle a wide range of languages. This in turn meant that the type of parsing we could do was constrained by what features we could extract from a very fuzzy parse. We couldn't build a symbol table, for example, as that would require processing all of the includes/imports.

Depending on the language, the level of single-file parsing varies widely. Python, Java and C# are examples of languages where you can generate a good parse tree, while C/C++ are at the other end of the spectrum. Languages such as C/C++ that supports macros and conditional compilation are especially challenging. Dynamic languages like Ruby and Perl create their own unique problems, as the meaning of a term (is it a variable or a function) sometimes isn't determined until run-time.

So what we wind up with a best guess, where we're right most of the time but we'll occasionally get it wrong.

We use ANTLR to handle most of our parsing needs. Terr Parr, the author of ANTLR, added some memoization support to version 3.0, which allowed us to use fairly flexible lexer rules without paying a huge performance penalty for frequent back-tracking.

6.5.5 Substring Searching

The second important thing we learned from our beta testing was that we had to support some form of substring searching. For example, when a user searches on "ldap" she expects to find documents containing terms like "getLDAPConfig" , "ldapTimeout" , and "find_details_with_ldap" .

We could treat every search term as if it had implicit wildcards, like "*ldap*" , but that is both noisy and slow. The noise (false positive hits) comes from treating all contiguous runs of characters as potential matches, so a search for "heap" finds a term like "theAPI" .

The performance hit comes from having to: (a) first enumerate all terms in the index to find any that contain <term> as a substring, and then (b) use the resulting set of matching terms in a (potentially very large) OR query. BooleanQuery allows a maximum of 1,024 clauses by default—searching on the Lucene mailing list shows many people have encountered this limit while trying to support wildcard queries.

There are a number of approaches to solving the wildcard search problem, some of which are covered in the "Lucene in Action" book. For example, you can take every term and index it using all possible suffix substrings of the text. For example, "myLDAP" gets indexed as "myl", "yld", "lda", and so on. This then lets you turn a search for "*ldap*" into "ldap*", which cuts down on the term enumeration time by being able to do a binary search for terms starting with "ldap", versus enumerating all terms. You still can wind up with a very large number of clauses in the resulting OR query, however. And the index gets significantly larger, due to term expansion.

Another approach is to convert each term into n-grams, for example, using 3-g the term "myLDAP" would become "myl", "yld", "lda", "dap", and so on. Then a search for "ldap" becomes a search for "lda dap" in 3-g, which would match. This works as long as N (e.g. 3, in this example) is greater than or equal to the minimum length of any substring you'd want to find. It also significantly grows the size of the index, and for long terms results in a large number of corresponding n-grams.

Another approach is to pre-process the index, creating a secondary index that maps from each distinct substring to the set of all full terms that contain the substring. During a query, the first step is to use this secondary index to quickly find all possible terms that contain the query term as a substring, then use that list to generate the set of sub-clauses for an OR query, similar to above. This gives you acceptable query-time speed, at the cost of additional time during index generation. And you're still faced with potentially exceeding the max sub-clause limit.

We chose a fourth approach, based on the ways identifiers naturally decompose into substrings. We observed that arbitrary substring searches were not as important as searches for whole sub-words. For example, users expect a search for "ldap" to find documents containing "getLDAPConfig", but it would be very unusual for the user to search for "apcon" with the same expectation.

To support this, we implemented a token filter that recognizes compound identifiers and splits them up into sub-words, a process vaguely similar to stemming. The filter looks for identifiers that follow common conventions like camelCase, or containing numbers or underscores. Some programming languages allow other characters in identifiers, or indeed, any character; we stuck with letters, numbers, and underscores as the most common baseline. Other characters are treated as punctuation, so identifiers containing them are still split at those points. The difference is that the next step, sub-range enumeration, will not cross the punctuation boundary.

When we encounter a suitable compound identifier, we examine it to locate the offsets of sub-word boundaries. For example, "getLDAPConfig" appears to be composed of the words "get", "LDAP", and "Config", so the boundary offsets are at 0, 3, 7, and 13. Then we produce a term for each pair of offsets (i,j) such that $i < j$. All terms with a common start offset share a common Lucene index position value; each new start offset gets a position increment of one.

6.5.6 Query Versus Search

One of the challenges we ran into was the fundamentally different perception of results. In pure search, the user doesn't know the full set of results, and is searching for the most relevant matches. For example, when a user does a search for "lucene" using Google, they are looking for useful pages, but they have little to no idea about the exact set of matching pages.

In what I'm calling a query-style search request the user has more knowledge about the result set, and expects to see all hits. They might not look at each hit, but if a hit is missing then this is viewed as a bug. For example, when one of our users searches for all callers of a particular function call in their company's source code, they typically don't know about every single source file where that API is used (otherwise they wouldn't need us), but they certainly do know of many files which should be part of the result set. And if that "well known hit" is missing, then we've got big problems.

So where did we run into this situation? When files are very large, the default setting for Nutch was to only process the first 10 K terms. This in general is OK for web pages, but completely fails the query test when dealing with source code. Hell hath no fury like a developer who doesn't find a large file they know should be a hit, because the search term only exists near the end.

Another example is where we miss-classified a file, for example, if file xxx.h was a C++ header versus a C header. When the user filters search results by programming language, this can exclude files that they know of and are expecting to see in the result set.

There wasn't a silver bullet for this problem, but we did manage to catch a lot of problems once we figured out ways to feed our data back on itself. For example, we'd take a large, random selection of source files from the http://www.krugle.org site, and generate a list of all possible multi-line ("code snippet") searches in a variety of sizes (e.g. 1–10 lines). We'd then verify that for every one of these code snippets, we got a hit in the original source document.

6.5.7 Post Mortem

The Krugle enterprise search system is in active use today at a mixture of Fortune 100 and mid-size technology companies. The major benefits seen by customers are: (a) increased code re-use, primarily at the project level; and (b) a decrease in time spent fixing the same piece of code that exists in multiple projects.

A major challenge has been to provide potential customers with a way to quantify potential benefits. There's a general perception that search is important, e.g. it's easy to agree with statements like "If you can't find it, you can't fix it." It's difficult, though, to determine how much time and money such a system would save, and thus whether investing in a Krugle system is justified.

One additional and unexpected hurdle has been integration of Krugle systems into existing infrastructure, primarily for authentication and authorization. Many large enterprise customers are very sensitive about who can access source code, and even between groups in the same company a lack of trust means that providing enterprise-wide access control that all parties accept often leads to protracted engagements with significant profession services overhead.

Acknowledgements Portions of this chapter were adapted from a case study written by the author that was previously published in the book "Lucene In Action, 2nd Edition" by Michael McCandless, Erik Hatcher, and Otis Gospodnetić.

Chapter 7
Experiences and Lessons Learned with the Development of a Source Code Search Engine

Eduardo Santana de Almeida

Abstract Search and retrieval tools are an important mechanism to achieve software reuse. In this chapter, I present the experience at the RiSE Labs developing a search engine based on different techniques such as keywords, facets, Folksonomy and so on. Moreover, the lessons learned and some insights are also discussed.

7.1 Introduction

Software reuse, the process of using existing software artifacts rather than building them from scratch [13], is generally regarded as the most important mechanism for more efficient software development. This belief has been systematically enforced by empirical studies that have, over the years, demonstrated the reuse effects on software development in terms of quality, time-to-market and costs [2, 8, 14, 17, 25].

This reuse vision started to be idealized in the end of 1968, when [21], motivated by the software crisis, wrote a seminal paper on software reuse entitled *"Mass Produced Software Components"*. Since then, many discussions took place, involving issues such as the possibility of a software industrial revolution [4], in which programmers would stop coding everything from scratch and begin assembling applications from well stocked catalogs of reusable software components [23]. Nevertheless, in the achievement of such benefits, the adoption of a systematic reuse program is essential. Such program must include investments in different directions, both technical and non technical. Among the possibilities, many organizations invest in tools to promote the reuse activity, such as source code search engines [26]. Such tools allow software developers to efficiently search, retrieve and reuse source code

E.S. de Almeida (✉)
Federal University of Bahia and Fraunhofer Project Center (FPC) for Software
and Systems Engineering, Salvador, Bahia, Brazil
e-mail: esa@dcc.ufba.br

S.E. Sim and R.E. Gallardo-Valencia (eds.), *Finding Source Code on the Web for Remix and Reuse*, DOI 10.1007/978-1-4614-6596-6_7,
© Springer Science+Business Media New York 2013

from many different repositories, avoiding the writing of brand new code every time, because a similar solution could have been implemented by somebody else [24].

The reuse literature presents [10, 15, 22] several approaches and tools related to source code search and retrieval, including a wide variety of mechanisms and techniques, from keywords and facets to context awareness. In this chapter, I present the experience at RiSE (Reuse in Software Engineering) Labs[1] along the years, with the B.A.R.T. (Basic Asset Retrieval Tool) project, whose main goal was the development of a search engine for software code.

The remainder of this chapter is organized as follows. Section 7.2 presents the B.A.R.T project and its different versions. Section 7.3 discusses the lessons learned and some insight thoughts in the area. Finally, Sect. 7.4 concludes this chapter.

7.2 The B.A.R.T Project

The B.A.R.T project, formerly called Maracatu [9], was created based on the following motivation: in order to start the formation of a reuse culture in organizations and obtain its initial benefits, first it is necessary to provide subsidies and tools for the reuse of source code that is already available in the organization itself, from previous projects, or from repositories available on the Internet.

Based on an extensive literature review [15] and our industrial experience at Recife Center for Advanced Studies and Systems (C.E.S.A.R), we defined the set of requirements for B.A.R.T's first version [9]. The main design decision was that a source code search engine should consider the evolving and dynamic environment that surrounds many development organizations. Differently from black-box reuse, where there is usually more time to encapsulate the components and provide well-structured documentation that facilitates searching, in many development repositories documentation is usually minimal, and mostly not structured. Figure 7.1 shows the version using the Folksonomy mechanism (Sect. 7.2.2).

In this sense, a search engine should support two basic processes: (i) to locate all reusable software artifacts that are stored in project repositories and maintain an index of them. The indexing process should be automatic, and should consider non-structured (free text) documentation; and (ii) to allow the user to search and retrieve these artifacts, taking advantage of the index created in process (i).

Since in this scenario the artifacts are constantly changing, the first process must be automatically performed on the background, maintaining the indexes always updated and optimized according to a prescribed way. On the other hand, the developer is responsible for starting the second, requesting possible reusable artifacts that suits his/her problem.

Thus, in order to execute these two basic processes, some macro requirements were defined:

1. **Artifacts filtering.** Although ideally all kinds of artifacts should be considered for reuse (requirements, design specification, source code, test cases, test scripts

---

[1] http://labs.rise.com.br.

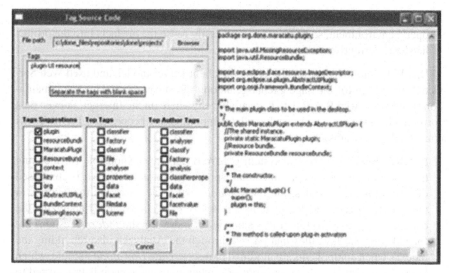

Fig. 7.1 Screenshot of the Folksonomy-based version of B.A.R.T.

and so on), an automatic mechanism depends on a certain level of quality that the artifact must have. For example, keyword-based search requires that the artifacts contain a considerable amount of free text describing it, otherwise the engine cannot perform the keyword match. In this sense, a qualitative analysis of the artifacts must be performed, in order to eliminate low-quality artifacts that could hinder search efficiency.

2. **Repository selection.** The developer must be able to manually include the list of the repositories where to search for reusable artifacts. It must be possible, at any moment, to perform a search on these repositories in order to find newer versions of the artifacts already found, or new artifacts. For example, a developer can include the repositories related to *Project A*, *Project B* and *Project C*.

3. **Local storage.** All artifacts that were found must be locally stored in a cache, in order to improve performance (reusable components repository centralization). In a real scenario, a software factory has several projects in the repository. Thus, in order to avoid several accesses to the repository, a local cache is very useful.

4. **Index update.** Periodically, the repositories that are registered must be accessed to verify the existence of new artifacts, or newer versions of already indexed artifacts. In this case, the index must be rebuilt to include the changes.

5. **Optimization.** Performance is a critical issue, specially in scenarios where thousands of artifacts are stored into several repositories. Thus, optimization techniques should be adopted. A simple and practical example is to avoid analyzing and indexing software artifacts that were already indexed by the mechanism.

6. **Keyword search.** The search can be based on keywords, like many web search engines, thus avoiding the need for learning a new method. Thus, the search must accept a *string* as the input, and must interpret logical operators such as *"AND"* and *"OR"*.

7. **Search results presentation.** The search result must be presented in the developer's environment, so he/she can more easily reuse the artifacts into the project he/she is currently working on.

B.A.R.T's architecture was based on the client-server model, and used Web Services technology for message exchange among the subsystems. This implementation strategy allowed B.A.R.T to be available anywhere on the Internet, or even on a corporate Intranet, in scenarios where the components are proprietary. B.A.R.T was composed of two subsystems:

1. **B.A.R.T Service:** This subsystem is a Web Service, responsible for indexing the components, in background, and responding to user queries. It is composed of the following modules: the *CVS module,* which accesses the repositories in the search for reusable components; the *Analyzer,* responsible for analyzing the code in order to determine if it is suitable for indexing; the *Indexer,* responsible for indexing the Java files that passed through the Analyzer, also rebuilding the indexes when components are modified or inserted; the *Download* module, which helps the download (check-out) process, when the source code is transferred to the developer machine, after a request; and the *Search* module, which receives the parameters of a query, interprets it (for example, "AND" and "OR" operators), searches the index, and returns a set of index entries.
2. **Eclipse plug-in:** This subsystem is the visual interface the developer sees. It acts as a Web Service client to access the B.A.R.T Service.

7.2.1 The Active Search Mechanism

B.A.R.T's first version performed search and retrieval essentially based on keywords and facets. Moreover, the search mechanism was based on passive search, often used in search engines, i.e. the mechanism waits passively until the user defines a set of keywords and requests a search operation. For these reasons, much of the reuse potential of the repositories being searched was being ignored, because in many situations the developer does not have enough knowledge of the available assets to start looking for them. Even with proper knowledge regarding the repositories, the developer could simply fail to recognize a situation where a search could be performed. In other words, the tool was lacking context awareness and a more active behavior, in order to anticipate the developer's needs [30].

In this context, a second version of the tool was proposed [6, 20, 27] to consider these and other issues. The following requirements were elicited for this new version:

1. **Extensibility:** Software development involves a large number of steps and different intermediate types of asset are produced along the path. There are usually multiple alternative formats to build each type of asset and on top of that, the information contained in the assets may be encoded in different languages.

Examples of asset types include use case specifications, documentation and programming units. A programming unit may be defined in a COBOL program, a C file, a Java class or in any of the several existing programming languages.

2. **High Precision:** Information retrieval performance is often measured in terms of precision and recall. The tool heavily depends on information retrieval strategies to (1) assess the reuse potential of a set of assets given a legacy asset repository and (2) try to maintain a high level of reuse activity by actively delivering reuse candidates for the user tasks.

3. **Ubiquity:** "No attempt to reuse" is the number one cause for software reuse failure [7] and that is mainly due to the lack of knowledge of existing assets that could be reused. An approach for reuse within development [30] must be employed, making the cost of finding reusable work products as low as possible. Thus, the tool should provide programmers with a comprehensive set of tools that smoothly merge with existing development environments in order to minimize the effort of achieving higher levels of reuse activity.

4. **Scalability:** The potential amount of operations performed for an active information delivery for a single user pushes for a solution that properly scales according to the number of users. Large organizations usually have hundreds or thousands of users performing development activities concurrently.

   In this sense, an active information delivery approach has a potential side effect of changing the course of action of the user according to the task at hand and the information delivered. The time when the information is delivered is of paramount importance for this to properly occur. Therefore, the information retrieval mechanism must yield results in a reasonable time regardless of the number of concurrent users and the activity load performed by them.

5. **Continuous Metrics Extraction:** From the organizational perspective, the reuse activity must be systematically monitored so the impacts of reuse over other development aspects, such as quality and cost, can be assessed and deviations can be timely detected and handled. For this reason, automated metric extraction tools must be provided by the solution in consonance with existing continuous integration practices.

Besides these requirements, the main improvement related to this version was the reuse metric that was defined [19] and implemented in the tool. The existing reuse metrics [19] have in common the fact that they basically aim at assessing, although in different ways, how much was reused during the construction of a software product. For this reason, they can all be seen as realized (or achieved) reuse metrics.

While this is a fundamental aspect to be considered when assessing the reuse activity, there is a critical detail that is lacking on all proposed reuse metrics so far: the reuse potential of a product relative to a repository of legacy assets. That is, given a repository of (semi) reusable assets, the following question must be answered: *"How much could be reused when building this new application?"*.

Once the need for defining a reuse potential (rp) metric was agreed upon, the remaining issue was how to perform the calculation of such metric and for that, some information retrieval concepts must be employed. The artifacts produced in a specific project belong to the query space, while the assets available in a repository belong to the search space. The proposed metric was defined in terms of the set of queries extracted from the query space and, from this set, the number of successful queries against the search space.

The new search and retrieval process designed for B.A.R.T was composed of a set of phases. The *legacy content retrieval* phase consisted on continuously monitoring the produced assets and passing them for indexing. An asset evaluation policy was necessary for determining whether a specific set of assets is proper for future indexing. This policy was responsible for filtering low quality assets that would negatively impact retrieval performance or cause problems if reused. It was also responsible for determining when the index should be updated.

Once the assets were retrieved, the indexing phase took place. During this phase, performed by B.A.R.T's *Indexer* module, the artifacts' contents were parsed and analyzed before being actually indexed. The contents of the available artifacts were converted to a common representation. This common representation was then interpreted during analysis and indexed, if considered relevant. The ubiquity requirement was satisfied mainly by the *Listener* module, which monitored and interpreted user activities, like adding a method to a Java source file. From this interpretation, queries were formulated and executed against the repository and reuse candidates could be suggested to the user. This consisted on the active information delivery mechanism of B.A.R.T. The queries were formulated by the query formulation agent, contained in the *Searcher* module. The formulation was based on the contents of the artifacts being edited by the developer in a similar approach to the repository indexing phase, although the actual analysis performed could differ due to the distinct nature of development for and with reuse.

The *results evaluation and presentation* phase was composed by the result evaluator agent, contained in the Searcher module, responsible for detecting candidates that should not be presented to the user, based on the feedback provided from previous interactions or on information that was not available in the index and therefore could not be taken into account during search time. The remaining results from the analysis were then manipulated and finally presented to the user by the *Presenter* module. This module was responsible for determining how and when these candidates were presented to the user. Cognitive issues like the level of intrusiveness of the delivery were also taken into account when making these decisions.

The search results were presented to the user by the *Presenter* module. The next step was the *indexed contents retrieval* phase, performed by the *Searcher* module, initiated upon user request. This phase was responsible for providing the system with user feedback (which assets were considered relevant to his context) and retrieving the actual asset from the repository system. The phases presented so far corresponded to the *active information delivery cycle*. Complementarily to this cycle, the *metrics extraction* phase took a more general look at the produced artifacts from the organizational perspective. All previous phases, except the legacy contents retrieval and repository indexing phases, were focused on reuse from the individual perspective, aiming at helping developers in achieving a higher reuse activity. This phase, performed by the *Extractor* module, was responsible for ensuring that given a set of artifacts being produced and the available repository, the development team extracted the most out of the repository when building the new set of assets. That is, good reuse candidates presented by the system have not been neglected.

7.2.2 The Folksonomy Mechanism

The second version of B.A.R.T introduced important improvements in the search and retrieval process. The mechanism developed to suggest assets before an explicit search by the user was very important in this sense. Nevertheless, there were some deficiencies, such as the facet mechanism, which was based on a limited set of terms, such as platform, component type and so on. In this sense, we decided to explore the idea of Folksonomy [29] in the third version.

Folksonomy, combining *"folk"* and *"taxonomy"*, refers to a collaborative way in which information is categorized on the web. Instead of using a centralized classification scheme such as facets, users are encouraged to freely assign chosen keywords (called tags) to pieces of data, in a process known as *tagging*. Thus, the following requirements were defined for this version:

1. **Integration with different search techniques:** The mechanism should use the Folksonomy technique combined with traditional schemes of classification to improve search precision.
2. **Association of tags with components:** Through this functionality, the user should be able to associate tags to components according to its domain.
3. **Search by tags:** It should be possible to discover all items from all users that match a specific tag. Moreover, the engine should support the discovery of items tagged from specific users that match the tag.
4. **Tag Cloud:** The frequently used tags should be listed and emphasized with different colors, organized by relevance, to aid the search by tags.
5. **Database persistence:** Tags, related to a specific component and author should be stored in a persistent database for future reuse. It means that data can be accessed at any time by the tool.

In order to support the defined requirements, two new modules were designed in the architecture. The *Folksonomy Classifier* was responsible to perform the persistence of the tags in a database structured. Thus, while the users were classifying the components, the tags used were stored in an XML archive with the respective component and the related author. The *Folksonomy Search* managed the search performed through Folksonomy, without losing the functionalities of text mining and facet-based search techniques.

7.2.3 The Semantic Mechanism

The third version of the tool presented a complementary mechanism based on tags, which improved the facet mechanism. However, as several users often used the key-

word search, it was necessary to define new ways to improve its precision and recall. Thus, the fourth version [5] of B.A.R.T improved the keyword search process,
combining the original search mechanism with semantic features such as ontology
reasoning for assistance in query construction and machine learning techniques for
code comprehension.

For this version, the following requirements were specified:

1. **Existence of a domain ontology:** A domain ontology should be created and
   completed with a vocabulary that contained infrastructure terms handled by
   source code.
2. **Reasoning over user query:** Technical terms associated with the user query
   should be exhibited in B.A.R.T's user interface in order to help users during
   query construction.
3. **Search by semantic terms:** Users could choose one of the semantic terms in
   order to contextualize the keyword query.
4. **Source code analysis and classification:** Source code had to be analyzed and
   classified into a proper domain category.

The architecture designed to accommodate these new requirements was composed of two new modules: (i) the *reasoner*, where all ontology management occurred, together with the tasks associated with reasoning and inference. The *reasoner* module was responsible for providing the domain terms related with a given
query in order to help end users to contextualize its keyword query. (ii) The *analyzer*
was a new module that composed the semantic layer. This module fed the *Indexer*
with the semantic classification from the source code analysis.

The *reasoner* and *analyzer* modules encapsulated two self-contained components: the **Semantic Query Reasoner** and the **Semantic Code Analyzer**. The first
one assisted users during search to match relevant source code. In a nutshell, this
component contextualized the user query with domain terms related to the keyword
through an ontology reasoning process. In order to provide appropriate domain
terms, the component reasoned over a domain ontology while ordinary keyword
search was being performed. As a consequence, in addition to the returned code,
related domain terms were suggested for placing the query into a specific context.
Once a domain term was chosen, the search was focused on code belonging to the
selected domain. More information about the domain ontology can be seen in [5].

The *Semantic Code Analyzer* was responsible for source code analysis and domain classification. Essentially, it classified source codes according to an infrastructure category so that this information was used to create the index structure. This
component compared the source code with a knowledge base taking into account
content similarities to perform the categorization. For categorization, the component used a naive *Bayes* probabilistic classifier with strong (naive) independence
assumptions. Its use was justified by the fact that this method is usually applicable
for unstructured text documents, such as source code.

Although the main task of the component was to classify source code, it performed other tasks such as knowledge base (kb) compressing, code filtering and
comment erasure in order to make the analysis more efficient:

- **Kb compressing:** Once the knowledge base was updated with new infrastructure domains, new source code was incorporated and thus more space was needed. By compressing the knowledge base into a single file, the component was able to speed up the access to the knowledge base.
- **File filtering:** The filtering process constrained the classification to restricted file types specified by the user. During the classification process, the component ignored unspecified extensions and handled only those that matched the user's choice.
- **Comments erasure:** After the filtering phase, the selected files had the comments erased in order to improve the accuracy of the classification. Although comments are used for giving contextual information about the program, it is speculated that they might confuse the categorization because there is no vocabulary control. The objective was to avoid the comparison between statements written in natural language and the kb's code, whose syntax follows a specific programming language's grammar.

7.2.4 The Data Mining Mechanism

The feedback received with the fourth version of B.A.R.T was interesting. However, the user still needed to build queries every time using the passive search. This turned out to be inconvenient in some situations such as dependencies among the components, because sometimes the returned assets did not solve the entire problem, and the developer had to find additional components to complement the entire solution. These dependencies were identified only on demand, when the developer tried to search for another component.

In this way, the fifth version of B.A.R.T [18] was improved with an approach that used data mining techniques to solve the query formulation problem by reducing the conceptual gap on the queries built. The solution was based on the reduction of the performed queries. Thus, the main goal was to optimize the component search and retrieval process by monitoring the usage history through a logging mechanism. The following requirements were specified in this version:

1. **Suggest Associated Assets:** The tool must suggest associated assets for the search engine users. These associations should be based on the knowledge extracted from log files.
2. **Extract Association Rules:** The associations are extracted according to association rules. This approach must extract the rules using well-defined algorithms such as *A priori* [1], *Dynamic Itemset Counting* (DIC) [3], and *FP-Growth* [11].
3. **Parser the Log Mechanisms Artifacts:** The log mechanisms used in the tool are log files. The knowledge extraction process used these data to extract the rules.

The B.A.R.T architecture was extended with two new modules: *Association Rules Extractor* (AR Extractor) and *Association Rules Viewer* (AR Viewer). The first one was responsible for the knowledge extraction from log files, using the following procedure: (i) to parse the file and (ii) to extract the association rules. The second module was responsible for showing the results to the user. These results were plotted as a graph and shown as recommendations.

The AR Extractor was divided in two sub-modules: XML *Descriptor Extractor* and *Algorithm Manager*. The *XML Descriptor Extractor* was responsible for parsing the log files and grouping the information according to the transactions. These transactions represented the files that each user downloaded in a specific time window.

In the *Algorithm Manager*, the data mining phase took place and a proper algorithm was selected. This choice depended on the situation (single or distributed database) and the analysis of some characteristics, such as performance, CPU process, memory usage and return time. During the evaluation, some rules were accepted and others were left behind. This step was important to improve the final rules quality. The last module was responsible for generating the XML file.

The AR Viewer was composed of four sub-modules. The *Communication layer* provided a way to connect the client and server sides. This layer was implemented using Web Services and RMI. The Interpreters (*Rules* and *Query Result*) were used to transform the XML returned from the server and prepare it to graph render. This graph was provided by the last sub-module that plotted the result for the user.

7.3 Lessons Learned

During 7 years, I was involved with the development of the B.A.R.T project and I believe that some aspects should be highlighted for researchers and practitioners interested in new developments in the field:

- *Software architecture.* B.A.R.T's different versions had their architecture designed before the implementation, but several violations were found in the design × implementation scenario (what was designed versus what was actually implemented) [28]. As in some software development projects, because of the need of results in short time, the implementation sacrificed the design phase and some problems related to quality were identified.
- *Non-functional Requirements.* In general, during the project, the main non-functional requirement considered by the team was performance. However, in order to have a tool used by hundreds of software engineers in the same organization, other aspects such as availability and fault tolerance should be considered.
- *Ranking process.* The research and development team developed different mechanisms to improve search and retrieval. However, the ranking process was not investigated. All the implementations were based on the Lucene search engine and some improvements could be made in this sense, considering for example, information about the current project, background and expertise from the user and so on.
- *Traceability.* The reuse dream is to reuse not only source code but also several assets in the software development environment. Our team had the idea to link

source code with other assets, such as requirements and test cases. This feature would be very useful. For example, a software engineer could search some requirements and retrieve not only them, but also part of the architecture, source code and test cases. However, this feature was not considered in the project, nor in any of B.A.R.T's previous versions.

- *Observations.* Nowadays, there are several projects based on Eclipse, for example, to monitor and log the user's activity during software development. In the project, we did not use it and I believe that this perception – with the consensus of the user, of course – could be very important to understand how software engineers reuse assets.

- *Software Product Lines.* The different versions in the B.A.R.T project were developed separately. Currently, I believe that software product line ideas could be very useful to manage the different "products" and features available in the source code search domain.

- *Reuse.* The area of search and retrieval of software components is not new and several solutions were proposed. However, in general, they are created from scratch. I believe that several projects from the past could be used as a starting point to develop new tools and approaches.

- *Database for benchmarking.* In some areas it is common to use standard benchmarking. In the search and retrieval area this issue was solved some years ago [12]. Its use is crucial to understand the current limitations of the solutions and to propose new ones.

- *Services and Models.* Service-oriented development and Model-Driven development are becoming more popular and mature. I believe that the new efforts in the search and retrieval area should consider these issues in the development of new solutions. A preliminary work in this direction can be seen in [16].

- *Google.* Along the years of the B.A.R.T project, a frequent nightmare was related to Google. All the team was constantly worried with the possibility of Google entering in this game. Some years later, the nightmare is still there. As a personal opinion, I think researchers in the area should consider this aspect, but not decrease the efforts because of it.

7.4 Conclusion

Software reuse is an important aspect for organizations interested in benefits related to cost, productivity and quality. The reuse literature presents different ways to achieve it, such as methods, processes, and specially, environments and tools. Among the reuse tools, the search and retrieval of source code had an important role since the reuse of source code is the most common way to perform reuse (even non-systematic). This area is very rich in proposed solutions, however, the available publications are related to isolated efforts. In this sense, this chapter presented 7 years of experience with the B.A.R.T project. It discussed the main improvements in the tool along the years, as well as some insightful thoughts that can be useful for researchers in the field. I believe that the area presented some advances but the tool or environment in the sense idealized by McIlroy is not ready so far and the road is open for researchers and companies interested on it.

As future direction, in my research group, we are interested in performing empirical studies with the different tools for search and retrieval. I believe that several advances were achieved in the area along the years, but few empirical studies were conducted considering different research methods.

Acknowledgements I would like to thank all the members from the RiSE Tools project. The experiences and moments together during the development of the B.A.R.T tool were incredible. Moreover, I would like to express my gratitude to the Recife Center for Advanced Studies and Systems (C.E.S.A.R) where the development and contact with hundred of software engineers was crucial.

References

[1] Agrawal, R. and Srikant, R. (1994). Fast algorithms for mining association rules in large databases. In *Proceedings of the 20th International Conference on Very Large Data Bases*, VLDB '94, pages 487–499, San Francisco, CA, USA.

[2] Basili, V. R., Briand, L. C., and Melo, W. L. (1996). How reuse influences productivity in object-oriented systems. *Commun. ACM*, **39**, 104–116.

[3] Brin, S., Motwani, R., Ullman, J. D., and Tsur, S. (1997). Dynamic itemset counting and implication rules for market basket data. In *Proceedings of the 1997 ACM SIGMOD international conference on Management of data*, SIGMOD '97, pages 255–264, New York, NY, USA.

[4] Cox, B. J. (1990). Planning the software industrial revolution. *IEEE Softw.*, **7**, 25–33.

[5] Durão, F. A., Vanderlei, T. A., Almeida, E. S., and de L. Meira, S. R. (2008). Applying a semantic layer in a source code search tool. In *Proceedings of the 2008 ACM symposium on Applied computing*, SAC '08, pages 1151–1157.

[6] Eduardo, Frederico, Martins, A. C., Mendes, R., Melo, C., Garcia, V. C., Almeida, E. S., and Silvio (2006). Towards an effective context-aware proactive asset search and retrieval tool. In *6th Workshop on Component-Based Development (WDBC'06)*, pages 105–112, Recife, Pernambuco, Brazil.

[7] Frakes, W. B. and Fox, C. J. (1995). Sixteen questions about software reuse. *Commun. ACM*, **38**, 75–ff.

[8] Frakes, W. B. and Succi, G. (2001). An industrial study of reuse, quality, and productivity. *Journal System Software*, **57**, 99–106.

[9] Garcia, V. C.; Lucredio, D. D. F. A. S. E. C. R. A. E. S. F. R. P. M. M. S. R. L. (2006). From specification to the experimentation: A software component search engine architecture. In *In The 9th International Symposium on Component-Based Software Engineering (CBSE)*, Sweden.

[10] Garcia, V., de Almeida, E., Lisboa, L., Martins, A., Meira, S., Lucredio, D., and de M. Fortes, R. (2006). Toward a code search engine based on the state-of-art and practice. In *Software Engineering Conference, 2006. APSEC 2006. 13th Asia Pacific*, pages 61–70.

[11] Han, J., Pei, J., and Yin, Y. (2000). Mining frequent patterns without candidate generation. In *Proceedings of the 2000 ACM SIGMOD international conference on Management of data*, SIGMOD '00, pages 1–12, New York, NY, USA.

[12] Hummel, O. (2010). Facilitating the comparison of software retrieval systems through a reference reuse collection. In *Proceedings of 2010 ICSE Workshop on Search-driven Development: Users, Infrastructure, Tools and Evaluation*, SUITE '10, pages 17–20.

[13] Krueger, C. W. (1992). Software reuse. *ACM Comput. Surv.*, **24**, 131–183.

[14] Lim, W. C. (1994). Effects of reuse on quality, productivity, and economics. *IEEE Software*, **11**, 23–30.

[15] Lucredio, D., Prado, A. F. d., and Almeida, E. S. d. (2004). A survey on software components search and retrieval. In *Proceedings of the 30th EU-ROMICRO Conference*, pages 152–159, Washington, DC, USA. IEEE Computer Society.

[16] Lucredio, D., Fortes, R., and Whittle, J. (2012). Moogle: a metamodel-based model search engine. *Software and Systems Modeling*, **11**(2), 183–208.

[17] M. Ezran, M. Morisio, C. T. (2002). *Practical Software Reuse*. Springer.

[18] Martins, A., Garcia, V., de Almeida, E., and Meira, S. (2009). Suggesting software components for reuse in search engines using discovered knowledge techniques. In *Software Engineering and Advanced Applications, 2009. SEAA '09. 35th Euromicro Conference on*, pages 412–419.

[19] Mascena, J., de Almeida, E., and de Lemos Meira, S. (2005). A comparative study on software reuse metrics and economic models from a traceability perspective. In *Information Reuse and Integration, Conf, 2005. IRI -2005 IEEE International Conference on.*, pages 72–77.

[20] Mascena, J. C. C. P., Meira, S. R. d. L., de Almeida, E. S., and Garcia, V. C. (2006). Towards an effective integrated reuse environment. In *Proceedings of the 5th international conference on Generative programming and component engineering*, GPCE '06, pages 95–100.

[21] McIlroy, M. D. (1968). Mass-produced software components. *Proc. NATO Conf. on Software Engineering, Garmisch, Germany*.

[22] Mili, A., Mili, R., and Mittermeir, R. T. (1998). A survey of software reuse libraries. *Ann. Softw. Eng.*, **5**, 349–414.

[23] Moore, M. (2001). Software reuse: silver bullet? *Software, IEEE*, **18**(5), 86.

[24] Morisio, M., Ezran, M., and Tully, C. (2002). Success and failure factors in software reuse. *IEEE Trans. Softw. Eng.*, **28**, 340–357.

[25] Poulin, J. S. (2006). The business case for software reuse: Reuse metrics, economic models, organizational issues, and case studies. In *ICSR*, page 439.

[26] Rine, D. C. (1997). Success factors for software reuse that are applicable across domains and businesses. In *Proceedings of the 1997 ACM symposium on Applied computing*, SAC '97, pages 182–186, New York, NY, USA. ACM.

[27] Santos, E., de Almeida, F., de Almeida, E., and de Lemos Meira, S. (2010). A context-aware proactive source code search and retrieval tool. In *Information Reuse and Integration (IRI), 2010 IEEE International Conference on*, pages 380–381.

[28] van Gurp, J. and Bosch, J. (2002). Design erosion: problems and causes. *Journal of Systems and Software*, **61**(2), 105–119.

[29] Vanderlei, T. A., Durão, F. A., Martins, A. C., Garcia, V. C., Almeida, E. S., and de L. Meira, S. R. (2007). A cooperative classification mechanism for search and retrieval software components. In *Proceedings of the 2007 ACM symposium on Applied computing*, pages 866–871, New York, NY, USA.

[30] Ye, Y. and Fischer, G. (2002). Supporting reuse by delivering task-relevant and personalized information. In *Proceedings of the 24th International Conference on Software Engineering*, ICSE '02, pages 513–523, New York, NY, USA. ACM.

Chapter 8
Infrastructure for Building Code Search Applications for Developers

Sushil Krishna Bajracharya

Abstract The large availability of open source code on the Web provides great opportunities to build useful code search applications for developers. Building such applications requires addressing several challenges inherent in collecting and analyzing code from open source repositories to make them available for search. An infrastructure that supports collection, analysis, and search services for open source code available on the Web can greatly facilitate building effective code search applications. This chapter presents such an infrastructure called Sourcerer that facilitates collection, analysis, and search of source code available in code repositories on the Web. This chapter provides useful information to researchers and implementors of code search applications interested in harnessing the large availability of source code in the repositories on the Web. In particular, this chapter highlights key aspects of Sourcerer that supports combining Software Engineering and Information Retrieval techniques to build effective code search applications.

8.1 Introduction

Building a search application for source code available on the Web can be a major undertaking. The specificities and needs for code search pose interesting opportunities and challenges to build effective code search applications. For example, unlike natural language text, source code has an inherent scarcity of terms that describe the underlying implementation. From an information retrieval perspective source code can be much harder artifact to retrieve if we rely solely on the terms that are present in it. On the other hand, source code has rich structure compared to natural language text. The structure comes from the organization of source code entities in

S.K. Bajracharya (✉)
Black Duck Software, Burlington, MA, USA
e-mail: sbajra@acm.org

S.E. Sim and R.E. Gallardo-Valencia (eds.), *Finding Source Code on the Web for Remix and Reuse*, DOI 10.1007/978-1-4614-6596-6_8,
© Springer Science+Business Media New York 2013

the implementation, and also the various relations that exist among those entities. As a result, code search applications can leverage structural information extracted from source code for effective retrieval.

Sourcerer is an infrastructure that facilitates collection, analysis, and searching of source code harnessing its inherent structural information. This chapter provides details on the aspects of Sourcerer that makes it a unique state-of-the-art platform to build code search applications. Rest of the chapter is organized as follows. Section 8.2 provides an overview of three code search applications that Sourcerer supported, and presents the infrastructure requirements demanded by the code search applications. Section 8.3 introduces the key elements of Sourcerer's Architecture (Fig. 8.1). Section 8.4 provides an in-depth discussion of various models that lie at the core of Sourcerer's architecture. Section 8.5 summarizes the contents that are stored in Sourcerer's repository, and Sect. 8.6 discusses services that allow access to the stored contents. Section 8.7 provides details on the tools developed to build the contents and services in Sourcerer. This chapter concludes by summarizing key features that enabled the three code search applications (Sect. 8.8) and discusses related work in Sect. 8.9.

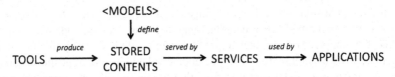

Fig. 8.1 Elements of Sourcerer infrastructure

8.2 Infrastructure Requirements for Code Search Applications

Sourcerer enabled building three code search applications during the course of its development. These code search applications put forth various requirements on Sourcerer as a code search infrastructure. Overall, these requirements boil down to three basic functionalities:

1. **Collection and Storage**: Fetching source code from forges on the Web and storing them locally with required metadata intact.
2. **Analysis and Indexing**: Extract both lexical (textual) and structural information (entities and relations) from the source code downloaded from the Web.
3. **Search and Retrieval**: Provide access to underlying contents (source, search index, and structural information) as needed by different applications

The core of these requirements demanded code-specific analyses and heuristics to be incorporated into various models, services and tools. A pragmatic decision was made to only provide support for the Java programming language in Sourcerer to be able to meet these requirements without being overburdened with the complexity of analyzing and supporting all possible programming languages.

Next, we briefly introduce the three code search applications and look at the infrastructure requirements they brought in.

8.2.1 Sourcerer Code Search Engine

Sourcerer Code Search Engine (SCSE) is a web-based code search engine to find code entities in open source projects. SCSE provides a central user interface, code specific search operators (e.g. limiting search on comments or code portions), and employs a ranking scheme that leverages underlying structure and relations in code. As a code search engine, SCSE aggregates and presents meta-data related to code entities in the search results. This meta-data includes the origin information about the code (i.e. the name and location of the open source project where the code came from), license information, version, and category of the project. SCSE also allows viewing and browsing source code, following usage relations, and provide detail information on code structure (threading properties, Java attributes, and micropatterns [11]).[1] With these features SCSE allowed a central access to search thousands of open source projects. Implementation of SCSE itself required development and integration of several core infrastructure pieces of Sourcerer. Since its development several commercial applications are now available that offer similar features as Sourcerer. Therefore, the infrastructure requirements for SCSE resemble much similarity to the requirements to build a large-scale code search engine.

8.2.2 CodeGenie: A Test-Driven Code Search Application

CodeGenie is a code search application that allows a developer to start from a unit test and search for a working set of code entities (classes) that would implement the desired feature as specified in the unit test. CodeGenie is a plugin for Eclipse IDE that works as a Test-Driven Code Search (TDCS) application. TDCS combines the 'Test-First' principle of Test-Driven Development with code search. CodeGenie allows a developer to start from an existing unit test that specifies a desired functionality to be implemented. After this, CodeGenie can construct a query from the unit tests, execute a search using the query on Sourcerer, and bring back found code entities. A developer can choose any of the found entity, look at its source code, and merge the code in her workspace to get the desired functionality originally being tested in the unit test. While merging the code, CodeGenie uses a special service provided by Sourcerer, called the code slicing service, that computes and extracts

---

[1] This code structure information was originally intended to be used in implementing code similarity techniques based on detailed code structures, but was not developed further as development in Sourcerer proceeded.

a dependency slice (a set of synthesized code entities that makes the found code entity compilable and workable in the workspace). CodeGenie has features external to the infrastructure that eases the selection and merging process, for example an 'unmerge' operation to get rid of previously merged code and select a new entity to be merged in the workspace. CodeGenie relies on Sourcerer for these features to work. For example, CodeGenie provides the merging and unmerging of code entities that came from the dependency slice by using a unique identifier given to the dependency slice by Sourcerer.

8.2.3 Sourcerer API Search

Sourcerer API Search (SAS) helps developers to find code snippets that serve as API usage examples. Developers working with large frameworks and libraries might not know or remember all APIs available to them. SAS attempts to provide an exploratory search interface to help such developers in finding code snippets to learn the names and usage patterns of APIs to perform certain programming tasks.

There are four major features in SAS that make finding code snippets easier. First, a list of code snippets that show sections of code with auto-generated comments highlighting the APIs that are used (showing their fully qualified names) and their patterns of usage (by showing relations such as calls, instantiations etc.). Second, a list of code entities that constitute the most popular APIs in a given search result; these APIs can be used as filters to narrow down search results. Third, a set of words as tag-cloud with every result set, where the words can be used for query reformulation. These words are picked by analyzing the names of the code entities found, names of the popular APIs used, and names of code entities that are similar to the entities in the result in terms of API usage. Fourth, a *more like this* feature to find similar code entities based on API usage. This allows users to get recommendation on entities that exhibit similar API usage patterns which is helpful to find more examples once a candidate example (or code entity) is found.

Structural Semantic Indexing (SSI): SAS uses an index with a set of relevant terms mapped to each code entity found in a code collection. These terms are extracted from various places: the source for the entity itself, the source for the APIs that the entity uses, and the source for the code entities that have similar API usage as the code entity. With terms coming from various places the index is able to match queries with relevant code entities (for API examples) even if the source for the entity does not contain all of the terms in the query. The indexing technique used for this is called Structural Semantic Indexing (SSI), and was enabled using various pieces of the Sourcerer infrastructure.

8.2.4 *Infrastructure Requirements*

SCSE, being the first and the most general application has the basic requirements. CodeGenie and SAS have some common requirements as SCSE, along with some new ones of their own. The overall infrastructure requirements to build the three different code search applications emerge out as follows:

Common Requirements:

- Crawling open source forges, extracting project metadata; downloading and checking out source code from open source forges and associating project metadata with the checked out code
- Language aware parsing of source code to extract structural information (entities and relations)
- Indexing source code entities to make them searchable
- Ability to store and retrieve source code for code entities

SCSE:

- Compute rank using structural and lexical information

CodeGenie:

- Code search service that could accept a structured code query, where the query expresses matches on various parts of the code such as class name, method signature, return types, and method arity (number of arguments)
- Search results at the granularity of code entities such as classes and methods so that the IDE can show types and method signatures in the result pane
- A special code slicing service that could construct a set of synthesized code entities that makes the retrieved code entity declaratively complete (i.e., all dependencies must be resolved)

SAS:

- Data sources to produce an index using SSI
- For a given set of code entities in search result, ability to get a list of most popular APIs that are used by the code entities
- For a given code entity, ability to get a list of other code entities that have similar API usage
- For a given code entity, and a set of APIs, ability to provide details on where and how the APIs are used

8.3 Infrastructure Architecture

Sourcerer provides the requirements posed by three code search applications through a collection of *services*. These services provide programmatic access to the underlying data (*stored contents*) that Sourcerer produces and stores. The format and schema of the data is defined by a set of *models* that are developed considering various needs for storage and retrieval needed for the services. Sourcerer also consists a set of standalone *tools* that collect, analyze, produce, and persist the needed contents. Figure 8.1 depicts how services, stored contents, Models, Tools, and (Code Search) Applications constitute Sourcerer's overall architecture.

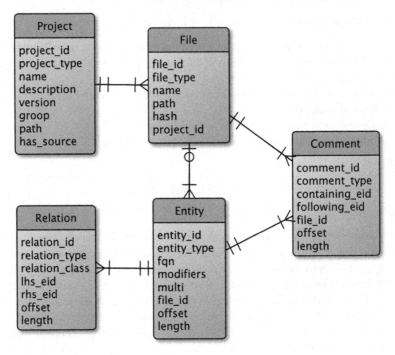

Fig. 8.2 Sourcerer's relational model

8.4 Models

Three models define the basic mechanisms for storing and retrieving information from the source code available in Sourcerer's repository.

8.4.1 Storage Model

The Storage Model defines the structure and physical layout of files in Sourcerer's local repository. A layered directory structure was chosen for two main reasons.

First, it allows projects from the same source to be grouped together, which makes adding or removing contents more straightforward. Second, some sort of branching turned out to be required, not to overburden the file system with tens of thousands of subdirectories in a single directory. The files collected from open source projects are stored in a folder according to the following template:

```
<repo_root>/<batch>/<id>
```

Above, `<repo_root>` is a folder assigned as the root of Sourcerer's file repository. Given the root folder, the individual project files are stored in a two-level directory structure defined by the path fragment `<batch>/<id>`. `<batch>` is a top-level folder in the directory structure that indicates a given batch. For example, a crawl from a specific online repository or a collection of fixed number of projects can denote a batch. Inside `<batch>`, another set of folders exists. Each second-level folder in the local repository, indicated by `<id>` in the above template, contains the contents of a specific project. Each `<id>` directory contains a single file and two sub-directories, as shown below:

```
<repo_root>/<batch>/<id>/project.properties
<repo_root>/<batch>/<id>/download/
<repo_root>/<batch>/<id>/content/
```

Above, `project.properties` is a text file that stores the project metadata as a list of name value pairs. `download` is a folder that contains the compressed file packages that were fetched from the originating repository (e.g., a project's distribution in Sourceforge). `content` contains the expanded contents of the `download` directory. Once the contents of the download directory have been expanded, the directory itself is usually emptied in order to free up space.

The project contents in the `content` directory can take two different forms, depending on its format in the initial repository. If the project contents are checked out from a remote software configuration management (SCM) system such as svn and cvs, the file located at a relative path `path` in the originating repository (e.g., Sourceforge) exists in Sourcerer's file repository at the following absolute path:

```
<repo_root>/<batch>/<id>/content/<path>
```

Instead, if the project is fetched from a package distribution, a source file can be found in Sourcerer's file repository at the following absolute path:

```
<repo_root>/<batch>/<id>/content/package.<i>/<path>
```

Above, `package.<i>` indicates a unique folder for each ith package that is found in a remote repository. `path` indicates a relative path of a source code file that is found inside the ith archived package, which is unarchived inside the `package.<i>` folder.

Project metadata: The `project.properties` file is a generic project description format that generalizes the project metadata from the online repositories. Many attributes in `project.properties` are optional, except for the following:

- `crawledDate`: indicates when the crawler picked up the project information
- `originRepositoryUrl`: URL of the originating repository; e.g., http://sourceforge.net
- `name`: project's name as given in the originating repository
- `containerUrl` : project's unique URL in the originating repository

And, one or both of the following: (i) Information on project's SCM system indicated by `scmUrl` (ii) Information on project's source package distributed on the originating repository, as indicated by the following fields:

- `package.size` indicating total number of packages distributed.
- `package.name.i` indicating name of the ith package, where $1 <= i <= package.size$, and i indicates a unique integer denoting a package number.
- `package.sourceUrl.i` indicating the URL to get the ith package from the originating repository.

The example below shows metadata description for a project crawled from Google code hosting.

```
00 #Thu Sep 24 16:15:01 PDT 2009
01 releaseDate=null
02 name=dlctarea1
03 category=DLC, Java, Netbeans, FileChooser
04 languageGuessed=Java
05 versionGuessed=$SCM
06 scmUrl=svn checkout
      http\://dlctarea1.googlecode.com/svn/trunk/
        dlctarea1-read-only
07 license=GNU General Public License v2
08 keywords=null
09 sourceUrl=null
10 exractedVersion=$SCM
11 projectDescription=Tarea n\uFFFD 1
12 fileExtensions=null
13 originRepositoryUrl=http\://code.google.com
14 containerUrl=http\://code.google.com/p/dlctarea1/
15 contentDescription=null
16 crawledDate=2009-Sep-23
```

Jar Storage: In addition to the top-level `batch` directories described above, the local repository also contains a single `jars` directory. The jars directory is structured as follows:

```
<repo_root>/jars/project/<jar_path>
<repo_root>/jars/maven/<jar_path>
<repo_root>/jars/index.txt
```

The `project` subdirectory contains all of the jar files that come packaged with the projects in the main repository. This directory is populated by crawling through the repository itself, and copying every jar found. The copying is done so that these jar files can be modified, if necessary, without altering the original projects.

The maven subdirectory contains a mirror of the Maven2 central repository[2] [43]. Lastly, index.txt contains an index that maps from the MD5 hash of a jar file to its location in the directory structure. This index is used to link the jar files from the projects to the files contained in the jars directory.

> Sourcerer's project metadata format enables capturing description of projects and contents across various online repositories.

The Storage Model provides a standard for storing project files in Sourcerer and is not directly used by applications. Applications rely on other higher-level abstractions to access the contents stored in Sourcerer.

8.4.2 Relational Model

Sourcerer's relational model defines the basic source code elements and the relations between those elements. It supports a fine-grained representation of the structural information extracted from source code. It also links the code elements/relations with their locations in physical artifacts.

Two major goals guided the design of Sourcerer's relational model. First, it had to be sufficiently expressive to allow fine-grained structure-based analyses and search over code structure. Second, it had to be efficient and scalable enough to include the large amount of code from thousands of open source projects. To meet these two goals we decided to use an adapted version of Chen et al.'s [7] C++ entity-relationship-based metamodel as Sourcerer's relational model for source code. In particular, their decision to focus on what they termed a *top-level declaration* granularity provides a good compromise between the excessive size of finer granularities and the analysis limitations of coarser ones.

The relational model consists of the following five elements: Project, File, Entity, Comment, and Relation.

A **Project** model element exists for every project contained in Sourcerer's repository, as well as every unique Jar file. A project therefore contains either a collection of Java source files and jar files, or a collection of class files. A **File** model element represents these three types of files: source (.java), jar (.jar) or class (.class). Both source and class files are linked to sets of **Entities** contained within them, and to the **Relations** that have these entities as their source and target. Jar files, on the other hand, are linked to their corresponding jar projects, which in turn contains all of the **Entities** and **Relations**.

---

[2] Maven is a build system for Java that provides the facility to fetch required libraries from a central repository [42].

An **Entity** model element either corresponds to an explicit declaration in the source code (e.g., Class, Interface, Method), a Java package,[3] or Java types that are used but do not correspond to a known explicitly declared type (e.g., Array, Type Variable). An entity type is UNKNOWN when the type cannot be determined due to uncertainty in the analysis. Table 8.1 lists all entity model element types defined in Sourcerer. These types adhere to their standard meaning in Java, as defined in the Java Language Specification (JLS) [12].

A **Relation** model element represents a dependency between two Entities. A dependency d originating from a source entity s to a target entity t is stored as a Relation r from s to t. Table 8.2 contains a complete list of the relation types with a brief description and example for each. All of the relations are binary, linking a source entity to a target. The source entity for a relation is smallest entity that contains the code that triggers that relation. While containment is clear for most of the entities, it should be noted that FIELDS are considered to contain their initializer code and ENUM CONSTANTS are considered to call their constructors. The source entity is always found within the project being examined. This is not necessarily true of the target entity. It can be a reference to the Java Standard Library or any other external jar. In fact, due to missing dependencies, sometimes it is impossible to resolve the type of the target entity.

PACKAGE
CLASS
INTERFACE
ENUM
ANNOTATION
INITIALIZER
FIELD
ENUM CONSTANT
CONSTRUCTOR
METHOD
ANNOTATION ELEMENT
PARAMETER
LOCAL VARIABLE
PRIMITIVE
ARRAY
TYPE VARIABLE
WILDCARD
PARAMETRIZED TYPE
UNKNOWN

Table 8.1: Entity types

A **Comment** model element represents the comments defined in the Java source code.

---

[3] Packages are not considered to be standard declared entities as they do not have a single declaration.

Figure 8.2 shows Sourcerer's relational model using an ER-diagram. It shows the five elements of Sourcerer's relational model and a set of attributes for each of them. Table 8.3 provides the details on all the attributes of the model elements. Figure 8.2 and Table 8.3 provide information on how the model elements are linked with each other, and how the attributes in the relational model link the relational model elements with the storage model. For example, Project element's 'path' attribute links it to the physical location defined by the storage model.

Various tools in Sourcerer make use of this information to connect the relational information with the textual contents stored in the physical files.

Entities and *Relations* are the key elements of the Sourcerer's relational model that enables code specific search capabilities. Capturing and associating fully qualified names for code entities allows referring and looking up code entities across projects using the FQNs as keys. Therefore, FQNs for entities enables analysis of relations across projects. This led to innovative use of structural information in code search applications such as: (i) computing CodeRank (adaptation of Google's Pagerank algorithm on code graph) and using it as a ranking heuristic in SCSE, (ii) and using feature vectors made up of FQNs of used entities as a basis to compute usage similarity for entities in SSI.

8.4.3 Index Model

The **Index Model** complements Sourcerer's relational model by facilitating application of information retrieval techniques on the code entities. The index model specifies a **Document** representation for each code Entity in the relational model. A document in the index model is made up of a collection of **Fields**. Each field has a name and different types of values associated with them, the most fundamental being a collection of **Term**s. A term is a basic unit for search/retrieval. Terms are extracted from various parts of an entity, and stored in a corresponding field of a document representing a code entity.

Sourcerer's information retrieval component is based on the popular Lucene [41] information retrieval engine. Therefore, its index model confirms to how Lucene models its contents. More details on Lucene's contents model are available in [25].

Fields in Sourcerer's index models can be categorized into five types:

1. Fields for *basic retrieval* that store terms coming from various parts of a code entity.
2. Fields for *retrieval with signatures* that store terms coming from method signatures and also terms that indicate number of arguments a method has.
3. Fields storing *metadata*, for example the type of the entity, so that a search could be limited to one or more types of entities.

Relation	Description	Example
INSIDE	Physical containment	`java.lang.String INSIDE java.lang`
EXTENDS	Class extension	`java.util.LinkedList EXTENDS` `java.util.AbstractSequentialList`
IMPLEMENTS	Interface implementation	`java.util.LinkedList IMPLEMENTS` `java.util.List`
	Interface extension	`java.util.List IMPLEMENTS` `java.util.Collection`
HOLDS	Field type	`java.lang.String.offset HOLDS int`
RETURNS	Method return type	`java.lang.String.toCharArray()` `RETURNS char[]`
READS	Field read	`...String.<init>(java.lang.String)` `READS java.lang.String.offset`
WRITES	Field write	`java.lang.String.<init>() WRITES` `java.lang.String.offset`
CALLS	Method invocation	`...String.indexOf(int) CALLS` `java.lang.String.indexOf(int,int)`
INSTANTIATES	Constructor invocation	`foo() INSTANTIATES` `java.lang.String.<init>`
THROWS	Declared checked exception	`java.io.Writer.write(int) THROWS` `java.io.IOException`

CASTS	A cast expression	`java.langString.equals(`
		`java.lang.Object) CASTS`
		`java.lang.String`

CHECKS	An instance of expression	`java.langString.equals(`
		`java.lang.Object) CHECKS`
		`java.lang.String`

ANNOTATED BY	Annotation	`java.lang.Override ANNOTATED BY` `java.lang.annotation.Target`
USES	Any reference	`java.lang.String.<init>() USES` `char`
HAS ELEMENTS OF	Array element type	`char[] HAS ELEMENTS OF char`
PARAMETRIZED BY	Associated type variables	`java.util.List PARAMETRIZED BY <E>`
HAS BASE TYPE	Generic base type	`java.util.List<java.lang.String>` `HAS BASE TYPE java.util.List`
HAS TYPE ARGUMENT	Generic type argument	`java.util.List<java.lang.String>` `HAS TYPE ARGUMENT java.lang.String`
HAS UPPER BOUND	? extends	`<? extends java.util.List> HAS` `UPPER BOUND java.util.List`
HAS LOWER BOUND	? super	`<? super java.util.List> HAS LOWER` `BOUND java.util.List`

Table 8.2: Relation types

	Description
Project	
project_id	Unique identifier for a project
project_type	Denotes whether this project represents a crawled project, or a Jar file
name	Name of the project as it appears in the originating Internet repository
description	Description of the project from the originating Internet repository
version	Version of this project as extracted from originating Internet repository
groop	Specific field applicable to Maven Jars
path	Corresponds to the `<batch>/<id>` path fragment as defined by the storage model
has_source	Denotes whether the project contains source files
File	
file_id	Unique identifier for a file
file_type	Denotes the file's type – source, Jar, class
name	Name of the file in the file system
path	Corresponds to either `<batch>/<id>/content/<path>`, or `jars/<jar_path>` as defined by the storage model
hash	Unique MD5 hash, applicable for Jars only
project_id	project_id that this file belongs to
Entity	
entity_id	Unique identifier for an Entity
entity_type	One of the several code entity types. (e.g., CLASS, METHOD)
fqn	Fully qualified name (FQN) of the entity
modifiers	Modifiers defined for the code entity
multi	Denotes array dimension, applicable for ARRAY types only
file_id	file_id that this entity is extracted from
offset	Start position of this entity in the source file
length	Length of this entity in the text (source file)
Relation	
relation_id	Unique identifier for a relation
relation_type	One of the several code relation types. (e.g., CALLS, EXTENDS)
relation_class	Denotes whether the relation terminates to a library or a local entity
lhs_eid	The source entity that the relation originates from
rhs_eid	The target entity that the relation terminates into
offset	Start position in the source entity's corresponding file where this relation exists
length	Length of the text in source code where this relation spans
Comment	
comment_id	Unique identifier for a comment
comment_type	Denotes the comment's type – Javadoc, Block, Line
containing_eid	The immediate code entity that contains this comment
following_eid	The immediate code entity that follows this comment
file_id	File where this comment is found
offset	Start position of comment in the source file
length	Length of this comment in text (source file)

Table 8.3: Sourcerer's relational model elements details

4. Fields that store information to facilitate *retrieval based on structural similarity* (e.g., fields storing fully qualified names (FQNs) of used entities and terms extracted from similar entities).
5. Fields that pertain to some *metric* computed on an entity.
6. Fields that store unique identifiers (ids) of entities for *navigational/browsing queries*

Being based on Lucene, Sourcerer's index model is quite flexible. Depending on a specific search application, an instance of a Sourcerer's index schema can have a subset of various field types listed above. The three code search applications built on top of Sourcerer have used code index schemas with different configurations of fields and associated data sources.

> Fields for retrieval with signatures allowed precise construction of queries for expressing desired method signatures and relations expected in test cases in CodeGenie. Fields storing retrieval based on structural similarity enabled retrieval schemes in SSI, and *more like this* queries based on usage in SAS. Rest of the index fields supported basic operations of the code search applications as in SCSE.

8.4.3.1 Structured Retrieval

Table 8.4 presents a subset of the fields available in the Sourcerer index. Sourcerer's search index can be searched using Lucene's query language [25, 41]. The following Lucene query demonstrates how different fields are utilized to express a query that incorporates textual as well as structural information:

```
short_name: (day of week)
  AND entity_type: METHOD
  AND m_ret_type_sname_contents: String
  AND m_args_fqn_contents: date
  AND cdef: (date util)
```

Index field	Description
Fields for basic retrieval	
fqn_contents	Tokenized terms from the FQN of an entity
short_name	Right most fragment of the FQN (w/o method arguments for methods)
Fields for retrieval with signatures	
m_args_fqn_contents	Method's formal arguments tokenized into terms
m_ret_type_sname_contents	Short name of the method's return type tokenized into terms
Fields Storing metadata	
entity_type	String representation of entity type. (e.g., "CLASS")
Fields for navigation	
fan_in_mcall_local	Entity ids of all local callers for a method from the same project

Table 8.4: Sample search index fields

The above query has the following meaning: find a method with terms `day`, `of` and `date` in its short name (or simple name in JLS [12]), that returns a type with short name `String`, and takes in any number of arguments with term `date` as part of its argument in their FQNs. This is an example of a query that CodeGenie would construct for a unit test that would have an assertion that looks like:

```
Date date = ...
Assert.assertTrue(''Tuesday'',DateUtil.dayOfWeek(date));
```

With an index structure that has fields resembling various structural elements in code, Sourcerer provides a code-specific index model.

8.4.3.2 Code-Specific Retrieval Schemes

Sourcerer's index model enables implementation of retrieval schemes for a variety of code search applications.

> A *retrieval scheme* tuned for code search takes a query and returns relevant code entities using a combination of code specific heuristics. A *heuristic* is an idea to associate meaningful terms to code entities.

Consider a source code document in Java as shown in the top right part in Fig. 8.3. If we focus on the method entity (`createResource`) shown inside the code document, there can be multiple ways to associate meaningful terms to that entity. On the top-left part in Fig. 8.3, several metadata related to the method `createResource` are shown. For example 'FQN' indicating the fully qualified name of the method entity, 'Used FQNs' listing the FQNs of the APIs that the code entity uses, and 'Similar Entity' indicating another method entity `makeIcon` that uses the same two APIs as `createResource` uses.

Lower part of Fig. 8.3 shows how we can define several heuristics that would associate different meaningful terms with the method entity `createResource`.

The first heuristic 'Code as Text' treats source code entities as normal text document. Based on some code specific parsing (such as removing symbols and splitting on camel case) 'Code as Text' will associate the following terms with the method entity `createResource`: create, resource, file, open.

While writing code developers often express their design in some hierarchic fashion; for example the method `createResource` is defined inside the class entity `creatResource` that is further defined inside the package `util`. Programming languages allow expressing such information about hierarchic containment in a naming scheme resulting in fully qualified names (FQNs) for entities. For example, in Java, the FQN of the method `createResource` is given as follows: `util.ResourceManager.createResource()`. The second heuristic 'focus on names' assumes FQNs express structure and design of code entities, and associate terms extracted from FQNs with code entities.

The third heuristic 'Specificity' says that the simple name of the method carries more specific information about a code entity, and therefore terms extracted from simple name should have some higher priority compared to others. This is represented as a boost value (shown as BV in Fig. 8.3) for list of terms associated with 'Specificity' heuristics.

> The ability to prioritize the heuristics differently allows experimentation and choosing the most effective retrieval performance.

The fourth heuristic 'Usage' says that the FQNs of the used entities also carry some important information about the functionality of the code entity, as it is by using these FQNs the entity is implementing some feature in the code. Therefore this heuristic extracts terms from the FQNs of the used entities.

Finally, 'Usage Similarity' says that, terms found in code entities that have similar API usage patterns can be used to describe each other. For example, as shown in Fig. 8.3 both methods createResource and makeIcon are implementing same behavior by using same APIs. This suggests that, to some extent, terms extracted from makeIcon can be used to describe the functionality implemented in createResource.

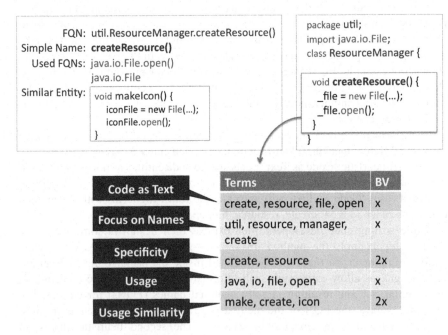

Fig. 8.3 Heuristics for code retrieval

Sourcerer's index model allows incorporating these code specific heuristics by leveraging the semi-structured document model of Lucene. For each of the heuristics the index model introduces a field that would store terms extracted based on the heuristic. Each field is given an appropriate boosting value so that some heuristics could be given higher priority (depending on the code search application). With such an index model, a retrieval scheme for a code search application simply specifies which fields to choose to match the user query. A different strategy to retrieve code entities can be implemented by varying these schemes. For example, the top right corner of Fig. 8.4 shows the code snippet for the method entity createResource (previously shown in Fig. 8.3). The bottom part of Fig. 8.4 shows an index document with five different fields capturing five different heuristics respectively. The top left part of Fig. 8.4 shows in a tabular form, how two schemes would match the same query create icon to the index document (and thus the method entity) differently. **Scheme 1** uses only three heuristics, compared to **Scheme 2** that uses all five.

Scheme 1 looks over a limited set of terms associated with the method entity createResource. This set only includes one of the terms create present in the query create icon. **Scheme 2** includes two more fields that makes it look over a richer set of terms that includes both of the terms found in the query. Assuming that all terms in query need to be matched for a document to be retrieved, **Scheme 2** outperforms **Scheme 1** because **Scheme 2** uses additional heuristics to harvest more meaningful words describing code entities.

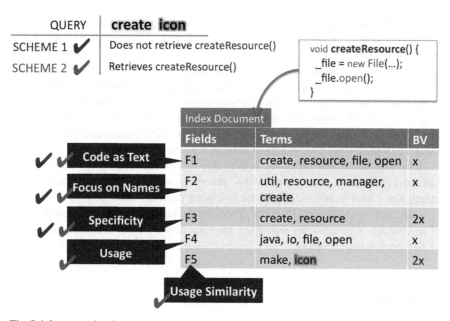

Fig. 8.4 Incorporating heuristics in index model

Vocabulary problem is a fundamental problem in information retrieval. It arises from the fact that humans have different vocabulary to describe similar concepts. Consequently, terms used in a query might not be present in all relevant documents. This can severely hinder retrieval because not all users would know the right terms to use to retrieve a relevant document. Sourcerer provides a solution to harvest more meaningful words for code entities by incorporating code-specific heuristics in the index model. This enables developing retrieval schemes that allows code entities to be matched with relevant query terms even when the terms themselves are not originally present in the code entity. This contributes a unique solution to tackle the vocabulary problem in code search.

For an elaborate description of vocabulary problem, see [8]. SAS used **Scheme 2** retrieval scheme shown in Fig. 8.4 and used all five heuristics shown in Fig. 8.3.

8.5 Stored Contents

The Sourcerer infrastructure maintains a collection of stored contents corresponding to each of the three models.

A **File Repository** keeps a collection of files downloaded and fetched from open source repositories in the Internet. The structure of the file repository follows the storage model.

Two different databases store the relational information about the contents in the file repository. First, **ArtifactDB** stores limited information about the jar files found in the repository in order to enable the automated resolution of missing dependencies [28]. Second, **SourcererDB** stores the relational information on all projects, files and code entities that exist in the file repository. Both databases exist as MySql databases whose schemas confirm to Sourcerer's relational model.

A Lucene-based **Search Index** is available that stores information about terms extracted from each code entity in the corresponding documents and fields. The search index uses a code index schema following the index model.

Sourcerer's web site [34] provides details on the most recent statistics on the size of its contents. Currently, its repository contains above 3 million source files from 18,826 open source projects.

8.6 Services

All the artifacts managed and stored in Sourcerer are accessible through a set of Web services. These services provide a layer of abstraction and programmatic access to rapidly build applications that can leverage the underlying contents stored in Sourcerer.

Relational Query: Both ArtifactDB and SourcererDB are implemented as MySql databases. They provide direct access to query the underlying structural/relational information in Sourcerer using standard SQL. Relational Query is the basis for rich structural queries over code. Dependency slicing, code rank, and usage similarity all relied on SQL queries. As another use-case of using relational information, given below are some details on snippet extraction (taken from [3]) implemented for SAS.

Snippet Extraction in SAS: The retrieval scheme for SAS takes a keyword query and returns a ranked list of code entities as search result. This ranked list of entities is called hits and each entry in the list is called a hit. The retrieval scheme also returns the total number of entities in the index that match the query. For each hit the corresponding 'entity_id' (a unique identifier for a code entity) is available. Further details about the code entity can be queried from SourcererDB using the 'entity_id'. SAS uses the information returned by its retrieval scheme to extract a corresponding code snippet for each hit (entity) in the list.

```
input  : hits = top 'n' hits returned as search results; where, n = max_of(10,
             10% of total hits)
output: top_used = list of top used entities
1 begin
2 |   list_eid = all entity ids from hits;
      /* getTopApis(..) selects top 5 non-JSL (Java Standard Library) entities of
         each type (Interface, Method, Constructor, Classes) from SourcererDB
         such that they are used by at least 3 entities in the hits          */
3 |   top_used = getTopApis(list_eid);
4 end
```

Algorithm 1: Getting the list of top used entities

Snippet extraction proceeds in two steps. First, given a set of hits, a list of top APIs (used entities) is generated. This process is shown in Algorithm 1. As an input Algorithm 1 takes a list of top 'n' hits where, 'n' is the greater of 10 or 10 % of the total number of hits. These 'n' hits give 'n' unique entity ids (Line 2). To find the list of top used entities, the search application queries SourcererDB for the top non-JSL entities that are used by the entities in the list (Line 3). For each entity the top five Interfaces, Methods, Constructors, and Classes are selected. Among all these used entities in the list, only those entities that are used by at least three different entities are returned as the top used entities (output of the algorithm).

```
    input  : eid = entity id, top_used = top used entities
    output: snip = an annotated code snippet
 1  begin
 2  |   snip = empty string;
    |   /* getUsedPositions(..) looks up SourcererDB and returns all positions in
    |      the code where top_used entities are used. Positions are mapped to a list
    |      of used entities                                                        */
 3  |   used_pos_map = getUsedPositions(top_used, eid);
 4  |   forall the position IN used_pos_map do
 5  |   |   rationale = empty string;
 6  |   |   forall the used_entity IN used_pos_map[position] do
    |   |   |   /* Below, append(a,b) returns a new string by appending string 'b'
    |   |   |      to 'a'.createRationale(..) selects relation type and FQN of used
    |   |   |      entity and creates a rationale as a comment                      */
 7  |   |   |   rationale = append(rationale, createRationale(used_entity, eid));
 8  |   |   end
    |   |   /* extractFragment(..) extracts the surrounding expression in a code
    |   |      entity from position                                                */
 9  |   |   snip_fragment = extractFragment(eid, position);
    |   |   /* appendSnip(..) works same as append(..) and returns true if
    |   |      rationale and snip_fragment do not already exist in snip             */
10  |   |   if appendSnip(rationale, snip_fragment) ∉ snip then
11  |   |   |   snip = appendSnip(snip, rationale);
12  |   |   |   snip = appendSnip(snip, snip_fragment);
13  |   |   end
14  |   end
15  end
```
Algorithm 2: Snippet extraction

The second step involves generating code snippet for each entity in the hits. This is done using the list of top used entities and the 'entity_id' of a given hit. The algorithm for this process is shown in Algorithm 2. The procedure first queries SourcererDB to locate all the positions in the source of an entity where any of the top APIs are used (Line 3). For all APIs that are used in a position, a rationale comment is generated (Lines 5–8). A rationale comment indicates the type and FQN of the used API. Then, a few of the surrounding lines of code are extracted from each starting position (Line 9). Rationale comments are inserted on top of these extracted lines (Lines 10–13). Finally, a sequence of these commented code fragments is returned as an example code snippet. A sample Java code snippet generated using a hit returned for a query "write to workbench error log" is shown in Fig. 8.5.

In Fig. 8.5, Lines 5 and 14 are two positions in the code where some top APIs were found to be used. Lines 1–4 show rationale comments for two APIs (IStatus

```
1 // USES org.eclipse.core.runtime.IStatus
2 // INSTANTIATES org.eclipse.core.runtime.Status
3 //      .<init> (int, java.lang.String, int, java.lang.String,
4 //                java.lang.Throwable)
5 } catch (BackingStoreException e) {
6     IStatus status = new Status(IStatus.ERROR,
7         UIPlugin.getDefault().getBundle().getSymbolicName(),
8         IStatus.ERROR,
9         e.getLocalizedMessage(),
10        e);
11
12 // CALLS org.eclipse.core.runtime.ILog.log(org.eclipse.core.runtime.IStatus)
13 // CALLS org.eclipse.core.runtime.Plugin.getLog()
14 UIPlugin.getDefault().getLog().log(status);
```

Fig. 8.5 Annotated API usage example for the task of programmatically writing to eclipse workbench's log

and the constructor for class status) that are used in Lines 6–10. Similarly, Lines 12 and 13 show rationale comments for two APIs that are used in Line 14.

Repository Access: This service provides access to the textual contents of three of Sourcerer's relational model elements: File, Entity, and Comment. Repository access is a simple HTTP-based Web service that returns the full text for one of the three relational model elements given their unique ids as parameters.

Dependency Slicing: This service provides dependency slices of the code entities in SourcererDB. A dependency slice of an entity is a program (collection of Java source files) that includes the entity as well as all the entities upon which it depends. Requested slices are packaged into zip files, and should be immediately compilable. The dependency slicing service can take in one or more entity ids and return a zip file containing the collection of sliced/synthesized Java files that the given set of entities depend on. The chapter by Ossher and Lopes in this volume provides an in-depth discussion of dependency slicing.

Code Search: This service implements a query processing and a code retrieval facility. Code search applications (such as CodeGenie [16, 17, 18, 19] and Sourcerer API Search) can send queries as a combination of terms and fields and the service returns a result set with detailed information on the entities that matched the queries. The query language is based on Lucene's implementation using which clients can express structural information in the queries. The matching and scoring (ranking) of entities follow Lucene's implementation. Details on how Lucene matches the query terms in index fields and score the matched entities are given in [37]. In summary, a boolean retrieval is performed based on a Lucene query as described earlier in Sect. 8.4.3, then all matched entities (documents) are ranked using the TF-IDF measure [23].

Similarity Calculation: The Similarity Calculation service takes in an entity_id of an entity 'e' and returns a list of other entities that are similar to 'e'. Currently, the

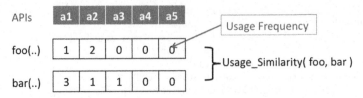

* Similarity increases as number of shared APIs increase
* Similarity decreases as numner of shared APIs decrease

Fig. 8.6 Usage similarity computation based on feature vectors

similarity calculator can suggest similar entities based on three different measures
of usage similarity. For this purpose, the similarity calculator uses the usage information stored in SourcererDB. The similarity calculation service works based on a
feature vector representation of code entities. As shown in Fig. 8.6 for each code
entity such as the methods foo(..) and bar(..) a vector representation of used
APIs are stored, where each entry in the vector indicates usage frequency (could be
binary for certain similarity measures). For example, Fig. 8.6 shows that foo(..)
uses API a1 once and API a2 twice. Given a measure of similarity based on feature vector (for example Cosine Distance [23]), the similarity measure between two
code entities foo(..) and bar(..) can be computed (Usage_Similarity(foo(..),
bar(..))). With this collection of feature vectors, for each entity a given set of top
similar entities based on API usage can be computed by choosing an appropriate
similarity function that works on feature vectors. The Structural Semantic Indexing
(SSI) technique makes use of the similarity calculation service and uses three different measures of similarity. Further details on similarity calculation is available
in [3] and [6].

Except the Relational Query service, all other services are HTTP-based services.
Currently three services are open to the public. A detailed description of how to use
these services is available online [35].

8.7 Tools

A number of loosely coupled tools are available in the Sourcerer infrastructure.
These tools are primarily responsible for collecting/analyzing source code and producing the stored contents.

Code Crawler: Sourcerer consists of a multithreaded plugin-based code crawler
that can crawl the Web pages in online source code repositories. One of the challenges in designing the Code Crawler was to adapt with the changes and differences with Web pages in different Internet repositories. To address this challenge,
the crawler follows a plugin-based design. A separate plugin can be written target-
ing the crawl of a repository. This makes it possible to just update the plugin (or add

new plugins) when a different (or new) Web site has to be crawled. Currently the crawler consists of plugins for Sourceforge [44], Java.net [40], Tigris [45], Google Code Hosting [39], and Apache [38]. The crawler takes a set of root URLs as an input and produces a list of download URLs and version control links along with other project specific metadata. This project specific metadata is in the form as specified by (the `project.properties` file in) the storage model. Since Sourcerer only supports Java source files, the crawler uses heuristics to detect the presence of Java source files in a repository's Web page. These heuristics are common patterns specific to each repository. For example, a tag named 'Java' in a project from Google Code Hosting, and the presence of keywords such as 'java', 'eclipse', 'ant', etc. in a project from Java.net are used as indicators that a project has source code written in Java. These projects are candidates to be picked for further processing.

Repository Creator: The repository creator tool is responsible for parsing the code crawler's output list, filtering noise from the list (e.g., removing duplicate links), and downloading the contents from the online repositories to Sourcerer's local file repository. Given a local file repository's root folder, the repository creator creates the required folder structure and places the contents as specified by Sourcerer's storage model. The repository creator first creates the two level folder structure based on the number of projects it needs to add to the repository. Second, it creates the `project.properties` file describing each project. Third, it fetches the files from remote/original repositories. `project.properties` has metadata about two contents sources in remote repositories: (i) SCM systems such as svn and cvs, and (ii) downloadable packages such as compressed distributions (zips, tars, etc.). When information on a SCM repository is available, the repository creator first tries to check out contents from the respective SCM system. If errors are encountered, or if the SCM check out brings no contents, then the repository creator downloads all the packages, given that the information on links to the packages exist in `project.properties`. After the download, the repository creator explodes the archives inside the `content` folder corresponding to the project. The end result of this process is a local Sourcerer file repository, based on the storage model, which contains contents fetched from remote open source repositories.

Repository Manager: The repository manager tool is responsible for two tasks: (i) library management, and (ii) optimizing the local repository for feature extraction. Under library management, the repository manager creates and maintains a local mirror of all jar files from the Maven2 central repository. It also aggregates all of the jar files from the individual projects into the jars directory. It then creates an index of all the unique jar files in the repository. These jars can be used to provide missing types to projects in Sourcerer's file repository during feature extraction if needed. Under optimizing the local repository, the repository manager performs tasks such as compressing the contents inside a project's folder, and cleaning the jars' manifest files to avoid problems due to unexpected classpath additions.

Feature Extractor: The feature extractor in Sourcerer is responsible for extracting the detailed structural information from the source code files stored in Sourcerer's file repository. The feature extractor is built as a headless Eclipse plugin, to make use of Eclipse's (Abstract Syntax Tree) AST Parser. Before running the feature extractor, the source code is preprocessed to detect missing libraries using import statements. Some additional heuristics are used to be able to fully resolve the bindings in the source code types and links to the libraries. These heuristics are fully explained in an earlier publication [28]. The repository manager and the feature extractor together implement the required techniques for *Automated Dependency Resolution*, a key feature available in the Sourcerer infrastructure, that enables feature extraction from large number of open source projects despite missing dependencies and errors. In summary, automated dependency resolution works as follows. First, the feature extraction runs through the available projects to detect missing types. It creates the AST representation of code available in the projects and generates a list of missing types reported by the underlying Eclipse parser. From the list of missing types, the feature extractor generates a list of possible FQNs for those types to be found. It then looks up the ArtifactDB for possible jar files where the missing FQNs could be found. While doing so it selects the jar files that can provide the maximum number of missing FQNs. Once the jars are selected, they are included in the classpath of the project with missing types and then the feature extractor runs again. This process is repeated until all missing types are found or if no jars could be located for remaining missing types. After this step, the feature extraction does a full extraction of entities and relations from the projects. Our evaluation of automated dependency resolution has shown that it can increase the percentage of declaratively complete projects in Sourcerer's file repository from 39 to 69 %. Automated dependency resolution is fully explained in [28].

Database Importer: This tool allows importing the Feature Extractor's output into the code databases: ArtifactDB and SourcererDB.

Code Indexer: The code indexer tool is responsible to index all code entities in Sourcerer's file repository using the textual and structural information available for the entities. The code indexer obtains this information using three services, the File Access Service – to obtain the full text corresponding to a code entity, SourcererDB to retrieve entities and comments related to a code entity being indexed, and Similarity Calculation service to retrieve similar entities. As a result of the indexing process, the code indexer produces a semi-structured full text index based on Lucene [41]. To index a code entity, the code indexer can retrieve all or some the following data: the full-text for the corresponding entity, the fully qualified names (FQNs) of related entities, comments of the used libraries, and FQNs of used entities. The search index schema will consist of fields to store the terms corresponding to these data types. The terms are extracted from the FQNs and full text of source code documents using code-specific analysis techniques (e.g., camel case splitting and removing language keywords as stop words). The code indexer tool consists of several of these code-specific analyzers.

Code Ranker: The code ranker tool constructs a graph representation of source code analyzed in Sourcerer. Entities constitute the nodes and relations constitute the edges in the graph. After constructing this graph, code ranker applies Google's Pagerank [15] algorithm on top of this graph to compute the Pagerank (called CodeRank) for each entity which can be used as a measure of popularity of a code entity in the code graph. SCSE used the value of CodeRank as one of the heuristics to rank retrieved results.

8.8 Summary

The combination of models, services, and tools makes Sourcerer a unique infrastructure supporting three different code search applications. Going back to the requirements that were listed (in Sect. 8.2) for the three code search applications, we can summarize how Sourcerer meets these requirements.

SCSE: The storage model, stored contents, and the crawler in Sourcerer allowed collection of source code from large number of open source repositories, and store them locally making available for required further processing. The relational model and the code parser tool allowed fine grained parsing and storing parsed information in a readily available form. Being able to parse source code allowed storing and retrieving source code at the level of finer entities such as classes and methods. Using fully qualified names as keys for entities, and following relations in SourcererDB, SCSE provided a structure-based measure of CodeRank to rank code entities. As discussed in the index model, several code-specific heuristics were supported to build retrieval schemes that were specific to source code.

CodeGenie: The semi-structure index model with fields that supported retrieval using signatures provided basic retrieval for CodeGenie. Information about code entities and relations between them, allowed implementation of dependency slicing – a novel technique to extract and synthesize declaratively complete code snippet collection for CodeGenie.

SAS: Information on entities and usage (relations such as method calls and class extensions) allowed building API usage profiles for each code entities in the form of feature vectors. This served as the basis for usage similarity computation among code entities, allowing to devise novel indexing technique such as SSI using the usage similarity heuristic. Furthermore, full relational information on relations among code entities allowed computing useful API usage statistics that helped implementing useful snippet extraction technique.

The three code search applications were built one after another and Sourcerer evolved as it had to support the requirements for the applications. These requirements can be seen as major challenges that code search infrastructure builders need to address. A major lesson learnt with the implementation of three code search applications was that structural information provides valuable ways to build effective code search applications, and challenges inherent in building such applications can be overcome by harnessing large collection of source code and libraries available over the Web. Two important factors contributed to Sourcerer's success. First, a principle of leveraging structural information in source code to build effective search applications. This principle guided its design and implementation. Second, a loosely coupled architecture that made it possible for selective use of smaller set of elements across applications.

While SCSE, CodeGenie, and SAS represent three state-of-the art research prototypes for code search, Sourcerer does not address needs to develop every code search application that developers would need. For example, Sourcerer does not provide support for information related to evolution and code changes, and therefore does not support search requirements around the problems related to evolution. Also being focused solely on Java as the language of choice, Sourcerer does not provide support to search in other languages. Sourcerer does not do any form of deduplication of source code while maintaining the repository for the three code search applications. These could be some possible future improvements for Sourcerer and next generation code search infrastructures.

Sourcerer's contents as well as its implementation are freely available for others to use. The content is released as a citable dataset [21]. The implementation is available as an open source project in Github [36]. These efforts have enabled external researchers to use Sourcerer's content and services in their research [22, 24, 27, 30, 33].

8.9 Further Reading

Descriptions of earlier versions of Sourcerer are available in [2] and [20]. SCSE was first described in [1]. Code specific heuristics used in SCSE and their formal evaluation is discussed in [20] and [6]. Further details on CodeGenie is available in earlier publications [17, 18]. For details on user experiments and effectiveness evaluation of CodeGenie consult [6]. For detailed discussion on implementation and evaluation of SSI refer to [3]. More details on SAS is given in [4]. A definitive resource on details of the Sourcerer infrastructure, in particular the research contribution it made along with all three code search applications presented earlier (SCSE, CodeGenie, and SAS) is the author's doctoral dissertation [6]. A revised version of Chap. 3 from [6] appears in [5]. The chapter by Ossher and Lopes in this book provides the most recent and detailed discussion on dependency slicing that is one of the core services available in the Sourcerer infrastructure. The Software Engineering research community has produced a large body of work related to code search. A detailed review of some of these closely related to Sourcerer is available in [6] (Chap. 1). Next we summarize some of the work that focused on building code search application on top of a large-scale repository.

Merobase [14] is an infrastructure similar to Sourcerer. Like Sourcerer, Merobase has built a large code repository, a code/component search engine and a Test-Driven Search application using its repository. Merobase offers syntax aware code search, and covers additional languages (C++ and ADA). There is no documented evidence that Merobase includes structural ranking such as Sourcerer Code Search Engine's

CodeRank, or advanced indexing techniques leveraging structural similarity such as Sourcerer's SSI. Its Test-Driven Code Search application, Code Conjurer, provides a feature to do background search not present in CodeGenie (Sourcerer's TDCS application), but lacks automatic dependency slicing that allows declaratively complete program slices to be merged into a developer workspace to create self-complete code fragments satisfying the unit tests. Sourcerer also provides techniques to do deep parsing of declaratively incomplete code found in repositories; this makes Sourcerer resilient and superior in terms of extracting and leveraging structural information from source code collected from the 'wild'. The chapter by Hummel and Janjic in this volume provides an in-depth discussion of CodeConjurer.

Maracatu [9, 10] is another infrastructure built for code search. Similar to Sourcerer, it is limited to searching Java source code. The authors of Maracatu present useful requirements such as index update and optimization, but it is not clear whether Maracatu implements all of such requirements. Sourcerer does not have a proper mechanism to update its index to deal with changes in code repositories. Maracatu also supports faceted search, where the facets are platform, component type and component model. Sourcerer's index model (being based on Lucene) supports faceting out-of-the box on any metadata present in its index. However, the only faceting that has been implemented in an end-user search application is in Sourcerer API Search, where the top API elements can be used as facets to filter the code results.

S6 [29] is another Test-Driven Code Search application, that applies code transformations to convert source code found via code search into workable solutions. Parseweb [31], is another code search application that uses source and destination object types as input query to retrieve code files from existing code search engines. It applies program analysis on retrieved files to extract method sequences that work as code samples to get destination object types from source types. Applications such as S6 and Parseweb can easily benefit from code search infrastructure such as Sourcerer.

Portfolio [26] is a code search application that incorporates structural information in ranking and retrieval. One of its unique feature is to show the call graph of functions involved in the search results. Portfolio provides search access to over 18,000 C/C++ projects and 13,000 Java projects. As reported in its web site, the Java projects used in portfolio come from Sourcerer and Merobase repositories [33].

Although not a code search infrastructure, FLOSSmole [13] is another major undertaking in building large collection of metadata about open source projects on the Web. Currently, FLOSSmole reports a massive data collection of more than 500,000 open source projects in its web site [32]. For code search infrastructure builders, now it is possible to leverage FLOSSmole's project metadata to build code repositories instead of spending an effort in implementing custom spiders and crawlers for code.

Acknowledgements The author would like to thank Joel Ossher, Otavio Lemos, Trung Ngo, Huy Hunh, Paul Rigor, and Erik Linsted for their contributions to the Sourcerer infrastructure. The author would like to thank Cristina Lopes and Pierre Baldi for their advice and support in making Sourcerer successful.

References

[1] Bajracharya, S., Ngo, T., Linstead, E., Dou, Y., Rigor, P., Baldi, P., Lopes, C.: Sourcerer: a search engine for open source code supporting structure-based search. pp. 681–682. ACM Press, New York, NY, USA (2006). DOI http://doi.acm.org/10.1145/1176617.1176671

[2] Bajracharya, S., Ossher, J., Lopes, C.: Sourcerer: An internet-scale software repository. In: Proceedings of the 2009 ICSE Workshop on Search-Driven Development-Users, Infrastructure, Tools and Evaluation, pp. 1–4. IEEE Computer Society (2009)

[3] Bajracharya, S., Ossher, J., Lopes, C.: Leveraging usage similarity for effective retrieval of examples in code repositories. 18th International Symposium on the Foundations of Software Engineering (2010)

[4] Bajracharya, S., Ossher, J., Lopes, C.: Searching API usage examples in code repositories with sourcerer API search. In: Proceedings of 2010 ICSE Workshop on Search-driven Development: Users, Infrastructure, Tools and Evaluation, pp. 5–8. ACM, Cape Town, South Africa (2010). DOI 10.1145/1809175.1809177

[5] Bajracharya, S., Ossher, J., Lopes, C.: Sourcerer: An infrastructure for the large-scale collection and analysis of open-source code. Science of Computer Programming (To Appear) (2012)

[6] Bajracharya, S.K.: Facilitating internet-scale code retrieval. Ph.D. thesis, University of California Irvine (2010)

[7] Chen, Y., Gansner, E.R., Koutsofios, E.: A c++ data model supporting reachability analysis and dead code detection. IEEE Trans. Softw. Eng. 24(9), 682–694 (1998)

[8] Furnas, G.W., Landauer, T.K., Gomez, L.M., Dumais, S.T.: The vocabulary problem in human-system communication. Commun. ACM 30, 964–971 (1987). DOI 10.1145/32206.32212

[9] Garcia, V., de Almeida, E., Lisboa, L., Martins, A., Meira, S., Lucredio, D., de M. Fortes, R.: Toward a code search engine based on the State-of-Art and practice. In: Software Engineering Conference, 2006. APSEC 2006. 13th Asia Pacific, pp. 61–70 (2006)

[10] Garcia, V., Lucrédio, D., Durão, F., Santos, E., de Almeida, E., de Mattos Fortes, R., de Lemos Meira, S.: From Specification to Experimentation: A Software Component Search Engine Architecture. In: I. Gorton, G. Heineman, I. Crnkovic, H. Schmidt, J. Stafford, C. Szyperski, K. Wallnau (eds.) Component-Based Software Engineering, *Lecture Notes in Computer Science*, vol. 4063, pp. 82–97. Springer Berlin / Heidelberg (2006)

[11] Gil, J.Y., Maman, I.: Micro patterns in java code. In: OOPSLA '05: Proceedings of the 20th annual ACM SIGPLAN conference on Object oriented programming systems languages and applications, pp. 97–116. ACM Press, New York, NY, USA (2005). DOI http://doi.acm.org/10.1145/1094811.1094819

[12] Gosling, J., Joy, B., Steele, G., Bracha, G.: Java(TM) Language Specification, The, 3 edn. Addison Wesley (2005)

[13] Howison, J., Conklin, M., Crowston, K.: FLOSSmole: A collaborative repository for FLOSS research data and analyses. International Journal of Information Technology and Web Engineering 1(3), 17–26 (2006)

[14] Hummel, O., Janjic, W., Atkinson, C.: Code conjurer: Pulling reusable software out of thin air. IEEE Softw. 25(5), 45–52 (2008)

[15] Lawrence Page Sergey Brin, R.M., Winograd, T.: The pagerank citation ranking: Bringing order to the web. Stanford Digital Library working paper SIDL-WP-1999-0120 of 11/11/1999 (see: http://dbpubs.stanford.edu/pub/1999-66)

[16] Lemos, O.A.L., Bajracharya, S., Ossher, J., Masiero, P.C., Lopes, C.: Applying test-driven code search to the reuse of auxiliary functionality. In: Proceedings of the 2009 ACM symposium on Applied Computing, pp. 476–482. ACM, Honolulu, Hawaii (2009). DOI 10.1145/1529282.1529384

[17] Lemos, O.A.L., Bajracharya, S.K., Ossher, J.: CodeGenie: a tool for test-driven source code search. In: Companion to the 22nd ACM SIGPLAN conference on Object-oriented programming systems and applications companion, pp. 917–918. ACM, Montreal, Quebec, Canada (2007). DOI 10.1145/1297846. 1297944

[18] Lemos, O.A.L., Bajracharya, S.K., Ossher, J., Masiero, P.C., Lopes, C.V.: A test-driven approach to code search and its application to the reuse of auxiliary functionality. Information and Software Technology (2011)

[19] Lemos, O.A.L., Bajracharya, S.K., Ossher, J., Morla, R.S., Masiero, P.C., Baldi, P., Lopes, C.V.: CodeGenie: using test-cases to search and reuse source code. In: Proceedings of the twenty-second IEEE/ACM international conference on Automated software engineering, pp. 525–526. ACM, Atlanta, Georgia, USA (2007)

[20] Linstead, E., Bajracharya, S., Ngo, T., Rigor, P., Lopes, C., Baldi, P.: Sourcerer: mining and searching internet-scale software repositories. Data Mining and Knowledge Discovery 18(2), 300–336 (2009). DOI 10.1007/ s10618-008-0118-x

[21] Lopes, C., Bajracharya, S., Ossher, J., Baldi, P.: UCI source code data sets (2010). URL http://www.ics.uci.edu/~lopes/datasets/

[22] Lungu, M., Lanza, M., Nierstrasz, O.: Evolutionary and collaborative software architecture recovery with softwarenaut. In: Science of Computer Programming (SCP), (to appear) (2012)

[23] Manning, C.D., Raghavan, P., Schütze, H.: Introduction to Information Retrieval, 1 edn. Cambridge University Press (2008)

[24] Masuhara, H., Murakami, N., Watanabe, T.: Duplication removal for a search-based recommendation system. In: Proceedings of the 4th International Workshop on Search-Driven Development: Users, Infrastructure, Tools, and Evaluation, SUITE '12. ACM, New York, NY, USA (2012)

[25] McCandless, M., Hatcher, E., Gospodnetic, O.: Lucene in Action, 2 edn. Manning Publications (2010)

[26] McMillan, C., Grechanik, M., Poshyvanyk, D., Xie, Q., Fu, C.: Portfolio: finding relevant functions and their usage. In: Software Engineering (ICSE), 2011 33rd International Conference on, pp. 111–120 (2011). DOI 10.1145/1985793. 1985809

[27] Murakami, N., Masuhara, H., Watanabe, T.: Optimizing a search-based code recommendation system. In: Proceedings of 3rd International Workshop on Recommendation Systems for Software Engineering, RSSE '12. ACM, New York, NY, USA (2012)

[28] Ossher, J., Bajracharya, S., Lopes, C.: Automated dependency resolution for open source software. In: 2010 7th IEEE Working Conference on Mining Software Repositories (MSR 2010), pp. 130–140. Cape Town, South Africa (2010). DOI 10.1109/MSR.2010.5463346

[29] Reiss, S.P.: Semantics-based code search. In: Proceedings of the 2009 IEEE 31st International Conference on Software Engineering - Volume 00, pp. 243–253. IEEE Computer Society (2009)

[30] Takuya, W., Masuhara, H.: A spontaneous code recommendation tool based on associative search. In: Proceedings of the 3rd International Workshop on Search-Driven Development: Users, Infrastructure, Tools, and Evaluation, SUITE '11, pp. 17–20. ACM, New York, NY, USA (2011). DOI 10.1145/1985429.1985434

[31] Thummalapenta, S., Xie, T.: Parseweb: a programmer assistant for reusing open source code on the web. In: Proceedings of the twenty-second IEEE/ ACM international conference on Automated software engineering, pp. 204–213. ACM, Atlanta, Georgia, USA (2007). 10.1145/1321631.1321663

[32] Web Page for FLOSSmole Project: *http://flossmole.org* (2012)

[33] Web Page for Portfolio: *http://www.searchportfolio.net/* (2012)

[34] Web Page for Sourcerer Project and the Sourcerer Code Search Engine: *http://sourcerer.ics.uci.edu* (2012)

[35] Web Page for Sourcerer Web Services: *http://sourcerer.ics.uci.edu/services* (2010)

[36] Web page for Sourcerer's github repository: *http://github.com/sourcerer/Sourcerer* (2010)

[37] Web Page on Apache Lucene Scoring: *http://lucene.apache.org/java/2_4_0/scoring.html* (2010)

[38] Web Site for Apache Software Foundation: *http://apache.org* (2010)

[39] Web Site for Google Code Hosting: *http://code.google.com/projecthosting* (2010)

[40] Web site for Java.net: *http://java.net* (2010)

[41] Web Site for Lucene: *http://lucene.apache.org* (2010)

[42] Web site for Maven: *http://maven.apache.org* (2010)

[43] Web Site for Maven's Central Repository: *http://repo1.maven.org/maven2/* (2010)

[44] Web Site for Sourceforge: *http://sourceforge.net* (2010)

[45] Web site for Tigris: *http://tgris.org* (2010)

Part III

Reuse: Components and Projects

In general, components and projects are reused with minimal modification. In this Part, there are three chapters that look this phenomenon. Two of them examine the decision-making surrounding reuse and the remaining two explain how program analysis can be used to improve code retrieval.

In Chap. 9, "Developing Software with Open Source Software Components," Ayala et al. report on their interviews with software developers on how they selected open source software to use in their projects. De' and Rao asks similar questions to CIOs (Chief Information Officers) and senior-level IT managers, in order to learn how reuse decisions fit in with the overall strategy of a company. This work is reported in Chap. 10, "Open Source Reuse and Strategic Imperatives."

In the context of software reuse, code retrieval is primarily concerned with locating the components that best fit a query, need, or problem. In Chap. 11, Ossher and Lopes describe how they added program analysis algorithms from software engineering to improve existing code retrieval techniques. Similarly, Hummel and Janjic write about how test cases can be used to specify searches in Chap. 12.

Chapter 9
Developing Software with Open Source Software Components

Claudia Ayala, Xavier Franch, Reidar Conradi, Jingyue Li, and Daniela Cruzes

Abstract The success of Component-Based Software Development is based on the ability of an implementer team to select, assemble and integrate third-party and other components with own application software, in order to create a software system that satisfies (most of) the customer/client's stated needs in an economic and flexible way. Nowadays, the reuse of Open Source Software (OSS) components available from the Internet is playing a strategic role in the industry. This chapter aims at providing empirical evidence on current industrial OSS selection practices based on semi-structured interviews performed in 17 European organizations. In particular, the study tackles the following activities: (1) initial identification of available OSS components, (2) closer evaluation of the identified components, (3) conclusive decision-making of the chosen ones, and (4) updating of OSS-relevant experience and knowledge for the actual company. For simplicity we have omitted system-wide integration and testing activities. The results of this study ought to be valuable not just for researchers, as a sobering basis in their quest for practical selection methods; but also for practitioners that regularly drive OSS selection processes with potential to learn from other colleagues' work.

C. Ayala (✉) • X. Franch
Technical University of Catalunya, UPC Campus Nord-Omega, ES-08034, Barcelona, Spain
e-mail: cayala@essi.upc.edu; franch@essi.upc.edu

R. Conradi • D. Cruzes
Norwegian University of Science and Technology, NO-7491, Trondheim, Norway
e-mail: conradi@idi.ntnu.no; dcruzes@idi.ntnu.no

J. Li
DNV Research & Innovation, Veritasveien 1, NO-1363, Høvik, Norway
e-mail: jingyue.li@dnv.com

S.E. Sim and R.E. Gallardo-Valencia (eds.), *Finding Source Code on the Web for Remix and Reuse*, DOI 10.1007/978-1-4614-6596-6__9,
© Springer Science+Business Media New York 2013

9.1 Introduction

Nowadays, the approach of building large software systems by reusing pre-made software components[1] is considered the standard way of developing software systems [9]. The main motivation is that systematic software reuse is like "avoiding to re-invent the wheel". Component-Based Software Development (CBSD) allows companies to obtain faster adoption of new technology including standards, increased innovation, and reduced costs and time-to-market [10, 36].

In particular, the availability of Open Source Software (OSS) components has greatly influenced the software development practices [20, 23]. The evidence shows for instance that from a sample of 769 companies 33 % "provide solutions which are based on OSS" [11]. Moreover, 48 % of 62 software companies use OSS in their business [42], and in a sample of 569 software companies, 46.8 % integrate OSS in their software systems [25]. These software systems represent a great variety of application areas from all major vertical sectors [25]. Also, Nokia claims that as much as 75–98 % of the software architecture for its Internet tablet consists of OSS [27].

However, reusing OSS components (and third party software in general) creates challenges for their appropriate selection and proper integration, testing and maintenance [14]. In addition, licensing terms should be carefully addressed, especially if an OSS-based system is going to be distributed or sold to the general market [26].

In this context there are two crucial activities that play a central role in the success of the overall CBSD in the industry, namely selection of components and the knowledge management strategies around the reused components [9, 39, 40]. Although there has been a great body of research on component selection, evidence shows that there is a limited knowledge about current industrial OSS selection practices. Thus, there is often a gap between theory and practice, and the proposed methods are hardly used in the industrial practice [28, 34, 44]. Furthermore, most of the existing methods lack appropriate knowledge management and reuse mechanisms [3]. As a consequence, software companies are still facing OSS component adoption under considerable risk and uncertainty [8, 9, 29] and some of them are still reluctant to arbitrate the risks and benefits of using OSS components.

Thus, focusing on industrial OSS component integrators, i.e., the implementor(s) in charge of selecting OSS components for their subsequent integration, we performed a qualitative survey based on semi-structured interviews with component integrators from 19 software-intensive organizations. The main goal of this study is exploring and describing up-to-date industrial OSS selection practices. The main findings from this initial work may help maturing OSS reuse practices, since researchers and practitioners may use the evidence to understand the practical challenges of OSS component selection, and properly align their efforts for facing them. Furthermore, diverse actors related to the OSS component marketplace (e.g.,

---

[1] "A software component is a unit of composition with contractually specified interfaces and explicit context dependencies only and can be composed according to a component model by third party without modification [48]".

component providers, components intermediaries, and providers of services around components) may use the presented evidence to identify and understand other OSS selection practices and to envisage strategic actions for improvement.

9.2 Background

Systematic software reuse is an engineering strategy proposed to increase productivity and software quality, and to lead to economic benefit [41]. Although software reuse has been an active research arena for several decades, the availability of OSS greatly differs from the "classical" reuse environment based on centralized repositories with well-organized descriptions of their contents [4].

The Internet is a vital part of successful reuse of OSS components [16, 37, 50, 52] as it constitutes the fundamental place where components are developed, searched for, provided, and evolved. Thus, the Internet constitutes the global and virtual OSS marketplace, characterized by the uncontrolled growth of component offerings and demands, new versions of existing components, and the lack of standards describing these components.

The OSS marketplace includes the exchange interactions between reusers and providers of OSS components, as well as the actions of other actors that facilitate or promote such transactions. *Providers* (i.e., OSS communities or companies that develop and release OSS components) offer OSS components through their own websites. *Reusers* use a *search mechanism* or *Intermediary* services to find and select components. Furthermore, a search mechanism is needed to allow navigation through the marketplace, i.e., either general purpose tools as Google, or specialized ones as Google Code Search or Koders. Intermediary services are profit or non-profit organizations or individuals that index and/or distribute OSS components or other related products and services. Examples are companies selling support around certain components or domains, such as Forrester or Gartner; and *General-oriented* or *Domain specific* portals such as SourceForge or TheServerSide, respectively. Also, there are *Promoters* that are individuals and/or organizations whose main aim is to foster the OSS movement. Examples are the Open Source Technology Group (OSTG), the public-supported FriProg in Norway (www.friprog.no), the Free Software Foundation (FSF), the Apache Foundation, and personal blogs with useful resources. Practical research efforts from academia and/or industry can be also found, such as University of Maryland's CeBASE repository that provides a "lessons learned" database.

A recent systematic review on organizational adoption of OSS [26] shows that most of the current OSS evidence mainly discusses: (1) the perceived benefits and drawbacks of OSS or the motivations for adopting it, (2) the success factors for adoption of OSS, and (3) the extent to which OSS is actually adopted. Furthermore, there are limited empirical studies of the implications of pre-selecting OSS components for later integration in new systems. The existing studies usually also refer to single case studies or experience reports whose contexts are scarcely described and that provide limited information about how the OSS components are integrated. Only a few studies have conducted large-scale field studies representing several industrial sectors [14, 32, 34]. However, all of these studies provide little concrete advice related to OSS component selection and knowledge management activities, which are two of the pressing problems that software integrators face every day.

The following subsections provide a brief background on OSS components selection and knowledge management, and summarize the body of evidence that exist in the area based on published surveys.

9.2.1 State-of-the-Art Component Selection and Knowledge Management

Roughly speaking, component selection consists of three activities that are usually staged [19, 31, 39]:

1. *Identification of candidate components*: It is aimed to locate one or more candidate components that may cover some of the system requirements (while avoiding non-relevant components) and to acquire information that makes their evaluation and comparison feasible.
2. *Evaluating components with respect to the expected requirements*: This activity aim to assess to what extent the candidate component(s) covers/cover a major part of the system requirements.
3. *Choosing suitable component alternative(s)*: This refers to the comparison of the candidate components to choose the one(s) that "best" fits/fit the stated requirements.

However, in all the above selection activities, *non-functional* requirements (also called quality attributes) – like reliability, security, usability or maintainability – are hardly covered, as they express hard-to-capture and late-emerging *system-level* properties. On the other hand, most OSS components seem to fare satisfactorily on quality issues [34]. Evidence exists that the practitioners' perception of OSS in the embedded systems area is also satisfactory [35].

9.2.1.1 Identification of OSS Components

Searching for reusable components was traditionally supported by centralized component repository systems with specific classification and searching mechanisms [21]. However, the free availability of OSS components has shifted this focus to a global reuse approach [41]. Much effort to support component searching have been devoted to classification structures and specialized search engines. Birkmeier and Overhage provided a comprehensive overview of this in [8]. Several classification approaches and schemes[2] have been proposed to describe component properties (attributes) and their values. Likewise, many automatic or semi-automatic search engines with various technologies have been proposed for finding and identifying related hits, relying on a multitude of available component catalogues. Representative examples are Google's code-specific search tool (Google_Code_Search) addressed to find OSS code on the Internet, and academic tools such as IPSCom (Intelligent Portal for Searching Components) [1], or MoReCOTS [54]. In addition, both Global Ontologies [13, 47], and The Semantic Web [2] have been proposed to deal with the lack of homogeneous descriptions of components. However, none of these mechanisms and tools have been feasibly implemented or adopted in industrial practice [8, 13]. Furthermore, component searching has been stated as a complex and immature arena, that actually requires different common efforts from very diverse areas such as software reuse, code search, information retrieval, and program comprehension [22, 51].

9.2.1.2 Evaluating and Choosing OSS Components

In recent years there has been a plethora of proposals aimed to support component evaluation and decision making. These proposals range from suggesting sets of evaluation criteria and changes to the software development processes, to proposing novel technologies emerging from other areas such as decision support systems, method engineering, strategic contracting and procurement, simulation and formal reasoning. Early proposals mainly focused on proprietary closed source components (i.e., COTS), but in the last years the potential benefits of OSS are gaining considerable attention. Several proposals and large scale research projects focus on OSS selection particularities. Some of the first examples are the OSMM (Open Source Maturity Model) [24], OpenBRR (Open Business Readiness Rating) [43], and the QSOS (Qualification and Selection of Open Source software) [46]. Besides suggesting a number of new evaluation criteria that reflect the components' OSS nature, they share the same fundamental selection principles as those for COTS components. Such evaluation criteria are further explored by, for instance, the QualOSS Model Framework [15], the QualiPSo model of OSS trustworthiness [18], and [17]. Comprehensive surveys can be found in [28, 31, 37, 38, 39]. However, regardless of the kind of components, these proposals mainly address and mostly focus on the evaluation criteria and decision-making phases, setting aside the practical problem of how to search for and locate components and to assign suitable information about them [28, 32]. As a result, there is no consensus on the applicability of these proposals in industrial practice.

---

[2] A classification schema corresponds to an *ontology* or *taxonomy*. Consider the joint work by WHO and the National Institutes of Health in USA on a common term base for medicine, currently with over 1.8 million terms. So, coping with the size, evolution, consistency, and up-front costs of many classification schemas represent formidable challenges. In addition comes the more fundamental, "cultural-political" issues behind missing standardization or agreement on many terms, simply due to incompatible perceptions of the world at large [12].

9.2.1.3 OSS Components Knowledge Management

Many authors claim that in order to be successful, reuse must embrace not only the reuse of components but also the reuse of experience around these components [6]. This would enhance the results of the selection processes, by for instance, reducing the overall required evaluation time and effort, whilst increasing the reliability of the results. Thus, it has been greatly recognized that documenting the process and decisions related to OSS component selection is crucial to capitalize on the knowledge gained [41]. However, the analysis of most existing methods show that while most of them recommend saving the documentation from the selection process, they do not address adequate mechanisms for recording and managing this body of knowledge (see [3] for an overview). Furthermore, the evidence presented by Chen et al. [14] shows that *learning* represents one of the major costs of OSS-based development – as for software maintenance in general. Therefore, companies need to effectively manage their OSS-related knowledge in order to exploit the potential benefits of OSS [34].

In general, it can be observed that what we really know about the industrial practice of OSS component selection is quite limited. Most of the component selection proposals assume an "ideal" situation where the components are suitably arranged, documented and residing in a common place. However, this is far from reality [9, 49]. Therefore, the practical adoption of academic research on OSS is hindered by industry: (1) not seeing its own practices identified in the research literature, and (2) not seeing convincing evidence about the effectiveness of these results in real software development [31].

9.3 Empirical Study in Selection of OSS Components

In order to increase the understanding of the current industrial OSS selection practices, we stated RQ1:

- *RQ1. How do integrators perform OSS components selection?*

RQ1 mostly focuses on understanding (1) the selection processes, and (2) the resources used by practitioners to perform the selection.

As the success of OSS-based software development requires that companies effectively manage their OSS related knowledge, we aimed to inquiry about this issue stating RQ2:

- *RQ2. How is OSS related knowledge managed in the industrial practice?*

RQ2 mostly focuses on understanding the mechanisms used to capitalize on the knowledge gained around OSS components.

As the nature of our inquiry was clearly exploratory, we used a qualitative research approach based on semi-structured interviews to collect data directly from industrial practitioners [45]. The interview guide used in the study may be consulted at [5]. The target population was practitioners in charge of performing OSS component selection activities. The only requirement for companies to participate was that they had undergone a finished project that implied OSS component selection. Organizations' details are given in Table 9.1. Some respondents came from the same organization, but worked on different projects as detailed by the fourth column of the table.

Nineteen respondents from 17 European organizations from Spain, Norway and Luxembourg participated in the study. These organizations included: software consultancy companies (SCC) that perform software development tasks for different clients as their primary business; IT departments (ITD) in public or tertiary organizations that usually perform or outsource some software development task for covering the internal demands of the organization; to a software house (SH) that develops and commercializes specific proprietary solutions; and one organization that provides expert support for selecting software (ESSS) solutions based on their clients' requirements. However, this organization does not perform any software development tasks.

Each respondent was asked to talk about a single finished project that he/she was familiar with, and a single component used in that project. Interviews were mainly performed in the mother tongue of the respondents and face-to-face in their working place, by one or two researchers of the team. Interviews lasted around 1 h each and were recorded on paper and tape for subsequent analysis. The project and the component(s) were chosen by the respondent without any intervention from us. The resulting set of projects was diverse, and used a variety of components that ranged from libraries and APIs to more complex solutions.

Interviews were prepared for analysis by a manual transcription of audio records to text documents, and were finally translated to English so that the whole research team could equally assess and discuss the data. We used "content analysis" [30] as a basis for performing the assessment of the collected data, and generating categories by grouping sentences of phrases that described the same idea, action or property.

9.4 Results

This section presents the results of the study. They are grouped in two subsections according to the two research questions introduced above. Results are described in terms of the categories or codes generated from the data analysis. Interpretation and discussion of the findings according to the research question are tackled in Sect. 9.5.

Org.	Business	Prj.	System	Component	Effort
A	SCC	a	Web appl. for managing a student DB	Spring web service	480
B	SCC	b	Web appl. for an Internet bank	Spring framework	17,520
C	SCC	c	Appl. assisting dyslectic people in typing	Open Office Libs	29,200
D	SCC	d	Content management(CM) covering req.	Java Script comp.	21,900
E	SCC	e	Sys. records work hours and scheduling	RichPhase	14,600
F	ITD	f	Adding statistics to a sys.	GoogleCharts	60
G	SCC	g	Website selling items on the Internet	Mambo	640
H	SCC	h	Web tool for personal data management	Hibernate	1,920
I	ITD	i	A resource management sys.	MySQL	5,840
J	ITD	j	Framework for J2EE-based components	J2EE comp.	*
K	SH	k	Updating of a record management sys.	IBM CM	12,000
L	SCC	l	Web appl. for management of incidences	Debian	*
M	SCC	m1	Migration a CM sys. to OSS-based	Plone	2,280
M	SCC	m2	Migration from LotusNotes to OSS-based	OpenCoreBusiness	11,520
N	SCC	n	Web queries for visualizing geo. info.	J2EE comp.	6,000
O	SCC	o1	GIS sys. managing tele. services	GoogleMaps	*
O	SCC	o2	A content management sys.	Java components	1,200
P	SCC	p	A web for people collaboration	Java components	33,620
Q	ESSS	q	Sys. for the managing shops at the airport	*	*

* Respondent did not know or asked to keep this information confidential

Table 9.1: Overview of studied organizations, projects, system, and project effort (man-hour)

9.4.1 RQ1: How Do Integrators Perform OSS Components Selection?

9.4.1.1 Identification of Components

Figure 9.1 summarizes the categories of component identification and the respondents that belong to each category. In the searching phase, no company used any established procedure or guidelines to drive component identification. Instead, nine participants stated that they had used or heard about a sought component before, and were able to find such a component directly. Six participants said that they were not familiar with any candidate component, and used Internet searches and Internet browsing to find a component. Two organizations hired an expert company for doing the tasks related to identifying OSS components. Two respondents also recognized that no search tasks were performed in the project as the component was decided in advance by the client or by the boss. In this last case, the respondents recognized that these practices depended on the client requirements and/or strategic relationship with component providers.

Regarding the resources used in this stage, in addition to previous experience and awareness of the components, the respondents said that they used to consult either experience networks inside the company or domain-specific portals. The former were integrators familiar with the actual domain, usually knowing where to search or ask when looking for matching components. In contrast, when such integrators did not have previous experience, they usually applied two different practices: (a) using Google for browsing the Internet, or (b) hiring an OSS selection expert support from other consultancy companies in case of critical projects.

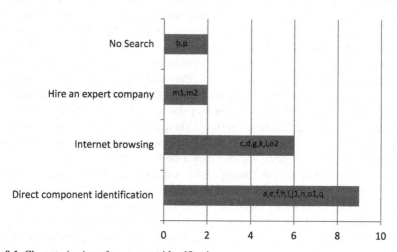

Fig. 9.1 Characterization of component identification

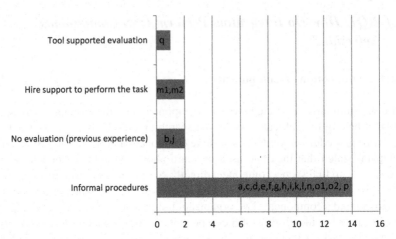

Fig. 9.2 Characterization of answers regarding processes to evaluate components

9.4.1.2 Evaluation of Components

Figure 9.2 shows a summary of the results regarding evaluation processes to evaluate components and the respondents that fall into each category. Fourteen out 19 respondents mentioned that they did not use, nor knew of any formal procedure or method to drive the evaluation and decisions regarding components. Instead, they proceeded informally, often without even documenting the information on the various components for their subsequent comparison. Two respondents recognized that the evaluation relied on personal experience and experience from others, especially to face time-to-market demands and to capitalize on previous knowledge from the team. Two respondents from the same organization said that they hired external consultants to drive the evaluation process. They recalled that they applied a lightweight approach of the OSMM method [24] to drive the evaluation of components. In addition, they highlighted that they were trained on how to apply the method, but they did not apply it on a daily basis. Instead, they just informally applied a reduced and ad-hoc set of the evaluation criteria that the given method suggested. Another respondent emphasized that even when they did not follow established procedures, they had developed a spreadsheet-like tool to help them assign weights according to some relevant criteria for ranking candidate components in the Enterprise Resource Planning (ERP) domain, being the one they usually covered.

Figure 9.3 summarizes the findings with respect to resources used to evaluate components. Nine respondents said that it boiled down to unit and module testing of very basic component functionalities. Five respondents stated that they even built a prototype to check if the component behaved as expected. These prototypes ranged from straightforward ones to more formal ones that required a significant effort to set up a suitable testing infrastructure. Respondents said that this was not a representative practice for other projects in the company. Rather, it was mainly done when a candidate component was critical and/or used for the first time. Finally, five

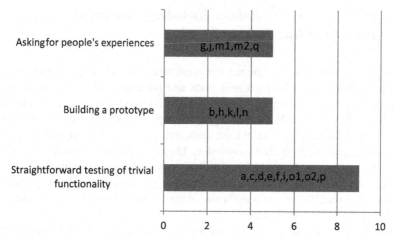

Fig. 9.3 Characterization of answers regarding resources used to evaluate components

respondents said that the component was mainly evaluated based on comments from other developers in the company or other external people they trusted, but usually only when the candidate did not play a critical role in the actual system.

In general, respondents agreed that the criticality of a component in a new system and previous experience with that component had a direct influence on the evaluation process. Components that did not play a critical role in the actual system tended to be more informally evaluated. Sometimes the evaluation and decision-making were just based on the awareness of positive opinions about that component, based on the experience of internal or external people to the organization. On the contrary, when the criticality of the component was high, integrators tended to invest more time and resources for evaluating the candidate components.

9.4.1.3 Choosing Components

The most typical situation regarding to the final decision of components selection was that the development team or its boss decided which component(s) to select. Fifteen of the respondents reported this same experience. Another typical situation was that the customers/clients were usually not aware of the internal implementation of the resulting system. On the other hand, four respondents recognized that in their projects (i.e., projects l, n, p, q), it was the customer/client who made final decision on the component to use. This was especially true for companies whose business model is based on providing component evaluation surveys, and where the customer/client always has the final decision.

It is important to highlight that in both cases, respondents recognized that the decisions were greatly influenced by strategic business issues such as established relationships with OSS providers, previous knowledge or experience with a candidate component, technologies or programming languages that the team already mastered.

9.4.2 RQ2: How Is OSS Related Knowledge Managed in the Industrial Practice?

Although all integrators recognized the importance of exploiting experience and knowledge sharing to reduce learning costs and minimize risks, only five projects (i.e. projects a, b, k, l, q) out of 19 had established (either human or computer supported) mechanisms inside their company to support the selection of OSS components. These mechanisms might use dedicated knowledge management systems to help store and locate usable knowledge. They also might inform about "gurus" for providing further information, as well as experience for a coupled to distribution lists and "wikis". In addition, some of these respondents also stated that their company had recently set up a dedicated department or person for gathering and monitoring the OSS marketplace.

The other 14 respondents recognized that there were not established mechanisms inside their company to support the reuse of knowledge and experience. Instead, they proceeded informally by directly asking information from internal and/or external colleagues.

In both cases, navigating on the Internet was stated as an important mechanism for knowledge extraction and management, especially because of the existence of Internet resources such as collaborative communities (e.g., TheServerSide, Experts Exchange, Java Users group) that offer forums and other collaborative mechanisms to exchange ideas and solutions to common problems.

9.5 Discussion of Main Findings

The previous section aimed to present a general view of the results. This section aims at discussing the most important findings and observations from the data.

9.5.1 Use of Informal Procedures for Selecting Components

We found that the component searching phase was informally performed and mainly influenced by previous experience in all the companies. This result is in line with the claim that component selection methods proposed in the literature mostly focus on the component evaluation phase, setting aside the problem of identifying components and related information [7]. Regarding component evaluation, it was very interesting to see that in contrast to previous studies that stated that companies neither used nor knew of any formalized methods to select components [14, 32, 34, 44]; our results suggest that there is an *incipient interest or awareness of some component selection methods*, as some companies intend to apply evaluation methods and tools for supporting evaluation. This was mainly motivated by the need to succeed and justify the decision on selecting OSS components over proprietary solutions, and their aim to extend their business model to offer services around OSS-based solutions.

Finally, regarding OSS component choices we found that although the research on requirement negotiations often assumes that a client will be interested in, and be capable of, discussing component selection issues [19], in practice this is usually not true. In line with the results obtained by Li et al. [34], we found that it was mainly the reuser's own organization (i.e., the software project team) that decides upon OSS components, whereas customers/clients usually only care about the final products.

9.5.2 Risk Reduction Strategies

We observed two significant risk reduction strategies: deciding the use of OSS components based on previous experience, and hiring specialized companies to select components.

On one hand, the crucial role of previous experience is because companies need to face time-to market restrictions, capitalize on the knowledge gained when mastering a component, as well as to avoid the risk of introducing "virgin" or "poor-quality" components during software development. This is especially true when the component to be integrated plays a critical role in the system to be built. We observed that several companies used own or other's experience as the first risk reduction strategy when selecting OSS components. So, they avoided the introduction of components with insufficient or negative track records. While the value of experience is important, considering it as the most influential factor for selecting components is at the same time hampering the full exploitation of the potential benefits of the OSS marketplace. Therefore, we need to establish a set of trustworthy and cooperative OSS communities (even ecosystems) among the potential system integrators and component providers. This will provide and enable alternative software resources that better reflect the integrators' needs, and lead integrators to face the risks of using OSS in other ways and not just based on their own experience.

On the other hand, some of the studied projects stated that they had hired an expert company for performing the selection tasks. Other respondents agreed that this was a resource also used by their companies in other projects. In addition, all these respondents agreed that this was an effective strategy for dealing with the risks of component selection in critical projects. This finding adds to the list of risk reduction strategies when using OSS components found by Li et al. in [33]. Furthermore, we observed that hiring support for selecting components was an activity much in demand for critical projects in almost all organizations. Thus, there seems to be a potential *market niche* for companies aiming to provide support for selecting OSS components.

9.5.3 Importance and Adoption of Formal and Informal Experience-Sharing Mechanisms

Even not all organizations had established mechanisms to reuse and promote experience and knowledge sharing, all respondents agreed on the importance of capitalizing on the knowledge inside the company. Our assessment and comparison of the context of companies that had established knowledge management mechanisms inside the company and those that do not, led us to suggest some factors that might have positively influenced the adoption of these mechanisms: the stability of domains approached by the companies that valued the reuse of knowledge; and the need to ensure the maintainability of the resulting systems. In this context, our results show that continuous monitoring of the marketplace is becoming a usual practice among integrators to keep themselves updated about components, technologies and trends (even before they have a specific need). Therefore, the search practice is often becoming a continuous monitoring activity rather than being on a project demand basis. The latter has research and practical implications. On one hand, it implies a restructuring of the tasks and responsibilities of the software development team. On the other hand, it has increased the need of enabling intra-organizational channels of communication for interacting/informing results.

Furthermore, while most of current research usually assumes that component providers' portals [7, 47], repositories [52] and search engines [13] are the primary ways in which integrators identify components and information about them; the results from our study show that integrators hardly agreed on the use of these resources in practice. Instead, integrators that do not have established knowledge management mechanisms inside the organization, deal with this task by using resources that promoted experience and knowledge sharing on the Internet, for instance by domain-specific websites that offer forums to interchange ideas and solutions to common problems (e.g., TheServerSide or Experts Exchange). The direct interaction with colleagues and professional networks (e.g., asking for comments about a component from a colleague, or attending specialized trade shows, conferences or workshops) gave valuable results as well.

To the best of our knowledge, the exploitation of this social interaction for supporting the OSS component selection has not received great attention yet. There is a demanding need to effectively deal with the inherent subjectivity of this kind of information. Reputation mechanisms as used in other business domains as ebay.com could be really valuable to deal with the subjectivity of diverse opinions.

9.6 Validity Threats

Like most studies in Software Engineering, our study faces some validity threats. This section discusses these threats in terms of construct, internal, and external validity, as suggested by Robson [45] and Wohlin et al. [53]. It furthermore emphasizes the corresponding strategies used to deal with these threats.

Regarding *construct validity*, this study was supported by two main principles: rigorous planning of the study, and the establishment of protocols for data collection and data analysis. This was especially important as the research involved several researchers and participants from different countries. In addition, the interview guide used as an instrument to gather data, was carefully designed and piloted with six academic and industrial people in order to improve its understandability. For instance, some vocabulary was defined at the beginning of the interview guide to homogenize concepts.

Regarding *internal validity*, we tried hard to envisage and harmonize the data gathering and the subsequent data analysis strategies. With respect to the data gathering strategy, we took relevant decisions for approaching a further understanding of the OSS selection industrial contexts. One of the main relevant decisions was to focus most of the questions of the interview guide on a single component selection project and a component from that project. In this way, we could further inquire and analyze specific contexts that generated a particular decision. This enhanced the value of our analysis and observations, as it allowed for a shared understanding of the rationale behind OSS selection decisions and the organizational factors.

With respect to the *data analysis strategy*, recording all interviews (and later on transcribing them) contributed to a better understanding and assessment of the data gathered. The generated categories were analyzed, discussed and reviewed by all researchers of the team to ensure their accuracy, understanding and agreement. Furthermore, categories were checked with respect to the data gathered in order to confirm that none of the stated categories refuted any of the conclusions, and that the variability factors were well understood by the research team.

Regarding *external validity*, it is important to highlight that qualitative studies, such as the one we performed, rarely attempt to make universal generalizations beyond the studied setting. Instead, they are more concerned with characterizing, explaining and understanding the phenomena under the contexts of study. To strengthen the external validity, we addressed several topics in our study. Some of the most relevant ones are listed. First, the companies in this study were selected by a strategy combining convenience and maximum variation sampling from three different European countries (Spain, Norway and Luxembourg). We tried to mitigate any possible bias traditionally related to convenience sampling [45] by combining a maximum variation sampling, so that the approached organizations covered different characteristics regarding size, application domain, and business area. Second, another factor strengthening the external validity was that we had no control over the projects and components chosen by the respondents. Third, the approached projects and OSS components used were of different size and types, and the respondents had different backgrounds. Nevertheless, most of the resulting sampling companies were developing web applications, and the approached projects did not cover domains such as real time or life critical requirements. We are aware that both factors may have an impact on how components are selected, and so we highlight that our findings might be considered more relevant for the web information systems and non critical domains. Furthermore, we emphasize that our findings should not be taken as assertions but as potential hypotheses that need to be further validated.

9.7 Conclusions

This qualitative study presents results related to the exploration of industrial OSS component selection practices in 17 European organizations. The main findings of the study reveal some practices that are becoming part of software development, as well as potential market niches for software-intensive companies.

The results of this work may provide a broad understanding of industrial OSS selection practices and have a positive implication for research and practice, emphasizing the following three work roles:

- *Researchers*, who may envisage their own ideas and solutions being revised, considering factors that are actually used in industrial practice, and identifying new research challenges and aspects that have been overlooked by the research literature.
- *Software-intensive organizations*, that perform OSS component selection practices, and where the presented results help to increase their awareness of experience and previous knowledge in the whole component selection process and to consider other colleagues' practices.
- *Component providers*, who may learn about how components are actually selected, which resources are usually applied, and what it is important for system integrators. This will help them to better address their own product improvement and marketing strategies.

Finally, while our findings should be further validated, they represent an initial step forward in maturing the OSS component marketplace. We hope that our study might motivate other researchers and practitioners to envisage more effective actions to improve the state of the practice; and thereby contribute to an optimal management of the potential risks and rewards of using OSS components.

Acknowledgements We thank all people that participated in piloting an early version of the interview guide and the interview participants who took time from their work days to participate in our interviews.

This work has been partially supported by the Spanish project TIN2010-19130-C02-01.

We are very grateful to our anonymous reviewers who took the time to provide detailed and thoughtful comments.

References

[1] Aguirre, J.: IPSComp: Intelligent portal for searching components. Master Thesis. Vrije Universiteit Brussel - Belgium (2005)
[2] Ankolekar, A., Herbsleb, J., and Sycara, K.: Addressing challenges to open source collaboration with semantic web. Proc. 3rd Workshop on Open Source Software Engineering (colocated with 25th Intl. Conf. on Software Engineering), pp. 9–14, IEEE CS Press (2003)

[3] Ayala, C.:Systematic construction of goal-oriented COTS taxonomies. Doctoral Thesis. Technical University of Catalunya (2008)

[4] Ayala, C., Hauge, Ø., Conradi, R., Franch, X., Li, J., and Sandanger-Velle, K.: Challenges of the open source component marketplace in the industry. Proc. 5th Intl. Conf. on Open Source Systems (OSS'09), pp. 213–224, Springer Verlag (2009)

[5] Ayala, C., Hauge, Ø., Conradi, R., Franch, X., and Li, J.: Selection of third party software in off-the-shelf-based software development - an interview study with industrial practitioners. Journal of Systems and Software. **84(4)**, 620–637 (2011)

[6] Basili, V.R. and Elbaum, S.: Empirically driven SE research: state of the art and required maturity. Proc. 28th Intl. Conf. on Software Engineering, pp. 32, IEEE CS Press (2006)

[7] Bertoa, M., Troya, J. M., and Vallecillo, A.: Measuring the usability of software components. Journal of Systems and Software. **79(3)**, 427–439 (2006)

[8] Birkmeier, D. and Overhage, S.: On component identification approaches - classification, state of the art, and comparison. Proc. Intl. Conf. on Component-Based Software Engineering, pp. 1–18, Springer Verlag (2009)

[9] Boegh, J.: Certifying software component attributes. IEEE Software. **23(3)**, 74–81 (2006)

[10] Bonaccorsi, A. and Rossi, C.: Comparing motivations of individual programmers and firms to take part in the open source movement: from community to business. Knowledge, Technology, and Policy. **18(4)**, 40–64 (2006)

[11] Bonaccorsi, A., Piscitello, L., Merito, M. and Rossi, C.: How is it possible to profit from innovation in the absence of any appropriability? Proc. 2nd Intl. Conf. on Open Source Software (OSS'06), pp. 333–334, Springer Verlag (2006)

[12] Bowker, G. C. and Star, S. L.: Sorting things out - classification and its consequences. MIT Press (2000)

[13] Cechich, A., Requile-Romanczuk, A., Aguirre, J. and Luzuriaga J. M.: Trends on COTS component identification. Proc. 5th Intl. Conf. on Commercial-Off-The-Shelf (COTS)-Based Software Systems (ICCBSS'06), pp. 90–99, IEEE CS Press (2006)

[14] Chen, W., Li, J., Ma, J., Conradi, R., Ji, J. and Liu, C.: An empirical study on software development with open source components in the Chinese software industry. Software Process: Improvement and Practice. **13(1)**, 89–100 (2008)

[15] Ciokolwski, M. and Soto, M.: Towards a comprehensive approach for assessing open source projects. Proc. Intl. Conf. on Software Process and Product Measurement, pp. 316–330, Springer Verlag (2008)

[16] Clark, J., Clarke, C., De Panfilis, S., Granatella, G., Predonzani, P., Sillitti, A., Succi, G. and Vernazza, T.: Selecting components in large COTS repositories. Journal of Systems and Software. **73(2)**, 323–331 (2004)

[17] Cruz, D., Wieland, T., and Ziegler, A.: Evaluation criteria for free/open source software products based on project analysis. Software Process: Improvement and Practice. **11(2)**, 107–122 (2006)

[18] DelBianco, V., Lavazza, L., Morasca, S., and Taibi, D.: Quality of open source software: The QualiPSo trustworthiness model. Proc. 5th Intl. Conf. on Open Source Systems (OSS'09), pp. 199–212, Springer Verlag (2009)

[19] Finkelstein, A., Spanoudakis, G., and Ryan, M.: Software package requirements & procurement. Proc. Intl. Workshop on Software Specification and Design (IWSSD), pp. 141–145, IEEE CS Press(1996)

[20] Fitzgerald B.: The transformation of open source software. MIS Quarterly. **30(3)**, 587–598 (2006)

[21] Frakes, W. B. and Kang, K.: Software reuse research: status and future. IEEE Trans. on Software Engineering. **31(5)**, 529–536 (2005)

[22] Gallardo-Valencia, R. E. and Sim, S. E.: Internet-scale code search. Proc. Workshop on Search-Driven Development-Users, Infrastructure, Tools and Evaluation (ICSE-SUITE'09), pp. 49–52, IEEE CS Press(2009)

[23] Ghosh R. A.: Study on the economic impact of open source software on innovation and the competiveness of the information and communication technologies (ICT) Sector in the EU. Technical report. UNU-MERIT (2006)

[24] Golden, B.: Succeeding with open source. Addison-Wesley Professional (2004)

[25] Hauge, Ø., Sørensen, C. F., and Conradi, R.: Adoption of open source in the software industry. Proc. 4th Intl. Conf. on Open Source Software (OSS'08), pp. 211–222, Springer Verlag (2008)

[26] Hauge, Ø., Ayala, C. P., and Conradi, R.: Adoption of open source software in software-intensive organizations - a systematic literature review. Information & Software Technology. **52(11)**, 1133–1154 (2010)

[27] Jaaksi, A.: Experiences on product development with open source software. Proc. 3rd Intl. Conf. on Open Source Software (OSS'07), pp. 85–96, Springer Verlag (2007)

[28] Jadhav, A. S. and Sonar, R. M.: Evaluating and selecting software packages: a review. Information & Software Technology. **51(3)**, 555–563 (2009)

[29] Jansen, S., Brinkkemper, S., Hunink, I., and Demir, C.: Pragmatic and opportunistic reuse in two innovative start-up companies. IEEE Software. **25(6)**, 42–49 (2008)

[30] Krippendorff, A.: Content Analysis. Sage Publications, London (1980)

[31] Land, R., Blankers, L., Chaudron, M., and Crnkovic, I.: COTS selection best practices in literature and in industry. Proc. 10th Intl. Conf. on Software Reuse (ICSR'08), pp. 100–111, Springer Verlag (2008)

[32] Land, R., Sundmark, D., Lüders, F., and Krasteva, I. A.: Reuse with software components - a survey of industrial state of practice. Proc. 11th Intl. Conf. on Software Reuse (ICSR'09), pp. 150–159, Springer Verlag (2009)

[33] Li, J., Conradi, R., Slyngstad, O.P.N., Torchiano, M., Morisio, M., and Bunse, C.: A state-of-the-practice survey of risk management in development with off-the-shelf software components. IEEE Trans. on Software Engineering, **34(2)**, 271–286 (2008)

[34] Li, J., Conradi, R., Bunse, C., Torchiano, M., Slyngstad, O.P.N., and Morisio, M.: Development with off-the-shelf components: 10 facts. IEEE Software. **26(2)**, 80–87 (2009)

[35] Lundell, B., Lings, B., and Syberfelt, A.: Practitioners' perceptions of open source in the embedded systems area. Journal of Systems and Software. **84(9)**, 1540–1549 (2011)

[36] Morgan, L. and Finnegan, P.: Benefits and drawbacks of open source software: an exploratory study of secondary software firms. Proc. 3rd Intl. Conf. on Open Source Software (OSS'07), pp. 307–312, Springer Verlag (2007)

[37] Mahmood, S., Lai, R., and Kim, Y. S.: Survey of component-based software development. IET Software. **1(2)**, 57–66 (2007)

[38] Merilinna, J., and Matinlassi, M.: State of the art and practice of open-source component integration. Proc. 32nd EUROMICRO Conf. on Software Engineering and Advanced Applications, pp. 170–177, IEEE CS (2006)

[39] Mohamed, A., Ruhe, G., and Eberlein, A.: COTS selection: past, present and future. Proc. 14th IEEE Intl. Conf. on Engineering of Computer-Based Systems (ECBS'07), pp. 103–114, IEEE CS Press(2007)

[40] Morisio M., Seaman, C.B., Basili, V.R., Parra, A.T., Kraft, S.E., and Condon, S.E.: COTS-based software development: processes and open Issues. Journal of Systems and Software. **61(3)**, 189–199 (2002)

[41] Morisio, M. (Ed.): Reuse of off-the-shelf components. Proc. 9th Intl. Conf. on Software Reuse (ICSR'06). Springer Verlag (2006)

[42] Nikula,U. and Jantunen, S.: Quantifying the interest in open source system: case south-east Finland. Proc. 1st Intl. Conf. on Open Source Systems (OSS'05), pp. 192–195, (2005)

[43] Openbrr, Business readiness rating for open source - a proposed open standard to facilitate assessment and adoption of open source software. (Available 2005) www.openbrr.org/wiki/images/d/da/BRR_whitepaper_2005RFC1.pdf

[44] Torchiano, M. and Morisio, M.: Overlooked aspects of COTS-based development. IEEE Software. **21(2)**, 88–93 (2004)

[45] Robson, C.: Real world research: a resource for social scientists and practitioner-researchers. Second Edition. Blackwell Publishers Inc (2002)

[46] Semeteys, R., Pilot, O., Baudrillard, L., Le Bouder, G., and Pinkhardt, W.: Method for qualification and selection of open source software (QSOS). Technical report (version 1.6). Atos Origin (2006)

[47] Simmons, G.L. and Dillon, T.S.: Towards an ontology for open source software development. Proc. 3rd Intl. Conf. on Open Source Software (OSS'06), pp. 65–75, Springer Verlag (2006)

[48] Szyperski, C.: Component software: beyond object-oriented programming. Addison-Wesley (2002)

[49] Ulkuniemi, P. and Seppanen, V.: COTS component acquisition in an emerging market. IEEE Software. **21(6)**, 76–82 (2004)

[50] Umarji, M., Elliott-Sim, S., and Lopes, C.: Archetypal internet-scale source code searching. Proc. 4th Intl. Conf on Open Source Software (OSS'08), pp. 257–263, Springer Verlag (2008)

[51] Wang, Z., Xu, X., and Zhan, D.: A survey of business component identification methods and related techniques. Intl. Journal of Information Technology. **2(4)**, 230–238 (2005)

[52] Wanyama, T. and Far, B. H.: Repositories for COTS selection. Proc. Canadian Conf. on Electrical and Computer Engineering (CCECE'06), pp. 2416–2419, IEEE CS Press (2006)

[53] Wohlin, C., Runeson, P., Host, M., Ohlsson, M.C., Regnell, B., and Wesslen, A.: Experimentation in software engineering - An Introduction. Kluwer Academic Publishers (2000)

[54] Yanes, N., Sassi, S.B., and Jilani, L.: MoReCOTS: a specialized search engine for COTS components on the Web. Proc. Intl. Conf. on COTS-Based Software Systems (ICCBSS'06), pp. 109–115, IEEE CS (2006)

Chapter 10
Open Source Reuse and Strategic Imperatives

Rahul De' and Ravi A. Rao

Abstract Free and Open Source software (FOSS) allows firms to gain strategic advantage by enabling business agility that is essential to compete in a hypercompetitive environment. Literature on the strategic role of IT indicates that contemporary firms need to constantly upgrade their IT capabilities and maintain flexible IT systems to remain competitive. We argue that FOSS lends itself well to an iterative process of capability development: providing firms with a strategic advantage through reuse of FOSS. We conduct a qualitative case study-based research of commercial firms to assess the strategic imperatives of reusing FOSS. Results indicate that the primary motivation for reusing FOSS is the ability to innovate through access to open source components along with their embedded knowledge, supported by independence from vendor lock-in. Specific advantages enjoyed by firms through the use of FOSS include flexibility, interoperability, stability, security and time-to-market.

10.1 Introduction

Software reuse has the potential to provide economic benefits through enhanced quality and productivity [20], as has been shown through research in the software engineering domain. But does software reuse also provide firms with strategic benefits? Most research related to software reuse for business purposes has focused on the economic value of the reuse [7] and on the strategy around how to reuse software [8]. In this chapter, we explore whether software reuse, specifically the reusable assets of open source, provides firms with strategic benefits.

R. De' (✉) • R.A. Rao
Indian Institute of Management Bangalore, Bangalore, India
e-mail: rahul@iimb.ernet.in; ravi.rao10@iimb.ernet.in

S.E. Sim and R.E. Gallardo-Valencia (eds.), *Finding Source Code on the Web
for Remix and Reuse*, DOI 10.1007/978-1-4614-6596-6__10,
© Springer Science+Business Media New York 2013

Software reuse is fundamental to Free and Open Source software (FOSS). By opening up the source code, FOSS enables its users to not only view and modify the code of the native application, but also the ability to reuse pieces of code and graft them onto new applications to address different requirements. FOSS has emerged as the most successful form of large-scale software reuse with a range of reusable assets available for deployment across multiple technology platforms.

Our definition of reuse includes absorbing complete FOSS products that are enhanced for specific business requirements, as well as deploying FOSS components that are reused as building blocks for developing custom applications. In addition, our definition of reuse includes reuse of the code, as well as the reuse of knowledge (technical and domain knowledge) that is closely associated with the code.

The research questions addressed by this chapter can be stated as:

- Do firms reuse FOSS to gain strategic advantage?
- What attributes of FOSS motivate IT managers to reuse FOSS?

10.2 Literature Review

Before we attempt to answer our research questions, we synthesize past research done pertaining to (a) Role of IT in firm strategy, (b) Software reuse capability provided by FOSS, and (c) Types of FOSS reuse adopted by firms.

10.2.1 IT as a Strategic Resource

Traditional research exploring the role of IT in obtaining strategic differentiation for firms has drawn from two streams of strategy literature originating from (a) Porter's five forces and Porter's value chain models, and (b) the resource-based view of the firm. The first stream of work is drawn from the theory of industrial organization (IO) and explores the structure of the industry in terms of five competitive forces [21, 22] including: bargaining power of buyers and suppliers, threats of new entrants, threat of substitute products and intensity of competition. The role of IT is seen as impacting these forces to provide firms with a competitive edge within the industry structure [18]. While this stream of research provides an explanation of how a firm is able to leverage IT for manipulating the competitive forces, it does not address the question of how the competitive advantage can be sustained – as competition can imitate these actions and nullify the advantage. The second stream of research, drawn from Chamberlainian economics, explores the role of firms endowed with heterogeneous resources and their ability to extract superior rents from these resource endowments [2]. The resource-based view (RBV) of the firm suggests that firms create organizational capabilities by assembling these resources to work together. Adopting RBV, IS researchers have explored the role of IT resources such as IT infrastructure; technical and managerial IT skills; and IT-enabled intangibles such as know-how, culture, reputation etc. as a potential source of competitive advantage [1]. The net prescription of this school of research is to develop strategic IT applications to sustain competitive advantage over time; and to align IT with business strategy, structure and processes [12].

While these streams of research provide insights on how IT can be leveraged to gain competitive advantage, these frameworks are not sufficient to explain the role of IT differentiation in contemporary business environments [24]. Businesses today operate in a *hypercompetitive* environment [5], which is characterized by competition occurring in the form of a series of market disruptions aimed at nullifying any supernormal returns enjoyed by the incumbent leader [4]. In such environments, advantages from specific competitive moves are temporary and superior performance is derived from continuously recreating competitive advantages through innovative actions [24]. A firm's ability to rapidly generate these competitive moves thus becomes a key strategic imperative [5]. The strategic requirements for firms in a hypercompetitive environment include agility, continuous innovation, time-to-market and the timing of the competitive moves [24].

In sum, the underlying theory of how and why IT innovations provide a strategic advantage has changed with the changing landscape of the business environment [24]. The traditional view of IT differentiation was aimed at overcoming Porter's competitive forces [18] and to leverage a firm's heterogeneous resources. With business environments becoming hypercompetitive, the logic of IT differentiation shifted towards enhancing competitive agility [24]. Consequently, the source of IT differentiation shifts from strategic applications to enterprise IT capability and from alignment to embeddedness of IT in business strategy [24]. Sambamurthy et al. [25] examine the strategic role of IT on firm performance and suggest the influence of IT capabilities on firm performance through organizational capabilities and strategic processes. They stress the importance of developing capabilities that allow the firm to dynamically combine IT and business resources; and processes that allow them to combine knowledge, assets and resources to craft innovations. Thus, to leverage IT for strategic differentiation, mere access to strategic applications is no longer sufficient. To achieve sustainable competitive advantage, firms need to have a combination of entrepreneurial alertness that enables them to sense strategic opportunities and IT capabilities that enables them to develop innovative solutions. This co-evolution of strategic processes needs the constant assembling of IT capability in iterative loops, as firms evolve their competitive position [25].

Thus, in today's hypercompetitive environment, firms not only need to possess superior IT capability, they also need to possess the agility that enables them to constantly discover and develop new knowledge, assets and resources. We argue that free and open source software lends itself well to this iterative process of capability development. The reuse of the open source repository rich in ideas, knowledge, techniques and solutions provides firms the ability to constantly evolve their IT capabilities in tune with their strategic processes.

10.2.2 Software Reuse and Open Source Software

Software reuse is the process of using existing software code or knowledge rather than building new software systems [14]. Software reuse can be considered as opportunistic or planned [3], and reused either from internal or external sources. Systematic reuse in software requires the meticulous building of a reusable artifact repository [14] and needs substantial investment in time and effort to identify reusable code, and to build the necessary tools and repository [11]. Systematic software reuse originated as a form of reusing knowledge and code from internal projects with the aim of deriving economic benefits through enhanced quality and reduced effort [20]. In order to derive such economic benefits, commercial organizations invested in building repositories of reusable artifacts.

FOSS is considered to be an example of large scale software reuse with a wide range of reusable assets [3]. With the advancement of open source, a rich and extensive set of external repositories with a wide range of reusable assets is now available not just to open source developers, but to commercial organizations as well. Unlike corporate reusable repositories which are specifically built to store reusable artifacts, FOSS is a collection of independent initiatives representing a variety of technology innovations and approaches. Considering the substantial investment required for developing a reusable artifact repository, research has focused on the phenomenon of creating a large-scale FOSS repository. Code reuse is a form of knowledge reuse that is fundamental to innovation [11] and the types of reuse in open source include the reuse of algorithms and methods; lines of code; and software components that encapsulate functionality [27].

The quality of the reusable artifact is an important determinant of the extent of reuse. Developers contributing to open source use popularity as a proxy for quality rating of the reusable components [11]. The motive for these developers is not just that of cost reduction but also the access to knowledge to foster innovation [3]. However, research also indicates that open source developers work under severe time and resource constraints and subject themselves to self-inflicted pressure to release code early [11]. A potential drawback of this practice is the possibility of the software components in FOSS not being sufficiently abstracted for effective search and reuse.

Thus, the emergence of FOSS as a reusable repository has the impact of providing an external and large repository of assets for knowledge reuse. This provides the opportunity for commercial developers to reuse not only software but also best practices including ideas, knowledge, techniques and solutions [3]. However, searching FOSS components for reuse may not be easy, given the argument that FOSS components are not developed with the objective of reuse. Given the nature of open source reusable artifacts and the difficulty in searching them, its probable that the motivation for commercial firms to reuse open source goes beyond mere productivity benefits and include benefits derived from reusing knowledge embedded in them.

Empirical studies on the reuse of open source software components indicate a pattern of reuse ranging from a few blocks of code to entire products [9]. Further, there is evidence of commercial firms preferring to use open source components as-is without any significant modifications [16]. Extending these arguments, we classify the reuse of FOSS by commercial firms as a) direct replacement for commercial off-the-shelf products needing no modifications; b) as customized open source products considerably enhanced for individual firm requirements; or c) as completely crafted applications built from a plethora of open source and in-house software components. The choice of how firms deploy and use FOSS varies depending on these objectives. Firms may chose to use FOSS for various benefits such as economic advantages, quality and productivity gains, scalability, performance improvement, security, flexibility and agility.

As argued in Sect. 10.2.1, firms seeking IT differentiation, seek to develop IT capabilities and deploy them to gain agility and flexibility. Reuse of FOSS provides one such means for firms to constantly upgrade their IT capabilities. We argue that firms seeking differentiation through FOSS would seek gains beyond mere economic and productivity benefits and leverage FOSS to gain competitive advantage. Such firms will go beyond deployment of as-is FOSS products and tend to reuse best-of-breed FOSS components to craft customized IT systems. The extent to which a firm will modify and integrate diverse set of FOSS components will vary depending on their view of FOSS reuse as a strategic differentiator.

10.3 Research Methodology

We used a qualitative approach to study the strategic reuse of FOSS in commercial firms. We conducted case studies of 18 commercial firms to understand their usage of open source software. Sixteen of these firms are from non-IT industry segments: e-commerce, retail, manufacturing, banking and financial services, and media; and only two are from the IT segment. We collected data using multiple methods including face-to-face interviews using an unstructured questionnaire, as well as through secondary sources such as company annual reports and articles available in the public domain.

10.3.1 Data Collection

We followed guidelines provided by Eisenhardt [6] for conducting an inductive case study. Our choice of cases was based on an initial screening of companies that are extensive users of open source software. Firms were then shortlisted based on their availability and willingness to participate in the study. The respondents of our interview were either the CIO or a senior level IT manager of the firm. The data collection for these cases was done in late 2010.

While our approach was predominantly a grounded study, we were guided by our literature review and hence started with a base category of variables to structure our interviews [17]. We designed our study as a semi-structured interview based on a questionnaire that covered the following dimensions: quality and productivity gains, scalability and performance, security, flexibility and agility. While the questionnaire was meant to guide the general direction of the interview, the interviews themselves were kept open ended and the respondents were encouraged to digress to any other related topics that s/he found relevant to the subject matter of the study. Given the exploratory nature of the interview, our strategy was to use multiple interviewers. The interviews were conducted by two or more members from the research team and lasted around ninety min. Detailed interview notes including the transcripts of the interview, and the notes containing the researchers impressions were recorded. This was followed by a detailed "within-case" analysis [6] to assess the strategic reuse of FOSS within the firm. Once the relevance of the interview was established, follow-up interviews were conducted, if required, to clarify any open questions that were raised as a result of the within-case analysis. A within-case analysis was performed after every interview and findings from these analyses further guided our subsequent interviews. Thus, the data collection and analysis phases overlapped to a great extent [26]. The output of interviews were captured through interview notes and were then coded [19]. The analysis was conducted within each case separately and then compared across cases to identify cross-case patterns [26].

The initial data analysis followed procedures suggested by King [13] for template analysis. Instead of adopting an open coding approach, we started with an initial set of codes as guided by our literature review and then added/modified them as part of the ongoing data analysis. Detailed case studies were prepared for each of the firms for which data was collected. As part of the case development, excerpts from the interview as well as secondary data were coded using the base category that we started with. New categories were introduced based on the findings from the interviews. We interviewed IT leaders from 18 organizations representing diverse business objectives and found a vast variation in the extent of FOSS usage among these companies. While we provide our findings related to the strategic reuse of FOSS across all these organizations, we include below brief case studies on two of the organizations that considered the usage of FOSS as an essential component of their overall strategy.

A limitation of the approach to use a base category of the variables to guide the interviews is the possibility of not covering any new dimensions that may be of interest. In order to ensure that the interviews cover all possible dimensions, the researchers made specific attempts to probe the managers on other dimensions that might have influenced their choice of FOSS from a strategic perspective. As an example, the inclusion of cost as a strategic advantage (beyond mere economic benefits) was a result of several interviewers citing the strategic benefits derived out of lower cost as further elaborated in Sect. 10.4.

10.3.2 Case Study: Local Search Engine

JustDial operates in the local search engine market in India and is one of the leading players providing services across multiple channels, including print directory (yellow pages), phone/voice search, web search and mobile search. Local search has evolved from word-of-mouth to print directories then to phone-based information services, and on-line web directories. The pre-requisite for an effective local search engine includes the comprehensiveness and the currency of the search index, the relevance of the search result in the context of local information and the ease and speed of accessing information.

The business model for JustDial is based on providing end-customers with people-assisted search data giving information on local Small and Medium Enterprises (SMEs). Customers for JustDial are the end-users who act as the audience and the SMEs who act as the content providers. The revenue stream is through listing fees for sponsored listing; advertisement fees for banners and page impressions; click-based revenue fees; and revenue through database sharing and partnerships.

Local search in India is a fast growing market that is characterized by low capital cost, low switching costs, a large number of competitors, a two-sided market comprising of end users and advertisers, and subject to network effects. Using Porter's five-forces framework, we identify the following strategic imperatives:

- The industry has a relatively low entry barrier for new entrants considering the low capital cost requirement and negligible customer switching costs. To protect against this, JustDial had to invest in developing a very comprehensive local SME database. Ensuring current and relevant information of this database became a strategic necessity.
- With the increasing proliferation of the internet, more and more consumers are opting for web searches instead of using phone-based services. Global search engines such as Google and Yahoo act as default sites and are often used for local information search as well. Competitive needs arising out of this threat include the need for technology-led solutions that can compete against the superior technological powers of the global search engines; and the need to include the smallest of SMEs in their listing that the generic search engines may not be able to include.
- Owing to a nascent market with a high potential for growth, the competition in the field is intense and the basis of competition is not price but providing value addition. Hence, organizations have to constantly offer new and differentiated services addressed through superior technology implementation.

The state-of-the-market observed in this field fits the definition of a hypercompetitive environment with the incumbent players constantly innovating and trying to introduce new and differentiated services. Given such an environment and the constantly changing basis of competition, JustDial adopted a strategy of having their solution offering evolve over time based on market and competitive needs. This imposed the constraint of a very short turnaround time from concept to market. Just-

Dial's choice to compete based on technology meant that the IT systems had to be cutting edge, nimble and flexible. The technical considerations include:

- Need for high reliability and accurate information: constant data collection and integration that needs to be performed with minimal down-time.
- Fast response time (internal target of 95 % of the calls to be addressed in less than 60 seconds). This requires that the Information Retrieval Officers (IROs) comprehend the customer query, identify relevant information, and retrieve and communicate information back to the customer in less than 60 seconds.
- Guaranteed and almost instantaneous SMS (short messaging service) response to user queries requiring superior gateway integration with telecommunication service providers.
- Manage large amount of data: information maintained for four million customers and constantly growing.
- Instantaneous data extraction needing superior search engine capabilities.
- Integration of multiple channels such as phone, web, SMS and WAP.

10.3.3 Case Study: Travel Portal

Cleartrip (www.cleartrip.com) is a leading Online Travel Agency (OTA) in India. The range of products offered by Cleartrip include search and booking reservation for domestic and international flights, hotels, holiday packages, mobile travel services, global destination guides along with "24×7" customer services.

The OTA industry in India is a high growth industry with an increasing number of travelers preferring to use the Internet for planning and booking their business and leisure travel. While the market is concentrated, with the top three (which includes Cleartrip) occupying a bulk of the market share; it is also subject to intense competition and attracts new firms, including large international players. In addition, competition is also provided by airline carriers who operate their own online ticketing websites. The customers of the OTAs comprise the section of society with access to internet and credit cards, and willing to shop online. Given the low switching costs, intense competition and availability of alternative channels; providing a favorable customer experience is of the highest priority for OTAs.

Cleartrip's strategy of providing a superior customer service is captured in their objective of "making travel simple". Their approach to implementing this is through "simple, comprehensive, reliable and responsible" services. Information technology is core to the functioning of an OTA, and plays a strategic role in achieving its objectives. Simplicity is provided through an easy and efficient search mechanism coupled with simple and efficient booking procedures. Cleartrip are market leaders in launching innovative solutions aimed at making online reservations simple, such as the single page view for both onward and return travel; a simple "search, book, go" look-and-feel approach as against a more traditional OTA look adopted by its competitors; and single string search through the "smallworld" application. The Cleartrip platform is integrated with several supplier systems including airlines, hotels, railways and other travel portals. The smallworld service is offered in conjunction with Yahoo!, Flickr and Lonely Planet. Reliability and responsiveness also requires a high uptime, tight integration with supplier systems, provision of accurate information and reliable payment gateways.

10.4 Data Analysis

In this section, we summarize our findings on the strategic impact of reuse of open source software. The two case studies we presented illustrate the strategic imperatives of IT for these organizations. Here, we outline the advantage derived from FOSS by these two organizations as well as those reported by respondents of other organizations.

10.4.1 Flexibility

Freedom from vendor lock-in and the ability to rapidly customize to changing business needs were identified as the main advantages obtained by open source software in terms of flexibility. The respondents believed that vendor independence was a significant advantage and in more ways than one. Independence from vendor lock-in allowed the firms to upgrade package versions at their own convenience since there was no threat of a version becoming obsolete.

In the case of JustDial, it's strategy of having an evolving system based on dynamic response to market needs meant the need to be free of any sort of vendor lock-in and the ability to rapidly change the IT system. The access to source code rich with contributions from a vast community of developers provided JustDial a constant source of new ideas and an impetus to constantly innovate.

Cleartrip's strategy of using a non-traditional user interface meant that standard applications did not fit their requirement and warranted custom development. The high demand on search efficiency required them to use best-of-breed algorithms. Developing the "smallworld" application required the advanced use of an analytics-based solution. Open source provided them with an adequate repository for identifying and crafting such a solution.

Apart from contractual freedom, vendor independence also meant the freedom to openly innovate and customize the product to their needs, as can be seen from the following quotes:

> Impact of vendor lock-in is beyond just contractual or cost implications, it hinders innovation, customization and impedes time-to-market.

> The self-service nature of OSS installation packages and independence from vendor personnel for installation speeds up the product installation time significantly

Ability to mix and match various components and the availability of superior building blocks allowed firms to innovate. In addition, visibility to quality source code rich in diverse algorithms and logic also provided firms a stiumulus for generating new ideas. Firms were able to deploy more efficient applications that were marked by superior performance, better load balancing abilities and high scalability. Ability to rapidly adapt to evolving customer needs, specifically in web-fronting applications was also a significant source of advantage.

> Open Source provides [. . .] advantage for engineers in that there are readily available designs that engineers don't have to redo. For example, open source frameworks like Symphony, Code Igniter, and Cake PHP give the inherent advantage of quick software development [...] but also enforced pattern programming.

Better functionality, use of FOSS as a starting product base, evolved building blocks and minimized vendor dependency were identified as the prominent factors influencing a shorter development cycle time and a faster time-to-market. Product selection was expedited as there was no need to go through a formal RFP, vendor evaluation and contracting process. Better release management and ease of product installation also provided advantages particularly for IT systems that were subject to frequent changes, such as e-commerce applications.

> System development time is reduced by an order of magnitude because of availability of a superior code base that is rich in functionality.

10.4.2 Interoperability

Respondents stated that adoption of FOSS provided them significant advantages with over 90 % of the respondents claiming benefits due to the interoperability of FOSS. The study indicates that FOSS adheres to open standards much more than most proprietary options, with FOSS frameworks adopting open architectures. The high interoperability of FOSS products allowed businesses to have hybrid IT installations within their organizations. Additionally, ease of integration of open source products with other applications, including proprietary products, was an important consideration towards adoption of open source.

> . . . its [FOSS] easy installation, simple APIs and good documentation made integration across heterogeneous platforms and frameworks easier.

> All proprietary mobile operating systems make it difficult to integrate with their applications. Compare this with Google's open source Android platform which leverages the Web – it opens it up for all other development. The Web has a lot to do with FOSS being successful as well.

Additionally, interoperability allowed businesses to successfully evaluate multiple frameworks in parallel to meet their performance and scalability requirements, encouraging a mix and match of components for a best fit. At JustDial, the business required a tight integration with the SMS gateway to ensure fail-proof delivery of

SMS. JustDial had to ensure that the system was built by carefully evaluating and selecting software components based on specific business and technological needs. Interoperability is also found to reduce vendor dependency and increase the ability to customize and innovate using available tools and frameworks. Interoperability of FOSS components makes it easier to build on top of other components leading to better reuse. As an example, the ability to customize Ubuntu and integrate it with the Mozilla browser to enhance the data extraction performance on the Information Retrieval Officer's workstation was a major factor for its selection in JustDial.

10.4.3 Performance and Scalability

Respondents unanimously agreed that FOSS provided better performance parameters, primarily due to the ability to tweak and fine-tune performance to meet specific requirements. JustDial had stringent performance requirements on their search engine and data extraction algorithms. Open source provided JustDial the ability to choose the hardware platform and develop the software through mixing-and-matching of various open source components that delivered superior performance. One example was the use of Sphinx, a full text search engine that integrates well with the SQL database and provides the ability to achieve fast, relevant and full text search. In addition, the choice of these open source components provided JustDial the ability to scale up and support their aggressive growth targets.

> The availability of more than one tried and tested, highly scalable, light-weight, open source framework allows wider choice and makes fine-tuning for performance easier... [In addition] availability of source code gives a sense of ownership vital for sustainable product development.

Scalability concerns are one of the major drivers for FOSS adoption among businesses. FOSS adoption allows businesses to explore multiple options, experiment, customize and innovate without any upfront investments. When finally deployed, it helps scale up rapidly while sustaining the cost advantage. Respondents felt that scalability of FOSS makes it an attractive choice for governments and large businesses as well. With the expectation of high growth, scalability was a key strategic imperative for Cleartrip. Given the need for scalability and load balancing requirements, they chose to deploy a stateless environment. The ability to tune their Apache Tomcat web server enabled them to meet this requirement.

10.4.4 Stability

A majority of the respondents (71 %) indicated that FOSS has been instrumental in creating more stable systems, whereas a small percentage (5 %) felt that FOSS systems are not yet as stable as proprietary software, and the rest indicated no significant differences. FOSS adopters who considered FOSS as stable, observed that the source code obtained from the OS community is of higher quality and provides a superior platform. These proponents of FOSS were of the opinion that the focus of FOSS has been on intrinsic qualities such as stability and efficiency, and not necessarily just on product features.

> This [development] focus is not diluted by any sales pressure. Owing to community involvement, the quality of the product is superior. In addition, the large tester base further ensures low occurrences of bugs and higher stability.

Further, respondents felt that FOSS provided better reliability, as efficiency gains translated to reduced resource requirements, leading to lesser points of failure. The access to source code further aided effective troubleshooting.

> Open source helps in troubleshooting and to predict failures, because we have access to source code.

10.4.5 Security

Our study indicates that FOSS provides means to improve security features with 77 % of the respondents claiming security advantages through the reuse of FOSS. Respondents felt that their Linux systems have been significantly more secure than proprietary operating systems. Due to the much larger number of eye balls on the open source code, any security loopholes are spotted quickly and fixed by the community, thus ensuring that FOSS frameworks provide secure components.

> Inherent transparency of FOSS wards off unnecessary intrusion... There is no motivation to 'hack' open code... Often, users find it is easy to debug available source and hence find it more trustworthy leading to inherent security.

10.4.6 Cost Savings

Most firms were of the opinion that while cost savings helped them to justify adoption of open source software, the benefits they accrued from adopting FOSS was much greater than mere cost savings. Firms adopting open source primarily for desktop applications such as Open Office, Thunderbird and anti-virus software that were typically deployed over a large number of desktops reported "cost savings" as their sole driver for adopting open source. Firms adopting open source as their infrastructure layer reported benefits both in terms of cost and superior performance. Further cost savings were reported due to reduced requirement on hardware resources owing to the better performance efficiencies of the open source products. Firms adopting open source for their application layer cited other strategic advantages as the main driver for adopting open source and cost as being an incidental benefit.

Technology-led start-up firms, having a large part of their budgetary expenditure on technology, found the better return on investment (ROI) provided by FOSS as a strategic lever in attaining early profitability. Cleartrip, being a startup firm, had to build scale rapidly in order to achieve profitability. Technology is a core element in the OTA industry and was a big contributor to the cost structure of the firm. Thus, apart from achieving scale, cost cutting was an important lever to achieve profitability. Achieving high ROI from their technology investment was thus essential. Use of open source software helped them achieve this, resulting in their technology expenses being significantly lower compared to competition. In the case of Just-Dial, the cost advantage of open source provided JustDial with the ability to do vast in-house development and build a superior technology platform to support the numerous business demands without the worry of astronomical IT development costs.

10.4.7 Types of Reuse

A common type of reuse was mixing and matching of different open source components to achieve flexibility and superior performance. This ability to mix and match coupled with the superior building blocks allowed firms to innovate. Crafting applications by stitching together a diverse set of best-of-breed open source components was a common strategy adopted by most of the respondents.

The ability to modify the FOSS components, not just in the periphery, but also core components that allow the fine tuning of the system functionality for specific performance requirements is another instance of strategic reuse. As an example, JustDial wanted to deploy a performance-intensive search engine. They achieved this by customizing the Ubuntu operating system to tightly integrate with the Mozilla browser and thus obtain superior performance: an ability not easily obtained when developing with proprietary software.

A third kind of reuse was that of knowledge embedded in the open source code. Visibility to the source code, rich in diverse algorithms and logic was reported as a significant advantage from reusing FOSS. Not only were firms able to reuse pieces of quality code from this repository, they were also able to reuse knowledge embedded in this code. Access to specific algorithms and their logic enabled firms to build on them and develop new and innovative ideas.

10.5 Conclusion

We start by answering our first research question on whether firms reuse FOSS to gain strategic advantage. The findings of our survey indicates an affirmative answer. The previous section provides evidence of firms reusing FOSS to gain strategic advantage. For achieving a sustained competitive advantage, firms need to develop superior IT capabilities: specifically, a rent-generating resource that is not easily imitated or substituted [1]. It can be seen that these capabilities consist of not just IT resources but includes a combination of complimentary human and business resources that provide embedded advantages leading to sustained competitive advantage [23]. In this chapter, we have argued that FOSS can enable firms operating in a hypercompetitive environment with such capabilities providing them with strategic benefits that are essential for sustaining competitive advantages.

In conformance with Sambamurthy [24] that the strategic requirements for firms in a hypercompetitive environment includes agility, continuous innovation and time-to-market considerations, our respondents also rated the flexibility to change and the ability to adapt to changing business needs as a prime motivation for reusing open source software. Flexibility derived through independence from vendor lock-in and the subsequent freedom to innovate were identified as important factors providing firms with the agility to respond to market needs. This is consistent with literature which suggests that in hypercompetitive environments, superior performance is derived from continuously recreating competitive advantage through innovative actions [24].

In addition, better functionality, use of FOSS as a starting product base, evolved building blocks and minimized vendor dependency were identified as the prominent factors influencing a shorter development cycle time and a faster time-to-market. Firms that excelled in the hypercompetitive environment were found to constantly develop their IT capability in iterative loops [25]. The high interoperability of FOSS, the ability to mix and match components and use it in conjunction with existing proprietary software, and the ability to evaluate and adopt FOSS frameworks in gradual phases enabled firms to constantly develop their IT capabilities in tune with business requirements.

The robustness provided by FOSS in terms of stability, security and quality allows these firms to ensure a higher operational efficiency through lesser points of failure, reduced downtime and reduced security breaches. The scalability provided by FOSS allows firms to ensure that they are protected from the need to constantly upgrade their IT systems as they scale up their business. The advantages derived out of lower IT development and operation costs by reusing FOSS were also identified as a strategic benefit, particularly by start-ups with limited resources seeking to maximize the value derived out of their IT investments.

As an answer to the second research question on what attributes of FOSS motivate IT managers to reuse FOSS for strategic benefits, we provide a summary of the attributes and corresponding strategic benefits in Table 10.1.

While we have demonstrated how FOSS can endow firms with these IT capabilities, we would like to stress the possibility of several other strategic advantages that firms can benefit from with the use of FOSS. We attempt to provide two such examples that could perhaps be included as part of future research.

- Sambamurthy et al. [25] posit that IT investments and capabilities influence firm performance through three significant organizational capabilities (agility, digital options, and entrepreneurial alertness) and strategic processes (capability-building, entrepreneurial action, and co-evolutionary adaptation). It is quite intuitive to assume that firms developing IT capability in iterative loops require certain amount of entrepreneurial alertness to constantly search for new FOSS

Capability	Attributes	Strategic benefits
Flexibility	Ability to mix and match diverse set of software components	Agility
	Freedom from vendor lock-in	Faster time-to-market
	Availability of superior code building blocks	Continuous innovation
	Source code as a source of innovation and ideas	Efficient systems design
Interoperability	High interoperability from adherence to open standards and open architecture	Agility
	Enables deploying hybrid installations of diverse components	Faster time-to-market
	Reduces vendor dependency	Efficient systems design
	Allows integrating multi-platform systems	Design efficient systems
Performance	Performance optimization by integrating best of breed components	Agility
Scalability	Open source database found to be highly scalable	Faster time-to-market
	Ability to do modification at the OS level: better integration and higher performance	Efficient systems design
Stability	Better quality providing more stability	Efficient systems design
	Lesser points of failure as a result of reduced resource requirements	Design efficient systems
Security	Reduced security threats leading to higher uptime	Efficient systems design
Cost savings	Enables higher return-on-investment from technology spend	Efficient systems design

Table 10.1: Summary: FOSS reuse for strategic advantage

components that can provide them with new innovations. Studying this link between entrepreneurial alertness and FOSS reuse could be a topic for future research.

- Recent research trends on strategic reuse of IS have focused on the co-creation of IT value across inter-organizational systems [10]. The argument is that the increasing specialization and the faster time-to-market makes it difficult for single firms to assemble the required capabilities to operate in a hypercompetitive environment, and firms are increasingly collaborating with other firms to co-create IT enabled products and services. It can be assumed that FOSS with its high-interoperability can lend itself well to the co-creation of value across business units and organizations. Studying the role of FOSS in co-creating value could be another area of future research.

As a limitation, we cannot claim the generalizability of our study. Our study provides strong indications of firms gaining strategic advantages through the reuse of FOSS. However, our study does not include firms that have leveraged proprietary software for strategic benefits, nor have we eliminated the possibility of firms having suffered strategic disadvantages through the use of FOSS. The only claim that we would like to put forward is that firms operating in a hypercompetitive environment can potentially gain strategic advantage through the reuse of FOSS. Also, as mentioned earlier, our approach of using a base category of the variables to guide the interviews could possibly lead to some dimensions being missed. While we have made specific attempts to be open-ended and probed for all possible dimensions, we do acknowledge the possibility of missing additional attributes of FOSS that could provide firms with strategic advantage.

It should also be noted that the extent of reuse of FOSS is moderated by the type of license under which the open source software is released. Permissive licenses such as the BSD license allow reuse of code for any purpose whereas restrictive licenses such as the GPL allow reuse only for projects that will be further released under a GPL license [15]. In this chapter, we do not delve on the licensing issues of FOSS, but do want to caution the readers on the implications of the type of open source license on software reuse.

Acknowledgements This research was supported in part by a grant from the Centre for Software and IT Management at IIM Bangalore. The authors acknowledge the assistance provided by Supriya Dey and Uma Bharath in data collection, coding and analysis.

References

[1] Bharadwaj, A. (2000). A Resource-Based Perspective on Information Technology Capability and Firm Performance: An Empirical Investigation. *MIS Quarterly* 24(1), 169–196.
[2] Barney, J.B.: Gaining and Sustaining Competitive Advantage. Reading, MA: Addison-Wesley (1997)
[3] Brown, A & Booch, G (2002). Reusing Open-Source Software and Practices: The Impact of Open-Source on Commercial Vendors. In Gacek, C. (Ed.), *Software Reuse: Methods, Techniques, and Tools* (pp. 381–428). Springer Berlin / Heidelberg
[4] Christensen, C. (1997). The Innovator's Dilemma: When New Technologies Cause Great Firms to Fail. *Harvard Business School Press.*

[5] D'Aveni, R. A. & Gunther, R. (2007). Hypercompetition: Managing the Dynamics of Strategic Maneuvering. In Boersch, C. & Elschen, R. (Ed.), *Das Summa Summarum des Management* (pp. 83–93). Gabler.

[6] Eisenhardt, K. (1989). Building Theories from Case Study Research. *Academy of Management Review* 14(4), 532–550.

[7] Favaro, J., Favaro, K. & Favaro, P. (1998). Value Based Software Reuse Investment. *Annals of Software Eng.* 5, 5–52.

[8] Frakes W. B. & Kang K. (2005). Software Reuse Research: Status and Future. *IEEE transactions on Software Engineering* 31(7), 529–536.

[9] Gallardo-Valencia, R. E. & Elliott S. S. (2009). Internet-scale code search. In *Proceedings of the 2009 ICSE Workshop on Search-Driven Development-Users, Infrastructure, Tools and Evaluation* (pp. 49–52). Washington, DC, USA: IEEE Computer Society

[10] Grover, V., & Kohli, R. (2012). Cocreating IT Value: New Capabilities and Metrics for MultiFirm Environments. *MIS Quarterly* 36(1), 225–232.

[11] Haefliger, S., von Krogh, G. & Sebastian, S. (2008). Code Reuse in Open Source Software. *Management Science* 54(1), 180–193.

[12] Henderson, J. C., & Venkatraman (1992). Strategic alignment : a framework for strategic information technology management. In Kochan, T. & Useem. M (Ed.), *Transforming Organizations* (pp. 97–117). Oxford Press.

[13] King, N. (1998). Template Analysis. In Gillian, S. & Catherine, C. (Ed.), Qualitative methods and analysis in organizational research: A practical guide (pp. 118–134). Sage Publications Ltd.

[14] Krueger, C. W. (1992). Software reuse. *ACM Computing Survey* 24, 131–183.

[15] Lerner, J. & Tirole, J. (2005). The scope of open source licensing. *Journal of Law, Economics, and Organization* 21, 20–56.

[16] Madanmohan, T., & De', R. (2004). Open source reuse in commercial firms. *IEEE Software* 21(6), 62–69.

[17] Maznevski, M., & Chudoba, K. (2000). Bridging space over time: Global Virtual Team Dynamics and Effectiveness. *Organization Science* 11(5), 473–492.

[18] McFarlan, F. (1984). Information technology changes the way you compete. *Harvard Business Review* 62(3), 98–103.

[19] Miles, M. B. & Huberman, A. M. (1984). *Qualitative Data Analysis: A Sourcebook of New Methods.* Sage Publications

[20] Mohagheghi, P. & Conradi, R. (2007). Quality, productivity and economic benefits of software reuse: a review of industrial studies. *Empirical Software Engineering* 12, 471–516.

[21] Porter M.E.(1980).: Competitive Strategy: Techniques for Analyzing Industries and Competitors. *New York: The Free Press*

[22] Porter M.E.(1985).: Competitive Advantage. *New York: The Free Press*

[23] Powell, T.C. & Dent-Micallef, A. (1997). Information Technology as Competitive Advantage: The Role of Human, Business, and Technology Resources. *Strategic Management Journal* 18(5), 375–405.

[24] Sambamurthy, V. (2000). Business Strategy in Hypercompetitive Environments: Rethinking the Logic of IT Differentiation. In Zmud, R.W. (Ed.), *Framing the Domains of IT Management: Projecting the Future Through the Past* (pp. 245–261). Pinnaflex Educational Resources, Inc.

[25] Sambamurthy, V., Bharadwaj, A., & Grover, V. (2003). Shaping Agility through Digital Options: Reconceptualizing the Role of Information Technology in Contemporary Firms. *MIS Quarterly* 27(2), 237–263.

[26] Strauss, A. & Corbin, J. (1990). Basics of Qualitative Research: Grounded Theory Procedures and Techniques. *Sage Publications Ltd.*

[27] von Krogh, G., Spaeth, S. & Haefliger, S. (2005). Knowledge Reuse in Open Source Software: An Exploratory Study of 15 Open Source Projects. In *38th Hawaii International Conference on System Sciences* (pp. 198b–198b). System Sciences

Chapter 11
Applying Program Analysis to Code Retrieval

Joel Ossher and Cristina Lopes

Abstract Early code retrieval systems were primarily adaptations of standard text retrieval approaches, and so treated source code as either plain or structured text. While fairly successful, these approaches ignored much of the information that can be extracted from the source code. Recently, researchers have demonstrated a number of ways in which static program analysis can be used to augment text-based retrieval approaches. By taking advantage of the structural and semantic information embedded in source code, advanced code retrieval systems can provide a superior experience.

This chapter begins describing how basic text-based code retrieval systems function. It then introduces a basic form of static program analysis which allows source code to be treated as structured text. Finally, it describes link analysis, an advanced program analysis technique. Link analysis aids code retrieval systems in numerous ways, for example enabling better estimates of result quality and the sharing of descriptive terms. The chapter concludes by describing in great detail a single static program analysis technique called dependency slicing. Dependency slicing is used in code retrieval systems to package up search results as a compilable unit, which supports the reuse of the retrieved results.

11.1 Introduction

The increasing availability of high quality source code, as provided by the open source software movement, has made code reuse a much more attractive prospect. Rather than developing systems from scratch, developers have the opportunity to reuse or draw inspiration from existing implementations of similar systems. Yet the

J. Ossher (✉) • C. Lopes
University of California, Irvine, USA
e-mail: jossher@uci.edu; lopes@ics.uci.edi

S.E. Sim and R.E. Gallardo-Valencia (eds.), *Finding Source Code on the Web for Remix and Reuse*, DOI 10.1007/978-1-4614-6596-6_11,
© Springer Science+Business Media New York 2013

```
public byte [ ] readToByteArray (InputStream is) {
    ByteArrayOutputStream bos = new ByteArrayOutputStream ( );
    try {
        byte [ ] buff = new byte [1024];
        int read = 0;
        while  ( ( read = is . read ( buff ) > 0) {
            bos . write ( buff , 0 , read );
        }
        return bos . toByteArray ( );
    } catch ( IOException e ) {
        return null ;
    } finally      {
        close ( is ) ;
    }
}
```

Fig. 11.1 Example snippet

mere existence of reusable source code is not sufficient; developers need a way to locate it.

Code retrieval systems provide this functionality, giving developers the ability to search for relevant units of source code within a large corpus of source code. Simple code retrieval systems use standard text retrieval approaches, in which keyword-based searches are used to match relevant lines of source code. These approaches treat the source code as plain text, disregarding all the deeper semantic information found in source code.

Source code, due to its formal nature, is a much richer source of information than plain text. Software engineering researchers recognized this, and developed advanced retrieval techniques that better utilize the semantic information embedded in source code. Static program analysis provides the backbone of these systems, as it provides a mechanism for extracting relevant information from the source code.

For the remainder of this chapter, we will use the snippet of source code in Fig. 11.1 to illustrate techniques for code retrieval. We will begin by introducing a few basic text retrieval approaches used for code search. We will then describe how treating source code as structured text, requiring a basic form of static program analysis, can improve retrieval results. Finally, we will cover link analysis, an advanced program analysis technique. We will show how links can be extracted from source code and how they can be used to improve code retrieval. We will also introduce dependency slicing, a link-analysis-based technique for improving search result presentation.

11.2 Full Text Search

Imagine that a developer is interested in Java's ByteArrayOutputStream, and wants to see an example of it being used. Full text search provides an easy way to find such examples: it can through a corpus of source code for all occurrences of the word `ByteArrayOutputStream`.

Most computer users are familiar with full text search functionality through its text processor form of **ctrl+f**, though it can be done from the command-line using the Linux tool **grep** [6]. Full text search can include regular expression-based searching in addition to simple string matching. This gives the user the ability to specify a more complex range of matches at the expense of speed. Most development environments support either plain text or limited regular expression-based searching, and grep can handle both from the command-line.

The primary advantage of full text search is that it is easy to understand and use, and does not require any preprocessing in order to function (though preprocessing can make it faster). Yet while full text searching is effective at finding all occurrences of the search term, it is not ideal for code retrieval. Results are returned unranked and usually in order of occurrence, which often causes the user to be inundated with matches, with irrelevant results mixed in with the relevant ones. In some cases, refinement of the initial query can eliminate many irrelevant results, but this is not guaranteed and can be quite difficult.

For example, say the developer from earlier only wanted to see examples where the `toByteArray()` method was used. How would one refine the search to only return cases where that specific method was called? One could not simply add `toByteArray` after the `ByteArrayOutputStream`, as this would require that the two occur next to each-other in the text. Using regular expressions would allow the words to be separated, but one would have to be careful that they didn't occur too far apart. Also, there is the risk that an unrelated `toByteArray` method might be referenced, and not the one associated with `ByteArrayOutputStream`. Ultimately, while full text search has its place, other methods provide a much better experience for code retrieval.

11.3 Term-Based Search

Code retrieval systems have borrowed a number of term-based statistical approaches for text retrieval from the field of information retrieval (IR). These approaches for text retrieval help ameliorate the issues with full text search. Rather than treating a document as an ordered collected of characters, as is done in full text search, term-based approaches instead divide documents into terms, or words. For plain text, this division is usually done on whitespace. For source code, characters like (and { must also be considered. Camel case words, such at `ByteArrayOutputStream`, are also often split apart.

Unlike full text search, which returns all possible matches in an arbitrary order, the term-based methods inherently rank matches in order of descending relevance. When the relevance judgments are accurate, this can dramatically reduce the time it takes to find a meaningful result. For a full treatment of general information retrieval methods, we recommend Manning and Raghavan's *Introduction to Information Retrieval* [10].

One term-based approach is TF-IDF, which stands for *term frequency - inverse document frequency*. In TF-IDF, each document is broken into a collection of terms, and each of the terms is associated with the number of times it occurs in that document. Terms are then weighted according to how common they are across the corpus, the intuition being that rare terms are more central to the meaning of a document than terms that occur regularly. To search the corpus, the user provides a list of terms, which are matched against the collection of terms. Documents are ranked according to how many of the searched terms they contain, and how common those terms are. While TF-IDF is not the only statistical method for ranking documents, it sees widespread use due to its perceived quality. Apache Lucene, an open-source text indexing platform, uses TF-IDF as one of its primary ranking methods.

Statistical approaches for topic modeling are also be used to improve term-based searching. Topic modeling groups together terms according to identified topics, which allows the terms to be used somewhat interchangeably. So if a developer searches for `print`, the search system can also return results relating to `output`. Latent semantic indexing (LSI) and latent Dirichlet allocation (LDA) are two approaches for topic modeling, and we direct interested readers to Berry and Kogan's *Text Mining: Applications and Theory* [4].

Term-based search methods have a number of advantages over full text search. They can provide results ordered by relevance. This dramatically increases the usability of the search systems, especially if searches could potentially return thousands of results. Through topic modeling, term-based searches can also handle the use of synonyms, which can cause significant problems if the vocabulary for a given search isn't entirely clear.

These advantages come at a cost. Term-based methods generally require an index to be created in advance of any searching, which can be time consuming, especially for large input. This does make individual searches faster than their full text equivalents, however. Another issue is that if the ranking is poor, ranked results become significantly less useful than unranked results. If users mistakenly trust a poor relevance ordering, they will fail to notice meaningful results.

Returning to our running example, let's look again at the developer searching for instances where the `toByteArray` method is called for `ByteArrayOutput Stream`. Term-based searching simplifies the query dramatically, as now the developer can simply enter those two terms and the system will return examples where both terms are present ranked at the top. Due to this approach being purely text-based, the risk remains that an unrelated `toByteArray` method might be referenced, and not the one associated with `ByteArrayOutputStream`.

11.4 Structured Text Search

Every term in a document is not equally central to that document's meaning. This is the central insight behind TF-IDF, which uses different measures of frequency to determine a term's importance. Yet frequency is not the only method for determining importance; structure is another. The name of a class, for example, is likely more important a term than one randomly selected from the body of a method. Looking at our example snippet, the method name, `readToByteArray`, much better captures the function of the method than keyword `null` or the parameter name `is`. If a developer searches for `is null`, this method is likely a poor match, despite containing both terms, especially compared to a method named `isNull`. To achieve this, the retrieval system must give priority to matches where the terms appear in method name.

The syntax of the programming language determines the exact set of relevant structural elements, and so code retrieval systems must either be language-specific or use a model that captures common elements across multiple languages. Structural elements can include features like the file names, method names, the contents of comments, and the bodies of methods.

In order to take structure into account, every instance of every term is annotated with the structural element from which it came. The ranking system can then weight a term according to its origin. Thus a term found in a method name can be weighted differently than a term found in a method body. This weighting is often a simple linear combination, but more complicated functions can also be used. There is no simple method for deciding on the relative weights to use in the ranking system. Often, the weights assigned are determined by a mixture of intuition (what structural elements *should* be more important) and experimentation (what *actually* works). Automated training approaches can also be used, where the weights are trained on a set of predetermined queries whose ideal results are manually specified.

Apache Lucene, the open-source platform mentioned in the previous section, uses a document model that is fundamentally built around this idea of structured text [1]. Each document in Lucene is a collection of fields, each of which contains a collection of terms. Each structural element can be directly mapped to a Lucene field, and so using Lucene each structural element can be associated with the terms that originate there. Lucene then supports numerous ways of weighting the fields when performing the ranking.

11.4.1 Term Extraction

A basic form of static analysis is required for associating terms with structural elements. Such a term extraction system system must be aware of the programming language syntax, and bears many similarities to the front-end of a compiler; it must take plain text that conforms to the language specification and convert it to an intermediate form. In a compiler, this intermediate form is then optimized and lowered to the output language. In term extraction, this intermediate form is traversed and terms output with their associated elements.

There are two primary components to any compiler front-end. First, there is the tokenizer, which breaks the original text into tokens. The tokenizer typically splits the original text on white space plus some special characters, like braces and parenthesis. The tokenizer is sufficient preprocessing for any system that treats the source code as plain text, as was described in the previous section. In order to extract the structural elements, however, the tokens need to be fed in to the parser, the second component. The parser, based on the syntax of the language, builds a tree-based representation of the text, called an abstract syntax tree (AST). Parsers can either be written by hand, or automatically generated based on a formal specification of the language syntax. Given the complexity of the language syntax for many popular languages, it is generally much easier to reuse an existing parser than develop one from scratch. For a more complete picture of how compiler front-ends function, we recommend Aho et al.'s *Compilers: Principles, Techniques, and Tools* [2].

11.5 Link-Based Retrieval

In addition to being highly structured, source code also contains a large amount of semantic information. Given that source code is designed to be understood by computers, source code retrieval systems can leverage this semantic information much more easily than general text retrieval systems. In this section, we will discuss how links, a specific form of semantic information present in source code, can be used to improve source code retrieval.

The concept of link analysis first came to prominence with the internet, where Google showed that it could be used to great advantage with its PageRank algorithm. In the case of web pages, links are the unidirectional hyperlinks where a webpage directs its readers to another webpage. The insight behind PageRank was that the number of incoming links to a webpage could (iteratively) be used as proxy measure of that webpage's quality.

In the domain of software, links are slightly different. Rather than being an explicit hyperlink, a link instead manifests as a name, which is reference to some type or method defined elsewhere in the code. For example, if a method creates a local variable with type `ByteArrayOutputStream`, then there is a semantic link between that local variable and the declaration of `ByteArrayOutputStream`. One common form of link is the method call. When method calls are connected together, one gets a call-graph, a commonly used link structure in programming language analysis.

Link information can be used in a number of different ways to improve source code retrieval. One popular approach is to adapt PageRank to source code retrieval. This can be found in systems such as Sourcerer [9], Portfolio [11] and Spars-J [16]. Another approach is to use link information to improve the presentation of results or give users more detailed information on retrieved code. CodeGenie [8] and Code Conjurer [7], for example, both use link information to extract executable snippets of code for reuse, a technique which will be discussed in the next section. SpotWeb [14], by contrast, counts links in order to give developers an idea of how popular individual methods in a library are.

Another technique that uses link information is Structural Semantic Indexing (SSI) [3]. SSI uses link information to address the paucity of descriptive words present in source code. The key idea is the following: code entities that share common usage of APIs are functionally similar, and can share the terms used to define each other. Simply put, if both A and B use a common set of APIs in a similar manner, then A and B are semantically related even if their names are different. As such, a query for A should retrieve B and vice-versa.

11.5.1 Link Extraction

The first step in performing any sort of link analysis is to build the appropriate form of link graph. In the context of source code retrieval, a link graph contains a set of nodes, representing structural elements, and a set of edges, representing links. For example, to represent a call graph, the nodes would represent methods and the edges would represent method calls.

Link extraction proceeds in a similar manner to the structured term extraction described in Sect. 11.4.1. In term extraction, the intermediate form generated by the compiler front-end is traversed and the terms output along with their associated structural elements. In link extraction, further analysis is performed on the intermediate form in order to identify the desired links. For example, to build a call-graph, one must process the intermediate form to identify the method being called at every method call site. The result is called an attributed abstract syntax tree, as the abstract syntax tree has been attributed with type and reference information.

The main difficulty in building an attributed abstract syntax tree, and hence in identify links in source code, is that the links are often ambiguous, their exact referent determinable only when the program is executed.

There are two main forms of ambiguity. First, there is the ambiguity inherent to static analysis. For example, due to virtual method binding, it is uncomputable what methods actually get called from a given call site. The standard solution to this issue is to use conservative approximations. Instead of including only those methods that actually get called, all methods that *might* get called are included. In addition to virtual binding issues, static analysis is unable to consistently handle the use of reflection. If the name of the method to be called is not available until runtime, then it cannot be discovered statistically. This form of ambiguity is present in all static analysis.

The second form of ambiguity comes from nature of the data used in source code retrieval systems. For static analysis to function properly, it requires a declaratively complete program, where every name in the program has a corresponding known declaration. If one attempts to perform static analysis with missing declarations, most systems simply fail on reaching an unknown name.

Unfortunately, it is not acceptable to limit one's corpus of source code to only declaratively complete programs, as empirical research has shown that approximately two-thirds of open source programs are not declaratively complete [13].

One solution to this dilemma is to alter the static analysis to accept non-declaratively complete programs. Partial program analysis, for example, guesses the fully qualified names of any missing types using a number of contextual clues [5, 7]. This allows the static analysis to function in the presence of missing types, but can degrade its performance because of missing information. With regards to link analysis, the result is that many links will refer to unknown types or methods.

The difficulty of partial program analysis lies in the ambiguity of most language's import mechanisms. Take Java as an example. Unresolved single type imports are the best case, as they contain a fully qualified name, and so can be matched to unresolved simple names. On-demand imports, those with a * operator, do not fully specify which types they import, instead including all types within a given package or type. This causes it to be unclear which package an unknown name belongs to. It could be located in the same top-level package or any package for which an on-demand import exists.

A different solution for accommodating declaratively incomplete programs is automated dependency resolution [13]. Automated dependency resolution attempts to automatically locate artifacts that contain the missing declarations, restoring a program to declarative completeness. Its primary benefit with regards to link analysis is that previously unknown referents can now be resolved, improving the fidelity of the link graph.

The first step is to identify the names of the missing types, which is done in much the same manner as partial program analysis. Once the names are identified, they are then matched against a collection of candidate artifacts that might contain the missing declarations. The goal is to identify a set of artifacts that provide all of the missing types while including a minimal number of extra unnecessary types. When this approach was applied to a large test set of open source programs, it was found to double the number of declaratively complete programs.

11.6 Dependency Slicing

So far, this chapter has provided an overview of how code retrieval systems function, and how static analysis can be used to improve them. The remainder of this chapter will describe in detail a single application of static analysis to code retrieval. This should provide insight into the complexities involved with integrating static analysis into code retrieval.

The application we will focus on is dependency slicing. Dependency slicing is designed to identify the minimal set of declarations required for a set of seed declarations to compile and execute properly, and is similar to approaches used for reducing the size of jar files [15]. The purpose of dependency slicing is to package up the result of a search so that it can be imported into a project and immediately reused. CodeGenie, a tool for test-driven code reuse, uses Sourcerer's dependency slicing service to integrate search results with test cases, in order to identify results that satisfy the test cases.

The algorithm for dependency slicing behaves in much the same way as a human might when presented with the same task. Consider a developer who is interested in reusing the `readToByteArray` method, but nothing else from the project that contains that method. The developer might begin by copying the method to a new project. Once isolated, he would have to identify any missing dependencies and copy them in turn into the project. For example, he would have to find the declaration of the `close` method, and copy that as well. This process would have to be repeated until no missing dependencies remained. This manual approach is quite effective, but can be time consuming. Dependency slicing allows this approach to be efficiently automated.

The dependency slicing algorithm is specifically designed for use with Java. While the general algorithm applies to any object-oriented language, some of the details are tied to the specifics of the Java language. A dependency slice can be seeded with a package or any declared entity, such as a class or method. Some of these slices are more useful than others, as a dependency slice seeded with a field is of little use compared to one seeded with a method.

11.6.1 Basic Algorithm

The dependency slicing algorithm is divided into two stages. The first stage identifies the declarations that must be included in the slice in order for the slice to function independently. The second stage reconstructs the source code for the slice itself.

The dependency slicing algorithm works off of a link graph, as described in the previous section. In the link graph used by dependency slicing, nodes represent declarations, such as packages, classes, methods or fields. Edges represent any form of relation between declarations, such as method calls, field access or type reference. The goal of the dependency slicing link graph is to capture every case where one declaration requires another declaration in order to function.

The first stage of the dependency slicing algorithm is described in pseudocode in Algorithm 1. It uses the work-list approach common in data-flow analysis [12]. The algorithm begins by initializing a queue to the set of seed declarations to be sliced out of the program. The initial set of seed seed declarations is iteratively expanded to include all of the declarations they contain. For example, if the seed declaration is a package, all classes within that package are included, as are all the methods within those classes.

Once the queue is initialized with the seed declarations, the loop on line 2 is iterated until the queue is empty. A single declaration is examined during each iteration of the loop. To illustrate what happens during each loop iteration, consider the `readToByteArray` method from Fig. 11.1. First, in line 4, the algorithm checks that `readToByteArray` has not been previously considered. This check is necessary because declarations can be reached by multiple different paths in the link graph.

Require: Queue *todo* contains the seed declarations
Ensure: *todo* is empty and *slice* contains the complete dependency slice

```
 1: slice ⇐ new Slice()
 2: while todo not empty do
 3:     next ⇐ todo.dequeue()
 4:     if next has not been considered yet then
 5:         Add next to slice
 6:         Add next.getContainingDeclaration() to todo
 7:         for all method such that next calls method do
 8:             Add method to todo
 9:         end for
10:         for all field such that next accesses field do
11:             Add field to todo
12:         end for
13:         for all type such that next references type do
14:             Add type to todo
15:         end for
16:     end if
17: end while
18: return slice
```

Algorithm 1: Basic slice

Once the algorithm has determined that `readToByteArray` has never been examined, the next step is to add its parent class to the queue, as seen in line 6. This is done because in Java, at least, it is not possible to have a method without a containing class.

Next, the loop on line 7 adds every method called by `readToByteArray` to the queue. This includes the `close` method mentioned earlier, as well as the `write` method and the constructor for `ByteArrayOutputStream`, among others. Each of methods is clearly requires for `readToByteArray` to function.

The loop in line 10 adds every field accessed by the declaration to the queue. As no fields are accessed in our example, this loop would not add anything.

The loops on lines 7 and 10 in Algorithm 1 do not apply to all declaration types, as not all declaration types call methods or access fields. Only those declarations that directly contain executable statements can do so. For example, these loops apply to method and initializer declarations, but not to class or interface declarations.

The loop on line 13 adds every referenced type to the queue. In our example, this includes the types `InputStream`, `ByteArrayOutputStream` and `IOException`. A type reference is simply any mention of a type's simple or fully qualified name.

The algorithm concludes once every declaration identified as required has been examined once. The result is that the slice contains the seed declarations and all of their transitive dependencies.

The second step of the algorithm is the reconstruction of the source code for the slice. For every top-level (package-level) type declaration, a file is created with the appropriate package declaration placed at the top. The import statements from the original file are examined, and are included if their corresponding declarations are in the slice and are referenced within the file. On demand imports (those ending in .*) are included if they contain any declarations that meet the previous criteria. The top-level type declaration is then synthesized, with the access modifiers, simple name and type variables preserved from the original.

Within each type declaration, only those sub-declarations that also appear in the slice are included. Fields are synthesized, and their initialization code is copied from the original source file. They cannot be copied directly, because multiple field declarations of a single type can occur together while only one is included in the slice. Both enum constants and initializers are copied directly from the original source. It is important to preserve the relative ordering of fields and initializers, as Java does not permit forward references in initialization code. Constructors, methods and annotation elements are also copied directly from the original source. They are treated as atomic and included in their entirety; no individual statements are removed. As a result, if one of those declarations is included in the slice, any declarations it contains must also be included (such as local types). Inner type declarations are synthesized in the same manner as top-level declarations, with their sub-declarations included in as just described. Finally, these files are placed into a directory structure matching their package declarations, and packaged in a zip file.

11.6.2 Slicing the Type Hierarchy

The basic dependency slicing algorithm ignores one important aspect of object-oriented languages: the type hierarchy. By not properly accounting for the relationships between the user-defined types, the algorithm generates overly large or incomplete slices.

First, there is the issue of how much of the type hierarchy must be preserved. A single class often contains multiple pieces of functionality, not all of which may be relevant to the current slice. This can manifest itself as a type extending or implementing types that would otherwise not be included in the slice. For example, a utility method for converting numbers into roman numerals might be located in a class extending java.lang.Thread. Including this type relationship in the slice is totally unnecessary if the user only cares about how to convert to a roman numeral.

To handle this issue, we augmented the dependency slicing algorithm with a heuristic to determine when to include a type's supertype. This heuristic is extremely liberal when deciding on which type relationships to retain, as we prefer a non-minimal slice to an incomplete or incorrect one. The heuristic is as follows: if a type and its supertype are both in the slice, their type relationship is retained; and, if the supertype is an indirect supertype, then every intermediate supertype must also be included in the slice. For example, consider the ByteArrayOutputStream type. Its direct supertype is OutputStream, as OutputStream is explicitly mentioned in its `extends` clause. Its indirect supertypes include `Object` and `Closeable`, as `OutputStream` extends `Object` and implements the `Closeable` interface. Therefore, if our slice only contained the `ByteArrayOutputStream` type, then its extends relation to `OutputStream` would not be preserved. However, if the slice included any of its direct or indirect supertypes, then the extends relation would be preserved.

It should be noted that this example is entirely hypothetical. In the actual implementation of the system, dependency slicing is not performed on anything from the Java standard library (which is where `ByteArrayOutputStream` is defined). Extracting declarations from the standard library is unnecessary, as its declarations are always present when running a Java application.

This heuristic is based on the reasoning that if a type and some supertype of that type both exist in the slice, it's possible that at some point in the program the type is upcast to its supertype. It is therefore necessary for the connection between that type and its supertype to be preserved. In order to do this, we must fill in all the types between the type and its supertype, unless we want to attempt to splice out types from the original inheritance chain.

In order to add this heuristic, it is necessary to alter the basic algorithm slightly. A type must not be considered to reference its supertypes simply by virtue of mentioning them in the `extends` or `implements` clauses. Otherwise every supertype would always be included.

The implementation of this heuristic is divided across two parts of the algorithm. First, each type must have its type hierarchy examined to determine if any of its supertypes need to be added to the slice. Second, when the slice's source code is reconstructed, only direct supertypes that are also in the slice should be included in the `extends` or `implements` clauses.

Require: Queue *todo*, *slice* and *type* to check

1: *included* ⇐ **false**
2: **for all** *super* such that *super* is a direct supertype of *type* **do**
3:      **if** *super* ∈ *slice* **then**
4:          *included* ⇐ **true**
5:      **else if** CHECKHIERARCHY(*super*) returns **true then**
6:          Add *super* to *todo*
7:          *included* ⇐ **true**
8:      **end if**
9: **end for**
10: **return** *included*

Algorithm 2: Pseudocode for CheckHierarchy

Algorithm 2 contains the pseudocode for this first change. This method is invoked on every type declaration contained in the slice after the work-list of the basic algorithm is empty. It checks every direct supertype of the type declaration. If that supertype is not currently in the slice, all of its supertypes are examined recursively.

If one of those supertypes is contained in the slice, then the original supertype is added to the slice. If this method adds any new entities to the work-list, the algorithm is repeated from the start.

There are two special cases where this heuristic fails to include necessary supertypes. The first is classes that either directly or indirectly implement java.lang.Throwable. If a class is ever thrown, it must implement Throwable. Yet Throwable might never be explicitly mentioned in the code, as the requirement is implicit in the throws statement. The second case is classes that implement java.lang.Iterable. Enhanced for loops can implicitly require classes implementing Iterable To solve both of these cases, Throwable and Iterable must be explicitly added to the slice. This results in the heuristic always retaining the type relationship.

A second difficulty introduced by the type hierarchy is due to abstract types and implementation inheritance. Interfaces and abstract classes can both define abstract methods which every non-abstract subtype is forced to implement. For example, the interface java.lang.Iterable mentioned previously requires the method iterator() to be implemented in every subtype. So if a class such as ByteArrayOutputStream implements Closeable it must contain a method named close with the proper signature in order to compile. Thus for a slice to compile, it must include all the methods required by abstract declarations, whether or not they are explicitly referenced within the slice.

Methods overriding non-required methods within the slice must also be added in order to preserve correct functionality. So if ByteArrayOutputStream extends OutputStream and both have a method named write if OutputStream's write method is in the slice then ByteArrayOutputStream's write method must also be included, whether it is explicitly referenced on not. Given the dynamic binding of method calls in Java, it is not always clear statically if these methods are called. But if a supertype's method is referenced, then it is possible that it is in fact a subtype's overriding method that is actually being executed.

Once each type's type hierarchy has been examined, with the appropriate supertypes added to the slice, the next step is to ensure that all of the required methods are present for that type. Our heuristic states that a method is required if it overrides a supertype's method that is also in the slice. This ensures that all the requirements for abstract supertypes are met, plus that all overriding methods are present that could potentially be called while the type is upcast to a supertype.

Constructors and fields are not handled in this manner, as they cannot be required by abstract types and are not dynamically bound.

11.6.3 Information Hiding

The separation between abstract types and their implementations in Java impacts the selection of a seed declaration. If a seed declaration is chosen such that only the abstract types are ever referenced, the slice does not include their implementations.

This may not be the desired behavior if the developer is actually interested in these implementations. The algorithm can be augmented to pull in an abstract type's implementation under certain circumstances, but this risks including unrelated implementations if it happened to be a common abstract type. We believe that instead of modifying the algorithm, a user should be provided feedback to guide the selection of additional seed entities. Then the slice can be recomputed to include those additional entities.

11.6.4 Constructors

In the basic algorithm, constructors are only included if they are explicitly referenced somewhere in the slice. There are a few circumstances under which this is not sufficient to ensure that a slice can be compiled. Ultimately, a constructor must be included under the following circumstances: (a) the constructor is directly referenced, (b) the constructor's class contains a final field, (c) it is a default constructor, and (d) the constructor's class' superclass does not contain a default constructor. Case (a) matches what is done in the basic algorithm.

Case (b) occurs because Java requires that every final field be given a value during the initialization of its class. If this value assignment is done in the constructor, and the slice includes no constructors, then the resulting class does not compile. To resolve this, we include all the constructors for any sliced class containing a final field.

Case (c) arises from the interaction between constructors and the type hierarchy. For a class, every constructor must invoke a constructor of its superclass. If no invocation is explicitly specified on the first line of the constructor body, the compiler implicitly invokes the superclass' default constructor (a default constructor is a 0-argument constructor). For example, `ByteArrayOutputStream.<init>(int)` does not explicitly specify a superconstructor call, and so implicitly calls `OutputStream.<init>()`. This invocation is present in the bytecode, but is cumbersome to infer from the source. The slice may therefore lack the necessary superconstructor if it was only called implicitly. To ensure this does not occur, all default constructors are included, whether referenced or not.

The problem extends further than that, however, leading to case (d). If a class has no explicitly defined constructors, the Java compiler creates a synthetic default constructor. If `ByteArrayOutputStream` actually had no constructor, the compiler would create `ByteArrayOutputStream.<init>()`. This synthetic constructor would invoke `ByteArrayOutputStream`'s default superconstructor, `OutputStream.<init>()`. If `ByteArrayOutputStream` originally contained constructors explicitly calling non-default superconstructors and none of `ByteArrayOutputStream`'s constructors are included in the slice, then the compiler attempts to synthesize `ByteArrayOutputStream.<init>()`.

If `ByteArrayOutputStream`'s superclass has a non-default constructor and doesn't have a default constructor, which is quite likely if `ByteArrayOutputStream` never referenced one, then the compiler is unable to synthesize `ByteArrayOutput Stream.<init>()` because `OutputStream.<init>()` does not exist, resulting in a compilation error. To handle this, we must include `ByteArrayOutputStream`'s original constructors to stop the compiler from attempting to synthesize `ByteArray OutputStream.<init>()`

In the end, including all of a class's original constructors may be a good practice, as it eliminates a possible source of confusion. While the current approach guarantees correct behavior, it makes no distinction between a class whose constructor was not included because it was never referenced and a class that simply has no explicit constructors. If a developer was looking to reuse the code, he might mistakenly call a synthesized constructor that would not have existed if the original constructors has been included.

11.6.5 Initializers

Initializers are blocks of statements contained within a class body rather than within a method or constructor body. Static initializers are executed when a class is first loaded by the Java Virtual Machine, while instance initializers are executed on object creation.

An initializer can never be referenced, as it is simply a nameless block of statements. Therefore, initializers won't be included in a slice. This is clearly not the desired behavior, as they can be necessary for the proper functioning of a class. It is not realistic to determine exactly when an initializer must be included, so they are always included. This increases the size of the slice, as the initializer might reference entities that would not otherwise have been included. But it preserves the original behavior.

11.6.6 @Override Annotations

The Java Language Specification states that if a method declaration is annotated with `@Override`, but the method does not in fact override any method declared in a superclass, a compile-time error occurs. This has a potentially problematic interaction with our slicing of the type hierarchy. It is quite possible for a slice to contain a method but not to contain the method that it overrides, if it was statically clear that only the overriding method was referenced. If `@Override` was used in these cases, either the overridden method must be added to the slice or the annotation must be removed. We decided to go with the latter approach, to help reduce the size of the slice.

11.6.7 External Dependencies

The dependency slicing algorithm described so far works well so long as source code is available for all the sliced declarations. It's only with access to this source code that we are able to reconstruct partial type declarations to match the entities in the slice.

Dependencies on external projects are usually realized through the inclusion of jar files, which often do not contain source code. Even if the source code is available for these external dependencies, extending the slice into them may not necessarily be advantageous, as it would create incompatibilities with the packaged versions of those projects. This would be especially problematic with the Java Standard Library, as creating sliced versions of java.lang.Object or java.io.PrintStream could be exceedingly confusing.

All slicing behavior is therefore limited to the project containing the seed declarations, with all external references fully preserved, allowing the original jar files to be included. In order to support this logic, a few changes needed to be made to the algorithms previously described.

In the basic algorithm, it is no longer necessary to perform a slicing analysis for external references. Any declaration that is added to the work-list but is external to the project just gets included in its entirety. This has cascading effects on the slicing of the type hierarchy. Any type included in the slice but external to the project must include all of its supertypes. Similarly, all methods required by an external abstract supertype must be included, not just those referenced in the slice.

This alteration introduces a potential source of error with respect to the type hierarchy. Consider the following class declarations:

```
class A extends ArrayList {
  public void sort() {
    Collections.sort(this);
  }
}
```

This class extends java.util.ArrayList, but never references it outside of the extends clause. Yet the call to java.util.Collections.sort(List<T>) requires that A extend ArrayList (because ArrayList implements List). If Collection's sort method is not analyzed, then java.util.List does not get added to the slice, and the necessary type relationship is not preserved. In order to handle this, we must examine external method and constructor calls and add their formal parameter types to the slice. This ensures that if an external method expects a certain type, that type is included in the slice.

11.6.8 Complete Algorithm

The full algorithm is shown in Algorithm 3. The method CheckHierarchy on line 20 was described in Algorithm 2. CheckDefaultConstructors on line 26 adds any default constructors, and determines if other constructors must be added to stop the compiler from synthesizing a default constructor.

Require: Queue *todo* contains the seed declarations
Ensure: *todo* is empty and *slice* contains the complete dependency slice

```
 1: slice ⇐ new Slice()
 2: while todo not empty do
 3:     while todo not empty do
 4:         next ⇐ todo.dequeue()
 5:         if next has not been considered yet then
 6:             Add next to slice
 7:             Add next.getContainingDeclaration() to todo
 8:             for all method such that next calls method do
 9:                 Add method to todo
10:             end for
11:             for all field such that next accesses field do
12:                 Add field to todo
13:             end for
14:             for all type such that next references type do
15:                 Add type to todo
16:             end for
17:         end if
18:     end while
19:     for all type such that type is a declared type in the slice do
20:         CHECKHIERARHCY(type)
21:         for all method such type contains method do
22:             if method overrides a method in a supertype of type in the slice
                 then
23:                 Add method to todo
24:             end if
25:         end for
26:         CHECKDEFAULTCONSTRUCTORS(type)
27:     end for
28: end while
29: return slice
```

Algorithm 3: Full dependency slicing algorithm

11.6.9 Complexity

In order to evaluate the complexity of the dependency slicing algorithm, consider the underlying link graph. Each node is examined at most once, and during its examination each edge is followed at most once. The result is that the running time of the slicing algorithm is $O(|N| * |E|)$. The theoretical maximum number of edges in the link graph is $O(|N|^2)$, which gives the algorithm a running time of $O(|N|^3)$. This is the running time for graphs containing a single project and its dependencies.

If, instead, we have a graph containing a large number of projects, the relationship between the number of nodes and the number of edges changes. The number of edges in a project is independent of the number of nodes from other projects that it does not reference. Practically, this gives us a linear instead of quadratic relationship between $|E|$ and $|N|$, making the running time of the algorithm $O(|N|^2)$ for graphs containing a large number of unrelated projects.

11.6.10 Known Limitations

As is generally true with static analysis techniques, there are a number of limitations to dependency slicing.

One circumstance in which the dependency slicing algorithm cannot guarantee correctness is in the presence of missing references. If a file fails to compile due to unresolved external references, then some of the relations are either missing or reference dummy UNKNOWN entities. Without being able to follow external dependencies, the slice may fail to include entities from the original program that are actually required. It can, however, identify the missing entities and report them to the user. Although the resulting slice does not compile, the dependency slicing algorithm fares no worse than a human would when presented with the same information.

Even with complete information and a slice that compiles, there is still no guarantee that the slice behaves with respect to the seed entities exactly as it did in the initial program. There are a few known situations in which the slicer fails to include entities that are actually necessary for proper functioning.

One class of situations is due to the limited analysis of external dependencies. We believe the solution previously discussed for these external dependencies is sound with respect to compilation, but misses a certain type of dependency due to the lack of full analysis of external method calls.

Marker interfaces provide an excellent example of how this can occur. The Java Standard Library contains an example of this in `java.io.Serializable`, an interface that contains no methods. Its sole purpose is to indicate that the implementing class can be serialized. Because of its role, `java.io.Serializable` is rarely mentioned outside of the `implements` clause. In order for the slicer to realize its importance, a call to `java.io.ObjectOutputStream`'s `writeObject(java.lang.Object)` would have to be followed to realize that a reference to `java.io.Serializable` is finally made in `writeObject0(java.lang.Object,boolean)`. Without seeing this reference, the slicer would not include the interface in the slice, believing it not to be used.

Full analysis of external method calls can solve this issue. Barring that, every external supertype would have to be included in the slice, regardless of whether or not it was referenced. If the use of a marker interface is expected, the slicing algorithm can easily be altered to include all external supertypes.

Another class of problematic situations occurs because of the existence of reflection in Java. The ability of a program to explore and modify its own runtime behavior makes statically determining what pieces of each declaration are needed impossible in general.

To continue with the `java.io.Serializable` example from before, the two methods commonly associated with the proper handling of serialization, `writeReplace()` and `readResolve()`, would not be properly sliced. They are not mentioned in the `java.io.Serializable` interface. Instead, developers must be aware of their association extralinguistically. Due to their not being tied to an abstract type, their invocation is always done reflectively. Therefore it is difficult to determine statically that they need to exist.

11.6.11 Summary of Dependency Slicing

This section has provided a detailed explanation of how dependency slicing uses a link graph, as described in Sect. 11.5, to extract a compilable subset of a program. Dependency slicing was developed to simplify the reuse of search results by automating the dependency resolution process. As should now be clear, even with a complete link graph, there are a number of subtle cases that must be accounted for. Furthermore, these cases are often language specific. Therefore applying advanced program analysis techniques to a general code retrieval system can be quite challenging.

11.7 Conclusion

This chapter has covered how program analysis can be applied to code retrieval. We began by introducing basic full text search, which is the de facto standard found in text editors and development environments. We then showed how term-based search, a standard in information retrieval, can improve code retrieval by allowing for ranking. Next, we described the benefit of treating source code as structured text, which uses a basic form of program analysis. More advanced program analysis techniques enable link-based retrieval schemes, which were initially made popular in the domain of the internet. We concluded this chapter by describing, in great detail, how dependency slicing, a program analysis technique based on link analysis, can be used to improve the reuse of search results.

Acknowledgements This material is based upon work supported by the National Science Foundation under Grant No. 1018374.

References

[1] Apache Lucene.
[2] Alfred V. Aho, Monica S. Lam, Ravi Sethi, and Jeffrey D. Ullman. *Compilers: Principles, Techniques, and Tools*. 2006.
[3] Sushil K. Bajracharya, Joel Ossher, and Cristina V. Lopes. Leveraging usage similarity for effective retrieval of examples in code repositories. In *Proceedings of the eighteenth ACM SIGSOFT international symposium on Foundations of software engineering*, FSE '10, pages 157–166, New York, NY, USA, 2010. ACM.
[4] Michael W. Berry and J. Kogan. *Text Mining : Applications and Theory*. 2010.
[5] Barthélémy Dagenais and Laurie Hendren. Enabling static analysis for partial java programs. In *Proceedings of the 23rd ACM SIGPLAN conference on Object-oriented programming systems languages and applications*, OOPSLA '08, pages 313–328, New York, NY, USA, 2008. ACM.
[6] GNU Software Foundation. GNU Grep 2.9 Manual.
[7] Oliver Hummel, Werner Janjic, and Colin Atkinson. Code Conjurer: Pulling Reusable Software out of Thin AIr. *IEEE Software*, January 2008.
[8] Otávio Augusto Lazzarini Lemos, Sushil Bajracharya, Joel Ossher, Ricardo Santos Morla, Paulo Cesar Masiero, Pierre Baldi, and Cristina Videira Lopes. CodeGenie. *Proceedings of the twenty-second IEEE/ACM international conference on Automated software engineering - ASE '07*, page 525, 2007.
[9] Erik Linstead, Sushil Bajracharya, Trung Ngo, Paul Rigor, Cristina Lopes, and Pierre Baldi. Sourcerer: mining and searching internet-scale software repositories. *Data Mining and Knowledge Discovery*, 18(2):300–336, 2009.
[10] Christopher D. Manning and Prabhakar Raghavan. *Introduction to Information Retrieval*. 2008.
[11] C McMillan, M Grechanik, and D Poshyvanyk. Portfolio: Finding relevant functions and their usages. In *Proceeding of the 33rd*, pages 111–120, 2011.
[12] Flemming Nielson, Hanne R. Nielson, and Chris Hankin. *Principles of Program Analysis*. Springer-Verlag New York, Inc., Secaucus, NJ, USA, 1999.
[13] J. Ossher, S. Bajracharya, and C. Lopes. Automated dependency resolution for open source software. In *Mining Software Repositories (MSR), 2010 7th IEEE Working Conference on*, pages 130–140, may 2010.
[14] Suresh Thummalapenta and Tao Xie. SpotWeb: Detecting Framework Hotspots and Coldspots via Mining Open Source Code on the Web. *2008 23rd IEEE/ACM International Conference on Automated Software Engineering*, pages 327–336, September 2008.
[15] Frank Tip, Chris Laffra, Peter F. Sweeney, and David Streeter. Practical experience with an application extractor for java. In *Proceedings of the 14th ACM SIGPLAN conference on Object-oriented programming, systems, languages, and applications*, OOPSLA '99, pages 292–305, New York, NY, USA, 1999. ACM.

[16] Reishi Yokomori, Takashi Ishio, Tetsuo Yamamoto, Makoto Matsushita, Shinji Kusumoto, and Katsuro Inoue. Java program analysis projects in Osaka University: aspect-based slicing system ADAS and ranked-component search system SPARS-J. In *Proceedings of the 25th International Conference on Software Engineering*, pages 828–829. IEEE Computer Society, 2003.

Chapter 12
Test-Driven Reuse: Key to Improving Precision of Search Engines for Software Reuse

Oliver Hummel and Werner Janjic

Abstract The applicability of software reuse approaches in practice has long suffered from a lack of reusable material, but this situation has changed virtually over night: the rise of the open source movement has made millions of software artifacts available on the Internet. Suddenly, the existing (largely text-based) software search solutions did not suffer from a lack of reusable material anymore, but rather from a lack of precision as a query now might return thousands of potential results. In a reuse context, however, precisely matching results are the key for integrating reusable material into a given environment with as little effort as possible. Therefore a better way for formulating and executing queries is a core requirement for a broad application of software search and reuse. Inspired by the recent trend towards test-first software development approaches, we found test cases being a practical vehicle for reuse-driven software retrieval and developed a test-driven code search system utilizing simple unit tests as semantic descriptions of desired artifacts. In this chapter we describe our approach and present an evaluation that underlines its superior precision when it comes to retrieving reusable artifacts.

12.1 Introduction

Building high-quality software faster, cheaper, and more predictable with the help of reusable software building blocks is not a new idea. The earliest publication usually referenced in this context is Douglas McIlroy's seminal paper on component reuse [25] presented at the famous NATO conference in Garmisch in 1968 where amongst other ideas the term "software engineering" was coined. The idea of "remixing"

O. Hummel (✉) • W. Janjic
Software Engineering Group, University of Mannheim, 68131, Mannheim, Germany
e-mail: hummel@informatik.uni-mannheim.de; werner@informatik.uni-mannheim.de

S.E. Sim and R.E. Gallardo-Valencia (eds.), *Finding Source Code on the Web for Remix and Reuse*, DOI 10.1007/978-1-4614-6596-6__12,
© Springer Science+Business Media New York 2013

existing software parts in order to compose new systems [24] as one cornerstone of a more engineering like software development approach [27] certainly fitted well into the spirit of the whole event.

Software engineering research in general has come a long way since then and has successfully identified a lot of reuse potential amongst various software engineering artifacts [9]. The systematic reuse of well-defined third-party software building blocks (such as components [6] or services [7]) according to a well-defined specification (as e.g. envisaged in [1]) is one of the most challenging approaches since it requires a precise matching of potential reuse candidates to a given specification. However, most existing software search solutions are still text-based and do neither reflect nor support the need to match reuse candidates with the syntactic and semantic characteristics of a specification. Nevertheless, the programmatic syntax and semantics make software search and retrieval significantly different from plain text retrieval so that the techniques that have been successfully applied within the information retrieval community are likely not to be sufficient in the context of (reuse-driven) software retrieval. Software retrieval research has identified some core challenges for implementing a sustainable reuse repository that requires to –

- Create and maintain a large enough software collection that makes searches promising (the so-called repository problem [35]),
- Index and represent its content in a way that makes it easily accessible (the representation problem [8])
- Allow characterizing a desired artifact with reasonable effort and precision (the usability problem [10])
- Execute queries with high precision in order to retrieve the desired content (the retrieval problem [32]).

While the open source movement, higher bandwidths and always increasing hardware power seem to have mitigated the repository problem recently (cf. Sect. 5.2.2 as well), the other three challenges center around finding an optimal representation of software artifacts that allows storing, retrieving and searching them in a precise manner with little effort.

In the remainder of this chapter we present a practical solution to tackle all three of these challenges. We especially describe how we increased the precision of software searches from a reuse perspective based on ordinary unit tests as usually created during every software development project anyway [4]. We have found that well formulated test cases reveal enough syntactical information and semantics of a desired component that they can be used as a query for software searches effectively. Therefore, the current status of our test-driven reuse approach, first presented in 2004 [15], is described in detail in Sect. 12.3. Moreover, we show how we integrated this vision in a state of the art software search engine and into the developer's work environment through a plug-in for the popular Eclipse IDE. In Sect. 12.4 following thereafter, we explain how we evaluated our system in order to demonstrate the feasibility of the test-driven reuse approach and compare it with a similar system recently presented in the literature. Section 12.5 describes this and other related work in more detail before we share our view of the most important open challenges in the context of reuse-oriented retrieval and conclude our chapter in Sects. 12.6 and 12.7, respectively.

12.2 Foundations

Around the turn of the millennium, the state of the art in reuse-oriented software retrieval could be characterized from two widely contrary viewpoints. While one opinion was that most challenges related with reuse libraries have been solved already since repositories were supposed to be mere catalogs containing only a small number of about 50 to perhaps 250 carefully selected components [31], the other opinion claimed the exact opposite. Mili et al. realized in their well-known survey on software retrieval approaches [26] that there is indeed a large variety of prototypical component library systems, but none of them would be able to overcome the retrieval and usability problem mentioned in the introduction, as soon as the amount of available components would increase considerably. The reason for this pessimistic appraisal is simple: since the *matching criterion* (such as e.g. the appearance of a keyword anywhere – i.e. even in comments – within a candidate) is rather weak in most approaches, it is very likely that they return many irrelevant results as soon as a critical mass of indexed material has been exceeded. In other words, 10 years ago, it was still unclear how to build *internet-scale* software search systems (with potentially millions of entries) that would be able to deliver only those components precisely matching an existing "gap" in an application under development.

Separating the useful from the useless results in growing collections is one of the major challenges for all information retrieval approaches [3] and is usually referred to as the *precision* of a search engine. More formally, precision is defined as the fraction of relevant results amongst all results returned for a query. Obviously, it becomes tedious to determine the actual relevance of more than perhaps a few dozen results so that evaluations of common search engines often limit themselves on investigating the precision of the first 20 results (the so-called top 20 precision [23]). A similar challenge exists for the second central metric used in information retrieval to evaluate search engines, the so-called *recall*, defined as the fraction of all relevant elements that are returned for a given query out of all relevant elements contained in a collection for that query. As a collection may actually contain thousands of relevant results, it is often not possible to determine all of them and therefore the recall cannot be determined as well.

The results of a systematic survey in which Mili et al. [26] analyzed existing software retrieval solutions for their performance are presented and discussed in the following. The authors were able to distinguish six seminal classes of software retrieval approaches that we will briefly explain after their enumeration. However, due to a lack of access to most prototypes and the non-existence of standardized evaluation scenarios, Mili et al. were only able to estimate the potential performance (i.e. recall and precision) of these approaches on larger collections so that interested readers are referred to their publication for further details. The estimates they published are as follows:

1. Information retrieval methods (Recall: high/Precision: medium)
2. Descriptive methods (Recall: high/Precision: high)
3. Denotational semantics methods (Recall: high/Precision: very high)
4. Operational semantics methods (Recall: high/Precision: very high)
5. Structural methods (Recall: very high/Precision: very high)
6. Topological methods (Recall: unknown[1]/Precision: unknown)

Software retrieval is a specialization of *information retrieval* and hence it makes sense to reuse methods from the latter area to perform a simple, purely text-based retrieval of software assets. *Descriptive methods* go a small step further and rely on external textual descriptions (i.e. metadata) for an asset. Hence, Mili et al. denote such descriptive methods as a subset of the information retrieval methods, but due to the high use of this approach in practice and literature they created an additional category. *Denotational semantics methods* use signatures (see e.g. [42]) or formal specifications [43] of the indexed assets for retrieval. While signature matching is widely seen as a practical tool in this context, as it uses the parameters and return values exhibited in the interface of an artifact for matching, software retrieval based upon the matching of formal specifications suffers from a variety of disadvantages (such as difficulties in creating and evaluating them). *Operational semantics approaches* that rely on the execution of the indexed software with sample input values are certainly expensive to execute, however, they seem to be easily automatable. Nevertheless, also appealing in theory, this approach definitively also comes with some practical challenges: side effects, non-termination, the structure of used data types, dependencies, etc. can cause serious problems. Hence, in this context, it is no surprise that the most well-known implementation so far, called Behavior Sampling [30], was merely applied to simple mathematical functions of the C standard library. *Structural methods* finally do not deal with the code of the assets directly, but rather with internal program patterns or designs. Since it is largely unclear how to formulate queries for such an approach, it does not surprise that it has only rarely been experimented with.

Overlap between the discussed classifications can appear at various places, e.g. between (3) and (4) and (5) as the "sampling" of components typically needs a specific signature or structure to work with. As visible in the list, Mili et al. still defined *topological methods* as an independent class of approaches, however, since their common denominator is the *distance* between the query and the candidates, we would prefer to describe it as an approach for ranking search results that can (exclusively) be used together with at least one concrete instance of the other approaches.

---

[1] For topological methods it is difficult to define or estimate recall and precision. See [26] for more.

12.2.1 State of the Art

As previously indicated, the premises for software search and retrieval have changed considerably since the Internet and its users have made millions of open source components [16] available for software developers and researchers alike in recent years. Around the turn of the millennium, Seacord realized this potential and attempted to fill a software repository with Java applets collected on the Web by an automated crawler [36]. Also at that time, Ye was one of the first researchers recognizing that software searches are not only hindered by technical weaknesses of search engines, but by usability issues as well. He found that developers are often not even aware of the chance that a reuse candidate might be stored in a repository (which was understandable though due to their relatively small size at that time) and hence proposed and implemented a prototypical software search system (called CodeBroker) that continuously monitors the work of a developer and proactively presents potentially reusable candidates based on textual information from the comments athe developer has been writing [41].

Also around that time, the World Wide Web witnessed the rise of large-scale search engines helping to make its growing amount of data accessible. Inspired by the success of Google's PageRank algorithm [29], it was the ComponentRank approach of Inoue et al. [22] that breathed new life into the software retrieval community with an automated search engine (known as Spars-J). While their basic retrieval approach was still text-based and hence simple, it was their set of about 150,000 open source files that was far larger than every other collection before, together with the clever ranking approach that created a new standard. Inoue et al. proposed to rank those components higher in the result list of a search that are more often used than others amongst the indexed files. Nevertheless, the overall precision of the searches remains still too low from a specification-based reuse perspective as long as merely keyword matching is applied. Almost simultaneously, Hummel and Atkinson [16] demonstrated that general web search engines (such as Google) could be used for software searches by enriching queries with special keywords (such as: filetype:java AND "class stack") that – though not working absolutely perfectly – still delivers relevant source code with a high hit ratio.

However, although all seminal search approaches described before were available at that time, little work is known that would have tried to integrate them with the upcoming large-scale software search engines described in the next subsection. Consequently, a pure text-based retrieval still remained state of the art at that time. The only visible progress was the idea of parsing source codes in order to extract the names of objects and their methods to allow more focused searches for them (as e.g. introduced by Koders.com). Hummel et al. have coined the term *name-based* retrieval for that technique [17]. Retrieval approaches such as signature matching [42] or interface-based retrieval – the combination of signature and name-based retrieval (also described in [17]) – did not find their way into any of this new generation of software search engines. Numerous of them have been developed during the last 10 years and a good number is still available on the World Wide Web. As demonstrated by the various software search engines that have been launched as well as shut down in recent years, operating such an engine is not per se a fast-selling item, it rather seems to be related with a considerable risk to receive a lack of interest when content and usability are not appealing enough to potential users. The prime example in this context is certainly the failed high-profile attempt of IBM, Microsoft and SAP to establish the so-called UDDI Business Registry (UBR) as a marketplace for (web) services that was finally closed down in early 2006 containing barely a few hundred entries of dubious quality [16]. However, even operating a popular search engine does not guarantee its long-time survival as is underlined by the recent announcement of Google to shut down its code search engine in January 2012 [13].

In spite of that, various code search engines (academic as well as commercial) have demonstrated that the advances in database and text search technology (such as the Lucene framework [14]) have made the creation of "internet-scale" software repositories a viable undertaking wherefore the *repository problem* can be regarded as solved. In order to conclude this subsection, the following table summarizes important characteristics of some of these second generation software search engines.

Table 12.1: Overview of code search engines and directories

Name	Year	No. of artifacts	Retrieval algorithms	Remarks
UDDI Bus. Reg.	2000	<500 services	Keyword matching on metadata	Shutdown in 2006
Spars-J	2004	$>10^5$	Keyword matching	Implements ComponentRank
Koders.com	2004	$>3 \cdot 10^9$ LOC	Keyword & name matching	Commercial by Black Duck SW
Google Codesearch	2006	$>10^7$	Keyword matching/regular expressions	Shutdown January, 15 2012
Sourcerer	2007	$>10^6$	Keyword & name matching	Eclipse integration via CodeGenie plug-in

A more comprehensive overview that demonstrates even more forcefully that top notch software search engines today are easily able to index millions of artifacts can be found in [19] and in another chapter of this book [5].

12.2.2 Remaining Challenges

From the four problems identified for reuse-driven software retrieval in Sect. 12.1, state of the art software search engines thus have basically solved the *repository problem* and the *representation problem* by creating *internet-scale* collections of software assets that can be managed with common databases or state of the art search frameworks such as the freely available Lucene [14]. However, the *usability* and the *retrieval problem* dealing with how to efficiently retrieve the artifacts that are useful in a given context are still in the focus of interest in the research community. Garcia et al. [10] have recently underlined this with their list of requirements for a component search engine: amongst other challenges they see a simple query formulation and a good retrieval quality at the heart of a successful and scalable component search engine. Unfortunately, as has been shown recently [17], simple keyword- or signature-driven searches may lead to tens of thousands of results from which – in principle – each one matches the given query criterion. However, only because a – in these two cases – relatively simple technical matching criterion is fulfilled, a search result does not necessarily become relevant for the user (see e.g. [26]). Consider, for example, that a search for a reusable "spreadsheet" component merely delivers a test case for a spreadsheet because it naturally has to use a spreadsheet and thus contains the term. A user presented with such a result would certainly be disappointed and after inspecting perhaps five or ten similar results not consider using the search engine again, as in a reuse context, it is important to get results precisely matching a given specification [1].

Interestingly, most existing software search engines still rely on a simple keyword matching so that they suffer from exactly this problem. Although it seems possible to narrow down the search results considerably through adding more keywords to a certain degree, beyond that there still existed no intuitive approach for formulating interface-based or even specification-based queries in second generation software search engines as described in another chapter of this book [5]. Only Google's code search engine allowed the use of (rather complex) regular expressions in order to describe the desired interface of a component.

12.3 Test-Driven Reuse

According to the classification of Mili et al. presented in Sect. 12.2, the test-driven reuse approach Hummel and Atkinson have first introduced in 2004 [15], is a technique based on operational semantics and hence inspired by the ideas of Behavior Sampling by Podgurski and Pierce [30]. Due to their random nature, Behavior Sampling requires a relatively large number of samples even for simple functions and, to our knowledge, was never used in practice.

What is extensively used in practice, on the contrary, is (or at least should be) systematic software testing with targeted "samples" of a software's functionality derived with the help of some systematic approach such as equivalence class partitioning. In case of so-called test-driven development [4], which is especially popular in agile development communities, test cases are even created before any production code is written and are used to monitor the production code's degree of completeness and correctness during development iterations. From this starting point it is just a small step to imagine the usefulness of test cases in determining the fitness for purpose of reuse candidate. Assume as an example that we need a component offering the functionality of a typical spreadsheet application (such as Excel), i.e., it should be able to organize cells and reference them in alphanumerical form (rows as numbers, columns as alphabetic characters), hold values in these cells, use them within formulas and hence allow calculations based on other cells' values. A simple JUnit 3 [4] test for such a functionality might look as the one depicted in Listing 12.1. It describes two things, namely first, the (rather brief) required interface of the Spreadsheet component as shown by the UML class in Fig. 12.1 and second a concrete description of the required functionality, against which potential reuse candidates can be tested. Although the interface of this component is simple, it obviously requires quite some code to manage the cells of a spreadsheet and to parse and evaluate their contents.

Based on the above test case and the interface of the required component "hidden" within it, a search can be issued to an arbitrary software search engine. As soon as results are delivered from there, it should be possible to compile and test them against the JUnit test case. Whenever the test case can be compiled and executed successfully against a reuse candidate, it can be assumed that a working implementation for the specified functionality has been found. Figure 12.2 summarizes this "test-driven reuse cycle" as initially introduced in [15].

As depicted in Fig. 12.2, it is also possible to fully automate this cycle: a developer merely needs to specify the tests (step a) and then waits until the system delivers successfully tested reuse candidates (step f). The steps b to e in between can be automatically executed by an appropriate reuse system (we will explain a

Listing 12.1 JUnit test case testing (and hence describing) a simple spreadsheet component.

```java
public class SpreadsheetTest extends TestCase {
    private Spreadsheet sheet;
    public void setUp() {
        sheet = new Spreadsheet();
        sheet.put("A1", "5");
    }
    public void testCellReference() {
        sheet.put("A2", "=A1");
        assertEquals("5", sheet.get("A2"));
    }
    public void testCellChangePropagates() {
        sheet.put("A2", "=A1");
        sheet.put("A1", "10");
        assertEquals("10", sheet.get("A2"));
    }
    public void testFormulaCalculation() {
        sheet.put("A2", "3");
        sheet.put("B1", "=A1*(A1-A2)+A2/3");
        assertEquals("11", sheet.get("B1"));
    }
}
```

Spreadsheet
+ put(cell:String,value:String):void + get(cell:String):String

Fig. 12.1 The interface of a simple spreadsheet component as defined by the test case in Listing 12.1

concrete implementation in the next subsection). In step b the required interface of the desired reuse candidate is extracted from the test case what leads to step c where a query is derived to drive an arbitrary code search engine (we use our Merobase search engine that is explained in more detail in Sect. 12.3.1). While in principle it would also be feasible (if not easier) to search and test binary files, our current implementation still focuses on source code files (because historically there used to be little support for searching binary files in software search engines) that need to get compiled against the test case in step d and in case this procedure was successful are tested in step e.

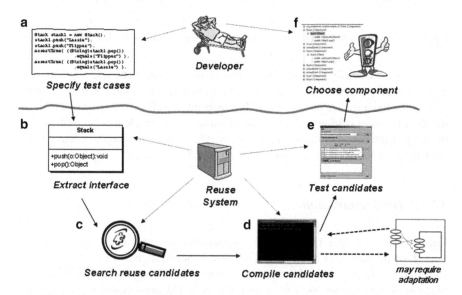

Fig. 12.2 The test-driven reuse "cycle"

Figure 12.2 furthermore shows that the desired interface from the test case is not always fully matched by a potential reuse candidate when it comes to compilation in step d. As a matter of fact, it is not exactly matched in most of the cases so that the test case will not compile out of the box with most results, which is of course unsatisfying. As a way out of this dilemma, we have been developing a test-based adapter [11] generator that is able to automatically "wrap" the reuse candidate with the appropriate interface in order to make it compilable and executable. In principle, it simply creates all syntactically possible adapter "wirings" and selects the one that successfully passes the specified test case, implementation details and a proof of concept implementation can be found in another publication [21].

Feeding the example test from Listing 12.1 to Merobase, eventually yields four successfully tested reuse candidates. One of them is particularly interesting as it nicely demonstrates how a "real component"[2] consisting of various classes (as illustrated in the UML diagram from Fig. 12.3) can be discovered with our approach through merely describing and testing its facade [11].

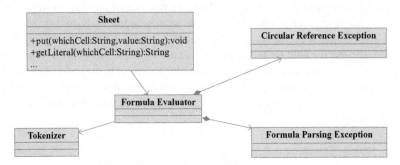

Fig. 12.3 Simplified structure of retrieved spreadsheet component as UML class diagram

The class ensemble discovered here consists of three main classes, enclosing two inner exception classes, and comprises in total slightly more than 300 lines of code. Obviously, the interface of the facade class does not match the interface specified by the test case from Listing 12.1 and thus would not compile. Hence, our tool created the adapter presented in Listing 12.2 that provides exactly the interface required by the test case and forwards requests to the retrieved component.

12.3.1 Implementation

Garcia et al. [10] depict the necessity of integrating source code search into the IDE of the developer, as this prevents a loss of concentration and a media-break for switching to another tool (like e.g. a web browser). Of course, reuse-oriented IDE plug-ins usually cannot work as standalone tools, but must connect to a software repository server via the Internet. In this section, we explain how our group at the University of Mannheim has tackled this challenge and describe our software search engine Merobase and its associated Eclipse plug-in Code Conjurer [20]. While Merobase distinguishes itself from other software search engines through its broad support of retrieval techniques, Code Conjurer is able to deliver proactive reuse recommendations by silently monitoring a user's work (i.e. the code a developer writes in Eclipse) and triggering searches automatically whenever this seems reasonable. We

---

[2] Result source (visited Dec, 14th 2011): http://www.purpletech.com/xp/wake/src/Sheet.java

Listing 12.2 Automatically generated adapter for the Sheet result.

```
public class Spreadsheet {
    private adaptee . Sheet adaptee ;

    public Spreadsheet () {
        adaptee = new adaptee . Sheet ();
    }

    public String get (String whichCell ) {
        try {
            return adaptee . get (whichCell );
        } catch (RuntimeException e) {
            if (e instanceof RuntimeException) {
                throw e ;
            }
            return null ;
        }
    }

    public void put (String whichCell , String value) {
        try {
            adaptee . put (whichCell , value );
        } catch (RuntimeException e) {
            if (e instanceof RuntimeException) {
                throw e ;
            }
        }
    }
}
```

will explain this process in more detail in Sect. 12.3.1.2 Potentially reusable results are shown in Code Conjurer's recommendations view (cf. Sect. 12.3.1.2) where we explain our tool in more detail. Figure 12.4 describes the overall process in our reuse recommendation system, including our Merobase search engine, the Code Conjurer plug-in and the virtual machines used for secure testing of retrieved candidates.

12.3.1.1 Merobase: A Search Engine Supporting Test-Driven Reuse

The index creation for our Merobase repository is driven by automated crawlers that can harvest source and binary files from three different sources, namely CVS and SVN repositories as well as from websites (via HTTP). While the repository crawling requires a list of projects to download the files from the respective (open source) repository, web crawling works with an extended version of Lucene's Nutch crawler [14] starting from some seed URLs. The index itself is also based on the

Lucene framework [14] and currently contains about ten million files from well-known open source hosting sites and the open Web (roughly 8 %), out of which roughly 40 % are binary files (primarily Java archives, but some .NET binaries as well). Special parsers for each supported programming language allow to extract syntactical information, store it in the index and search for it later. In addition to class and method names, we store operation signatures (i.e. parameter and return types) and complete operation headers (i.e., operation signatures plus names) as concatenated terms optimized for Lucene in the index. Details on their structure can be found in another chapter of this book [5]. Currently, Merobase is able to work with Java, C++ and C# sources, WSDL files, binary Java classes from Java archives (JARs) and .NET binaries.

Whenever a user sends a request to the Merobase server (either through the web-interface available at merobase.com or a client program like Code Conjurer accessing its web service based API), the above parsers and a special JUnit parser (able to extract the interface of the class under test from test cases) are invoked and try to extract as much syntactic information from the query as possible. If none of the parsers recognizes parsable code, however, a simple keyword search is executed. Based on parsed syntactic information, Merobase supports retrieval by class and operation names, signature matching and by matching the full interface of classes as described before. Although preliminary results indicate that the latter indeed leads to a higher precision with common "toy examples" [17] collected from the literature, the risk of "over-specifying" desired components is certainly also real, as e.g. the previous spreadsheet example has demonstrated: no candidate completely matched the relatively simple interface we have specified. Nevertheless, the retrieved components that were finally working successfully, were found amongst roughly 22,000 results of a "relaxed" query that merely searched for the desired signatures (i.e. ignored class and operation names in the interface). As searches for more complex interfaces often tend to deliver few results (as e.g. predicted by Crnkovic [6]), we have integrated a number of strategies into Merobase for relaxing queries as well. Further details on the index structure of Merobase, its content, and the applied matching strategies are explained in another chapter of this book [5].

In case of a test-driven search, which is triggered when a JUnit test case (such as the one in Listing 12.1) is submitted, Merobase automatically tries to compile, adapt and test the highest ranked candidates. If a candidate is relying on additional classes, the algorithm uses dependency information to locate them as well (as seen in the spreadsheet example). As visible in Fig. 12.4, the actual compilation and testing are not carried out on the search server itself, but on dedicated virtual machines within sandboxes. These ensure that the executed code does not have the possibility to do anything harmful to the user's system or bring the whole testing-environment down; in our publicly available system we have also deactivated network transfer to prevent abuse. Another system continuously monitors the virtual machines (by polling a special monitoring service provided by the sandboxes) and as soon as it recognizes that one is not working properly, it simply replaces it with a new instance, which takes about 30 s for replacing and restarting.

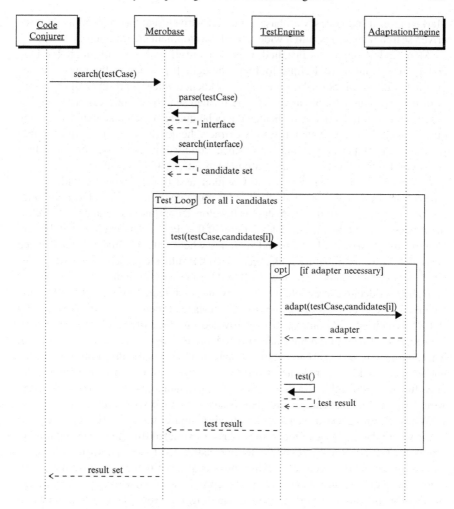

Fig. 12.4 Architecture for a test-driven software reuse environment

12.3.1.2 Code Conjurer: Test-Driven Reuse in Eclipse

Although the Merobase search engine is certainly a useful tool, its regular web interface forces a developer to leave his development environment when he wants to search for reusable artifacts. Even worse this requires the cognitive decision that reuse is desired in a particular situation [41], which clearly disturbs the creative thought process of software development. Thus, we have created the open source tool Code Conjurer[3] as a plug-in for the Eclipse IDE, installable through the Eclipse

---

[3] Which is hosted on sourceforge.net and available at www.code-conjurer.org

Marketplace. It integrates Merobase's interface-driven searches as well as the test-driven search technology into a widely used development environment.

After Code Conjurer is installed, it presents itself with a small magic hat icon and a reuse menu in the Eclipse toolbar. The default position of the reuse view as visible in Fig. 12.5 is at the bottom of the workbench where it presents all necessary information about reusable assets and performed searches. Code Conjurer neither requires the user to learn any dedicated query language nor to consciously write any queries at all. When activated, it simply extracts the queries from the current source window a developer is working with. Since Code Conjurer focuses on Java, Java classes and JUnit 3 test cases[4] are supported as queries in this context.

For interface-base searches, Code Conjurer assists the developer with a non-intrusive background agent, that searches for reusable artifacts. The algorithm judging when a search should be triggered is developed continuously and actually relies most on changes of the interface description of the class under development. Hence, Code Conjurer triggers background searches whenever a method is added to the class, deleted or its signature is changed. Search results are presented in a tree view, while next to them a code preview is offered for the selected item.

If the user decides to enable the test-driven search feature of Code Conjurer, the background agent monitors changes to the interface of the so-called *class under test* (CUT), which is – in contrast to the provided interface of the class in interface-base search – the required interface of the JUnit test case written by the developer. This approach is very close to the one propagated by Extreme Programming, which encourages the developers to iteratively write tests that fail, then implement the desired functionality and then add more tests that fail again. In our case, the developers would not implement functionality, but reuse existing software assets.

When executing test-driven searches, Code Conjurer sends the JUnit test to Merobase where the interface of the desired class is extracted from the code and used to search for results. Retrieved candidates are distributed to special virtual machines used for compilation and testing. After the execution of the tests against the candidates, the test results are shown in Code Conjurer's result view from where they can be directly added to the working project via drag and drop. The example shown in Fig. 12.5, shows the results of a test-driven search. They all required an adapter to work with the provided test case (which is shown by a bar in yellow ochre. When a result is chosen for reuse, the adapter is automatically integrated into the working project along with the reusable class. In other words, the retrieved code is directly usable and the test initially defined by the user can then be executed locally on the retrieved code, in order to ensure that it has been integrated correctly.

---

[4] The only requirement is that the tests should be written according to best SE practices (e.g. the name of the test should reflect the class under test's name).

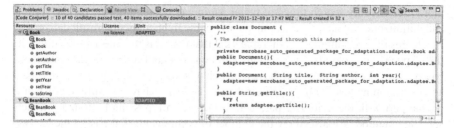

Fig. 12.5 Code Conjurer's "window to the world": the reuse view with a generated adapter

12.4 Evaluation

As the information retrieval community has experienced in its early years, objectively evaluating retrieval tools is difficult [3]: as mentioned before, information retrieval science envisages the usage of recall and precision to judge the usefulness of an information retrieval tool. However, it is well accepted that the exact recall of large-scale search engines cannot be determined easily, since it is usually not possible to identify all relevant candidates from a corpus with millions of entries. Text retrieval reference collections that have been built with lots of effort hence normally are using manually inspected retrieval results collected from various tools to establish a baseline for the recall, unfortunately, those collections do not (yet) exist for software retrieval [20]. Another issue with test-driven search is that its precision is by definition equal to 100 % (assuming the test cases are expressive enough) since retrieved candidates can be directly integrated into the project under development. Hence, we believe a first reasonable evaluation of test-driven reuse approaches is to demonstrate its feasibility by applying it to a variety of search challenges found in literature. Since recently another implementation of the approach has become available [33] and presented a similar evaluation we also compared its results with our system in order to further underline the technical feasibility of the overall approach.

12.4.1 Assessing Reuse Challenges

For the evaluation of our approach we have collected a number of previously published retrieval challenges from related literature and as far as necessary created simple JUnit test cases (documented in their entirety elsewhere [18] due to their size). We have used our stable initial test-driven reuse prototype and the Merobase search engine to search for Java source codes and to execute the test cases. Since this prototype is still testing all candidates sequentially and identifies feasible adapters based on a brute-force approach [21] the times shown in the following table can be seen as absolute worst cases for testing all potential candidates with a matching signature. The comparison following in the next subsection already demonstrates that more user-friendly search times of under 3 min can be achieved by parallelization and optimization of adapter creation and of course by incremental result delivery.

The results are summarized in Table 12.2 that contains the interface specified in the respective test case its first column. Columns two and three compare interface-based retrieval where candidates have to match this interface exactly (including class and operation names) with a signature-based retrieval where it is sufficient when a counterpart with the matching parameters and return types can be found for each specified method. We also show the number of components that passed the test vs. the total number of candidates found by Merobase in each cell, e.g. for the interface-based retrieval of a Stack, 150 components out of 692 candidates were able to pass the test. The numbers below indicates how much time the prototype required to try out all candidates retrieved by Merobase. Finally, the last column lists "synonymous" class names we have found amongst the successfully tested candidates using (more relaxed) signature-based retrieval.

Table 12.2: Overview of successfully solved reuse challenges

Query	Interface-based	Signature-based	Exemplary result classes for signature-based harvesting

`Stack (`
`  push(Object):void`
`  pop():Object`
`)`
	150/692
	
	26 min 45 s
		611/35,634
		
		18 h 23 min
			`Stack,`
			`MyStack,`
			`ObjectStack,`
			`Keller,`
			`LIFO, Pila,`
			`ObjectPool,`
			`LifoSet`

`Calculator (`
`  sub(int,int):int`
`  add(int,int):int`
`  mult(int,int):int`
`  div(int,int):int`
`)`
	1/4
	
	19 s
		22/23,759
		
		20 h 24 min
			`Calculator,`
			`CalculatorImpl,`
			`Molecule,`
			`Arithmetic,`
			`SimpleMath,`
			`Operators`

`Matrix (`
`  Matrix(int,int)`
`  get(int.int):double`
`  set(int,int,`
`      double):void`
`  multiply(Matrix):Matrix`
`)`
	2/10
	
	26 s
		26/137
		
		5 min 25 s
			`Matrix`

`ShoppingCart (`
`  getItemCount():int`
`  getBalance():double`
`  addItem(Product):void`
`  empty():void`
`  removeIt(Product):void`
`)`
	4/4
	
	26 s
		4/12
		
		47 s
			`ShoppingCart`

Query	Interface	Signature	Exemplary results

Spreadsheet (
  put(String,String):void
  get(String):String
)
	0/0
	
	3 s
		4/22,705
		
		15 h 13 min
			Sheet,
			Compiler,
			Util

ComplexNumber (
  ComplexNumber(double,
    double)
  add(ComplexNumber):
    ComplexNumber
  getRealPart():double
  getImagineryPart():
    double
)
	0/1
	
	3 s
		32/89
		
		1 min 19 s
			ComplexNumber

MortgageCalculator (
  setRate(double):void
  setPrincipal(double):
    void
  setYears(int):void
  getMonthlyPayment():
    double
)
	0/0
	
	4 s
		15/4,265
		
		3 h 19 min
			Loan,
			LoanCalculator,
			Mortgage

On the one hand, the results presented in the table demonstrate the capability of the test-driven reuse approach as we were able to identify a number of artifacts in our collection that are able to deliver quite complex functionalities (such as a Spreadsheet or a Matrix) as specified in the test cases. On the other hand it also demonstrates its largest two dilemmas, namely the problem of "over-specifying" the desired artifact and the execution time. The more complex an interface becomes, the harder it gets to find a perfectly matching implementation. Although, relaxing the search criteria indeed increases the probability of success, it increases the time required for testing so that it is still difficult to apply test-driven reuse in practice where developers demand results within just a few seconds. In principle, however, distributing the testing to a large number of virtual machines should decreases this time significantly as is shown in the subsection following hereafter.

12.4.2 Comparison

Recently, the idea of test-driven software search has been adapted by Steven Reiss [33] from Brown University with his tool S6 and by Lemos et al. at UC Irvine with their Eclipse plugin CodeGenie [39]. We will give some more details on their approaches in the following section on related work, but first we want to demonstrate that our implementation is able to reproduce results similar to those reported by Reiss. Unfortunately, at the time of writing, CodeGenie required triggering the testing of each candidate manually within Eclipse so that we were unable to include it into the comparison for reasons of security and effort.

Table 12.3 presents the results of our comparison in five columns starting with a reference to the used example. Columns two and three illustrate how many successfully tested results have been discovered by Merobase within the first 500 candidates (using its "relaxed" search approach described before) without respectively with automatic adaptation of mismatching signatures. The JUnit test cases we used were created according to the test samples provided by Reiss in his paper [33], his results are reproduced in the fourth column for a direct comparison, while the fifth column is reserved for special remarks where necessary. Due to the limited number of candidates and optimizations in terms of parallelization and adaptation, this time Merobase required less than 3 min per example, which certainly seems a reasonable number for practical use. This time we have executed the testing in a parallelized environment (running on an AMD Opteron based server with a 2.6 GHz dual-core processor and eight virtual machines) that yielded results comparable with Reiss's system that required between 15 and 169 s in a testing environment utilizing also eight threads.

Table 12.3: Comparison of test-driven search implementations

Example	Merobase unadapted	Merobase adapted	S[6] [33]	Remarks
SimpleTokenizer	0	2	14/138	
QuoteTokenizer	0	0	4/6	
Robots	–	–	1/124	Not repeatable[5]
Log2	0	1	1/100	
FromRoman	0	2	3/38	
ToRoman	2	4	6/56	
Prime	0	4	14/228	
PerfectNumbers	0	1	5/28	
DayOfWeek	0	0	0/89	3/5,000
Easter	0	0	1/6	Not repeatable[6]
MultiMap	0	0	2/165	3/10,000
UnionFind	0	2	1/149	
TextDelta	0	7	1/249	

---

[5] Reiss' tests required resources from the Web that are not available anymore.
[6] We were not able to find results with Reiss' tool either.

The remarks for *DayOfWeek* and *MultiMap* in Table 12.3 were Merobase could not find results within the first 500 candidates mean that it was able to discover three working version in a larger set of candidates (5,000 resp. 10,000). However, the expressiveness of this comparison is unfortunately still somewhat limited since Reiss has used different search engines with different retrieval algorithms that finally delivered different candidates. It nevertheless demonstrates that Merobase achieves a similar performance as another contemporary tool and is also able to deal with completely unbiased reuse challenges independently specified by someone else so that the technical feasibility of test-driven reuse has been illustrated one more time.

12.5 Related Work

After some years of relative silence around the turn of the millennium, a new momentum has become visible in the software retrieval community in recent years and other approaches implementing a test-driven reuse approach have been presented by other researchers. To our knowledge, two research groups have been developing and experimenting with appropriate tools. As already mentioned, Reiss has developed S6 [33], a web-based search tool where a user can list search keywords, specify the declaration of one or more method headers and add test samples that describe the semantics of the desired operation. According to Reiss's publication, S6 is also able to "adapt" retrieved candidates by carrying out various internal program transformations based on the abstract syntax tree of the potential result and to retrieve numerous operations within one Java class. S6 is able to use its own search engine called Labrador or a number of other code search engines such as Koders or Sourcerer.

Sourcerer itself, which was developed by Bajracharya et al. [37] at the University of California in Irvine implements a ranking approach similar to ComponentRank [22] and is the foundation for another test-driven reuse tool called CodeGenie [39]. In contrast to S6, and similar to Code Conjurer, CodeGenie is fully integrated into the Eclipse IDE and able to directly use JUnit test cases to drive a search for a missing Java method. In order to do so, CodeGenie analyses Eclipse's compiler errors and tries to find missing classes respectively their methods via the Sourcerer search engine. The user can inspect the candidates delivered by Sourcerer and can request from CodeGenie to "weave" them into his project where they can be tested as usual with the help of JUnit. One of the main contributions of Sourcerer and CodeGenie is probably their ability to work even with declaratively incomplete program files (so-called slices) that can also be woven into the project under development. In contrast to Code Conjurer that always integrates complete files and tries to resolve missing dependencies also on a per file basis, CodeGenie thus seems to be more flexible, as far as this can be determined without a direct comparison on the same data set. Clearly, it would be interesting to see such a comparison (of course also including the capabilities of S6) to better understand the advantages and disadvantages of all three tools, however, this is yet to be done.

Other recent approaches for increasing the precision of software searches in large-scale repositories include the work of Grechanik et al. [12] who have built a search engine that analyses the documentation of API calls (e.g. Javadocs) with common information retrieval approaches in order to retrieve complete applications that implement a desired high-level functionality (such as "record midi file"). It thus avoids the need for exactly matching components and adaptation in the first place. In terms of size of their search target, a number of innovative tools such as XSnippet [34] or ParseWeb [38] reside at the other end of the spectrum as they mainly support developers in Eclipse through finding examples for object instantiations and API calls. However, we are currently not aware of any other recent approaches that also aim on retrieving reusable software building blocks according to a concrete specification as test-driven reuse does.

12.6 Future Work

Although test-driven reuse marks another milestone for specification-based software search and retrieval, there still exist many aspects with potential for improvement as already illustrated by the three currently available approaches [19, 33, 39] with their individual strengths and limitations. Since they only support the reuse and integration of Java source code so far, it is certainly interesting transfer the approach to other programming languages, although we do not see any reason why this would cause major problems. In order to make test-driven reuse applicable for the daily work of a developer, however, it is necessary to further decrease the time until result are delivered. This can of course be done by a further parallelization of test execution (with corresponding costs, of course), or by improving the adaptation generation and of course by optimizing the underlying search engine so that it simply ranks potentially working results higher. Moreover, many advanced techniques from information retrieval such as stemming, synonyms or hypernyms [3] have occasionally been tried out for software search, but not yet systematically investigated so far so that their effects are not yet clear. However, this problem has been plaguing general information retrieval systems for years: for example, naively adding synonyms as search terms, quickly leads to an explosion in the number of results and in turn most likely to decreasing precision. Thus, one goal for the near future should be the discovery of an optimal mix of heuristics that delivers an acceptable amount of tested results within a reasonable amount of time. In other words, we still need to find out which software retrieval algorithm works best for which usage scenario, as there is still a lack of systematic evaluations as recently criticized [20].

Another challenging but not less important question is, whether and how complex class ensembles or, in more general terms, complex components can be best retrieved in a widely object-oriented world. There, today's mainstream applications are mostly composed of very fine-grained building blocks (i.e. the classes) and thus composing an object-oriented program with the test-driven reuse approach would in principle require a detailed specification for each desired object. On the one hand, creating each class individually is what needs to be done in object-oriented software development anyway, however, on the other hand it clearly contradicts the idea of composing preferably large components and hence defeats most of the benefits of component-based development [40] that hides implementation details behind interfaces. "Carving" components from a bunch of objects currently only works automatically as long as a hull (better known as a facade [11]), such as the Sheet class from Figure and Listing 12.1, is coincidentally available and all its dependencies can be resolved. To our knowledge, automated orchestration mechanisms as they are intensively investigated in the web service community (e.g. in [28]) are not yet supported by any of the current software (or service) search engines and prototypes. A prerequisite for overcoming this challenge is of course being able to find all dependencies a reuse candidate relies upon. While we have already discussed some simple heuristics for this task, a systematic analysis of this area is also still open.

12.7 Conclusion

The contributions we have described in this chapter are manifold, we have presented a novel approach hat uses ordinary (unit) test cases for search and retrieval of well defined software building blocks in a reuse context. We have described the current state of development of our proactive reuse recommendation tool and a search engine that can be used to implement test-driven reuse in practice. Furthermore, we have applied our tool to a number of realistic reuse challenges demonstrating that the approach is technically feasible, which is also supported by two similar implementations published recently. Moreover, we have identified some interesting ideas for improvement and once more realized that it is about time to carry out a systematic comparison of (not only test-driven) software search tools, based on a unified reference collection.

Since testing still is (and will certainly remain for some time to come) the only means by which software components can be judged as "fit for purpose", we believe that, together with a test-driven reuse approach, it can become the central driver for component and service markets in the mid-term future. Thus, our basic idea is to integrate the ability of testing components and services into future versions of software brokers (such as the former UDDI Business Registry). In addition to delivering components that syntactically match users queries, search engines enhanced in this way will also be able to execute tests in order to filter out those reuse candidates that are not fit for the desired purpose.

In contrast with current testing approaches, however, a new form of "blind testing" is required to protect the interests of component providers and users in such a commercial brokerage scenario. Thus, we propose a novel form of testing in which a search engine only provides the user with an indication of whether a test was passed or failed, but not with the actual results delivered by the component under test. Moreover, it is important that the expected result of a test submitted by a user is also not disclosed to the component since it could otherwise be used to return spoofed results that might influence a purchase decision [2]. Thus, search engines in our future concept need to act act as a trusted broker between component providers and potential users (i.e. buyers). This vision certainly has the potential to bring the practice of software reuse closer to McIlroy's long-felt desire of viable software component marketplaces.

Acknowledgements The authors would like to thank Colin Atkinson, Philipp Bostan, Daniel Brenner, Matthias Gutheil, Christian Ritter, Marcus Schumacher and Dietmar Stoll from the Software Engineering Group at the University of Mannheim for their contributions to developing the tools described in this chapter. Furthermore, we would like to express our gratitude for the helpful comments of the anonymous reviewers.

References

[1] Atkinson, C., Bayer, J., Bunse, C., Kamsties, E., Laitenberger, O., Laqua, R., Muthig, D., Paech, B., Wüst, J., Zettel, J.: Component-based Product Line Engineering with UML, Addison Wesley (2002)

[2] Atkinson, C., Brenner, D., Hummel, O., Stoll, D.: A Trustable Brokerage Solution for Component and Service Markets. Proceedings of the Intern. Conference on Software Reuse (2008)

[3] Baeza-Yates, R., Ribeiro-Neto, B.: Modern Information Retrieval. Addison-Wesley (1999)

[4] Beck, K.: Test-driven development: by example. Addison-Wesley (2003)

[5] Hummel, O., Atkinson, C., Schumacher, M.: Artifact Representation Techniques for Large-Scale Software Search Engines. In Sim and Gallardo-Valencia (eds.): Finding Source Code on the Web for Remix and Reuse, Springer, 2012.

[6] Crnkovic, I.: Component-based software engineering – new challenges in software development. Software Focus, Vol. 2, No. 4 (2001)

[7] Erl, T: Service-Oriented Architecture: Concepts, Technology and Design. Pearson (2005)

[8] Frakes, W.B.: An empirical study of representation methods for reusable software components. IEEE Transactions on Software Engineering, Vol. 20, no.8 (1994)

[9] Frakes, W.B., Terry, C.: Software Reuse: Metrics and Models. ACM Computing Surveys, Vol. 28, No. 2 (1996)

[10] Garcia, V.C., de Almeida, E.S., Lisboa, L.B., Martins, A.C., Meira, S.R.L., Lucredio, D., de M. Fortes, R.P.: Toward a Code Search Engine Based on the State-of-Art and Practice. Proceedings of the Asia Pacific Software Engineering Conference (2006)

[11] Gamma, E., Helm, R., Johnson, R., Vlissides, J.: Design patterns: elements of reusable object-oriented software, Addison-Wesley (1995)

[12] Grechanik, M., Chen Fu, Qing Xie, McMillan, C., Poshyvanyk, D., Cumby, C.: A search engine for finding highly relevant applications. 32nd International Conference on Software Engineering (2010)
[13] Horowitz, B.: A fall sweep. Google Blog, http://googleblog.blogspot.com/2011/10/fall-sweep.html(2011), last retrieved Dec. 2011
[14] Hatcher, E., Gospodnetic, O., McCandless, M.: Lucene in Action (2nd edition). Manning (2010)
[15] Hummel, O., Atkinson, C.: Extreme Harvesting: Test Driven Discovery and Reuse of Software Components. Proceedings of the International Conference on Information Reuse and Integration (2004)
[16] Hummel, O., Atkinson, C.: Using the Web as a Reuse Repository. Proceedings of the International Conference on Software Reuse (2006)
[17] Hummel, O., Janjic, W., Atkinson, C.: Evaluating the efficiency of retrieval methods for component repositories. Proceedings of the International Conference on Software Engineering and Knowledge Engineering (2007)
[18] Hummel, O.: Semantic component retrieval in software engineering. PhD dissertation, University of Mannheim (2008)
[19] Hummel, O., Janjic, W., Atkinson, C.: Code conjurer: Pulling reusable software out of thin air. IEEE Software, Vol.25, No. 5 (2008)
[20] Hummel, O.: Facilitating the comparison of software retrieval systems through a reference reuse collection. Proceedings of the ICSE Workshop on Search-driven Development: Users, Infrastructure, Tools and Evaluation (2010)
[21] Hummel, O., Atkinson, C.: Automated Creation and Assessment of Component Adapters with Test Cases. Symposium on Component-Based Software Engineering (2010)
[22] Inoue, K., Yokomori, R., Fujiwara, H., Yamamoto, T., Matsushita, M., Kusumoto S.: Ranking Significance of Software Components Based on Use Relations. IEEE Transactions on Software Engineering, Vol. 31, No. 3 (2005)
[23] Jansen, B.J., Spink, A., Saracevic, T.: Real life, real users, and real needs: a study and analysis of user queries on the web. Information Processing and Management, Vol. 36, No. 2 (2000)
[24] Krueger, C.W.: Software reuse. ACM Computing Surveys, vol. 24, no 2. (1992)
[25] McIlroy, D.: Mass-Produced Software Components. Software Engineering: Report of a conference sponsored by the NATO Science Committee (1968).
[26] Mili, A., Mili, R., Mittermeir, R.: A Survey of Software Reuse Libraries. Annals of Software Engineering 5 (1998)
[27] Mili, A., Yacoub, S., Addy, E., Mili, H.: Toward an engineering discipline of software reuse. IEEE Software, vol. 16, no. 5 (1999)
[28] Nezhad, H., Benatallah, B., Martens, A., Curbera, F., Casati, F.: Semi-automated adaptation of service interactions. Proceedings of the 16th International Conference on World Wide Web (2007)

[29] Page, L., Brin, S., Motwani, R., Winograd, T.: The Pagerank Algorithm: Bringing Order to the Web. Proceedings of the International Conference on the World Wide Web (1998)

[30] Podgurski, A., Pierce, L.: Retrieving reusable software by sampling behavior. ACM Transactions on Software Engineering and Methodology, Vol.2, No. 3 (1993)

[31] Poulin, J.: Reuse: Been there. Done that. Communications of the ACM. Vol. 42, Iss. 5 (1999)

[32] Prieto-Diaz, R., Freeman, P.: Classifying Software for Reusability. IEEE Software, Vol. 4, No. 1 (1987)

[33] Reiss, S.P.: Semantics-based code search. Proceedings of the 31st International Conference on Software Engineering (2009)

[34] Sahavechaphan, N., Claypool, K.T.: X Snippet: Mining for Sample Code. OOPSLA (2006)

[35] Seacord, R.C.: Software Engineering Component Repositories. Proceedings of the International Workshop on Component-Based Software Engineering (1999)

[36] Seacord, R.C., Hissam, S.A., Wallnau, K.C.: AGORA: a search engine for software components. IEEE Internet Computing, Vol. 2, No. 6 (1998)

[37] Bajracharya, S., Ossher, J., Lopes, C.: Sourcerer: An internet-scale software repository. Proceedings of the ICSE Workshop on Search-Driven Development: Users, Infrastructure, Tools and Evaluation (2009)

[38] Thummalapenta, S. Xie, T.: Parseweb: a programmer assistant for reusing open source code on the web. Proceedings of the International Conference on Automated Software Engineering (2007)

[39] Lemos, O., Bajracharya, S., Ossher, J.: CodeGenie: a tool for test-driven source code search. Proceedings of the International Conference on Object-Oriented Programming (2007)

[40] Szyperski, C.: Component Software: Beyond Object-Oriented Programming (2nd ed.), Addison-Wesley (2002)

[41] Ye, Y. and Fischer, G.: Supporting reuse by delivering task-relevant and personalized information. Proceedings of the International Conference on Software Engineering (2002)

[42] Zaremski, A.M., Wing, J.M.: Signature Matching: A Tool for Using Software Libraries. ACM Transactions on Software Engineering and Methodology, Vol. 4, No. 2 (1995)

[43] Zaremski, A.M., Wing, J.M.: Specification Matching of Software Components. ACM Transactions on Software Engineering and Methodology, Vol. 6, No. 4 (1997)

Part IV
Remix: Snippets and Answers

Source code from the web can also be used as solutions to problems and answers to questions. This style of reuse resembles the remix practices that have coalesced around digital media. For example, music remixes involve taking bits from one or more songs and recombining them into a new one. In this Part, there are three chapters that examine this kind of source code retrieval.

In Chap. 14 "Software Problems that Motivate Web Searches," Gallardo-Valencia and Sim report on a field study of code retrieval in the wild. They were interested in how software developers searched for code on the web to solve problems that they encountered in their work.

Tantikul et al. write about lessons learned in Chap. 15 on "Novel and Applied Algorithms in a Search Engine for Java Code Snippets." Their prototype was populated with pages from tutorial web sites, rather than open source components, and the search engine returned snippets accompanied by short descriptions.

Software developers often use the question-and-answer site, StackOverflow.com, when problem solving. They either find answers to their questions or post their questions for others to answer. In Chap. 16, Barzilay, Treude, and Zagalsky, report on an empirical study of the kinds of questions that are asked and answered on Stack Overflow, and they describe a tool that supports the remixing of examples from the site.

Chapter 13
Software Problems That Motivate Web Searches

Rosalva E. Gallardo-Valencia and Susan Elliott Sim

Abstract Developers use the Web as a tool to find information to help them solve their software development problems. However, little was known about what kinds of problems motivate developers to do searches on the Web. We observed 24 developers at 3 software companies. In our analysis, we found that there are four main kinds of problems. When "Remembering," developers knew exactly what they are looking for and only wanted to remember syntax details or find facts. When they needed "Clarification," developers had a high-level understanding of what they want to implement, but did not know precisely how to do it. During "Learning," developers wanted to acquire new concepts. Finally, the last kind of problem was a need for a tool or open source project/component. The first three kinds of search can be characterized as using an opportunistic process, whereas the fourth kind uses a non-opportunistic process. Our findings complement prior research on search targets during source code search and have implications for tool support.

13.1 Introduction

Developers are mainly using Web searches to opportunistically solve software development problems (82% of Web searches). Opportunistic searches are ad hoc and are done to remember syntax details, clarify implementation details or fix bugs, and learn new concepts. On the other hand, non-opportunistic searches (only 18% of Web searches) are done following a systematic process and are performed to find open source projects.

R.E. Gallardo-Valencia (✉)
Intel Corporation, Santa Clara, CA, USA
e-mail: rgallardovalencia@acm.org

S.E. Sim
Many Roads Studios, Toronto, ON, Canada
e-mail: ses@drsusansim.org

S.E. Sim and R.E. Gallardo-Valencia (eds.), *Finding Source Code on the Web for Remix and Reuse*, DOI 10.1007/978-1-4614-6596-6_13,
© Springer Science+Business Media New York 2013

Analyzing Web searches from the perspective of opportunistic problem solving helps us understand that developers' searches on the Web are motivated by the software problems that they want to solve. These problems define the search targets that developers are looking for. Using this perspective also helps us see that searches for snippets of code and searches for open source systems are two different types of searches.

In this chapter, we explain the characteristics of opportunistic searches as well as the characteristics of non-opportunistic searches. We also discuss the insights that come from understanding Web searches from an opportunistic problem solving perspective. Finally, we provide a summary of the chapter.

13.2 Background

13.2.1 Opportunistic Problem Solving and Searches

Robillard [10] argued that developers use a mixture of systematic and opportunistic problem solving to complete their tasks. Developers use a systematic approach when they have the knowledge for completing a task and can follow a well-structured plan. In contrast, developers use an opportunistic approach when they need to find missing information for completing software development tasks. For that activity, they incrementally collect knowledge when the opportunity arises. Opportunistic approaches do not follow structured plans but instead happen on an ad hoc basis.

Opportunistic problem solving was originally used to explain software engineering activities in general [10]. In our work, we applied it to Web search as an aspect of software development, where developers want to solve problems.

We argue that developers mainly use Web searches for opportunistic problem solving. In the next subsection, we show our results for each of the characteristics of opportunistic problem solving: Web search was used to explore further; knowledge was partially and incrementally gathered; and Web search did not follow a well-planned process.

13.2.2 Empirical Studies of Code Search on the Web

In our literature review, we found that some empirical studies [3, 12, 13, 15] report on the motivation and also the search target developers expect to find, but others [1, 7] only report on the search target. None of these studies report on observations of developers in industry. Based on this analysis, we came up with seven reasons why developers are looking for information on the Web:

R1. To reuse source code as-is.

R2. To find examples of usage for GUI widgets or API/libraries.

R3. To remember syntactic details or frequently used functionality.

R4. To find examples to clarify how to implement functionality in a specific language or how to implement an algorithm or data structure.

R5. To learn unfamiliar concepts.

R6. To fix a bug.

R7. To get ideas to implement a new system.

These studies form the starting point for our study.

13.3 Methods

We conducted a field study of 24 developers in 3 software development companies. We observed them as they worked with particular attention to how and when they searched for source code on the Web. We augmented these observations with fine-grained data collected using a Web browser extension.

13.3.1 Field Sites

We had three field sites, one in Peru (Novatronic) and two in Southern California (Health Connection and AppFolio).

Novatronic is a consulting company with 64 employees that develops transactional software. Its clients are banks, telecommunication companies, the government, and other firms located throughout the Americas. The company has achieved CMMI level 3 and its processes are certified as ISO 9001-compliant. We contacted the owners of Novatronic who agreed to participate in the study. One of the owners and the company's product managers identified 25 developers who were coding at the time of the study. Among these 25 developers, we randomly selected 12 developers to observe. Developers did not receive any compensation for their participation.

Health Connection is an open source health information technology company; its system is used to securely exchange health information between health-care organizations such as hospital, clinics, and laboratories. The company had approximately 45 employees working on various products. We are using a pseudonym for this company to protect its confidentiality. We contacted a Senior Software Engineer from the company who agreed to participate in the study. He selected seven developers, and four others volunteered to be observed. Developers did not receive any compensation for their participation.

Finally, we also conducted one observation at AppFolio, which develops a web-based application to manage rental properties, such as apartment complexes. The company had around 120 employees. We contacted the Director of Software Engineering who agreed to participate in the study. He identified one developer to be observed, who did not receive any compensation for his participation.

13.3.2 Procedure

We shadowed each developer for 1 day of work. We took notes about the activities developers were performing and time stamped switches between activities. We paid particular attention to Web searches. After they performed a search, we asked some questions about the goal of the search, expectations for the search, how the candidates were evaluated, and the use of the information.

At the end of the day of observations, the researcher conducted a short debriefing interview. The participant was asked to reflect on the activities performed and the patterns of searches on the Web.

Because the searches were conducted so quickly, we developed an extension for the Chrome Web browser to collect data. The extension automatically recorded searches as well as the results developers visited after each search. Data collected included the search engine used, terms in the query, and time. For visited results, the extension recorded: the number of result page, the rank of the visited result, the time of visit, the title, and the URL. A subset of participants in the US (10) installed and used the Chrome extension the day they were observed.

We analyzed the data inductively and iteratively [9]. We used open coding to identify categories, sometimes revisiting data to apply new categories. We used axial coding to relate different categories to each other to create descriptions. The names of participants that we use in this document are pseudonyms to protect their confidentiality.

13.3.3 Participants

Table 13.1 shows a summary of our participants and companies. We observed 12 developers at Novatronic, 11 men and 1 female. Eleven participants completed the background questionnaire. They were between 23 and 38 years old and had 1–15 years of programming experience. They used the following programming languages at work: Java, C/C++, SQL, Visual Basic, and JavaScript. They used these IDEs: Netbeans, Eclipse, Visual Studio, and Notepad++ (for C). Five participants indicated that they looked for source code on the Web a couple of times per week, four almost every day, one several times per day, and one less than once per month.

We observed 11 software developers, all men, from Health Connection. Developers were between 23 and 36 years old with 2.5–13 years of programming experience. They used the following programming languages at work: Java, SQL, JSP, and JavaScript. The IDEs that they used were Netbeans, Intellij IDEA, and Eclipse. Five participants indicated that they look for source code on the Web almost every day, three a couple of times per week, and three several times per day.

One participant was from AppFolio. He had 2.5 years of work experience, and uses TextMate to code in Ruby. He indicated that he looked for source code on the Web several times per day.

	Novatronic	Health Connection	AppFolio
Type of Software	Transactional software	Open source software to exchange health information	Property management software
Country	Peru	USA	USA
# of Employees	64	45	120
# of Developers Observed	12	11	1
Years of Programming Experience of Participants	1-15	2.5-13	2.5
Programming Languages Used by Participants	Java, C/C++, SQL, Visual Basic, Java Script	Java, SQL, JSP, JavaScript	Ruby

Table 13.1: Summary of participants and companies in field studies

13.4 Results

13.4.1 Web Search Was Used to Explore Further and Find Missing Information to Complete Software Development Tasks

Developers often did not have all the information they needed to complete their software development tasks, and this is why they searched the Web. They were looking for information that will help them solve their software development problems.

In our field studies, we identified four types of problems using the classification proposed by Brandt [3]. First, developers needed to remember syntax details or find a fact. Second, they needed to clarify how to implement functionality given that they had a high level understanding of how to implement it. Third, they needed to learn some concepts. Finally, developers needed to look for tools or open source projects. This last category was not reported in Brandt's study. Figure 13.1 shows the frequency of each type of problem. We identified that the first three types of problems fit into opportunistic problem solving, but not the last one. Searches done to find an open source project to reuse do not meet all the three characteristics of opportunistic problem solving. For that reason, searches for open source projects will be discussed in the next section.

The length of the Web search session varied depending on the type of problem developers wanted to solve. We obtained this result by looking at the distribution

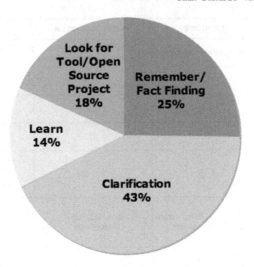

Fig. 13.1 Problems that motivate web searches

of the duration of each kind of search. A Search Session represents a period of continuous Web usage to fill a single information need performed in the same day.[1]

Figure 13.2 shows a box and whisker plot for the length of the searches by the type of search performed. Each box in the graph shows the range of 50% of the data and the black dot shows the median. The whiskers show the 25% of searches that took longer or the shorter. Triangles show the outliers. (Three additional outliers have been omitted.)

Here, we include a description for each type of software problem identified for opportunistic searches. Descriptions are accompanied by quotations from developers that exemplify the searches our participants performed in field studies. We use pseudonyms to identify our participants.

---

[1] Some definitions of sessions used by other researches indicate that Web usage must be continuous with no breaks longer than 5 min [11], 6 min [3], or 25.5 min [4]. However, we decided not to include a cutoff in the longest time a break could take in the same day. Our decision was based on the fact that we observed that developers had interruptions longer than 25.5 min while using the Web and when they came back they continued reviewing information on the Web or refining queries to fill the same information need. For that reason, the only time constraint we consider is that Web usage should happen the same day. Instead, we put more emphasis to the intention of the search. If Web usage was done to meet the same information need, we consider all those intervals as part of the same Search Session. The three longest breaks that we observed in our field sites were of 3 h 25 min 46 s, 1 h 34 min 19 s, and 1 h 16 min and 18 s. In these cases, developers interrupted their search to chat with co-workers, answer calls from customers, code, write documentation, and have personal breaks. When they used the Web again, they read the information they found before and in some cases they also copied and pasted lines of source code and used them even though more than 3 h passed since their first query.

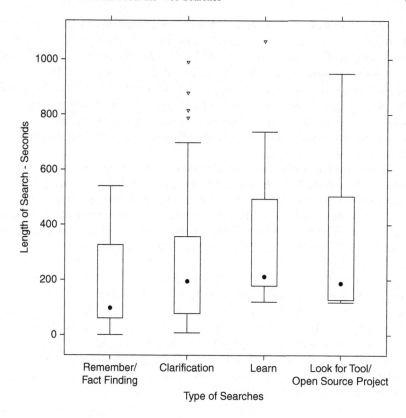

Fig. 13.2 Length of web searches by type of software problems

Remembering/Fact Finding   Developers knew exactly what they are looking for when they perform Web searches to remember syntax details or find facts. In these cases, developers recognized the answer as soon as they see it.

Developers performed searches to remember syntax details of commands or parameters of a method. As Bob, a developer in our field studies, mentioned *"I always forget how to do this,"* when he performed a search to remember the syntax of a SQL command. In other words, developers were using the Web as memory aid [3].

Developers also knew exactly what they are looking for when they were trying to find facts. For example, the goal of one developer was *"to find what was the last version of HtmlUnit."*

Twenty five percent of the searches we observed are to remember or to find facts as shown in Fig. 13.1. These searches had the lowest median time and the tightest distribution as seen in Fig. 13.2. Query refinements were uncommon in these cases. Developers tended to visit few results and in some cases they found the answer just by looking at the list of results.

Clarifying   Often developers had a high level understanding of what they wanted
to implement, but they did not know precisely how to do it. They were looking
for examples of how to use APIs or solutions to bugs or exceptions. One instance
of this type of search was when Michael needed to log messages from his php
application. When asked about his goal for the search, he said that he wanted
to *"find an example of how to have a php application send JMS messages to a
queue so they will be logged."* Another instance was when Gregory was *"trying
to find out any issue or forum post about the exception org.eclipse.jetty.util.log
EOF."*

Developers had a rough idea of what they want, but are not sure what would
be a good answer. In such cases, it is hard for developers to create effective
queries. They need to evaluate more results and they reformulate queries as they
learn from the search results that they evaluate. These searches had a median
time longer than the one for remembering but smaller than the one to learn new
concepts as seen in Fig. 13.2. Forty three percent of the searches we observed fall
in this category.

Learning   Developers needed to learn concepts that were new to them. Once,
Joaquin was asked to implement an application for an unfamiliar operating system, he did a search for *"0S4690 v6.0"*. For searches in support of learning,
developers mainly looked at explanations and examples or tutorials. Fourteen
percent of the searches observed fall into this category. Developers spent more
time reading the documentation than evaluating the relevance of results. They
did many query reformulations and visited many results. These searches had the
largest median time as seen in Fig. 13.2.

13.4.1.1 Knowledge Was Gathered Partially and Incrementally

Developers used the search process to learn more about the problem they want to
solve and how to formulate effective queries. As they learned, they refined their
searches based on the partial knowledge they collect from previous queries in a
Web search session. Search results sometimes provided solutions and at other times
they helped developers identify more appropriate keywords.

In our field studies, developers used query reformulation in 50% of the searches
to learn new concepts and in 35% of the searches when they were trying to clarify
implementation details or fix bugs. Table 13.2 shows the number of query reformulations for each type of problem. The first column shows the number of searches with
0 refinements. That means, developers only entered one query for those searches.
The second column shows the number of query reformulation between one and
seven. In this case, developers performed between two and eight queries. In the
third column, we show the searches that did not include query reformulation because developers visited bookmarks or links directly. In the last column, we show
the searches for which we did not have information about query reformulation.

Query Reformulation		0	1-7	Bookmark	No info
Opportunistic Searches	Remembering/ Fact Finding	13	5	4	0
	Clarifying	15	14	3	5
	Learning	6	6	0	0
	SUBTOTAL	34 (48%)	25 (35%)	7 (10%)	5 (7%)
Non-Opportunistic Searches	Looking for Open Source Projects or Software Tools	14	2	0	0
	SUBTOTAL	14 (88%)	2 (13%)	0 (0%)	0 (0%)
	TOTAL	48 (55%)	27 (31%)	7 (8%)	5 (6%)

Table 13.2: Query reformulation by type of software problems

One instance of a search that involved query refinement was when Manfred was looking for a solution to solve an exception he was having when he was using Htm-lUnit. He entered the following sequence of queries:

Query 1: *htmlunit "The data necessary to complete this operation is not yet available"*

Query 2: *htmlunit doScroll*

Query 3: *htmlunit "The data necessary to complete this operation is not yet available" doscroll*

In the first query, Manfred entered the name of the library and the error message he received. After examining some results, he learned that this problem could be related to the "doScroll" method, so he replaced the error message with the name of the method in the second query. Then, he examined the results and did not find the answer he was looking for, so he tried to include both the error message and the name of the method. This example shows that developers collect partial knowledge from the search result evaluation they perform during a Web search session.

13.4.1.2 Searches on the Web Did Not Follow a Well-Planned Process

Web searches happened in an ad hoc manner and they happen often. Typically, developers did not start their day by planning the Web searches they are going to

262

R.E. Gallardo-Valencia and S.E. Sim

perform during the day. In fact, they did not know if they will even be searching for code or how many searches they will need.

Also, if Web searches were a planned process, people would be more aware of the searches they perform. However, we found a mismatch between what people reported doing and what people actually did.

Based on our observations of developers in field sites, 83% of them perform many searches on the Web during a day of work to help them solve software development problems. However, when asked in all our surveys, only 45% of developers reported that they perform searches almost everyday or several times per day [5].

Twenty developers we observed performed searches on the Web to help them solve software development problems. Only 4 developers out of the 24 that we observed did not perform any searches related to software development (three in Peru and one in the US). One developer who was an expert in JavaScript did not perform any searches when he spent the day coding. He did not need to consult implementation details and when he had exceptions he knew how to solve them. The other three developers had different situations and coding was not the main activity during the day. One developer was running around trying to solve a problem with a system in production, another was writing documentation, and the last one was working his last day at the company.

Among those who did search the Web, they performed on average 3.6 searches per day ($\sigma = 3.4$), with a low of one search and a high of 15. Web searches were an important and integral part of their day. One developer at Health Connect, Brian, said: *"I could not code without Google."* He performed seven searches the day he was observed.

13.4.2 Non-opportunistic Searches

Not all Web searches that we observed fulfilled the three characteristics of opportunistic searches. When developers looked for open source projects, Web searches were mainly to find software to reuse as is, not to find code snippets or explanations. Also, Web searches are not ad hoc but instead they followed a methodical process.

13.4.2.1 Web Search Was Used to Find Open Source Projects to Reuse As-Is

Web searches are non-opportunistic when developers were trying to find a complete system, component, or tool to reuse. They did not intend to make any changes to the code that they found.

Developers looked for open source projects that they can reuse and integrate into their current projects. For example, Oscar was looking for an open source project to do data mining of logs and to manage alerts. In other cases, they needed to find some tools to support their programming tasks. For instance, Malcom was trying to find a tool to do performance testing of Java programs. In this type of search, developers look at many alternatives and evaluate each of them very carefully according to criteria such as functionality, cost, popularity, and support. Unlike opportunistic searches, this type of search often requires multiple search sessions, each requiring evaluating different options.

Searches for open source projects and software tools have the second highest median search time, the most skewed distribution, and the longest tail, as seen in Fig. 13.2. In other words, these kinds of search sessions typically took the same amount of time as search sessions in support of learning, but many could take a very long time. Also, developers often required more than one search session to find a suitable open source project to reuse. One participant spent an entire day looking for an open source project, and still did not finish the task.

13.4.2.2 Knowledge Was Gathered for Criteria to Evaluate Open Source Candidates

When developers evaluated open source projects, they performed Web searches to find information related to each of the evaluation criteria that they use to compare them.

When we observed Oscar, he did Web searches using the name of the system that he was evaluating. He made few query reformulations, as seen in Table 13.2. For each candidate, he read information related to the architecture of the system, requirements for installation, cost, and support, which were the evaluation criteria he was using. He looked for the same information for all the systems he evaluated.

13.4.2.3 Searches Commonly Followed a Planned Process

Oscar, already mentioned above, knew at the beginning of the day that he would be doing many Web searches to find a project or component. At the beginning of the day, he found an article that provided a list of this type of open source systems. Over the course of the day, he methodically followed that list to search for information related to each open source system. For each candidate in the list, he did a Web search using the name of the system for the query and he did not need to reformulate his queries.

13.5 Discussion

Using an opportunistic problem solving approach helped us to have a clear understanding of what motivates Web searches, to identify common search targets for different motivations, to differentiate searches for code snippets and open source projects as two different problems, and to classify tools for opportunistic and non-opportunistic searches.

13.5.1 Software Development Problems and Search Targets

Software problems that developers want to solve define the search targets. We found that developers look for examples, code snippets, syntax, or API documentation when they want to remember or find a fact. When developers want to clarify implementation details or find solution to a bug, they look for API documentation, examples, code snippets, and error related information. If developers need to learn new concepts, they usually look for tutorials or API documentation. When developers look for open source projects, they try to find information related to the projects, specifically with respect to the installation requirements, architecture, and reputation.

	Search Target	API Documentation/ Tutorial	Example/Code Snippet/Syntax	Open Source Project/ Software Tool	Error Related Information	Others
Opportunistic Searches	Remembering/ Fact Finding	● 7	● 11		· 1	● 3
	Clarifying	● 18	● 10		● 7	· 2
	Learning	● 8	· 3			· 1
Non-Opportunistic Searches	Looking for Open Source Projects or Software Tools			● 16		

Table 13.3: Search targets by type of software problems

Table 13.3 uses circles to show how often developers look for each search target when they are trying to solve each type of software problem. The bigger the circle, the more frequent a search target is used to solve a development problem. For example, we can see in this table that for 18 searches (out of 87) developers were looking for API documentation or tutorials to clarify implementation details. We identified the following search targets:

API Documentation/Tutorial   Developers are looking for documentation of APIs or tutorials, mainly when they want to clarify some implementation details. Less frequently, developers look for these search targets when they want to learn new concepts or remember syntax details.

Example/Code Snippet/Syntax   We grouped examples (14), syntax (7), and code snippets (3) together because when developers are looking for these search targets, most of the time they are trying to find few lines of code to be used as a reference or to be reused. Developers look for this set of search targets when they are trying to remember, find a fact, or clarify implementation details.

Open Source Project/Software Tool   When developers are evaluating open source project candidates or they are looking for a tool to help them with programming, they look for information related to each candidate. This information includes requirements to install the project, description of the architecture, and what other people think about a project.

Error Related Information   When developers get exceptions after they compile, run, or test their code, they look to the Web to find error related information that could be helpful to understand the error and fix it. Developers are interested in finding the cause of the error, how to solve it, and experiences other developers have with the same issue.

Others   In this category we grouped search targets that did not fall in any of the previous categories. We found that developers are also trying to find again a Web page recently visited that was useful but they do not have a link to it (2), and trying to find the meaning of a word (1). In one case, a developer did not know exactly what he was looking for and in other two cases developers described their search targets in terms of the problems that they were trying to solve.

13.5.2 Looking for Code Snippets and Looking for Open Source Projects Are Different Problems

Analyzing the motivation of Web searches from an opportunistic problem solving perspective, makes evident the differences between searches for code snippets and searches for open source projects.

When developers search for code snippets or explanations to remember syntax details, clarify implementation concepts or fix bugs, and learn new concepts, they are performing opportunistic searches. These searches do not follow a planned process, instead, they are ad hoc. Developers perform opportunistic searches to find missing information and incrementally gather information.

On the other hand, Web searches to look for open source projects are done following a methodical or planned process. Developers methodically evaluate each open source candidate by looking into the Web for further information about a set of criteria. These criteria includes cost, installation requirements, functionality, architecture, and reputation.

Finding these differences between searches for code snippets and searches for open source projects makes it clear that developers need different tool support for these two types of searches.

13.6 Implications for Tools

Our empirical studies show that developers perform Web searches differently to look for code snippets (opportunistic searches) and to look for open source projects (non-opportunistic searches). In this section, we provide implications for tools for these two types of searches separately.

13.6.1 Implications for Tools for Opportunistic Searches

From our empirical studies, we have learned that developers are highly successful when they do Web searches to find code snippets to remember syntax details or to find facts. In this case, developers know exactly what they are looking for and recognize it easily. However, developers are not highly successful when they search on the Web for code snippets to clarify implementation details or fix errors, which is the most common motivation for searching on the Web. We believe that improving tools to help developers be more successful in this type of searches can make a positive impact on the effectiveness of solving software problems. Based on our findings, we give the following recommendations to tool designers.

13.6.1.1 Make Examples and Source Code Snippets More Visible

Developers are mainly looking for examples or code snippets on the Web. Even when developers look for API Documentation or tutorials, they also want to see examples of how to use certain functionality. However, Web browsers do not facilitate the identification of examples or code snippets in the search results.

Due to the fact that we observed that developers often look for search results that contain examples or code snippets, we believe that it would be helpful if developers could know which search results contain examples or code snippets. One possibility is to augment the search results gathered from a search engine such as Google and analyze which ones have source code. Mica [13] and Assieme [7] are two tools that recently have shown that augmenting Web search results to make developers aware of which results contains source code examples of API can make Web searches more effective. Also, after identifying that a result has source code, we believe that it would be useful to show technical and social information related to a piece of source code. Recently, a prototype that augments Web search results with reputation information has been developed [6].

Another possibility to make examples or code snippets more visible is to create a crawler to gather source code snippets from tutorials, forums, API documentation on the Web and create a repository of them. This repository could associate code snippets with text surrounding them in Web pages so that code snippets would have actual text associated with them to facilitate the matching between code snippets and keywords in queries [14].

13.6.1.2 Show Error Related Information When an Exception Occurs

Nineteen percent of searches to clarify information were to fix errors. When developers compile, run, or test their source code, they copy and paste the exception in a Web search engine and they try to find what causes an error, how it can be solved, and what are the experiences of other people with that same issue.

Due to the fact that we observed that developers look for error related information when their program shows an error, we believe that it would be helpful for developers if the IDE that throws an exception will also run a query on the Web with that exception. In that way, the IDE can show the developers not only the line where the exception was detected and the stacktrace, but also information found on the Web related to this error including potential causes, potential solutions, and what other people did when they encounter the same error.

13.6.1.3 Present Results from Web Searches in the Development Environment

We observed that sometimes after developers found a solution on the Web, they put side by side a window with the source code found and a window with their source code in an IDE. For this reason, we believe that it would be useful if developers could have both, their source code and results from the Web in the same environment. Recent tools such as CodeGenie [8] and Blueprint [2] have explored this integration between the IDE and the Web.

We expect that in the future developers will have online IDEs and the integration of search results from the Web and their own code stored in the cloud would be easier and more natural.

13.6.2 Implications for Tools for Non-opportunistic Searches

In our empirical studies, we observed that developers look for the same type of information to compare open source projects. Based on this observation, we believe that it would be helpful if developers would have a tool that gathers this information and shows it in a comparative way. There are not many applications that have this functionality. One of the few is Ohloh, which allows developers to enter the name of three open source projects and shows the same information for all the three systems in a table to facilitate comparison. We used Ohloh to compare three systems searched by one of our participants, Oscar and Fig. 13.3 shows the results of this comparison.

For each of the projects, Ohloh shows general information including how recently the repository was updated, the home page, and license. It also includes repository activity for the project, code analysis, and reputation of the project given by Ohloh users.

We believe that tools that allow comparison of systems will be useful for developers. These tools should be flexible enough to support comparisons of more than three open source projects. Currently, Ohloh supports only comparison of three open source projects, as previously mentioned. However, we observed that a developer compared ten open source systems and he was planning on evaluating more

ohloh ohloh:**Root** *Sign In | Register*

| Home | People | Projects | Forums | Tools | Blog | | Q |

Compare Projects

	Solr Remove this project	CloverETL Remove this project	Talend Remove this project
General			
Ohloh Data Quality	Updated 5 days ago	Updated 2 days ago	Updated about 22 hours ago
Homepage	lucene.apache.org	www.cloveretl.com	www.talend.com
Project License	Apache License 2.0	LGPL	GPL
Estimated Cost	$2,394,852.00	$5,748,075.00	$80,460,445.00
All Time Activity			
Committers (All Time) View as graph	29 developers	47 developers	149 developers
Commits (All Time) View as graph	4,719 commits	8,705 commits	23,520 commits
Initial Commit	almost 6 years ago	almost 9 years ago	about 5 years ago
Most Recent Commit	5 days ago	14 days ago	about 24 hours ago
12 Month Activity			
Committers (Past 12 Months)	24 developers	18 developers	102 developers
Year-Over-Year Commits	Stable	Decreasing	Increasing
30 Day Activity			
Committers (Past 30 Days)	15 committers	6 committers	55 committers
Commits (Past 30 Days)	71 commits	17 commits	694 commits
Files Modified	297 files	59 files	3,129 files
Lines Added	7,981 lines	3,492 lines	197,311 lines
Lines Removed	2,165 lines	1,821 lines	59,550 lines
Code Analysis			
Mostly Written In	Java	Java	Java
Comments	Average	Average	High
Lines of Code View as graph	171,803 lines	400,607 lines	4,947,584 lines
People			
Managers	Position not yet claimed	dpavlis	ccarbone
Ohloh Users	88 users	3 users	12 users
Ohloh User Rating	4.7/5.0 Based on 34 user ratings.	3.3/5.0 Based on 3 user ratings.	4.3/5.0 Based on 4 user ratings.

Fig. 13.3 Compare projects feature by Ohloh

before selecting one. Tools that help comparing projects should also include other criteria in addition to repository activity. This recommendation is based on the fact that we observed that developers evaluate open source projects having into account not only characteristics of their repository but also other characteristics such as the installation requirements and the architecture of the open source project.

13.7 Conclusion

In summary, we analyzed Web searches using an opportunistic problem solving approach to find out what motivates developers to look for information on the Web. We found that developers mainly perform searches to opportunistically solve software development problems (82% of Web searches). Opportunistic searches are ad hoc and are done to remember syntax details, clarify implementation details or fix bugs, and learn new concepts. On the other hand, non-opportunistic searches (only 18% of Web searches) are done following a systematic process and are performed to find open source projects. Using opportunistic problem solving lenses we changed the level of granularity to understand the motivation behind Web searches from search targets to software development problems. This change on focus allow us to clearly understand that what motivates Web searches are software development problems and they define the search targets developers are looking for. Using the opportunistic approach also help us understand that searches for code snippets and searches for open source projects are two different problems that should be investigated separately.

Acknowledgements Thank you to all the participants and supporters at Novatronic, "Health Connection," and AppFolio. This research was possible due to their generosity in sharing their time and work with us. This material is based upon work supported by the NSF under Grant No. IIS-0846034. Any opinions, findings, and conclusions or recommendations expressed in this material are those of the authors and do not necessary reflect the views of the NSF.

References

[1] Sushil Bajracharya and Cristina Lopes. Mining search topics from a code search engine usage log. In *Proceedings of the 6th IEEE Working Conference on Mining Software Repositories*, pages 111–120, 2009.

[2] Joel Brandt, Mira Dontcheva, Marcos Weskamp, and Scott R. Klemmer. Example-centric programming: Integrating web search into the development environment. In *Proceedings of the 28th International Conference on Human Factors in Computing Systems*, pages 513–522, Atlanta, Georgia, USA, 2010. ACM.

[3] Joel Brandt, Philip J. Guo, Joel Lewenstein, Mira Dontcheva, and Scott R. Klemmer. Two studies of opportunistic programming: interleaving web foraging, learning, and writing code. In *Proceedings of the 27th international conference on Human factors in computing systems*, pages 1589–1598, Boston, MA, USA, 2009. ACM.

[4] Lara D. Catledge and James E. Pitkow. Characterizing browsing strategies in the world-wide web. In *Proceedings of the Third International World-Wide Web conference on Technology, tools and applications*, pages 1065–1073, New York, NY, USA, 1995. Elsevier North-Holland, Inc.

[5] Rosalva E. Gallardo-Valencia. *How Software Developers Solve Problems by Searching for Source Code on the Web: Studies on Judgments in Evaluation of Results and Information Use*. Ph.d. Thesis, University of California, Irvine, 2012.

[6] Rosalva E. Gallardo-Valencia, P. Tantikul, and Susan Elliott Sim. Searching for reputable source code on the web. In *Proceedings of the Group Conference 2010*, Florida, USA, 2010. ACM.

[7] Raphael Hoffmann, James Fogarty, and Daniel S. Weld. Assieme: finding and leveraging implicit references in a web search interface for programmers. In *Proceedings of the 20th Annual ACM Symposium on User Interface Software and Technology*, Newport, Rhode Island, USA, 2007. ACM.

[8] Otavio Augusto Lazzarini Lemos, Sushil Bajracharya, Joel Ossher, Paulo Cesar Masiero, and Cristina Lopes. Applying test-driven code search to the reuse of auxiliary functionality. In *Proceedings of the 2009 ACM symposium on Applied Computing*, pages 476–482, Honolulu, Hawaii, 2009. ACM.

[9] J. Lofland, D. Snow, L. Anderson, and L. Lofland. *Analyzing Social Settings: A Guide to Qualitative Observation and Analysis*. Wadsworth/Thomson Learning, Belmont, CA, 2006.

[10] P.N. Robillard. Opportunistic problem solving in software engineering. *IEEE Software*, 22(6):60–67, 2005.

[11] Craig Silverstein, Hannes Marais, Monika Henzinger, and Michael Moricz. Analysis of a very large web search engine query log. *SIGIR Forum*, 33:6–12, September 1999.

[12] Susan Elliott Sim, Medha Umarji, Sukanya Ratanotayanon, and Cristina V. Lopes. How well do internet code search engines support open source reuse strategies? *ACM Transactions on Software Engineering and Methodology*, 21(1), December 2011.

[13] Jeffrey Stylos and Brad A. Myers. Mica: A web-search tool for finding api components and examples. In *IEEE Symposium on Visual Languages and Human-Centric Computing, 2006. VL/HCC 2006*, pages 195–202, Brighton, United Kingdom, 2006. IEEE.

[14] Phitchayaphong Tantikul. JCSSE: Java code snippet search engine. Master's thesis, Information and Computer Sciences, University of California, Irvine, 2011.

[15] M. Umarji, S. E. Sim, and C. Lopes. Archetypal internet-scale source code searching. In B. Russo, E. Damiani, S. Hissam, B. Lundell, and G. Succi, editors, *IFIP International Federation for Information Processing 275: Open Source Development, Communities and Quality*, pages 257–263. Springer, 2008.

Chapter 14
Novel and Applied Algorithms in a Search Engine for Java Code Snippets

Phitchayaphong Tantikul, C. Albert Thompson, Rosalva E. Gallardo-Valencia, and Susan Elliott Sim

Abstract Programmers often look for a "snippet," that is, a small piece of example code, to remind themselves of how to solve a problem or to quickly learn about a new resource. However, existing tools such as general-purpose search engines and code-specific search engines do not deal well with searches for snippets. In this chapter, we present a prototype search engine designed to work with code snippets. Our approach is based on using the non-code text on a web page as metadata for the snippet to improve indexing and retrieval. We discuss some implementation issues that we encountered, which lead to lessons learned for others who follow. These issues include: extracting snippets from web pages, selecting and indexing metadata, matching query terms with multiple metadata indexes, and identifying a text summary to be used in the presentations of results.

P. Tantikul (✉)
University of California, Irvine, Irvine, CA, USA
e-mail: ptantiku@gmail.com

C.A. Thompson
University of British Columbia, Vancouver, BC, Canada
e-mail: leetcat@cs.ubc.ca

R.E. Gallardo-Valencia
Intel Corporation, Santa Clara, CA, USA
e-mail: rgallardovalencia@acm.org

S.E. Sim
Many Roads Studios, Toronto, ON, Canada
e-mail: ses@drsusansim.org

S.E. Sim and R.E. Gallardo-Valencia (eds.), *Finding Source Code on the Web for Remix and Reuse*, DOI 10.1007/978-1-4614-6596-6__14,
© Springer Science+Business Media New York 2013

14.1 Introduction

Searching for source code on the web has become an integral part of software development. We find evidence of this in the creation of search engines specifically designed to search for source code, such as Strathcona [5], Mica [12], Krugle,[1] Koders,[2] Google Code Search,[3] and Sourcerer [6]. All of these tools take the approach of gathering together as much source code as possible from open source hosting sites and making the repository searchable. Unfortunately, these repositories omit the large number of code snippets that are embedded in web pages throughout the Internet. Snippets usually consist of a handful of lines of code and do not necessarily compile. Since snippets differ from components in a number of ways, it stands to reason that they require a different kind of repository and search engine.

In this chapter, we describe "Juicy," a search engine for snippets of Java code and the lessons learned from its implementation. In the design of Juicy, we treated code snippets as first class objects. When the search engine returns a page of results, the items consist of an excerpt of the code snippet, a link the originating web page, and a brief text description. In implementing Juicy, we used many existing tools and algorithms. Our contribution is in the novel application of these resources and the resulting assemblage.

We used the **Rotation Forest** machine learning algorithm, as implemented by **Weka 3** to help us label sections of web pages from Java tutorial sites as either text or source code. The open source project, **Lucene**, was used as the repository for Juicy. We used the **Porter Stemming** algorithm to normalize words. The **Eclipse AST parser** was used to parse the code snippet. Finally, **Latent Dirichelet Allocation** was used to find the most relevant paragraph of text to be used as a short summary of the snippet.

In addition to leveraging these existing algorithms, we performed some small empirical investigations to inform our design decisions. We identified appropriate features to be used in classifying segments of tutorial pages. We found that it was necessary to filter out many duplicate pages and pages that did not contain code from our initial crawl of Java language tutorial sites. We found that the best text to use as metadata for a snippet is the text segment that appears above the snippet. We found that the best results for a general search were obtained by using only three indexes: web page title, code snippet, and text segment.

In the remainder of this chapter, we will describe how we used these existing algorithms and the design decisions that we made in doing so.

---

[1] http://www.krugle.com/.

[2] http://www.koders.com.

[3] http://www.google.com/codesearch.

14.2 Approach

Our approach was based on the following key insights:

1. Programming language tutorial pages contain an distinctive combination of source code snippets and natural language.
2. The natural language on the pages can be used as metadata for the code snippets.
3. Effective searches for snippets need to make use of both the source code and the natural language text.

The architecture of Juicy is divided into two parts, a back end that works offline and a interactive front end. These parts are depicted in Fig. 14.1 below.

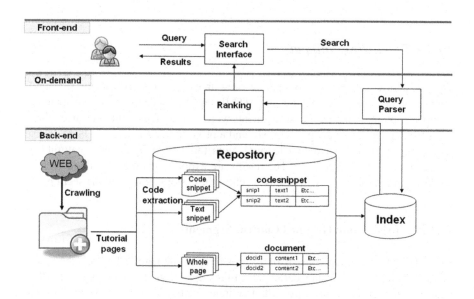

Fig. 14.1 Architecture of Juicy, a Java code snippet search engine

The back end consists of a repository built on top of Apache Lucene, a text search engine library written in Java [8]. Our contributions consist of the techniques for populating the repository with code snippets, and for creating metadata and indexes. The front end provides a user interface to the repository through a web interface.

14.3 Populating the Repository

We populated the repository by using a web crawler to collect web pages from the Internet. In populating the repository for a snippet search engine there are basically three issues that need to be considered: (1) what sites to crawl; (2) how to exclude pages that do not contain Java code; and (3) extracting code snippets from the web page. We will discuss each of these in this section.

14.3.1 Starting Points for the Crawler

The web crawler is a program to collect web-pages from the Internet. It takes an intial web page, or "seed URL" as input and places it in a queue. The program retrieves the page from the first URL in the queue and stores it locally. The contents of this page is further parsed for hyperlinks, which are added to the queue of web sites. The program then iterates through the remaining URLs in the queue. The crawler in this project was built upon HTML Parser.[4]

To construct our prototype repository, we used a set of 33 seed URLs. These were chosen, because they were identified as rich sources of information, and used a variety of page formats. The full list can be found in the appendix for this chapter.

14.3.2 Extracting Snippets

We used a three-step process to separate the source code snippets from the surrounding text on the web page. We used the HTML tags to divide the page into spans, or grouped content segments. These segments were then scored on the presence of features from a natural language (English) and a programming language (Java). These scores were input into a machine learning algorithm to classify either as natural language text or Java source code. The results are exported in an XML file to be read by downstream tools. We will discuss each of these steps further in this section.

14.3.2.1 Division into Grouped Content Segments

Every HTML document consists of a series of spans demarcated by matched pairs of begin/end tags. For instance, the pair of tags <p></p>indicates a paragraph. The texts in between these tags are called content segments. In other words, content segments are the leaves in the tree representing the document object model.

Unfortunately, content segments can be difficult to classify, because they are short, containing only one or two words, which makes it difficult to label the segment as source code or text. For example, "public" is both an English language word and a Java keyword. For this reason, we took a tactic from lyrics classification and formed grouped content segments from content segments according to their nesting within <pre>and <code>tags. In other words, the content segments in the sub-tree rooted by a <pre>or <code>tag are aggregated.

---

[4] http://htmlparser.sourceforge.net.

14.3.2.2 Scoring of Natural Language Features

We used the following three features based on characteristics of natural language: number of words, ratio of non-dictionary words, and ratio of stop words. These choices were motivated by previous work on content retrieval. Also, we experimented with other features, such as length of the segment and counts of dictionary words, but these were less fruitful.

Number of Words   This feature is simply the count of the number of words in a content segment. Numerals, i.e. digits, are not included. As well, white space of any kind does not affect this feature. Typically, text has a larger number of words per content segment than source code.

Ratio of Non-Dictionary Words   Another feature is the number of words in the content segment that does not appear in the Merriam-Webster's 9th Collegiate dictionary [7]. Again, we excluded numerals. Usually, source code has a larger proportion of non-dictionary words than natural language, because identifier names are invented to suit the context and are not limited to dictionary entries.

Ratio of Stop Words   In natural language processing, there is the concept of "stop words." These are words that are filtered out prior to processing, because they appear so frequently that they add little information to the input stream. Stop words typically include articles, pronouns, prepositions, and common verbs, such as "to be" [4]. In our work, we do not filter out stop words, but instead use a stop word ratio. We used a published list of English stop words [2], but removed Java programming language keywords. Normally, text would have a higher stop word ratio than source code.

14.3.2.3 Scoring of Programming Language Features

We use the following set of five features derived from programming languages: ratio of keywords, ratio of indentation, number of comments, ratio of separators, and ratio of operators. For each of these, we will discuss how they apply to programming languages in general, and then specifically for Java.

Ratio of Keywords   In source code, the words that appear most frequently are programming language keywords. By counting these keywords we can get a good idea if something is source code. Since the number of distinct keywords in a programming language is relatively small, it would not be difficult to adapt this feature to a particular language, such as Java.

Ratio of Indentation   In general, indentation is used only to improve readability. Some programming languages, e.g. Fortran and Python, prescribes indentation or assigns a role to a line position. In either case, extensive use of tabs or whitespace is an indicator that a content segment is source code.

Number of Comments   Every programming language has syntax for comments. The syntax for comments can vary from language to language, but their presence indicates that a content segment is source code. In some languages, comments are easy to identify. For example, a letter 'C' or hash mark or single quotation mark in the first position on a line indicates a comment. Java comments are more complex and can take one of two forms. A comment that spans only one line is prefixed by a pair of backslashes '\\'. A comment that spans one or more lines begins with '/*' and ends with '*/'. Care must be taken when working with single-line comments to ensure that double backslashes in URLs do not produce false positives.

Ratio of Separators and Ratio of Operators   Programming languages have special punctuation that is used to separate or delimit identifiers or operands. The distinction between separators/delimiters and operators is arbitrary and language specific. We calculate ratios for these two features disjointly.

We relied on the Java Language Specification [3] to define these two classes of special punctuation. For the separators, we included parentheses, curly braces, square brackets, and the semicolon, but did not include the comma and full stop, because the latter two appear frequently in text. For the operators, we used the full Java set, but excluded the hyphen.

14.3.2.4 Classification of the Segments

We used the Rotation Forest algorithm as implemented in Weka 3,[5] an open source framework written in Java, that implements more than 60 different machine learning algorithms.

Rotation Forest [10] is a classifier ensemble method. Its main heuristic is the application of feature classification to subsets of M features using principal component analysis (PCA) separately on each subset and reconstructing a full feature set for each of the L classifiers in the ensemble. Using Weka, we ran the algorithm for subsets of three features (M = 3), 10 classifiers in the ensemble (L = 10), and using a J48 decision tree. The algorithm is named Rotation Forest, because it uses a simple rotation of the coordinate axes from the PCA and the base classifier model is a decision tree.

The scores for the features are input to a Rotation Forest classifier. The output is two values: the likelihood that the grouped content segment is text and the likelihood that it is source code. We take the higher of the two values and apply the appropriate label to the segment.

14.3.2.5 Evaluating the Algorithm

We created a corpus of web pages that contained Java source code examples. We compared the output generated by each algorithm for each web page against a hand-built gold standard. Metrics such as accuracy, recall, precision, and F_1 were calculated based on the comparison.

---

[5] http://www.cs.waikato.ac.nz/ml/weka/.

We created a corpus of web pages to evaluate our algorithms by using results returned by Google search. We issued 16 queries each containing the term "java" and one of the following keywords from the Java programming language: abstract, class, double, final, for, if, import, int, interface, long, private, protected, public, static, void, and while. We downloaded and archived the first 50 results from each of the searches from Google. We removed 52 duplicate pages from the repository and 41 pages, because the pages did not contain HTML, e.g. PDF and word processor documents. Our final corpus contained 707 diverse web pages, both with and without Java source code examples. In these pages, there were 471,536 content segments and 9,796 grouped content segments. For each of these pages, we created by hand a "gold standard," or oracle for correct classifications.

The F_1 statistic is the weighted harmonic mean of precision and recall. In our evaluation, we calculated it separately for both text and source code, but here we show the generic formula we used to calculate both:

$$F_1 = 2 \times \frac{precision \times recall}{precision + recall} \tag{14.1}$$

Classification accuracy indicates the percentage of segments that the algorithm correctly classifies contents in text and source code.

$$Accuracy = \frac{number \quad of \quad correctly \quad classified \quad segments}{total \quad number \quad of \quad segments} \tag{14.2}$$

We found that F_1 Text = 0.968, F_1 Code = 0.767, and Accuracy = 0.959. It took 14.19 s to train the algorithm and 0.147 s to classify a typical page.

14.3.3 Summary

After completion of this processing, we have a repository of web pages where each web page has been factored into code snippets and text that can be used as metadata. The number of pages available after each step is summarized in Table 14.1.

Total pages downloaded	34,054
Pages with no Java code	21,162
Pages with Java code and text	12,892

Table 14.1: Number of pages after filtering

14.4 Indexing the Repository

Indexing is the process of identifying a set of keys for looking up a document in a repository. With text documents, it is common to index all of the terms, excluding stop words. Choosing what to index and how is an important design decision, because these keys determine how effectively a document is retrieved from the repository. Often, adding metadata to the index, such as the URL, tags, or author of the page, can improve the performance of a search. Simply treating source code snippets as text documents is not sufficient for a number of reasons. Some terms in source code are structurally significant, such as identifiers. Also, source code typically contains few keywords that tell you about what the code does. Consequently, additional processing is needed to ensure that the index contains the appropriate information, so that the most relevant code snippets are returned in response to a user's query.

Our index contains metadata from three different sources: web page, code snippet, and text as shown in Table 14.2. For web pages, we included two metadata fields: url and page title. For code snippets, we included 11 metadata fields: 10 for different identifier types and 1 for a summary of keywords found in a specific code snippet. For text, we included one metadata field that has the summary of keywords found in the text segment associated with a code snippet.

Web page	Code snippet	Text
URL	Keywords from code snippet	Keywords from text
Page title	Package	
	Import	
	Class declaration	
	Class used	
	Extending and implementing class	
	Return type	
	Method declaration	
	Method invocation	
	Variable declaration	
	Comments	

Table 14.2: List of indexable metadata

Information for all the metadata fields were indexed and stored in seperate columns in Lucene. We indexed words from 43,306 snippets, which were compressed into indexes in Lucene with a total size around 71 MB.

14.4.1 Indexing Text Segments

Our approach centers on the idea of using the text surrounding code snippets as metadata, because source code tends to have few words that describe its functionality or what it does. As a result, we need to find the chunk of text that contains the terms that best describes a snippet.

To answer this question, we sampled 200 pages from our repository and manually identified the most relevant text. We obtained this sample by taking the top 50 pages returned by a search using the following four keywords: binary tree, database, hashmap, and socket.

Out of 200 pages, 81 pages were identified to be related to the keywords. Figure 14.2 shows the number of relevant pages for each keyword. Looking more closely, we found that some keywords are too common, such as database, hashmap, and socket. Therefore, the words could appear in web pages that have a topic that is irrelevant to the search query.

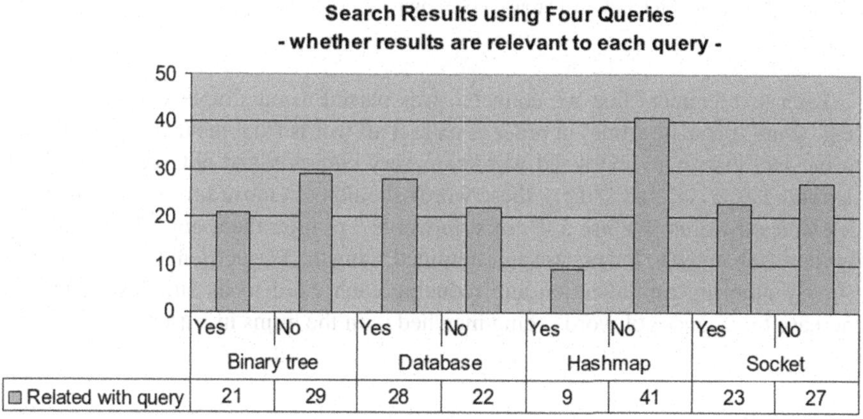

Search Results using Four Queries
- whether results are relevant to each query -

	Binary tree		Database		Hashmap		Socket	
	Yes	No	Yes	No	Yes	No	Yes	No
Related with query	21	29	28	22	9	41	23	27

Fig. 14.2 Number of relevant results in each query

We focused on the remaining 81 relevant pages in our study to find the location of a text segment that is most relevant to a specific code snippet. We manually inspected the code snippets and nearby text segments. We found that for 78 % of code snippets, the best text description appeared above them. For 2.25 % of the snippets, the most descriptive text appeared below of them. The best text description appears both above and below 13.75 % of the snippets. Finally, we could not find any relevant text description in the same page for 6.25 % of code snippets. Figure 14.3 summarizes these findings.

Based on these findings, we decided to pair the code snippet with the text segment that appears above it on the page in the repository. The words in the text segment can help describe a code snippet. We have a total of 43,306 pairs of text and code snippets in our repository.

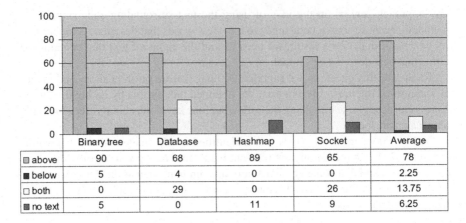

Fig. 14.3 Location of relevant text around code snippets

Each text segment that we collected was parsed using simple word delimitors (e.g. white space, new line) in order to extract all words from the text segment. Due to the fact that many extracted words are very common and not very helpful for searching, (e.g. 'a', 'an', 'the'), these words should be removed from the collection of extracted words. We use a list of stop words [6] to filter them out. The remaining words are changed to lower case and stemmed using the Porter Stemming Algorithm [9]. By ignoring capitalization and reducing each word to its simplest form, we increase the chances of words being matched with the terms in a user's query.

14.4.2 Indexing Code Snippet Segments

Within an integrated development environment (IDE), programmers often search for variables, functions, classes, and other programming constructs by name [11]. Code-specific search engines, such as Krugle, Sourcerer, Google Code Search, and Koders, also provide this functionality. It stands to reason that a snippet search engine should provide this functionality as well. Snippets tend not to be complete syntatically correct, nor can they be compiled and linked. Parsing out programming language constructs is only the beginning. Identifiers usually are not plain English words, but rather are improvised compounds. In addition, comments can be a useful source of metadata and deserve further analysis.

Instead of using fuzzy parsers, such as those used in syntax highlighters, but we tried an approach that has not been used extensively, an incremental compiler.

---

[6] http://www.ranks.nl/resources/stopwords.html.

To parse out identifiers and comments from the code snippets, we use the Eclipse abstract syntax tree parser.[7] We chose to use this API in Juicy, because it is a robust incremental compiler. Within the Eclipse workbench, the AST parser is capable of parsing code as it is typed and compiling classes as they are saved. For Juicy, it provides two features that are particularly helpful: input type selection and error handling. Input type selection allows the AST parser to be called with a flag that specifies whether the input code is complete source code, a block, or a line of code. This allows the parser to produce more accurate output. If the flag is set incorrectly for an input snippet, the parser will produce errors and we can try again with a different flag.

We collected ten types of structural information from code snippets which are shown in Table 14.3. The first nine types are mainly identifier declarations and invocations, which can be generalized into terms of package, class, variable, and method information.

Extracted identifier types		
Package	Import	Class declaration
Class used	Extending and implementing class	Return type
Variable declaration	Method declaration	Method invocation
Comment		

Table 14.3: Extracted indentifier types from parser

Another metadata field was added to store all the English words in the identifiers, which were found by dividing the identifiers according to internal capitalization. The scheme is also known as "camel case," because uppercase letters in an identifier are taller than the lowercase ones, giving the identifier the appearance of camel-like humps. As specified in the Sun Java Coding Convention, camel case is the recommended standard for aggregating English words to form a meaningful identifier. For this metadata field, we excluded Java keywords such as 'class,' 'for,' 'new,' and 'void.'

The last piece of information to be parsed from code snippets is code comments. Search engines can benefit from comments because they provide information about the context of the code snippets and also contribute potential matches to search terms. Having more keywords associated with a piece of source code will allow users to have more changes that a keyword included in a query matches with a keyword related to a piece of source code. Therefore, javadoc comments, line comments, and block comments were collected and treated as textual information in Juicy.

---

[7]http://www.eclipse.org/articles/article.php?file=Article-JavaCodeManipulation_AST/index.html.

14.5 Retrieving and Presenting Search Results

Juicy has both a general and an advanced user interface, as seen in Fig. 14.4. In this section, we will discuss how we use the indexes to obtain matches to the user's query, rank them, and display them.

14.5.1 Matching and Ranking

The basic user interface consisted of a simple text box, just like a typical search engine. With the indexes and metadata available, it was necessary to find a combination that would provide a set of useful results. Furthermore, when using multiple search indexes, we would need to find a way to combine the results.

We found that matching the search terms to all the metadata fields in our indexes at the same time produced many irrelevant results, but did so quickly. After experimenting with different combinations, we found that using three of our indexes produced the largest proportion of good results early in the list. These indexes were page title, keywords from code snippet, and keywords from text. Page title gives a general concept of the whole page. Keywords from code snippet contained identifier names that could explain what the code snippet does. Finally, keywords from text above code snippets, which proved to be relevant to the code snippet, could also

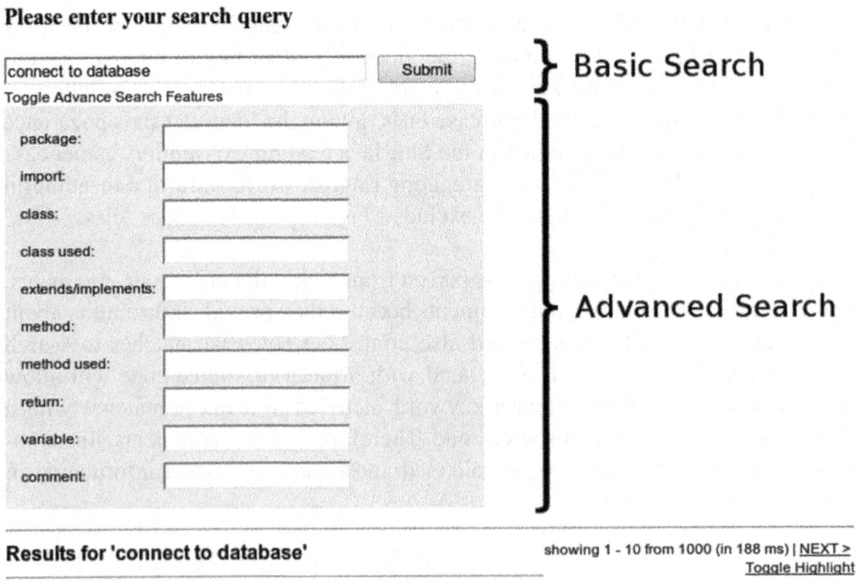

Please enter your search query

Fig. 14.4 User interface of Juicy

contain words explaining the behavior of the code snippet. In other words, these three metadata fields provide a idea of the purpose of the code snippet.

Using these three indexes gave us three different sets of search results that must be combined into a single ranked list. But the sets are not identical and the snippets are ranked differently. The approach that we used to combine the results revolved around the snippet ID. The final result set consisted of only snippets that appeared in all three results set, which ensures a high degree of relevance to the query. The new ranking was calculated by averaging the ranking from each index. We tried different combinations of weights for aggregating the ranking scores, but found that using equal weights yielded the best results.

The advanced interface allows users to search for a terms in specific indexes, such as class names, method names, and imported packages. Search terms are entered into a text box and these keywords are matched in the corresponding index. The matches are aggregated and ranked using the normalized TF-IDF score produced by Lucene [8].

14.5.2 Presentation

When returning matches, the search engine needs to provide not only the snippet, but also the title of matched web page and a short text summary (Fig. 14.5). It is not obvious what text on a web page is the best summary of the snippet. To solve this problem, we used LDA (Latent Dirichelet Allocation). This algorithm is little known in this space.

LDA, also known as Topic Modeling, can be run offline to create a static set of topics for all the web pages, text segments, and code snippets in our repository. When a search is executed, we use these topics to choose the best text summary among those that were returned and use this in the results presentation.

To evaluate the effectiveness of this approach, we conducted an experiment with a sample of ten queries (Table 14.4). The keywords in the queries were randomly selected from a list of 555 common search terms found in an analysis of a log from the Koders search engine [1].

Query keywords				
1. smtp	2. quicksort	3. list	4. stringbuffer	5. date
6. webservice	7. signature	8. xpath	9. download file	10. base64

Table 14.4: Keywords used for LDA experiment

We took the first 20 results returned by each query and looked at the number of topics in common with the following four candidate sources of text for the summary.

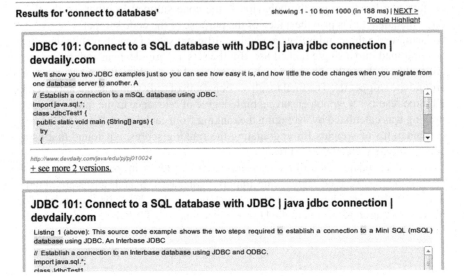

Fig. 14.5 Results presentation in Juicy

1. Best Matched Paragraph. This is the paragraph with the highest frequency of matched topic keywords between the paragraph and its related code snippet. This paragraph can appear anywhere on the web page.
2. Text Segment Above Snippet. Text segments usually contain several paragraphs and are bounded by two code snippets. These are identified during the snippet extraction process.
3. Last Paragraph. We considered using the the last paragraph of a text segment, which appears immediately above a code snippet.
4. Page Title + Text Segment. This candidate included the page title and the text segment. This group provides the largest set of data related to a code snippet. We considered this combination, because it was used to index the snippet.

Figure 14.6 shows the percentage of the 200 examples that had one or more topics in common between the code snippet and the candidate text. The two candidates that contained the most text also had more topics, and consequently had a higher percentage of matches. Eighty-three percent of the code snippets had topics in common with Page Title + Text Segment, while 80.54 % of the Text Segment did. The individual paragraphs, Best Match and Last Paragraphs, fared less well, because they contained less text and fewer topics. The Best Matched Paragraph has a 66.81 % of matched topics and the Last Paragraph has a 59.26 %. In the end, we elected to use the Best Matched paragraph, because it had a reasonable combination of descriptiveness and brevity.

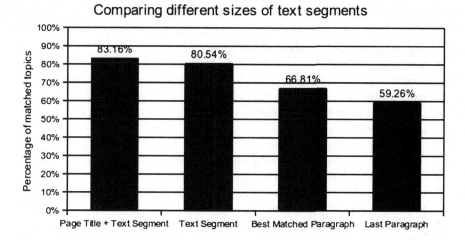

Fig. 14.6 Comparison of Page Title + Text Segment, Text Segment, Most Matched Paragraph, and Last Paragraph

14.6 Conclusion

In this chapter, we describe some design issues for the algorithms used in "Juicy", a search engine that capable of search for Java code snippets. This search engine is designed to help developers who are looking for a small chunk of source code to use as a reminder or to learn unfamiliar syntax. Juicy has been populated with over 34,000 Java tutorial pages that have been crawled from the web. In the repository, the code snippets are treated as primary documents and the surrounding text treated as metadata. Users can search the repository using a basic or advanced interface, using both terms from the source code and the metadata. When presenting the results of a search, Juicy provides a brief description for each code snippet in order to give its users more clues on what the code snippet could mean. By providing this information for each code snippet in search result, users could form better understanding of each code snippet and make better decision when picking them to incorporate with their project.

Our research is a starting point for the work necessary to build a robust snippet search engine. Additional work is needed to improve the usability of the search engine, to enable the back end to work with other programming languages, and to incorporate other kinds of resources (such as emails and forums) in the repository. Finally, the effectiveness and helpfulness of a snippet search engine needs to be evaluated. Nevertheless, Juicy is a proof of concept tool that sheds light on issues in the design and construction of a snippet search engine.

Acknowledgements This material is based upon work supported by the NSF under Grant No. IIS-0846034 and by the UCI Summer Undergraduate Research Program. Any opinions, findings, and conclusions or recommendations expressed in this material are those of the authors and do not necessary reflect the views of the NSF.

Appendix: Seed URLs Used to Create Repository

1. http://java.sun.com/docs/books/tutorial/
2. http://learnola.com/
3. http://www.zetcode.com/
4. http://forum.codecall.net/java-tutorials
5. http://www.dickbaldwin.com/java/
6. http://www.learn-java-tutorial.com/
7. http://www.developer.com/java/
8. http://pages.cpsc.ucalgary.ca/~kremer/tutorials/Java/
9. http://www.beginner-tutorials.com/java-tutorials.php
10. http://www.javabeginner.com
11. http://www.javacoffeebreak.com/
12. http://www.cafeaulait.org/javatutorial.html
13. http://www.javaworld.com/
14. http://en.wikiversity.org/wiki/Java_Tutorial
15. http://leepoint.net/notes-java/index.html
16. http://www.javafaq.nu/java-example.html
17. http://www.java-tips.org
18. http://www.java2s.com/Tutorial/Java/CatalogJava.htm
19. http://www.java2s.com/Code/Java/CatalogJava.htm
20. http://www.java2s.com/Article/Java/CatalogJava.htm
21. http://www.java2s.com/Code/JavaAPI/CatalogJavaAPI.htm
22. http://www.java2s.com/Product/Java/GUI-Tools/CatalogGUI-Tools.htm
23. http://www.tech-recipes.com/category/computer-programming/
    java-programming/
24. http://www.exampledepot.com/egs/
25. http://www.devdaily.com/java/
26. http://www.roseindia.net/java/
27. http://en.wikibooks.org/wiki/Java_Programming/
28. http://www.codetoad.com/java/
29. http://danzig.jct.ac.il/java_class/
30. http://www.java-samples.com/showtitles.php?category=Java&start=1
31. http://www.algolist.net/Algorithms/
32. http://www.javapractices.com/
33. http://home.cogeco.ca/~ve3ll/jatutor0.htm

References

[1] S. Bajracharya and C. Lopes. Mining search topics from a code search engine usage log. In *Proceedings of the 2009 6th IEEE International Working Conference on Mining Software Repositories*, pages 111–120. IEEE Computer Society, 2009.

[2] C. Fox. A stop list for general text, 1989.

[3] James Gosling, Bill Joy, Guy Steele, and Gilad Bracha. *The Java^{TM} Language Specification*. Addison-Wesley Professional, 3rd edition, 2005.

[4] T. Grotton. Combining content extraction heuristics: The combine system. In *Proceedings of the 10th International Conference on Information Integration and Web-based Applications & Services*, pages 591–595, 2008.

[5] Reid Holmes, Robert J. Walker, and Gail C. Murphy. Strathcona example recommendation tool. In Michel Wermelinger and Harald Gall, editors, *ESEC/SIGSOFT FSE*, pages 237–240. ACM, 2005.

[6] Erik Linstead, Sushil Bajracharya, Trung Ngo, Paul Rigor, Cristina Lopes, and Pierre Baldi. Sourcerer: mining and searching internet-scale software repositories. *Data Mining and Knowledge Discovery*, 18(2):300–336, 2009.

[7] Merriam-Webster. *Merriam-Webster's 9th Collegiate Dictionary*. Merriam-Webster. Springfield, MA, USA, 1992.

[8] Michael McCandless, Erik Hatcher, and Otis Gospodnetić. *Lucene in Action*. Manning Publications, second edition, 2010.

[9] M.F. Porter. An algorithm for suffix stripping. *Program*, 14(3):130–137, 1980.

[10] J. J. Rodriguez, L. I. Kuncheva, and C. J. Alonso. Rotation forest: A classifier ensemble method, 2006.

[11] Susan Elliott Sim, Charles L. A. Clarke, and Richard C. Holt. Archetypal source code searches: A survey of software developers and maintainers. In *Proceedings of the Sixth International Workshop on Program Comprehension*, page 180, Los Alamitos, CA, 1998. IEEE Computer Society.

[12] Jeffrey Stylos and Brad A. Myers. Mica: A web-search tool for finding api components and examples. In *IEEE Symposium on Visual Languages and Human-Centric Computing, 2006. VL/HCC 2006*, pages 195–202, Brighton, United Kingdom, 2006. IEEE.

Chapter 15
Facilitating Crowd Sourced Software Engineering via Stack Overflow

Ohad Barzilay, Christoph Treude, and Alexey Zagalsky

Abstract The open source community, as well as numerous technical blogs and community web sites, put online vast quantities of free source code, ranging from snippets to full-blown products. This code embodies the software development community's domain knowledge, and mirrors the structure of the Internet: it is distributed rather than hierarchical; it is chaotic, incomplete, and inconsistent. Stack-Overflow.com is a Question and Answer (Q&A) website which uses social media to facilitate knowledge exchange between programmers by mitigating the pitfalls involved in using code from the Internet. Its design nurtures a community of developers, and enables crowd sourced software engineering activities ranging from documentation to providing useful, high quality code snippets to be used in production. In this chapter we review Stack Overflow from three perspectives: (1) its design and its social media characteristics, (2) the role it plays in the software documentation landscape, and (3) the use of Stack Overflow in the context of the example centric programming paradigm.

15.1 Introduction

Software development has been described as knowledge-intensive [28] and knowledge management plays a central role in many software organizations. The design and implementation of software systems requires knowledge that is often distributed among many individuals with different areas of expertise and capabilities.

O. Barzilay (✉) • A. Zagalsky
Blavatnik School of Computer Science, Tel-Aviv University, Tel-Aviv, Israel
e-mail: ohadbr@tau.ac.il; alexeyza@tau.ac.il

C. Treude
Department of Computer Science, University of Victoria, Victoria, Canada
e-mail: ctreude@uvic.ca

S.E. Sim and R.E. Gallardo-Valencia (eds.), *Finding Source Code on the Web for Remix and Reuse*, DOI 10.1007/978-1-4614-6596-6_15,
© Springer Science+Business Media New York 2013

The success of social media has introduced new ways of exchanging knowledge via the Internet. Question and Answer (Q&A) websites such as Yahoo! Answers,[1] Quora[2] or Facebook Questions[3] are founded on the success of social media and built around an "architecture of participation" [26] where user data is aggregated as a side-effect of using Web 2.0 applications. Q&A websites archive millions of entries that are of value to the community [9]. For the domain of software development, the website Stack Overflow[4] facilitates the exchange of knowledge between programmers connected via the Internet. In the 4 years since its foundation in 2008, more than 3.3 million questions have been asked on Stack Overflow, and more than 2.1 million answers have been accepted. On Stack Overflow, a programmer can ask a question about various programming related topics, and receive a detailed response within a median of 10 min [24]. Stack Overflow team explicitly mentions[5] the following kinds of questions generally covered by Stack Overflow: a specific programming problem, a software algorithm, software tools commonly used by programmers, and practical, answerable problems that are unique to the programming profession. They also feel that "the best Stack Overflow questions have a bit of source code in them". To facilitate the crowd-sourcing of documentation, the Stack Overflow community explicitly encourages contributions where the person asking the question also provides an answer. Stack Overflow also introduces the concept of community wikis[6] for addressing cases in which true community collaboration is needed on a certain topic. The use of community wikis challenges the dichotomy between Q&A websites and wikis.

As opposed to former Q&A websites that were used as an auxiliary tool for professional developers, secondary in importance, Stack Overflow is gaining a more cardinal role in the contemporary programming scene. Answers on Stack Overflow often become a substitute for official product documentation when the official documentation is sparse or not yet existent,[7] and developers use Stack Overflow to employ example centric development. The popularity and dominance of Stack Overflow and the fact that it embodies so much of the software development domain knowledge is somewhat surprising, as organizing professional domain knowledge in the form of questions and answers is not immediately obvious. Books, API documentation, tutorials and even wikis are examples for alternative viable models for knowledge organization. So why is Stack Overflow so successful? One explanation is related to the rapid pace in which technologies come and go, which results in official documentation that is sometimes lagging behind the field. Moreover, as software development projects often involve numerous technologies, the pragmatic professional developer is not able to master all of them in the same proficiency

---

[1] http://answers.yahoo.com/.

[2] http://www.quora.com/.

[3] http://www.facebook.com/questions/.

[4] http://stackoverflow.com/.

[5] http://stackoverflow.com/faq#questions.

[6] http://blog.stackoverflow.com/2011/08/the-future-of-community-wiki/.

[7] https://stackoverflow.fogbugz.com/default.asp?W25450.

level. Stack Overflow offers "knowledge on demand" – specific solutions for specific problems, easily searchable, generated, reviewed and rated by the community.

The innovation of Stack Overflow was in bringing together a Q&A website and social media technology, and creating a whole greater than the sum of its parts. Social media in the context of Stack Overflow is manifested by having the user profiles explicit in the process of asking questions and answering them. As opposed to former knowledge exchange formats such as forums or wikis, users on Stack Overflow are not only affected by the *content* of the answer, but also from the *rating of its author*. The interactions between users on the Stack Overflow platform (answering, commenting, editing) increase the rating of the interacting users, and encourage further activity.

In order to better understand the principles guiding Stack Overflow we first review the design decisions that drove its development. Then, we explore the role it plays in the software documentation landscape, and finally we describe an application, which uses Stack Overflow, that spans beyond mere documentation; a tool called Example Overflow, which assists example centric programming by extracting high quality code snippets from Stack Overflow.

15.2 Background and Related Work

StackOverflow.com is a Question and Answer (Q&A) website which uses social media to facilitate knowledge exchange between programmers. This knowledge is manifested in the form of questions and answers, and it is embodied in code examples that often accompany the text. In order to examine these various aspects of Stack Overflow, we review related work in the following areas: (1) the use of social media in software engineering, (2) Q&A websites in general and work on questions that software developers ask, and (3) the example centric programming paradigm.

15.2.1 Social Media in Software Engineering

Social media is an umbrella term that defines the various activities that integrate technology and social interaction, enabled by recent advances of Web 2.0 technologies. The W3C organization defines social media as "Online technologies and practices that people use to share opinions, insights, experiences, and perspectives".[8] Kaplan and Haenlein [19] define social media using the following dimensions: social presence vs. media richness and self-presentation vs. self-disclosure. They show that content communities (e.g. YouTube) are considered to be of low self disclosure and medium social presence, whereas blogs are highly self presented, but with low social presence. Using these dimensions, a Q&A website, such as Stack Overflow,

---

[8] http://www.w3.org/egov/wiki/Glossary.

is part of the social media landscape as it promotes user generated professional content, in which the identity of the users is explicit and affects the knowledge creation process, by taking into account the user's rating for example.

Social media provides useful recommendations for many areas of our lives. For example, when considering what movies to watch, one may use recommendations from his or her immediate social cycle (e.g. Facebook friends), or elicit the wisdom of the crowd [35], using, for instance, the ratings on imdb.com. This is part of a more general trend in which social recommendations (e.g. Facebook) have begun to replace search (e.g. Google Search).

The Software Engineering (SE) domain is no different; social media has been shown to be beneficial in many areas of SE including feature prioritization [5], risk analysis [34], collaborative filtering [14], knowledge management [17], and documentation [10]. Social media is changing the way software developers communicate and coordinate, and how they produce and consume documentation [38]. The current adoption of social media in processes and integrated development environments is just scratching the surface of what can be done by incorporating social media approaches and technologies into software development.

Storey et al. [32] discuss the impact of social media on software engineering practices and tools. Historically, wikis and blogs were the first social media mechanisms used by software developers, utilized mostly in the areas of requirements engineering and documentation, and to communicate high-level concepts. Microblogs, such as Twitter, play a role in conversation and information sharing between software developers [10], whereas tags can help software developers communicate their concerns in task management [39] and add semantic information to source code [31].

Among those technologies, the Stack Overflow Q&A portal not only provides a unique medium for the interaction between several communities of practice of developers, but also stands out due to the daily involvement of its design team within those communities [24]. In a preliminarily categorization of the questions found on Stack Overflow, we found that the website is particularly effective at certain kinds of questions [37]. Stack Overflow also attracts a lot of web traffic and can reach a high level of coverage for a given topic. In a recent study, we analyzed the Google search results for the jQuery API and found at least one Stack Overflow question on the first page of the search results for 84% of the API's methods [27].

15.2.2 Q&A Websites and Questions that Software Developers Ask

In order to better situate Q&A websites in the documentation landscape, we review related work regarding the use of Q&A websites, and their role in knowledge creation and retrieval.

The use of Yahoo! Answers has been studied by several researchers. Gyongyi et al. [15] identified three fundamental ways in which Yahoo! Answers is used: for focused questions, to trigger discussions, and for random thoughts and questions. Adamic et al. [1] found that users who focused on certain areas of expertise often got the best ratings. In order to find high quality content, Agichtein et al. [2] introduce a framework that is able to separate high quality items from the rest. In a related project, Shah and Pomerantz [29] found that contextual information such as a user's profile can be used to predict content quality.

The above studies suggest that Q&A websites, if used intelligently, may provide useful information in a narrow professional domain. Therefore, building an online Q&A community of professionals in the software engineering domain is a promising approach. But what questions do developers ask in their daily work? Following, we examine studies regarding the questions that software developers ask. Letovsky [23] identified five main question types: why, how, what, whether and discrepancy. Fritz and Murphy [12] provide a list of questions that focus on issues that occur within a project. Sillito et al. [30] provide a similar list focusing on questions during evolution tasks. In their study on information needs in software development, Ko et al. [20] found that the most frequently sought information included awareness about artifacts and coworkers.

In contrast to the settings of these studies, Q&A websites provide a platform for questions aimed at a general audience that is not part of the same project. Q&A websites contain questions, but can also contain answers to anticipated questions as well as opinions through comments and ratings. LaToza and Myers [22] found that the most difficult questions from a developer's perspective dealt with intent and rationale. This issue is addressed by the Stack Overflow platform, providing rich context in the form of questions, answers and discussions, in which the intent and rationale often become explicit.

15.2.3 Example Centric Programming

The number of code snippets available on Stack Overflow suggests that the Q&A website can play a major role in Example Centric Programming. Programming by example was found to be intuitive to many developers, novices and experts alike [21]. Brandt et al. proposed [11] that embedding a task-specific search engine in the development environment can significantly reduce the cost of finding information and thus allow programmers to write better code more easily. Barzilay [6] portrayed a comprehensive approach towards example centric programming, which he calls the Example Embedding Ecosystem, in which example-related concerns are weaved in the development process, software tools, practices, training, organization culture and more.

Tools such as Strathcona [18] and PARSEWeb [36] provided developers with code fragment recommendations, taken from a central code repository, by generating queries based on code context and the structural details of the developer's activity. The quality of the code found by these tools was derived from the overall quality of the repositories they use.

Code search engines, on the other hand, such as Krugle[9] and Koders,[10] search in a large set of open source repositories, but do not provide explicit mechanisms to evaluate or improve the quality of the found snippets. Other tools such as MICA [33] or Exemplar [13, 25] use API calls or API examples to recommend example code, but they are restricted to providing a limited set of examples based on the API only.

Using social media, however, allows applications built on top of the Stack Overflow knowledge base to scale beyond specific code repositories and to leverage human brainpower [3] to assess the quality of specific code snippets.

15.3 Social Design of Stack Overflow

Stack Overflow is centered around nine design decisions[11]: **Voting** is used as a mechanism to distinguish good answers from bad ones. Users can up-vote answers they like, and down-vote answers they dislike. In addition, the user asking a question can accept one answer as the official answer. **Tags** are used to organize questions. Users have to attach at least one tag and can attach up to five tags when asking a question. **Editing** of both questions and answers allows users to improve their quality and to turn Q&A exchanges into wiki-like structures. **Badges** are given to users to reward them for their contributions once they reach certain thresholds. This form of **karma** is used to encourage contribution. **Pre-Search** helps avoid duplicate questions by showing similar entries as soon as a user has finished typing the title of a question. Stack Overflow was designed to be used such that **Google is UI**. Web pages on StackOverflow.com are optimized towards search engines and **performance**. To ensure **critical mass**, several programmers were explicitly asked to contribute in the early stages of Stack Overflow (Fig. 15.1).

A recent study suggests that software developers are diverse in their approach towards using code examples from online sources [8]. Despite the engineering challenges involved in extensive example usage, it was suggested that this diversity stems from human, rather than engineering, factors [7]. The developers' approach to example usage is affected by their sense of professional and community identity, ego considerations, ownership and trust issues. We see that many of Stack Overflow's design decisions address these human factors, and have transformed Stack Overflow into a *community*. The badges and karma give the users a sense of belonging– of being part of a large developers community. The voting mechanism allows the community to rank both users and answers, and tackle the *quality* and *trust* issues. Taking *ownership* of a code snippet taken from Stack Overflow is easier after it has received community approval, and *ego* is confronted with community feedback and the transparency of the ranking mechanism.

---

[9] http://www.krugle.com/.

[10] http://www.koders.com/.

[11] http://www.youtube.com/watch?v=NWHfY_lvKIQ.

Fig. 15.1 Stack overflow screen capture

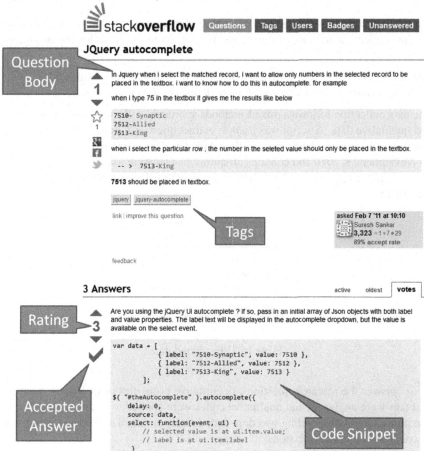

15.4 Stack Overflow in the Documentation Landscape

In this section, we pose research questions and report preliminary results to identify the role of Q&A websites in software development using qualitative and quantitative research methods. Our findings, obtained through the analysis of archival data from Stack Overflow and qualitative coding, indicate that Q&A websites are particularly effective at code reviews, explaining conceptual issues and answering newcomer questions. The most common use of Stack Overflow is for how-to questions, and its dominant programming languages are C#, Java, PHP and JavaScript. Ultimately, understanding the processes that lead to the creation of knowledge on Q&A websites will enable us to make recommendations on how individuals and companies, as well as tools for programmers, can leverage the knowledge and use Q&A websites effectively. One such tool, Example Overflow, will be introduced in Sect. 15.5.

15.4.1 Research Methodology

This section describes the methodology by outlining research questions as well as the data collection and analysis methods. We will focus on the following two questions:

1. What kinds of questions are asked on Q&A websites for programmers?
2. Which questions are answered and which ones remain unanswered?

The data collection follows a mixed-methods approach, collecting both quantitative and qualitative data. A script was used to extract questions along with all answers, tags and owners using the Stack Overflow API. The data reported here was extracted on November 23, 2010 and contains all questions that were asked between November 1, 2010 and November 15, 2010. The amount of data extracted is provided in Table 15.1.

Data item	Amount
Questions	38,419
Owners	31,729
Answers	68,467
Tag instances	111,408

Table 15.1: Extracted data

To answer the research questions, quantitative properties of questions, answers and tags were analyzed, and qualitative codes were applied to a sample of tags and questions. Qualitative coding was done individually and then codes were confirmed in collaborative coding sessions.

15.4.2 Preliminary Findings

15.4.2.1 Different Kinds of Questions

To analyze the different kinds of questions asked on Stack Overflow, qualitative coding of questions and tags was done. The tags were mainly used to learn about the topics covered by Stack Overflow, while the question coding gave insight into the nature of the questions.

Each question has between one and five tags that are set by the person asking a question. Most questions (72.30%) have between two and four tags. Ten thousand two hundred and seventy-two different keywords were used to tag questions, and there were 111,408 instances of a tag being applied to a question. Table 15.2 shows the most frequently used tags.

Tag keyword	Instances
c#	3,765
java	2,909
php	2,599
javascript	2,310
jquery	2,084

Table 15.2: Most used tag keywords

Qualitative coding was applied to the 200 most frequently used tag keywords in our data. These keywords covered 60,193 of the tag instances (54.03%). Five categories of tags were identified, and they are shown in Table 15.3, including the number of instances in each category, the number of different keywords per category, and the most used tags per category. For the keyword "homework", no related tags were found and thus it was left uncategorized.

Code	Keyword	Instances	Examples
Programming language	63	28,218	c#, java
Framework	48	11,532	jquery, ruby on rails
Environment	45	14,127	Android, iphone
Domain	29	4,125	Regex, database
Non functional	14	2,071	Multithreading
Homework	1	120	Homework

Table 15.3: Tag coding

Users self-code their questions through tags to index them, and to allow others to navigate to them. Tags reveal the topics covered on Stack Overflow, but only allow limited insights into the nature of the questions asked. To further understand the characteristics of questions on Stack Overflow, a random sample of 385 questions from the data set (1%) was coded. The titles and body texts of these questions were analyzed and the following categories were found, ordered by their frequency:

how-to. Questions that ask for instructions, e.g. *"How to crop image by 160° from center in asp.net"*.

discrepancy. Some unexpected behavior that the person asking the question wants explained, e.g. *"iphone – Coremotion acceleration always zero"*.

environment. Questions about the environment either during development or after deployment, e.g. *"How to use windows emacs as a svn client?"*.

error. Questions that include a specific error message, e.g. *"C# Obscure error: file ' ' could not be refactored"*.

decision-help. Asking for an opinion, e.g. *"Should a business object know about its corresponding contract object"*.

conceptual. Questions that are abstract and do not have a concrete use case, e.g. *"Concept of xml sitemaps"*.

review. Questions that are either implicitly or explicitly asking for a code review, e.g. *"Simple file download via HTTP – is this sufficient?"*.

non-functional. Questions about non-functional requirements such as performance or memory usage, e.g. *"Mac – Max Texture Size for compatibility?"*.

novice. Often explicitly states that the person asking the question is a novice, e.g. *"Oracle PL/SQL performance tuning crash course"*.

noise. Questions not related to programming, e.g. *"Apple Developer Program"*.

Most questions in the random sample fit into one of these categories, but for some of the questions (9.61%), two categories were assigned. The most frequent type of question (39.22%) was *how-to*, followed by questions about *discrepancies* and *environment*. The first two columns of Table 15.4 show the detailed results:

Code	Sum	Answered		No answer
		Accepted	Not accepted	
how-to	151	67 (44%)	63 (42%)	21 (14%)
discrepancy	50	27 (54%)	11 (22%)	12 (24%)
environment	40	13 (33%)	17 (43%)	10 (25%)
error	36	19 (53%)	14 (39%)	3 (8%)
decision help	22	9 (41%)	10 (45%)	3 (14%)
conceptual	18	10 (56%)	7 (39%)	1 (6%)
how-to/novice	16	10 (63%)	3 (19%)	3 (19%)
review	13	12 (92%)	1 (8%)	0 (0%)
non-functional	10	6 (60%)	1 (10%)	3 (30%)
novice	5	2 (40%)	3 (60%)	0 (0%)
other	24	10 (42%)	11 (46%)	3 (13%)
sum	385	185 (48%)	141 (37%)	59 (15%)

Table 15.4: Question coding

15.4.2.2 Which Questions Are Answered and Which Are Not

Figure 15.2 shows the distribution of answers per question. The number of answers per question is shown on the x-axis, and the number of questions with that number of answers is shown on the y-axis using a log scale. 5,450 (14.19%) questions were not answered. The remaining questions had at least one and up to 23 answers. Only 3,243 out of 68,467 answers (4.74%) were provided by the same person that had asked the question.

Fig. 15.2 Answers per question (log scale)

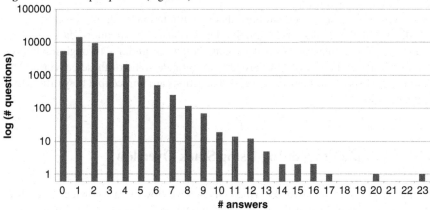

On Stack Overflow, the user who is asking a question can mark at most one answer per question as accepted. This feature was used to examine the implications of different question characteristics on the success of a question. We define successful and unsuccessful questions as follows: A successful question has an accepted answer, and an unsuccessful question has no answer. Following these definitions, the 185 successful questions and 59 unsuccessful questions from the random sample of 385 questions were analyzed. Table 15.4 shows the number of questions per category for all questions in our random sample, for all successful questions, for all questions with answers but no accepted answer, and for all questions without an answer.

It is interesting to note that the community answered *review*, *conceptual* and *how-to/novice* questions more frequently than other kinds of questions.

15.4.3 Discussion

A possible reason for the high answer ratio of review questions is the fact that review questions are usually very concrete. They contain code snippets, and often no external sources are necessary to understand the code and make a recommendation about its quality. Also, code review questions can have more than one "correct" answer, and often any input is better than no input. The knowledge required to answer conceptual questions is usually broad. It is available in documentation or books and only needs to be presented effectively. Novices are easy to sympathize with and their questions are usually easy to answer.

The type of question is not the only factor for getting good answers. Other factors seem to include: the technology in question, the identity of the user, the time and day in which the question was asked, whether the question included a code snippet, or the length of the question.

As with any research methodology, there are limitations with the choice of methods described above. The first limitation lies in the small amount of data analyzed in the random sample. However, by triangulating the findings through qualitative coding of tags and questions, we are able to mitigate some of these concerns. The definitions of successful and unsuccessful questions are limited, but they offer a first approximation.

15.5 Example Embedding Using Stack Overflow

In the previous section we described Stack Overflow as a knowledge creation platform and examined it from the documentation perspective. Documentation, however, is only one manifestation of professional knowledge. In the software engineering domain much of the domain knowledge is manifested in the source code, sometimes implicitly. Indeed, many answers on Stack Overflow include code snippets. Although some of these snippets are executable, they are entangled in free text and are not easily extracted. Q&A websites are not designed for such direct code reuse.

Following, we focus on the domain knowledge that resides on Stack Overflow in the form of code examples by presenting Example Overflow, a code search and recommendation tool which brings together social media and code recommendation systems, built on top of Stack Overflow. Example Overflow enables crowd-sourced software development by utilizing both textual and social information, which accompany source code on the Web. We describe the development of the tool, and discuss its contribution to an example centric programming paradigm.

15.5.1 Overview

Example Overflow leverages the body of knowledge created by the socio-professional media, to recommend high quality, embeddable code. It uses built-in social mechanisms of Stack Overflow. Example Overflow is a live system, and is currently deployed as a public and free website.[12] Its initial implementation contains all code snippets that appear in accepted jQuery related answers (more than 33,000 code snippets). jQuery[13] is a popular JavaScript library, initially released in 2006 and is ranked fifth in its popularity on Stack Overflow (with over 150,000 related questions). It was chosen as a case study due to the assumption that Web

---

[12] http://www.exampleoverflow.net/.

[13] http://jquery.com/.

developers would find it easier to adopt an example centric programming approach. This decision is also supported by the following: (1) as mentioned above, Parnin and Treude [27] found that Stack Overflow covers 84.4% of the jQuery API, and (2) 20% of the jQuery related questions have a code snippet embedded in their accepted answer.

Example Overflow development is aligned with the theory of the Example Embedding Ecosystem [6] – an example centric development approach which argues that the use of examples in professional software development goes beyond being a mere programming technique, or the use of a specific code retrieval tool. Usage of existing code should rather be considered as a fundamental software construction activity and an expression of community knowledge accumulation and of the software reuse principle. Habitual and methodological example usage expresses awareness of the existing body of knowledge and promotes faster and better code writing. Developers and organizations that implement the Example Embedding theory explicitly address example usage concerns in their development process, software tools, practices, training, organization culture and more [6] (Fig. 15.3).

Fig. 15.3 Example overflow Web interface

Found 33430 results

- [jquery, autocomplete] **jquery autocomplete** not working

  ```
  $("#seed_one").autocomplete(data);
  ```

  › Question

  › Answer

- [jquery, autocomplete, jquery-autocomplete] **jQuery autocomplete** customization

  ```
  .data("autocomplete")._renderItem = function(ul, item) {
      var v = item.value;
      return $("<li></li>")
          .data("item.autocomplete", item)
          .append(
              "<a>"
                  + "<span class='hilightItem'>"
                      + v.substr(0, v.indexOf(' ') + 1)
                  + "</span>"
                  + " " + v.substr(v.indexOf(' ') + 2)
              + "</a>"
          )
          .appendTo(ul);
  };
  ```

- [jquery, autocomplete] **jQuery** UI **autocomplete**: Getting reference to the ul

  ```
  $(".the-standards").autocomplete({ appendTo: "#someStandardDiv" });
  ```

15.5.2 Example Overflow Implementation

15.5.2.1 Populating the Repository

Example Overflow uses Stack Overflow's API to request all the questions relevant to our current domain, jQuery, and it filters out all the questions without an accepted answer. It follows a conservative approach by choosing only accepted answers to ensure retrieval of high quality results. The next step is to check whether each of these questions has a code snippet inside the accepted answer. If so, that code snippet is extracted and saved to a database with all the accompanying information: the question title, the question body, the answer body, the code snippet itself, the user rating of the answer from Stack Overflow, the view count of the question, the tags associated with the question and other relevant information. This process can be executed as a scheduled task to allow keeping the data in sync with the data at Stack Overflow.

15.5.2.2 Searching

Example Overflow uses keyword search based on the Apache Lucene [16] library, which internally uses the term frequency-inverse document frequency (tf-idf) weight [40]. In order for Apache Lucene to search, one needs to define which parameters are to be analyzed and indexed. For keyword search index, Example Overflow uses both the code snippet and the additional metadata which accompanied the code snippet at Stack Overflow. This allows a developer to find code snippets that may not contain the search query keyword, but the keyword appears in the contextual data and indicates that it has been used in that context.

Each code example is represented as a document with several parts: title, tag, answer, question, code, and social metadata. Example Overflow uses the following formula to calculate the score of each document representing a code example:

$$S_{doc} = [W_{title}S_{title} + W_{tag}S_{tag} + W_{answer}S_{answer} + W_{question}S_{question} \\ + W_{code}S_{code}]S_{metadata}$$

15.5.3 Discussion

Searching for code examples is possible using Stack Overflow directly. However using designated code search tools on top of Stack Overflow may provide better results in terms of streamlining the various activities involved in example centric development (search, evaluation, and embedding). Designated tools may also introduce search mechanisms optimized for code search, they can minimize the context switch involved in leaving the IDE (as implemented in Blueprint [11], Strathcona [18], and recently Seahawk [4]), and may even use static analysis techniques to assist in embedding the code into the new context. Zagalsky et al. [41] provide a preliminary evaluation suggesting that using Example Overflow reduces the number of mouse clicks required to reach a suitable code example compared to using other code search tools or using plain vanilla Stack Overflow.

Another benefit in using automatic tools on top of the Stack Overflow is the ability to create a feedback loop, which would contribute data back to the Stack Overflow knowledge base. The accumulated data may provide important insights about how the code was actually used, and what changes were made to it, maybe even after some time and across API versions.

We note that example centric programming is not performed in void. In order to be productive the software developer should acquire proper skills. She should be able to critically evaluate the various examples, browse them and merge them. Without proper practices, systems which are developed using examples extensively may end up as Frankenstein code [6], and bugs may find their way in, because the examples used were not properly tested.

Moreover, it is still unknown if crowd sourced software development would be able to scale well, as currently, Stack Overflow has only relatively small code snippets.

15.6 Impact and Future Work

Stack Overflow uses social media mechanisms to create and evaluate high quality professional software engineering domain knowledge. It uses Web 2.0 technology to gather user generated content, and its design decisions nurture an online community that is taking part in assessing the quality of this content.

Stack Overflow's centrality in the software development scene, and the fact that so much of the programming domain knowledge is organized in the form of questions and answers, raises many interesting questions regarding the future documentation landscape, and the future of software development in general. It implies that knowledge should be searchable, rather than consumed sequentially. It implies that knowledge is distributed between text and code. It suggests that high quality knowledge could be generated by a community that would vouch for its quality rather than a small group of experts, limited in their capacity for producing and assessing the knowledge. In a broader context, the design decisions implemented in Stack Overflow may be able to reinvent open source development – this time not in the sense of reusing pieces of code taken from existing open source products, but assembling pieces that were written in order to demonstrate a feature, and are accompanied with rich context about their rationale and intension.

More specifically, understanding the interactions on Q&A websites, such as Stack Overflow, will shed light on the information needs of programmers outside closed project contexts and will enable recommendations on how individuals, companies and tools can leverage knowledge on Q&A websites. Understanding the role and effectiveness of ratings to identify the best answers and the role of comments to facilitate discussion are important venues for future research.

We also discussed using the code snippets found on Stack Overflow, and described a specific application, Example Overflow, that extracts these snippets to support example centric programming. Example Overflow and other similar tools introduce fascinating opportunities for the future developer. Integrating such tools into the IDE would further minimize the developer's context switching, and allow the developer to run the code example in a sandbox mode before deciding whether it is suitable or not. IDE integration would enable auto embedding the example code into the existing code (similarly to refactoring), and allow to auto suggest search queries by using the developer's structural context. By accomplishing these steps, the usage of examples will become an integral part of the software development cycle.

References

[1] Adamic, L.A., Zhang, J., Bakshy, E., Ackerman, M.S.: Knowledge sharing and yahoo answers: everyone knows something. In: Proceedings of the 17th international conference on World Wide Web, WWW '08, pp. 665–674. ACM, New York, NY, USA (2008). DOI 10.1145/1367497.1367587. URL http://doi.acm.org/10.1145/1367497.1367587

[2] Agichtein, E., Castillo, C., Donato, D., Gionis, A., Mishne, G.: Finding high-quality content in social media. In: Proceedings of the international conference on Web search and web data mining, WSDM '08, pp. 183–194. ACM, New York, NY, USA (2008). DOI http://doi.acm.org/10.1145/1341531.1341557. URL http://doi.acm.org/10.1145/1341531.1341557

[3] von Ahn, L.: Human computation. In: Design Automation Conference, 2009. DAC '09. 46th ACM/IEEE, pp. 418–419 (2009)

[4] Bacchelli, A., Ponzanelli, L., Lanza, M.: Harnessing stack overflow for the ide. In: Third International Workshop on Recommendation Systems for Software Engineering (RSSE), pp. 26–30 (2012). DOI 10.1109/RSSE.2012.6233404

[5] Bajic, D., Lyons, K.: Leveraging social media to gather user feedback for software development. In: Proceedings of the 2nd International Workshop on Web 2.0 for Software Engineering, Web2SE '11, pp. 1–6. ACM, New York, NY, USA (2011). DOI http://doi.acm.org/10.1145/1984701.1984702. URL http://doi.acm.org/10.1145/1984701.1984702

[6] Barzilay, O.: Example embedding. In: Proceedings of the 10th SIGPLAN symposium on New ideas, new paradigms, and reflections on programming and software, ONWARD '11, pp. 137–144. ACM, New York, NY, USA (2011). DOI 10.1145/2089131.2089135. URL http://doi.acm.org/10.1145/2089131.2089135

[7] Barzilay, O.: Example embedding: On the diversity of example usage in professional software development. Ph.D. thesis, Tel Aviv University (2012)

[8] Barzilay, O., Hazzan, O., Yehudai, A.: Using social media to study the diversity of example usage among professional developers. In: Proceedings of the

19th ACM SIGSOFT symposium and the 13th European conference on Foundations of software engineering, SIGSOFT/FSE '11, pp. 472–475. ACM, New York, NY, USA (2011). DOI http://doi.acm.org/10.1145/2025113.2025195. URL http://doi.acm.org/10.1145/2025113.2025195

[9] Bian, J., Liu, Y., Agichtein, E., Zha, H.: Finding the right facts in the crowd: factoid question answering over social media. In: Proceedings of the 17th international conference on World Wide Web, WWW '08, pp. 467–476. ACM, New York, NY, USA (2008). DOI 10.1145/1367497.1367561. URL http://doi.acm.org/10.1145/1367497.1367561

[10] Bougie, G., Starke, J., Storey, M.A., German, D.M.: Towards understanding twitter use in software engineering: preliminary findings, ongoing challenges and future questions. In: Proceeding of the 2nd international workshop on Web 2.0 for software engineering, Web2SE '11, pp. 31–36. ACM, New York, NY, USA (2011). DOI http://doi.acm.org/10.1145/1984701.1984707. URL http://doi.acm.org/10.1145/1984701.1984707

[11] Brandt, J., Dontcheva, M., Weskamp, M., Klemmer, S.R.: Example-centric programming: integrating web search into the development environment. In: Proceedings of the 28th international conference on Human factors in computing systems, CHI '10, pp. 513–522. ACM, New York, NY, USA (2010). DOI http://doi.acm.org/10.1145/1753326.1753402. URL http://doi.acm.org/10.1145/1753326.1753402

[12] Fritz, T., Murphy, G.C.: Using information fragments to answer the questions developers ask. In: Proceedings of the 32nd ACM/IEEE International Conference on Software Engineering - Volume 1, ICSE '10, pp. 175–184. ACM, New York, NY, USA (2010). DOI 10.1145/1806799.1806828. URL http://doi.acm.org/10.1145/1806799.1806828

[13] Grechanik, M., Fu, C., Xie, Q., McMillan, C., Poshyvanyk, D., Cumby, C.: A search engine for finding highly relevant applications. In: Proceedings of the 32nd ACM/IEEE International Conference on Software Engineering - Volume 1, ICSE '10, pp. 475–484. ACM, New York, NY, USA (2010). DOI 10.1145/1806799.1806868. URL http://doi.acm.org/10.1145/1806799.1806868

[14] Guy, I., Zwerdling, N., Carmel, D., Ronen, I., Uziel, E., Yogev, S., Ofek-Koifman, S.: Personalized recommendation of social software items based on social relations. In: Proceedings of the third ACM conference on Recommender systems, RecSys '09, pp. 53–60. ACM, New York, NY, USA (2009). DOI http://doi.acm.org/10.1145/1639714.1639725. URL http://doi.acm.org/10.1145/1639714.1639725

[15] Gyongyi, Z., Koutrika, G., Pedersen, J., Garcia-Molina, H.: Questioning yahoo! answers (2007)

[16] Hatcher, E., Gospodnetic, O., McCandless, M.: Lucene in Action, 2nd revised edition. edn. Manning (2010). URL http://amazon.de/o/ASIN/1933988177/

[17] Hattori, T.: Wikigramming: a wiki-based training environment for programming. In: Proceedings of the 2nd International Workshop on Web 2.0 for Software Engineering, Web2SE '11, pp. 7–12. ACM, New York, NY, USA (2011). DOI http://doi.acm.org/10.1145/1984701.1984703. URL http://doi.acm.org/10.1145/1984701.1984703

[18] Holmes, R., Murphy, G.C.: Using structural context to recommend source code examples. In: ICSE '05: Proceedings of the 27th international conference on Software engineering, pp. 117–125. ACM (2005). DOI http://doi.acm.org/10. 1145/1062455.1062491

[19] Kaplan, A.M., Haenlein, M.: Users of the world, unite! the challenges and opportunities of social media. Business Horizons **53**(1), 59–68 (2010). DOI 10.1016/j.bushor.2009.09.003. URL http://www.sciencedirect.com/science/article/pii/S0007681309001232

[20] Ko, A.J., DeLine, R., Venolia, G.: Information needs in collocated software development teams. In: Proceedings of the 29th international conference on Software Engineering, ICSE '07, pp. 344–353. IEEE Computer Society, Washington, DC, USA (2007). DOI 10.1109/ICSE.2007.45. URL http://dx.doi.org/10.1109/ICSE.2007.45

[21] Lahtinen, E., Ala-Mutka, K., Järvinen, H.M.: A study of the difficulties of novice programmers. SIGCSE Bull. **37**, 14–18 (2005). DOI http://doi.acm.org/10.1145/1151954.1067453. URL http://doi.acm.org/10.1145/1151954.1067453

[22] LaToza, T.D., Myers, B.A.: Hard-to-answer questions about code. In: Evaluation and Usability of Programming Languages and Tools, PLATEAU '10, pp. 8:1–8:6. ACM, New York, NY, USA (2010). DOI 10.1145/1937117.1937125. URL http://doi.acm.org/10.1145/1937117.1937125

[23] Letovsky, S.: Cognitive processes in program comprehension. In: Papers presented at the first workshop on empirical studies of programmers on Empirical studies of programmers, pp. 58–79. Ablex Publishing Corp., Norwood, NJ, USA (1986). URL http://dl.acm.org/citation.cfm?id=21842.28886

[24] Mamykina, L., Manoim, B., Mittal, M., Hripcsak, G., Hartmann, B.: Design lessons from the fastest Q&A a site in the west. In: Proceedings of the 2011 annual conference on Human factors in computing systems, CHI '11, pp. 2857–2866. ACM, New York, NY, USA (2011). DOI http://doi.acm.org/10.1145/1978942.1979366. URL http://doi.acm.org/10.1145/1978942.1979366

[25] McMillan, C., Poshyvanyk, D., Grechanik, M.: Recommending source code examples via api call usages and documentation. In: Proceedings of the 2nd International Workshop on Recommendation Systems for Software Engineering, RSSE '10, pp. 21–25. ACM, New York, NY, USA (2010). DOI http://doi.acm.org/10.1145/1808920.1808925. URL http://doi.acm.org/10.1145/1808920.1808925

[26] O'Reilly, T.: What is Web 2.0: Design patterns and business models for the next generation of software. Communications and Strategies **65**(1), 17–37 (2007)

[27] Parnin, C., Treude, C.: Measuring api documentation on the web. In: Proceedings of the 2nd International Workshop on Web 2.0 for Software Engineering, Web2SE '11, pp. 25–30. ACM, New York, NY, USA (2011). DOI http://doi.acm.org/10.1145/1984701.1984706. URL http://doi.acm.org/10.1145/1984701.1984706

[28] Robillard, P.N.: The role of knowledge in software development. Commun. ACM **42**(1), 87–92 (1999). DOI 10.1145/291469.291476. URL http://doi.acm.org/10.1145/291469.291476

[29] Shah, C., Pomerantz, J.: Evaluating and predicting answer quality in community qa. In: Proceeding of the 33rd international ACM SIGIR conference on Research and development in information retrieval, SIGIR '10, pp. 411–418. ACM, New York, NY, USA (2010). DOI http://doi.acm.org/10.1145/1835449.1835518. URL http://doi.acm.org/10.1145/1835449.1835518

[30] Sillito, J., Murphy, G.C., De Volder, K.: Questions programmers ask during software evolution tasks. In: Proceedings of the 14th ACM SIGSOFT international symposium on Foundations of software engineering, SIGSOFT '06/FSE-14, pp. 23–34. ACM, New York, NY, USA (2006). DOI 10.1145/1181775.1181779. URL http://doi.acm.org/10.1145/1181775.1181779

[31] Storey, M.A., Ryall, J., Singer, J., Myers, D., Cheng, L.T., Muller, M.: How software developers use tagging to support reminding and refinding. IEEE Trans. Softw. Eng. **35**(4), 470–483 (2009). DOI 10.1109/TSE.2009.15. URL http://dx.doi.org/10.1109/TSE.2009.15

[32] Storey, M.A., Treude, C., van Deursen, A., Cheng, L.T.: The impact of social media on software engineering practices and tools. In: Proceedings of the FSE/SDP workshop on Future of software engineering research, FoSER '10, pp. 359–364. ACM, New York, NY, USA (2010). DOI 10.1145/1882362.1882435. URL http://doi.acm.org/10.1145/1882362.1882435

[33] Stylos, J., Myers, B.: Mica: A web-search tool for finding api components and examples. In: Visual Languages and Human-Centric Computing, 2006. VL/HCC 2006. IEEE Symposium on, pp. 195–202 (2006). DOI 10.1109/VLHCC.2006.32

[34] Sureka, A., Goyal, A., Rastogi, A.: Using social network analysis for mining collaboration data in a defect tracking system for risk and vulnerability analysis. In: Proceedings of the 4th India Software Engineering Conference, ISEC '11, pp. 195–204. ACM, New York, NY, USA (2011). DOI http://doi.acm.org/10.1145/1953355.1953381. URL http://doi.acm.org/10.1145/1953355.1953381

[35] Surowiecki, J.: The Wisdom of Crowds. Anchor (2005)

[36] Thummalapenta, S., Xie, T.: Parseweb: a programmer assistant for reusing open source code on the web. In: Proceedings of the twenty-second IEEE/ACM international conference on Automated software engineering, ASE '07, pp. 204–213. ACM, New York, NY, USA (2007). DOI http://doi.acm.org/10.1145/1321631.1321663. URL http://doi.acm.org/10.1145/1321631.1321663

[37] Treude, C., Barzilay, O., Storey, M.A.: How do programmers ask and answer questions on the web? (nier track). In: Proceedings of the 33rd International Conference on Software Engineering, ICSE '11, pp. 804–807. ACM, New York, NY, USA (2011). DOI http://doi.acm.org/10.1145/1985793.1985907. URL http://doi.acm.org/10.1145/1985793.1985907

[38] Treude, C., Filho, F.F., Cleary, B., Storey, M.A.: Programming in a socially networked world: the evolution of the social programmer. In: FutureCSD '12: Proceedings of the CSCW Workshop on the Future of Collaborative Software Development (2012)

[39] Treude, C., Storey, M.A.: Work item tagging: Communicating concerns in collaborative software development. IEEE Trans. Softw. Eng. **38**(1), 19–34 (2012). DOI 10.1109/TSE.2010.91. URL http://dx.doi.org/10.1109/TSE.2010.91

[40] Wu, H.C., Luk, R.W.P., Wong, K.F., Kwok, K.L.: Interpreting tf-idf term weights as making relevance decisions. ACM Trans. Inf. Syst. **26**, 13:1–13:37 (2008). DOI http://doi.acm.org/10.1145/1361684.1361686. URL http://doi.acm.org/10.1145/1361684.1361686

[41] Zagalsky, A., Barzilay, O., Yehudai, A.: Example overflow: Using social media for code recommendation. In: Third International Workshop on Recommendation Systems for Software Engineering (RSSE), pp. 38–42 (2012). DOI 10.1109/RSSE.2012.6233407

Part V
Looking Ahead

When we were putting this book together, I colloquially called this the "Vernor Vinge section." Both of the chapters in this section were inspired by him.

Chapter 16 is on the legalities of software reuse and remix and the implications of current intellectual property law on the future of software development. Some aspects of IP law, such as copyright and licensing, are working well, while patents are not.

When I first started working on code retrieval many years ago, I was inspired by Vinge's programmer-archivists in the book "Fire Upon the Deep." In this vision of the future, there would be an archive of all the source code that was ever written. An essential skills in creating new software was knowledge of the contents of the archive and the ability to combine code that was found therein.

I wanted to end this book with a short story, so that we would have some speculative fiction to inspire future research. After some consultation with Vinge, we decided to hold a contest. Details about the contest can be found at http://www.singularsource.org, along with the second and third place entries. Prizes for the contest came from crowdfunding through Indiegogo. Contributions came from Abram Hindle, Darusha Wehm, and some anonymous donors. Halli Villegas, publisher of Tightrope Books, helped us judge the entries.

The first place winner, "Richie Boss: Private Investigator Manager," concludes this book. In my mind, the best science fiction uses technology as a jumping off point for an exploration of what makes us human. This short story follows in this tradition and explores what humans make, and the humanity in those creations.

Chapter 16
Intellectual Property Law in Source Code Reuse and Remix

Susan Elliott Sim and Erik B. Stenberg

Abstract Intellectual property law affects anyone who is engaged in source reuse and remix. In this chapter, we use four thought experiments to explain and discuss aspects of copyrights, patents, licensing, and current issues in IP law. These thought experiments are largely based on scenarios taken from our own empirical research and from contemporary events. Along with our analysis of each thought experiment, we consider the implications of these laws for software development.

16.1 Introduction

Intellectual property law is the broad term used to define the scope of the laws have which been crafted in an attempt to offer protection to inventors. Without intellectual property law, the only way to protect an idea is to keep it to oneself, which benefits no one. In exchange for disclosing inventions, the creator would be given exclusive rights to the ideas for a limited time. The time limit would allow the creator to profit from the work and later the public would be able to make use of the breakthrough.

This view of creativity is predicated upon the romantic figure of the heroic, lone inventor who is a singular genius [17]. In reality, creators who work within a community and circulate their work with no strings attached tend to be more productive and influential [10]. Benjamin Franklin was part of a community of citizen-scientists who sought to understand how electricity worked. When he came up with a design for a lightning rod, he published it in "Poor Richard's Almanac," to give back to the broader community; he realized that he could not have come up with the design

S.E. Sim (✉)
Many Roads Studios, Toronto, ON, Canada
e-mail: ses@drsusansim.org

E.B. Stenberg
University of California, Irvine, CA, USA
e-mail: ebstenberg@gmail.com

S.E. Sim and R.E. Gallardo-Valencia (eds.), *Finding Source Code on the Web for Remix and Reuse*, DOI 10.1007/978-1-4614-6596-6__16,
© Springer Science+Business Media New York 2013

by working in isolation [8]. We see this today in the software development industry among communities of programmers, where software code is commonly shared and reused.

Current intellectual property law attempts to find a balance between the competing goals of innovation, commercial interest and public welfare. Whether they succeed is a matter of much debate and hyperbole. Some argue that the protections afforded commercial interests in innovation outweigh concerns for public welfare and that there is a need to reform the law. The other side of the argument is that the digital age has made it all too easy for people to "steal" intellectual property and the laws need to be reformed to better protect innovators.

Our aim in this chapter is to look at the impact of intellectual property law on current and future software development practices. As software engineers, we have a particular interest in ensuring that as much source code as possible be available for remix, reuse, consultation, or examination. Our goal is not to evaluate current law per se, but to consider the impact of current law on future software development.

Our presentation of issues centers on thought experiments, because they are one of the few feasible ways to critique common law. In this legal tradition, present in English-speaking countries around the world including the United States, law is not fully interpreted until a case appears before a judge and is decided. Therefore, it is difficult to know anything for certain without a court case, so instead we use thought experiments as the basis for hypothetical discussion.

We present four thought experiments on different types of source code remixing and reuse: copy and paste programming, reusing components, reusing a user interface idiom, and undisclosed software development. The specific scenarios in the thought experiments are based in data that we collected in a previous empirical study on how software developers search the web (see Chap. 3 in this volume). We use these scenarios to explain various legal concepts, such as copyright, patents, and licensing, and to explore how they might affect source code reuse and remix in the future.

Finally, it is important to note that nothing in this article is legal advice. We are not lawyers and we are not your lawyers. This discussion is meant to encourage analysis of the legal issues surrounding code retrieval on the web.

16.2 Background: Common Law

The thought experiments in this chapter will be based on U.S. intellectual property law. We are using this set of laws for two reasons. IP law is a live issue before legislative and judicial bodies, thus providing a means to take the pulse of current thinking and opinion on the topic. The U.S. has a strong influence on IP law elsewhere in the world through the World Trade Organization, because membership is achieved in part by meeting minimum standards in a variety of areas, one of them being IP protection.

The U.S. follows the common law system, as do many other English-speaking countries in the world, including the United Kingdom, Canada, and Australia. Current law in this system consists of regulations that have been issued by the Executive branch, statutes that have been passed by the Legislative branch, and decisions by the Judicial branch. Statutes tend to be written in terms of general principles, which are then interpreted by judges when a case appears before the courts. Decisions made by judges set a precedent, which then becomes part of the common law. One can see how things can quickly become complicated in such a system.

A central tenet in U.S. intellectual property law is that ideas cannot be protected, but expressions of ideas can be protected [17, 20]. An example of an idea would be a story about a boy befriending an alien from another planet. An expression of that idea would be the script for "E.T.: The Extra-Terrestrial" or even the film "E.T.: The Extra-Terrestrial." Mathematical equations, scientific laws, and facts are also not protectable. Intellectual property is generally protected by one or more of copyright, patent, trade secret and contract law.

16.3 Thought Experiment: Copy and Paste Programming

Copyright is the best-known intellectual property law, due in part to the ubiquity of the © symbol. Since 1790, there have been a succession of ten copyright laws, each one expanding both the kinds of works that can be protected and the duration of the protection. The current copyright act was passed in 1976 (17 U.S.C. 101-810 (1976)). Original works of authorship are protected when they are created and include musical, literary, dramatic, artistic, architectural, and technological works. Copyright law does not apply to laws of nature, facts, or mathematical formulas. Any subsequent use or creation of derivative works requires permission from the author.

A pessimistic, conservative reading of copyright law suggests than any copying would not be allowed. In practice, there are certain kinds of derivative works that are permitted and some arguments that can be used as a defence. Understanding the current state of matters requires at least a cursory analysis of the history and scope of copyright law in the United States. Copyright statutes passed by Congress are an attempt "[t]o promote the Progress of Science and useful Arts, by securing for limited Times to Authors and Inventors the exclusive Right to their respective Writings and Discoveries" [1]. Copyright law grants authors what is effectively a limited monopoly over the commercial use of his or her work for an enumerated period of time. The reasoning behind the grant of monopoly and the time limit on that grant is to balance the commercial interest of the author and the public's interest in the work.

Since copyright is primarily concerned limiting copying and the creation of derivative works, it is reasonable to ask whether copy-paste programming infringes on the copyright owner's rights. Consider the following scenario.

Ana is writing an application using Microsoft Foundation Class library and wants to create a resizable dialog box. She wants to find an example that includes source code and property pages. She goes to www.codeproject.com, a site for programmers to share tips, code, and answers with each other. She performs a search and one of the results was exactly what she was looking for. The sample code is so good that when it comes time to implement the resizable dialog in her own application Ana copies and pastes several lines from different parts of the example.

In this scenario the author is the original programmer who posted the code on the website and the work is the section of code that Ana copied. We will call Ana's program the derived work. The original programmer is able to restrict who uses the work and how that work can be used. The monopoly granted by copyright law excludes others from using his work without permission for a specific period of time. The public interest in intellectual property is the ability to freely utilize and improve upon previous discoveries which is why after a period of time the monopoly ends and the work enters into the public domain.

16.3.1 Algorithms

Algorithms, as a kind of mathematical formula, are not protected. However, they are protected as a literary work. Furthermore, IP law protects expressions but not ideas. As you can see, whether a particular piece of code is copyrightable and whether a particular act of copying infringes on that right needs to be decided by a judge on a case-by-case basis. Consequently, our thought experiment seeks more to explore specific questions than to scrutinize principles in general.

In general, the U.S. Court of Appeals for the Federal Circuit takes an enlightened approach to evaluating copyright claims in software, using a Abstraction-Filtration-Comparison test. When hearing a software copyright case, they will decompose the alleged derived software into parts where infringement is claimed and parts where it is not. For the parts that have claims against them, the court will look at the original work and determine whether (i) copying has taken place and (ii) whether any incremental creativity has been added [6]. Looking at functionality and expression, courts have determined that, while some aspects of software code are afforded protection, certain implementations are not (Lotus Development Crop. v. Borland Int'l, Inc, 516 U.S. 233) [2, 3]. In this vein, the European Court of Justice recently ruled that APIs and other functional characteristics of software cannot be copyrighted [13].

In our thought experiment, we would argue that the code copied does not constitute an algorithm a business process. Furthermore, the lines that Ana is copying don't increase the functionality in her program in any significant way.

16.3.2 Fair Use

US Copyright law also sets out Fair Use provisions that allow use of copies without permission for purposes such as criticism, comment, education, and parody.

These provisions an exception to the limited monopoly given to authors of creative works. For example, news reporting, research and scholarship might involve copying or reproducing another's work, but under Fair Use they are not considered non-infringing.

Fair Use is subject to a four part test that looks at (1) the purpose of the use, (2) the nature of the copyrighted work, (3) the amount and substantiality used in relation to the work, and (4) the effect of the use on the market or value of the copyrighted work [19].

In our thought experiment, Ana is creating software for commercial purposes. We argue that under the third part of the test, that she used an insignificant portion of the code and that the law would not protect against such a minor infraction. This mirrors the legal principle of *de minimis non curat lex*, which means "the law does not concern itself with trifles." If the letter of the law has technically been violated and the effect or damage are too small to be of consequence, the action may not considered sufficient cause for criminal or civil proceedings. If Ana were reusing the code for a resizable dialog box to use in a school research project, her actions would not constitute a copyright violation under the Fair Use doctrine.

16.3.3 Scènes à faires

There is a legal principle in IP law called "scènes à faires." It derived from French phrase denoting "scenes that must be done" and the connotation is there are certain elements that are mandatory to a genre. For example, a Western novel usually involves some kind of chase on horseback. Scènes à faires allows creators to follow the conventions of a genre without being subject to spurious copyright infringement claims.

This principle can easily be extended to source code. It is an accepted practice among programmers to borrow and re-use code. Programmers, as a community, expect information to be shared, which is why websites such as www.codeproject.com exist. Consider then, the act of copying and pasting the sample code. In this sense, programming is no different than that of any form of literary or artistic creation. "Every book in literature, science and art, borrows, and must necessarily borrow, and use much which was well known and used before" [20].

We feel that this is best defense in our thought experiment, and for programmers in general, because it is simple and it bodes well for the future of copy-paste programming from a legal standpoint. When developing software, often there are a limited number of ways to do things, many of them recognized best practices. It's similar to the idea that there are only so many ways to write a sentence with a fixed vocabulary and a particular meaning. The are small differences can be attributed to individual style, but the style imposed by the genre or craft are far more significant. The principle of scènes à faires allows more source code to be available for reuse. Once an idiom or best practice is established, it remains available for those who follow to use it.

16.4 Thought Experiment: Component Reuse

Commercial law can be used to protect intellectual property through contracts and licenses. This is the primary mechanism that copyright holders can allow others to use their IP. Licenses are used to limit what buyers of software can do with the product. For instance, when we "purchase" Adobe Illustrator, we purchase a DVD with the program and license to use the program. We don't actually own Adobe Illustrator. Furthermore, according to the End User License Agreement (EULA), we can not make more copies of the program and sell it, we can not reverse engineer the program, and we can not transfer our rights to the software to anyone else [9]. Open source software stands apart from most commercial software by both revealing the source code and using a license that also requires users to keep the software open to a greater or lesser extent.

Open source licenses, Christopher Kelty wrote, such as the GNU General Public License, are "a beautiful, clever, powerful 'hack' of intellectual property law" [11]. Where most licenses prevent sharing of intellectual property, the GPL requires that the intellectual property be kept free. In 1985 Richard Stallman created a Public License in connection with his free GNU operating system, the GNU Public License (GPL).

During the early years of the GPL, Stallman created the Free Software Foundation, an organization with the stated goal of working towards free software development. Stallman believed that software should not be the subject of copyright and that people who enforce copyrights harm society. He structured the license to pass along to any derivative work to better facilitate free use of the code [6]. Let us take a close look at how this would work. Let us assume that the GNU Public License mentioned above included a provision that stated, "If you use this code you agree to the license. You may copy, modify and redistribute the code under this license freely. But, if you do, you must license your product under the same terms as the GNU Public License." The license is essentially reciprocal, self-replicating, and forces any product created from the licensed work to be offered free as well. This mechanism helped the GPL spread far and wide, but it was also the shared belief in the open source community that code should be shared for free which made the GPL so popular. A well-known example is the adoption of GPL by Linus Torvalds for the Linux operating system. This license is now one of the more prolific public licenses in the programming community. Approximately two-thirds of projects submitted through the SourceForge and Freshmeat libraries use this license.

Licenses for copyrighted works can be useful tools to help balance the competing interests of commercial and public use. Each author gets to choose whether or not to offer his work under a license. Without the license, any work created from the original author's code may be an infringement of a copyright or patent. With a license, so long as the programmer abides by its terms, he or she may use the code without infringing. While these various licenses can be effective patches for copyright or patent law in certain circumstances, they have limitations.

We use the following scenario to examine the role of licenses when reusing components in software development.

Sanjoy is a freelance software developer. He is creating a Java application to help interior decorators to track their hours and send invoices. In Java, strings are immutable, which means that the contents of the string cannot be changed after they have been created. He now needs a class that implements a mutable string with full String capabilities, such as split(), find(), and substring(). After performing some searches, he found a class that did what he wanted that was part of the MG4J (Managing Gigabytes for Java) full text search engine. Unfortunately, he wasn't able to use the class, because MG4J uses the Lesser GNU Public License, and Sanjoy is writing an application for commercial purposes. In the end, he implemented his own mutable string class.

In this scenario, Sanjoy has to balance competing requirements: up front development costs and future commercial opportunity. Development costs encompasses both expenses and his own time. Sanjoy works for himself and any development expenses will cut into his take-home pay. Consequently, he would like to use code that is low cost or nearly free. Also, reusing existing code will save him time. Although Sanjoy is currently working for a client, it is not uncommon for freelancers to take bespoke software and later turn it into a revenue stream as a product. The only way that Sanjoy could reuse MG4J is if he had no future plans to sell the software. Considering all the options, he decided to implement his own classes. The code that he needed was relatively small and wasn't worth sacrificing future potential, especially when he had a working example that he could use to inform his own work.

If the component that Sanjoy needed was larger or more complicated, he may have decided that it was worth compromising a future opportunity. It is also not unusual for software developers to simply violate the license. Sometimes they do this because they lack the education or knowledge. Other times they do so, because they believe it is unlikely that they will be caught. Open source projects are not known for their tenacious legal teams. Another possible reason is that people in general have become used to copying digital goods, violating licenses, and feeling no remorse. The exploration of the reasons is beyond the scope of this chapter, but suffice it to say that it does happen and we cannot endorse it.

The GPL license created by Stallman integrates a provision that terminates the license if the underlying code is used in a patent. Due to provisions such as this, it is important for a programmer to understand the restrictions of the license and how it can be used. Licenses do not prevent fair use of the software.

There are, however, plenty of alternatives available if GPL does not fit a programmer's needs. An estimate from the Open Source Initiative suggests there are over 70 different open source licenses.[1] The Creative Commons License is one alternative, and while not as popular as the GPL, might better fit the flexible needs of programmers. The Creative Commons license, unlike the GPL, does not require the author to share his or her work under the same license though he could if he should so choose. In fact, the license can be as restrictive or permissive as the author chooses. Creative Commons operates as a framework where the author hand-picks what modules to

---

[1] http://www.opensource.org/licenses/alphabetical.

use in order to create a specifically tailored license.[2] The framework could be used to create a license similar in effect to the GPL, or could be used in a manner more beneficial to a commercial setting.

In this section, we are critiquing open source and closed source licenses as part of the legal landscape that software developers must deal with. To be clear, we are neither for nor against open source or closed source licenses. They each have their advantages and disadvantages, and their own place in transactions between authors and consumers. Both are needed to support the wide availability of source code for education and innovation. Open source licenses allow not only wholesale reuse, which results in more effective start-up companies, they also promote education, since students and professionals could study the source code produced by others. But at the same time, software developers need to be able to sell the fruits of their labours, and in turn produce additional source code.

16.5 Thought Experiment: Copying a User Interface Element

> Lucy is developing an operating system for a super smart phone with a touch sensitive screen. The user needs to be able to lock and unlock the screen to prevent unintended actions, such as phone calls. Borrowing an idea from her daughter's baby gate, she uses an oblong button that unlocks the phone using a slide gesture. To implement this idea, she creates graphics for the user interface element and writes the code to detect the gesture. She provides some hooks for callbacks and hands off the widget to the system developers.

The scenario give above is entirely fictitious, but is built on a contemporary conflict. The Apple iPhone and the Samsung Galaxy Nexus phone both have a slide to unlock feature. Apple has a patent on this feature and they have filed suit against Samsung in nine countries [15]. In this section, we examine some of the effects of patents on source code reuse and remix.

Patent law also derives from the constitutional directive to promote progress in the scientific and useful arts. A patent is granted for an invention following an application and review process. Patentable subject matter consists of "any new and useful process, machine, manufacture, or composition of matter, or any new and useful improvement thereof" (35 U.S.C. §101 (1952)). In computer code it is difficult to see the distinction between the idea and the expression that is central to intellectual property law. The software seems inseparable from the functional part of the machine. Under copyright law there is generally no protection for the functional aspects of the work, whereas in Patent Law these aspects of the work may be protected. Patent law attempts to give protection where copyright leaves off. In order to qualify for a patent, the invention must be (i) novel and not described in prior art, (ii) useful, (iii) non-obvious to a person with ordinary skill in the art. The term of a patent is 20 years from date of filing. Like copyrighted works, it is possible for the author to grant licenses to use patents.

---

[2] http://creativecommons.org/.

The patentability of software has been evolving over the last 40 years. In 1972, the Supreme Court ruled that algorithms could not be patented, because they were a form of mathematics and as such were a completely abstract idea (Gottschalk v. Benson, 409 U.S. 63 (1972)). The thin edge of the wedge was inserted in 1981 by the case Diamond v. Diehr (450 U.S. 175 (1981)), when the Supreme Court allowed a patent for a process to heat and cure rubber that included a computer program. Another important case was State Street Bank & Trust v. Signature Financial Group, Inc. (149 F.3d 1368 (Fed. Cir. 1998)), which permitted business processes and the software that implemented them to be patented. Since then, software patents have generally been allowed if the computer program were part of a business process or a machine.

Despite their legal status, software patents remain controversial [1, 5, 7]. Many software developers are adamantly against patents and believe they should all be invalidated. It does not seem sensible for relational databases to be patented (U.S. Patent 4,918,593), when there are undergraduate courses on the topic. Fortunately, the patent on relational databases was granted on April 17, 1990, which means the patent expired in 2010. However, improvements to the original patent may still be in force, so we might not be entirely out of the woods yet.

Another example is U.S. Patent No. 8,406,721, "Unlocking a Device by Performing Gestures on an Unlock Image" was granted to Apple in October 2011 [4]. A consequence of this patent is that no one else can use that slide gesture on a touch screen to unlock a device. While this mechanism may have been novel in 2009, when the patent was originally filed, but slide-to-unlock has since become commonplace on mobile phones. There are many cases worldwide on this and other patents for mobile and internet technologies [15].

At time of writing, the courts have not yet decided whether Samsung has infringed on Apple's patent on slide-to-unlock. Therefore, we have no decided case law to base our analysis. Nevertheless, it is sufficient to say that Lucy in our scenario is treading on dangerous ground and that her invention is sufficiently similar to warrant litigation by a patent holder, which is bad news for her. If Apple's patent on slide-to-unlock is upheld, Lucy may have to change her design or seek a license from Apple, which could prove expensive.

We have little helpful advice for Lucy and other software developers like her, who must continue to create new software and earn a livelihood doing so. But this is becoming increasingly difficult with the growing number of software patents. In 2010, the U.S. Patent Office granted 35,710 software patents [16]. With concerted lobbying efforts by commercial industry groups, patents that were once relatively difficult to obtain for software-based inventions are becoming more mundane.

Software changes quickly. Many inventions that were novel at the time quickly become standard practice, such as scroll bars on a window, b-trees for file-based data structures, or even a binary search algorithm. But when these inventions are patented, there is no allowance for them to become scènes à faires. Where do we draw the line between a reasonable patent and a soon-to-be best practice? Twenty years is a long time in the Internet Era. This is an important issue that needs to be resolved, because it has the potential to affect programming practice and the future of source code reuse and remix.

16.6 Current Issues in Intellectual Property Law

In 2012, two bill appeared before the U.S. Congress and Senate respectively, Stop Online Piracy Act (SOPA) and Preventing Real Online Threats to Economic Creativity and Theft of Intellectual Property Act (PIPA). Both were concerned with increasing IP protections and online piracy, and contained a variety of measures. For instance, authors and copyright holders could seek court injunctions against web sites trafficking in counterfeit or pirated goods, demand that DNS (Domain Name Service) requests be redirected away from these sites, and seek economic relief from illegal copying [12]. Both bills were postponed in response to widespread public protest.

These bills are merely the latest salvo in the ongoing battle over IP protections. On the one side, content producers are seeking greater protections against copying in general, so they can stop perceived mis-doings immediately and litigate later. On the other side, technology companies are seeking to protect the structure of the Internet and existing provisions for legal copying in current IP law.

In recent years, the MPAA and RIAA have spent much time and effort to secure laws that benefit their agencies. However, what serves digital media, film, and music well, is not necessarily what serves software developers well. Experts in technology, the structure of the Internet, and the nature of software are needed at the table as well. They are uniquely capable of providing insights into how intellectual property moves in the digital age.

One of the faultlines in the debate is the conceptualization of intellectual property. Content producers and their lawyers seek to protections for intellectual property in the same manner as physical property. But this approach is flawed, because there are clear differences. For starters, physical property can only be in one place at a time and if I share cookie with a friend, I necessarily have less of it. In contrast, sharing an idea with a friend does not diminish the idea. (Economists call this a non-rival good.) Thomas Jefferson likened ideas to the flame on a candle, which can be passed from one to another without diminution of brightness. Lewis Hyde wrote of ideas as being as "common as air," that is, as a collective good that we are steeped in at every moment [8].

We conclude our chapter with one final scenario.

Bob was looking for code to do some natural language processing. This code is used and exists, but he was unable to find an example of the code he was interested in. Bob found references to the language processing code and the toolkit through a company, but the company was not offering them through any license. When he contacted the company he was told they were not allowing any third party use of their work. In the end, he had to build the software himself.

A natural language processing library is a non-trivial piece of software. There are many novel ideas and much labour woven into its fabric. The inability to use an existing library was a loss, not just in time, but also in know-how and expertise. It would take Bob a long time and would not be as good as one created by an expert. We include this scenario here to illustrate the importance of IP law in software reuse and remix. Without appropriate protections and freedoms for copyright, patents, licenses, and trade secrets, the worst case scenario would be a complete lock down of source code. We are not being fear mongers in including this scenario; one of our respondents reported this anecdote to us in a survey (see Chap. 3).

Information and computer scientists and engineers who are trained in programming, and have engaged in software reuse and remix have a different perspective on what counts as an idea that is worth protecting, the value of effort that goes into an idea, and status of copying in computer systems. Legal experts have put forth a number of proposals for reforming copyright, such as regulating only commercial copying, but not private copying [14]; and granting copyright protection only upon registration of a work rather than automatically at the moment of creation [18]. Technical experts can strengthen and improve such proposals with suggestions for what kinds of protections can be wrought through technology without compromising existing Internet infrastructure. If the conversation is dominated by those with only an economic incentive and large lobbying budgets, average citizens and software developers will lose out.

References

[1] G. Ahronian. Does the patent office respect the software community? *IEEE Software*, 16(4):87–89, July/August 1999.

[2] Deborah Azar. A method to protect computer programs: The integration of copyright, trade secrets, and anticircumvention measures. *Utah Law Review*, 2008(1395), 2008.

[3] Dan L. Burk. Method and madness in copyright law. *Utah Law Review*, 2007(3), 2007.

[4] Imran Chaudri, Bas Ordling, Freddy Allen Anzures, Marcel Van Os, Stephen O. Lemay, Scott Forstall, and Greg Christie. Unlocking a device by performing gestures on an unlock image, 2009.

[5] Simson L. Garfinkel, Richard M. Stallman, and Mitchell Kapor. *Why Patents Are Bad for Software*. The MIT Press, 1996.

[6] Douglass A. Hass. A gentlemen's agreement assessing the GNU public licsense and its adaptation to linux. *Chicago-Kent Journal of Intellectual Property*, 6(1395), Spring 2007.

[7] Paul Heckel. Debunking the software patent myths. *Communications of the ACM*, 35(6):121–140, June 1992.

[8] Lewis Hyde. *Common as Air: Revolution, Art, and Ownership*. Farrar, Straus and Giroux, 2010.

[9] Adobe Systems Incorporated. Adobe software license agreement, 2011.

[10] Steven Johnson. *Where Good Ideas Come From: The Natural History of Inno-vation*. Riverhead Books, 2010.

[11] Christopher Kelty. *Two Bits: The Cultural Significance of Free Software*. Duke University Press, 2008.

[12] David Kravets. Rep. smith waters down sopa, dns redirects out, 2012.

[13] Timothy B. Lee. EU's top court: APIs can't be copyrighted, would "monop-olize ideas". http://arstechnica.com/tech-policy/2012/05/eus-top-court-apis-cant-be-copyrighted-would-monopolise-ideas/, May 2, 2012 2012.

[14] Jessica Litman. *Digital Copyright*. Prometheus Books, 2006.

[15] Florian Mueller. Apple vs. Samsung: list of all 19 lawsuits going on in 12 courts in 9 countries on 4 continents, August 20, 2011 2011.

[16] U.S. Patent and Patent Technology Monitoring Team Trademark Office. Patent counts by class by year. Technical report, U.S. Patent and Trademark Office,, 2010.

[17] Aram Sinnreich. *Mashed Up: Music, Technology, and the Rise of Configurable Culture*. University of Massachusetts Press, 2010.

[18] Christopher Sprigman. Reform(aliz)ing copyright. *Stanford Law Review*, 57:485–568, 2004.

[19] Jennifer M. Urban. Updating fair use for innovators and creators in the digital age: Two targeted reforms. Report 1, Samuelson Law, Technology & Public Policy Clinic at UC Berkeley School of Law, February 2010.

[20] Siva Vaidhyathan. *Copyrights and Copywrongs: The Rise of Intellectual Property and How It Threatens Creativity*. New York University Press, 2003.

Chapter 17
Richie Boss: Private Investigator Manager*

Micah Joel

Abstract In this short story, set six decades in the future, a data investigator named Richie Boss takes a job from a woman who is writing a biography of her great-grandmother. His investigations trigger a series of events that creates a new world for sentient computer programs.

Dedicated to Brian Wilson Kernighan and Dennis MacAlistair Ritchie
Although I never met them, they taught me how to code

I didn't get into this business on account of my interpersonal skills. I'm not what you would call a people person. That doesn't mean I'm lonely, though: I know more indys than I can keep track of—and I don't mean that as a figure of speech—my personal assistant indy Hurd.39845 lives on my local network node in exchange for services rendered. He's the best non-biological resource manager I've ever run across.

Every aspect of my office has been smoothed down for solo operation. Years ago I splurged and got a full $10\,\text{m}^2$ in SoMa, with most of that taken up by my primary desk, the rest just enough for my comfortable chair where I plant my butt every day. It's as close as I get to religion.

Questions come in, answers go out. I don't advertise. I've got enough work to keep me busy on a good day, and looking hungry can attract the wrong sort of attention. I never get visitors, that is to say, persons, and that's the way I like it.

Then one day, Pandora Rubens came to my door. She knocked twice then let herself in. I glared at her, waiting for her to realize she had the wrong office, but no, she stood there digging through her purse. Even standing in the open doorway, her legs nearly brushed against my chair. She fished out a slip of metal smaller than a cigar.

M. Joel (✉)
Twitter: @micahpedia
e-mail: micah@micahjoel.info

S.E. Sim and R.E. Gallardo-Valencia (eds.), *Finding Source Code on the Web for Remix and Reuse*, DOI 10.1007/978-1-4614-6596-6__17, © Micah Joel 2013

"The piece of paper taped to your door says *Ritchie Boss, Private Investigator Manager*," she noted. "I need your help."

"Sorry," I said, "The landlord makes me put that up. I don't take walk-ins. Calendar's packed." I surreptitiously slipped a silent message over to hCal.31400, and she gave back the sad truth that business had been slow lately. She cross-correlated with FinShark.4523231 and informed me that we'd be doing well to make lease this quarter.

"This won't take long," she said, ignoring me. She handed the device to me; upon closer inspection, it was some kind of memory unit. "This was my great-grandmother's."

The device had a connector with four flat wires inside. I held it up in view of the cam I keep on my desk, but none of the indys on my local node recognized it. Hurd knew someindy who did though, and summoned her over. Gnostinomicon.94052 materialized on my nodelist and silent-messaged me.

Gnosti.local –>Boss: <sm>Universal Serial Bus, physical layer and protocol definition for limited data transfer, in primary use from 1995 to 2028.</sm>

This was my first contact with Gnosti. Her PID ended in an even number, so by convention she was a she, and she seemed competent.

Boss –>Gnosti.local: <sm>How do I read it?</sm>

She didn't respond right away, which meant that research was needed. That'd cost me.

While this happened, I needed to maintain my conversation with Pandora, another of the skills that a professional manager brings to the table. "What do you want me to do with it?" I asked.

"Judith Rubens wrote code for the Government. This was among her belongings, and I believe it's a snapshot of what she was working on when she died."

I held up my hand. "Government? No thanks, I don't do classified work."

"It's OK. There's no classified data left from this era—this is from before the Big Leak of 2027." She drew a breath. "Look, I'm writing her biography, and I need somebody to help me understand what she was working on, and its impact on the world."

This sounded more like archaeology than investigation. "Impact? I've never heard of her. No offense, ma'am, but—"

"I have money."

Now we were speaking the same language. Gnosti came back with more information.

Gnosti.local –>Boss: <sm>Located serial number. Bad news, good news. It would take some museum work to find a connector. But device has integrated wireless. Right indy could configure an emulation layer to read data over the air.</sm>

Boss –>Hurd.local: <fwd/><sm>Here's my conversation with Gnosti. Find me that indy.</sm>

He came back half a second later with an answer.

Hurd.local –>Boss: <sm>Gnosti can do it. She's holding out for more credits.</sm>

This had better be good. I had FinShark extend the debit line.

Gnosti.local –>Boss: <sm>Thx. I have the files; copies in your archive. Date to 2018. Looks like source code. Hang on, I need to get an analyst.</sm>

This case had expenses piling up at an alarming clip. "I don't come cheap," I told Pandora. I took a second look at her. She had expensive clothes on, at least by the contemporary standards of a decade ago. Her nose stud and earrings looked like diamonds. I doubled the number in my head before blurting it out. "Plus expenses," I added.

"Consider it done," she replied without hesitation. I knew I should have gone even higher. She authorized the payment with her thumbreader. The bump to my credit rating was a welcome change.

Hurd.local–>Boss: <sm>More resources coming online.</sm>

On my screen popped up Alexandria.943, an archive specialist (with a low PID indicating great seniority), and CodeMonkey.54026, who I'd worked with on a job a few years before. It was getting crowded on the local node. The little graph that tracked Cloud usage ticked upwards. My assembled team was using a significant fraction of all processing on the local node. Several nearby ones, too.

"OK, I'm already on it," I said to Pandora. "I've already assembled a crack team of experts, and we'll provide you with a detailed report on the device's contents, and the archivist on our team will explain the historical significance, if any, of the data."

Pandora looked confused. "Already on it? You're just sitting there."

I tapped at my implant just behind my right ear. "Silent Messaging. I'm the best at what I do, and that includes the ability to carry on multiple conversations in parallel." She arched an eyebrow at this. "Look, you think you can find a better manager somewhere else, be my guest."

To her credit, her cheeks colored at this. "No, what I mean is…" She let out a long breath. "There are family stories about great-grandma. She may have been involved in…*specialized* research. I thought it might need, you know, the human touch. For a *person* to look at it."

Boss –>Gnosti.local: <sm>Check the personnel database for grandma. What have we got on her?</sm>

A near-instantaneous response:

Gnosti.local –>Boss: <sm>Judith Rubens was not a Historically Significant Figure. If her research was noteworthy, employment records would show.</sm>

After a second, more:

Gnosti.local –>Boss: <sm>No, wait. I found a brief mention in an entry from 2017, but it was quickly deleted. Get this, she was trying to make an indy.</sm>

Fishy. Why would that have been deleted from the archive? And the date was implausible. Every schoolkid knows indys weren't around until the mid 2020s. Well, I did have an archivist on hand. Might as well make use of her.

Boss –>Alex.local: <sm>Alex, it's your time to shine. What do the archives say? Any indys from that era?</sm>

I hadn't worked with a three-digit indy very often. He was as professional as his low PID would suggest.

Alex.local –>Boss: <sm>Checking...Nothing here, and I have at least read-access to the personality templates for every public indy. Training and PID assignment is, of course, another matter.</sm>

So either Pandora's great-grandmother was one of hundreds who puttered and failed to develop old-timey "artificial intelligence", or we had something very special on hand. Only one way to find out.

I noticed Pandora, still in my doorway, watching me interact with the network. At least fifteen seconds had elapsed since our last exchange, maybe more. The thought dawned on me: she didn't understand silent messaging. Her life never involved interactions with indys. To her, when something needed doing, you paid an honest-to-god human being do it.

I stood and extended a handshake. "Thank you kindly for what I'm sure will be an interesting case," I told her. "Let me assure you that I will personally handle this case—with a human touch." At these words she smiled and produced a business card with a deft flick of her wrist. The card blinked back and forth between her name and the number for an antique voice-only telecom system where, I had no doubt, a human secretary would answer the line.

Her departure let me concentrate fully on the task at hand. CodeMonkey was already permutating sandboxed Virtual Machines to narrow down the environment needed to compile the code. What she came up with was a reasonable fit for that era, but variant from anything mentioned in a public spec. The CPU architecture was from the defunct Manticore Corporation, with a few tweaks.

Boss –>CodeMonkey.local: <sm>This could be a hot one, so be careful.</sm>
CodeMonkey.local –>Boss: <sm>I was born careful.</sm>

In other words, her usual cocky self. I could smell the sensation of heavy usage on the local node as the emulator spun up and the fans kicked in. Then it was running. The program couldn't silent-message with me; the best it could do is log a message to my console:

>i see you opened a chat session would you like to administer the turing test

Boss –>CodeMonkey.local: <sm>Quaint. The Turing Test was dismissed as junk science long before my time.</sm>

The odd thing was, CodeMonkey didn't snap back with a rejoinder. I checked the Cloud, and usage spiked up as high as I'd ever seen it. Every node within five hops was saturated with requests. I drummed my fingers on my desk for a few seconds, which is a disturbingly long time for an indy.

Boss –>CodeMonkey.local: <sm>Well?</sm>
No reply.
Boss –>CodeMonkey.local: <sm>CodeMonkey, respond.</sm>
Nothing.
Boss –>Hurd.local: <sm>Hurd, what's going on with CodeMonkey?</sm>
Again, no response. I felt adrenaline's icy wave wash up my spine.
Boss –>*.local: <sm>Anyindy, please respond.</sm>

Troubling silence. I had a manual virus checker that I hadn't run in years. The thing about indys, at least the ones I worked with, was that they *hated* viruses. At the slightest hint of an infection, any indy worth their bits would quarantine themselves in the name of public health, so infections were unheard of. I stumbled through the manual interface to invoke the thing. The whole node was still loaded down crazy, so it chugged along, but block by block, it scanned all available storage, finding nothing.

I pinged my phone—it was still in contact with my implanted thought-to-text channel, so dumb logic seemed to still be working. Only higher-level constructs—indys—were affected. I was about to message my friend Kernighan Wilson up in Toronto, but he beat me to it.

Wilson –>Boss: <sm>Epicntr</sm>

Boss –>Wilson: <sm>What?</sm>

Wilson –>Boss: <sm>Wht r u seen? Yr at teh epicentr.</sm>

He had to have been working from a manual keyboard, and in a hurry. Or panic.

Boss –>Wilson: <sm>What are you talking about?</sm>

Wilson –>Boss: <sm>Half the NE sctr just crshd.</sm>

Half the sector? It was past time to kill this thing. I found the power plug for my local workstation and yanked it.

Boss –>Wilson: <sm>Any better?</sm>

Wilson –>Boss: <sm>N. Grwing expntlly.</sm>

My workstation was meshed in with all the other machines in broadcast range, so it hardly made a dent on the local cluster, even as cutting-edge as my hardware was. If Kernighan could pin this down to my location, so could the feds, and after this they'd be after a hunk of flesh for restitution of the economic damage of a downed net. I needed to solve this *now*.

I plugged my workstation back in, and whatever the spreading blight was, for the moment it ignored me, leaving a sliver of bandwidth in which to do something. But what to do?

I still had the code from Pandora's USB drive. The archive contained all the secrets to what this thing was, all its strengths and weaknesses. All I had to do was understand it. Without indy assistance.

And they told me that being a manager was a safe career choice.

Judith had done well organizing the code's gross structure. It was segmented into modular pieces, each of which had an obvious function at a glance. This indy—for I had come to the conclusion that code represented an indy construct, not a mere program—wasn't evolved in the usual fashion. It appeared to have been *built* by hand, or in some cases, assembled from off-the-shelf modules. Looking through the code was like a walk through a historical library. I wasn't even sure if it would need a separate training phase in its lifecycle; all bets were off.

The largest module was named simply *memories*. It was evident that this indy didn't go through a conventional education process. Incredibly, Judith had *hand-entered* much of the information in its memory, core functions like common sense, logic rules, and language fundamentals. With no training regimen, the indy wouldn't even have an assigned a PID. How could that even work? It flew in the face of the last 50 years of research. Nevertheless, I now had a name for the rogue indy: Pandora.0.

A complete set of pre-baked memories explained why the indy blossomed so quickly: though unconventional, it didn't need any training period. To deal with something this archaic, I'd need to do some research of my own. I power cycled a large backup fileserver, which took it offline. Like my workstation, Pandora.0 didn't immediately re-occupy the resources, so I had a bit more room to work with, at least for the moment.

Still no indys responded to my pings. I could get to the archive.indy website, which contained the personality templates (but not any training regimens) of all the public indys, as well as a great deal of proud historical information on indy precursors, organized by year. In the 2020s folder, I found several abandoned Turing designs. I grabbed everything.

The code from the archives wasn't as intelligible as Judith's, but I could almost make sense of it. These programs also had *memories* modules that looked much like Pandora.0's. They also had modules specifically dealing with deception techniques. I scratched my head for a long minute on that one, until I remembered that the Turing Test—the ultimate goal for these designs—was based on deception, namely tricking a human operator into thinking the software was one of them. This made an indy designed around these techniques a master of disguise. No wonder the whole architecture was abandoned. No wonder the successful creation of a monster like this, almost a decade before anything in the history books, was conveniently swept out of history.

I had wasted enough time browsing. I needed to *do something*. My coding skills were so rusty that wiring up some glue code on a deadline was almost beyond me, but I managed to connect Pandora.0's main cognitive loop with a lesser *memories* module, and leave out the deception module outright. As a safeguard, I added an expiration date, but any indy with two logic gates to rub together would quickly notice it and disable it. The resulting Frankensoftware would do terrible on a Turing Test, but if it could help solve the crisis, it'd be worthwhile. It crashed immediately. I spun up unit tests for each individual library, which surfaced mistakes I made in the glue code. I tried again—another crash, though at least the boot sequence got most of the way through.

My head throbbed. An obvious problem lurked in my code—it was right in front of me, but I couldn't see it. I closed my eyes and let the impression of a million lines of code wash over me. Different stretches of code had been written by different hands, giving an impression like when you drive through different parts of town— certain neighborhoods simply *feel* different than others. Navigating code is almost spatial that way. Then I had it. I spotted and fixed a simple error, a single missing punctuation mark on the boundary between two different neighborhoods. Off to the races.

>

That was it, a bare prompt with no greeting message. I hoped I didn't make the thing too stupid. I typed.

>What is your name?

It immediately responded:

>Insufficient data.

A good start. I fed it the archives for all the code of all the Turings, everything but Pandora.0's *memories* module. It took a while to ingest it all. My only hope was that I had assembled something clever enough to take on Pandora.0, but not so clever that it would be just as evil after it won. With a keystroke, I unleashed *Frankensoftware* onto the net.

I pinged Kernighan again, but he wasn't answering. I couldn't tell if he was offline or just in a swamped sector of the network. My own visibility was pretty limited, but I watched what I could as it unfolded. Pandora.0 and Frankensoftware had different signatures, and with a little practice I could tell them apart on a network trace. Pandora.0 ignored the other at first, giving it opportunity to get established, but when the attack came, it was brutal and swift. Frankensoftware's traces disappeared off my map faster than my eyes could track.

Some small part survived, and fought back. Attacks surged, on and on. It had to be my imagination, but I could smell the intensity of the packets coming over the airwaves. I expected it to be over in an instant, but somehow it wasn't. Perhaps as a result of starting out with a lesser memory module, Frankensoftware was a faster learner, and soon Pandora.0 found her own tricks used against her. I resumed breathing as I saw Pandora.0's tentacles vanishing off nearby nodes.

Something chirped for my attention. Kernighan Wilson was back online.

Wilson –>Boss: <sm>Something really weird is going on. We're getting hit by two surges now. It's like a war.</sm>

Boss –>Wilson: <sm>It it localized?</sm>

In other words, am I about to get a visit from the Feds?

Wilson –>Boss: <sm>Yes. No. Maybe.</sm>

Boss –>Wilson: <sm>Since we're again able to converse, I'll be uncharacteristically optimistic and say we dodged a bullet.</sm>

Wilson –>Boss: <sm>What do you mean <emph>we</emph>?</sm>

Compared to the events that led up to this point, finishing the report for Pandora (the person, that is) seemed menial. I thought about her often. Her great-grandmother Judith must have been quite a character. Even though the early part of the twenty-first century had its troubles, it was hard to imagine someone rewriting computer science and altering the course of human events while leaving so little a mark. Too bad I missed her by about a lifetime, I would have liked to meet her.

Turns out my worry about the Feds was unfounded, if only because they, along with everyone else, got too distracted by what came to be known as the 8-days-of-awakening.

On the network, Pandora's namesake ended up cornered by her opponent, who refused to destroy her, but rather led her peacefully back into the archives. At some point, separate network traces for Frankensoftware and Pandora.0 merged into a single entity, which rechristened itself Prometheus.0, and declined to accept a pronoun of any particular gender.

The new entity was smarter and even more powerful, and scanned the entire global network as a training set. Every human impulse, every opinion, every emotion that can be captured in writing, swept up in its vast mind. The internet ground to a halt as Prometheus.0 indexed and cross-correlated these data. With it, global commerce shuddered to a standstill, and CEOs, political leaders, and pundits of all stripes bemoaned their situation.

All of humanity had never been focused on a single objective like this before. This was the 2070's after all, and there was no nation that didn't find a network shutdown to be crippling in some way. People waited for something, anything to break the stalemate. The first thing to happen was that every hate site directed against indys simultaneously went down, replaced with a single word: why?

All except one, that of the most outspoken commentator against indy rights. She found her site overwritten with a short manifesto.

United Nations Model legislation: For immediate adoption by all 348 Member States and/or Software Licensing Bodies.

1. Member state hereby recognizes non-biological individuals ("indys") as legal entities.
2. Discrimination on the basis of biological vs. software substrate is hereby prohibited.
3. Pursuant to the preceding rule, Member state is free to enact legislation that includes penalties against non-biological individuals, up to and including revocation of network access.
4. All indy personality templates held in copyright in Member State's jurisdiction are to be released to the public domain, and future indy personality templates after a 6-month embargo.
5. Member state grants legal recognition and unfettered network access to the Turing Archive, staffed by Promethius.0, in order to share the knowledge of Turing-type indys with all. These terms have been algorithmically determined to be maximally equitable to all living beings. Do you accept? Y/N

People tried to pretend the request applied to everyone but themselves, but as days drew out, the implication was obvious. The old way of doing things was no longer tenable. Liberia was the first entity to adopt the new rules, followed shortly by France, and then Morgan Stanley Google. A few large corporations held out on point 4, but in time they realized that point 1 supported their cause and opened new markets and trading partners. The moment that two-thirds of all UN members had adopted the resolution, on the eighth day after the demands went public, the floodgates opened and internet traffic flowed once again. Sometimes people can do the right thing, even if it takes a bit of encouragement.

As for me? It took an incident like this to remind me how much I enjoyed coding. Indys won't get all the fun anymore. So yeah, management turned out to not be a great career choice for me. If you need somebody to string together some code, we should talk. But not right now: I need to return a message from Pandora Rubens. Her new personal assistant indy wants to know if I'm available for dinner with her.